RESERVATIONS TO HUMAN RIGHTS TREATIES AND THE VIENNA CONVENTION REGIME:

CONFLICT, HARMONY OR RECONCILIATION

Edited by

Ineta Ziemele

Deutsches Institut für Menschenrechte

Springer-Science+Business Media, B.V.

A C.I.P. Catalogue record for this book is available from the Library of Congress.

Printed on acid-free paper.

ISBN 978-90-04-14064-6 ISBN 978-94-017-6019-5 (eBook)
DOI 10.1007/978-94-017-6019-5

Originally published by Martinus Nijhoff in 2004.
Softcover reprint of the hardcover 1st edition 2004

http: //www.brill.nl

Brill Academic Publishers incorporates the imprint Martinus Nijhoff Publishers.

RESERVATIONS TO HUMAN RIGHTS TREATIES AND THE VIENNA CONVENTION REGIME: CONFLICT, HARMONY OR RECONCILIATION

Deutsches Institut
für Menschenrechte

THE RAOUL WALLENBERG INSTITUTE
HUMAN RIGHTS LIBRARY
VOLUME 17

TABLE OF CONTENTS

TABLE OF CONTENTS

FOREWORD

Quite early in the history of the European Commission and European Court of Human Rights, questions arose about the validity and consequences of reservations made by Contracting States when signing or ratifying the European Convention on Human Rights ('the Convention'), making them the subject of a reflection process which has been on-going ever since and caused the Court to gradually elaborate on the relationship between the Convention and international law.

One could say that it all started with the case of *Belilos* v. *Switzerland*[1], in which the Swiss Government referred, by way of preliminary objection, to the interpretative declaration it had made in respect of Article 6 § 1 of the Convention. The Court took the view that the said declaration was to be considered as a reservation within the meaning of former Article 64 (now 57) of the Convention, which meant that its validity had to be examined in the light of the requirements of that provision. In the end, the reservation was found to be invalid, as it failed to meet the requirements of Article 64.

A more difficult question to be resolved, however, was that of the effects of such a finding. In their submissions to the Court, the Swiss representatives had argued that there was disagreement on this issue. Under the contract theory of treaties, they pleaded, a State which made an invalid reservation simply was not a party to the treaty, whereas in a closed or integrated system, a State which had submitted an invalid reservation remained bound by the whole treaty, the reservation thus having no effect. As an intermediate solution, a State which had made an invalid reservation would continue to be a party to the treaty, but the provision in respect of which the reservation was made would be inoperative, either permanently or at least until the State had reformulated the reservation. The Court hardly discussed this argument and flatly held that it was "beyond doubt that Switzerland is, and regards itself as, bound by the Convention irrespective of the validity of the declaration".[2]

A few years later, a similar issue arising in the case of *Loizidou* v. *Turkey* gave the Court an opportunity to further elaborate on those questions. The case was concerned *inter alia* with the access of the applicant, a Cypriot

---

[1] *Belilos* v. *Switzerland,* judgment of 29 April 1988, Series A no. 132.

[2] On this, *see* L. Wildhaber, 'swiss Reservations and Interpretative Declarations to the European Convention on Human Rights and the Temeltasch, Belilos and Weber Cases', *Chicago-Kent Law Review* (1991), p. 451.

national living in Nicosia, to her property in northern Cyprus.[3] Before the Court, the respondent Government pointed to the territorial limitation it had included in its declarations made under former Articles 25 and 46 of the Convention, to the effect that the right of individual petition to the Commission and the jurisdiction of the Court were recognized only in respect of 'acts or omissions of public authorities in Turkey performed within the boundaries of the national territory of the Republic of Turkey'. The facts of the case thus fell outside the Court's jurisdiction, the Turkish Government argued.

After an extensive analysis of the validity of those limitations, the Court took the opposite view. Referring for the first time to Article 31 of the *Vienna Convention on the Law of Treaties* in the context of reservations and/or limitations to the Convention, it indicated that the validity of the territorial limitations at issue had to be examined by reference to the ordinary meaning to be given to the terms of Articles 25 and 46 in their context and in the light of their object and purpose, as well as to 'any subsequent practice in the application of the treaty which establishes the agreement of the parties regarding its interpretation'. In respect of 'the object and purpose' of the Convention, the Court noted that a system as the one in effect advocated by the respondent Government, whereby Contracting parties would be free to subscribe to separate regimes of enforcement of Convention obligations depending on the scope of their acceptances, would diminish the effectiveness of the Convention as a constitutional instrument of European public order (*ordre public*) to such a far-reaching extent that a power to this effect should have been expressly provided for, which however was not the case. In the end, the Court found the territorial limitations at issue to be invalid.

As in the *Belilos* case, it then remained for the Court to examine whether, as a consequence of this finding, the validity of the acceptances themselves could be called into question. On this point, the Court was more explicit than in the *Belilos* case, stressing *inter alia* that in addressing this issue it had to bear in mind the special character of the Convention as an instrument of European public order (*ordre public*) for the protection of individual human beings and its mission, as set out in Article 19, to ensure the observance of the engagements undertaken by the High Contracting parties. The Court also considered that the issue of the severability of the

[3] *Loizidou* v. *Turkey*, judgments of 23 March 1995 (preliminary objections, Series A no. 310), 18 December 1996 (Reports 1996-VI) and 29 July 1998 (Reports 1998-IV).

invalid parts of Turkey's declarations could not be decided by reference to the statements of her representatives, which were expressed subsequent to the filing of the declarations. In this connection, the Court observed that the respondent Government must have been aware, in view of the consistent practice of Contracting parties under Articles 25 and 46 to accept unconditionally the competence of the Commission and Court that the impugned restrictive clauses were of questionable validity under the Convention system and might be deemed impermissible by the Convention organs. The Court concluded that the restrictions at issue could be separated from the remainder of the text leaving intact the acceptance of the optional clauses.

In its judgment on the merits, the Court went a step further in explicating the relationship between the Convention and international law. It stated that the Convention must be interpreted in the light of the rules of interpretation set out in the *Vienna Convention on the Law of Treaties*. Article 31 § 3 (c) of that treaty indicated that account is to be taken of any relevant rules of international law applicable in the relations between the parties. The Court added that the principles underlying the Convention could not be interpreted and applied in a vacuum. Mindful of the Convention's special character as a human rights treaty, it must also take into account any relevant rules of international law when deciding on disputes concerning its jurisdiction pursuant to Article 49 (now Article 32 § 2) of the Convention[4]. On this basis, the Court took into account the fact that the "Turkish Republic of Northern Cyprus" (TRNC) was not regarded as a State under international law and therefore refused to attribute legal validity to some provisions of the "TRNC Constitution".[5]

Scholars identified four factors which could explain the Court's approach in *Belilos* and *Loizidou*. The first was the "age" factor. States which had ratified the Convention at an earlier stage had attached far less reservations, so that there was a danger of inequality between the Contracting parties. The Court apparently felt it could privilege the integrity of the guarantees of the Convention as against the need to secure a strictly

[4] The same principle has been since repeated in several other cases, including *Bankovic and others* v. *Belgium and 16 other Contracting States* (dec) [GC], no. 52207/99, § 57; *Al-Adsani* v. *United Kingdom* [GC], no. 35793/97, § 55.

[5] However, remedies available in the TRNC may be regarded as domestic remedies for the purposes of Article 35 of the Convention (former Article 26) (*see Cyprus* v. *Turkey* [GC], no. 25781/94, § 102. The Court added that this approach in no way amounted to an indirect legitimisation of a regime which is unlawful under international law (§ 101).

contractual participation. Second was the 'isolation' factor: whereas reservations normally operate reciprocally, with the effect that the decision invalidating a reservation would lead to conflicts and denunciations, the Convention as a typical human rights treaty claims an objective rather than a reciprocal effect, with the result that the impact of decisions such as in *Belilos* remained isolated. A third factor related to the role of the supervisory organs: under the framework of the Convention, the Court must have the final word as to the validity of reservations, which in turn lessens the sovereignty of the States parties and the value of the contract theory. Finally, and perhaps most importantly, the Court considered the Convention as an 'integration mechanism', which aims at establishing a common European public order in the field of human rights, which must transcend and replace the particular legal orders of the individual States parties.[6]

Even though the UN Human Rights Committee followed the same approach as the Court[7], other scholars were much more critical of it, pointing to the fact that while the intention to keep the States which made reservations within the system was understandable, the real issue was whether the States concerned had agreed to be bound by a treaty in the absence of the reservations declared invalid. The *Belilos* and *Loizidou* approach totally disregarded the fact that at the heart of any treaty-based commitment there could only be agreement. Human rights treaties made no exception in this respect.[8]

---

[6] S. Marks, 'Reservations Unhinged: The Belilos Case before the European Court of Human Rights', 39 INT. & COMP. L.Q. 300 (1990), p. 64. In the same sense, H. J. Bourguignon, 'The Belilos Case: New Light on Reservations to Multilateral Treaties', 29 VA. J.INT'L. 347 (1989), at p. 371, pp. 385–386.

[7] C.C.P.R./C/2/Rev.1/Add.6 (11 November 1994).

[8] *See* A. Pellet, Special Rapporteur, Second Report on Reservations to Treaties, A/CN.4/477/Add.1, 13 June 1996, cited by J.-P. Cot, "La responsabilité de la Turquie et le respect de la Convention européenne dans la partie nord de Chypre", *Revue trimestrielle des droits de l'homme* (1998) p. 102 (pp. 105–106). In this connection, it may also be worth noting the recent judgment in the case of *Assanidze* v. *Georgia* (no. 71503/01), in which the Strasbourg Court confirmed a presumption of territorial competence of the Republic of Georgia in respect of the Ajarian Autonomous Republic with the following reasoning: "For reasons of legal policy – the need to maintain equality between the State Parties and to ensure the effectiveness of the Convention – it could not be otherwise. But for the presumption, the applicability of the Convention could be selectively restricted to parts only of the territory of certain State Parties, thus rendering the notion of effective human-rights protection underpinning the entire Convention meaningless while, at the same time, allowing discrimination between the State Parties, that is to say between those which

This is precisely the question here: should human rights treaties in general and the Convention in particular be interpreted any differently from other treaties in respect of reservations? Should a distinction be made in this context between the validity of a reservation – which the Strasbourg Court confirmed in a number of instances[9] – and the effects of a reservation found to be invalid?

These questions and many others arising in this context call for an updated and comprehensive approach, as the one which is adopted by the present book. Its excellent contributions by well-known experts provide a detailed overview of the legal situation regarding reservations in respect of each of the most relevant present day human rights treaties, as well as discussions and proposed answers to the delicate and complex questions arising in this field. Professor Ineta Ziemele is to be most warmly congratulated on her initiative to edit the present collection of studies, a timely contribution to the on-going debate on harmony between human rights treaties and international law.

Luzius Wildhaber

President of the European Court of Human Rights

---

accepted the application of the Convention over the whole of their territory and those which did not" (§ 142).

[9] *See* the judgments in the cases of *Chorherr* v. *Austria* (A 266-B) and *Brannigan and McBride* v. *United Kingdom* (A 258-B). For an in-depth analysis of this issue, *see* the partly dissenting opinion of Judge Valticos in the *Chorherr* case.

EDITOR'S PREFACE

Questions relating to reservations to human rights treaties have been on the international law agenda for quite some time. Different important dates could be chosen, but one of them would certainly be the 1951 Advisory Opinion of the International Court of Justice on *Reservations to the Convention on the Prevention and Punishment of the Crime of Genocide.*[10] One can say that there has always been some discomfort about reservations in relation to international obligations of States applicable to individuals. This apprehension was brought to the forefront of the international normative process with General Comment No. 24 of the Human Rights Committee and the work of the International Law Commission on reservations to treaties.

This book is yet another contribution to the debate on reservations to human rights treaties. It emanates from the conference on the topic held in December 2002 at the Raoul Wallenberg Institute for Human Rights and Humanitarian Law in Lund, Sweden.[11] The initiators of the meeting were the German Institute for Human Rights and the Raoul Wallenberg Institute. The book consists of contributions presented at the conference, but it is not limited either to issues and observations made during the conference or to the participants of the conference. It is organised in two parts. Part I contains articles on practices of human rights monitoring bodies at the United Nations and the Council of Europe contributed by current or former experts of these committees or other experts in the field. Part II contains some highlights of the doctrinal debate on the topic. The book would have been incomplete without the Second Report of the ILC's Special Rapporteur Alain Pellet on Reservations to Treaties. The Report appears as Annex 1 in the book.

The book shows that differences in opinions among scholars and even within the various monitoring procedures continue to prevail. Several key questions have generated a variety of answers. Can the reservations' regime, as codified in the 1969 *Vienna Convention on the Law of Treaties*, adequately address human rights relationships? Is there a danger of further fragmentation of international law if human rights treaties were to be treated differently as concerns the reservations' regime applicable to these treaties?

These questions derive, in fact, from another prior question concerning the character of human rights treaties. Already during written and oral

---

[10] See Request for Advisory Opinion and Documents of the Written Proceedings, Part I, *ICJ Reports*, 1951.

[11] List of Participants is reproduced in Annex 2.

pleadings in front of the ICJ in the framework of the 1951 Advisory Opinion procedure the general question of classification of treaties and the Genocide Convention in particular was prominently present.

What remains unsettling about human rights treaties is their dual character. It has been argued that because individuals do not enter into international treaties on an equal footing with States, one can hardly consider human rights treaties as contractual in nature. At the same time, human rights treaties continue to derive their validity and binding force from the traditional rules of law of treaties. It is probably correct to say that human rights treaties contain both contractual rules between two States concerning their co-operation for the protection of human rights and the rules that States subscribe to in relation to individuals. During the 1951 Advisory Opinion proceedings it was suggested that the latter set of rules should be seen as normative rules, or that the Genocide Convention should be considered as a social or law-making treaty, and that this understanding should limit the right of States to enter into reservations.[12]

In short, today the question remains whether the enjoyment by individuals of international human rights is an issue altogether different from 'the exchange of reciprocal benefits and obligations' between States. More importantly, can the special, or at least a different, character of this issue be recognised within the existing structures and/or procedures of international law? It is in relation to these questions that different possibilities are proposed. The traditional approach would argue for the reinforcement of the role of States both in their respect for human rights and the available choices within an international law context. A more unorthodox approach would argue in favour of an ever-growing role for individuals in international fora, as supported by relevant international procedures. Therefore, the battle today takes place on the third ground, i.e., between the States and human rights monitoring procedures with respect to their respective competencies in relation to reservations. It can be safely said that this battle has no real potential of challenging the traditional structures of international law nor is it proposed in this book. But it is an important element of an on-going normative process. The fact that this debate has assisted in sharpening the questions and available options within the treaties concerned and in the broader context of general international law can be considered as a step in the right direction.

Before presenting to the reader the debate that follows in this book, the Editor wishes to express her appreciation to the Publications Office of the

---

[12] *Ibid.*, p. 378 *et seq* (Statement by Sir Hartley Shawcross).

Raoul Wallenberg Institute and Ms Carin Laurin, Mr Miles Hogan and Mr Jason Naum in particular for all the assistance rendered in the preparation of the publication.

Ineta Ziemele

Lund (Sweden)

TABLE OF CASES

INTERNATIONAL COURT OF JUSTICE

Reservations to the Convention on the Prevention and Punishment of the Crime of Genocide Advisory Opinion of 28 May 1951, *ICJ Reports 195*: xiii, 153

North Sea Continental Shelf Cases, Judgement of 20 February 1969 *ICJ Reports 1969*: 223

Military and Paramilitary Activities In and Against Nicaragua Merits, Judgement of 27 June 1986, *ICJ Reports 1986*: 64

Convention on the Prevention and Punishment of the Crime of Genocide Case (*Bosnia and Herzegovina* v. *Yugoslavia*), Provisional Measures *ICJ Reports 1993*: 240

EUROPEAN COURT OF HUMAN RIGHTS

Kjeldsen and Others v. *Denmark*, Publications of the Eur. Court H.R., Series B no. 21, 44-45: 100, 130

Luedicke, Belkacem and Koç v. *Germany*, judgment of 28 November 1978, ECHR, Series A no. 29:124

Temeltasch v. *Switzerland*, Commission's report of 5 May 1982, DR 31, p. 120 (§ 49), application no. 9116/80: 109, 112, 116, 123, 124, 179

Belilos v. *Switzerland,* judgment of 29 April 1988, Series A no. 132: vii, 44, 62, 109, 110, 112, 114, 115, 116, 120, 123, 155, 180, 208

Chrysostomos and Others v. *Turkey*, admissibility decision of 4 March 1991, applications nos. 15299, 15300 and 15318/89, *HRLJ* 12 (1990): 121, 130, 134, 208

Brannigan and McBride v. *United Kingdom,* judgment of 26 May 1993, Series A 258-B: xi

Chorherr v. *Austria*, judgment of 25 August 1993, Series A no. 226-B: xi, 116, 121

TABLE OF CASES

HUMAN RIGHTS COMMITTEE

TABLE OF CASES

ICTY

Prosecutor v. *Anto Furundzija*, Case No. IT-95-17/1, 10 December 1998, para. 160–61: 93, 229

IACHR

Effect of Reservations on the Entry into Force of the American Convention (Articles 74 and 75), advisory opinion, Inter-American Court of Human Rights of 24 September 1982, in 67 ILR 558: 181

CONSTITUTIONAL COURTS

Pratt and Morgan v. *the Attorney General for Jamaica*, 2 A.C. 1, 1994: 50

INTRODUCTION:

OPENING OF THE CONFERENCE ON RESERVATIONS TO HUMAN RIGHTS TREATIES*

*Percy MacLean***

Dear Göran, friends of the 'human rights community', ladies and gentlemen, let me welcome you to the first international conference organized by the newly founded German Institute for Human Rights in cooperation with the widely known and respected Raoul Wallenberg Institute of Human Rights and Humanitarian Law.

We are very happy to be here today in Lund. I would like to thank and acknowledge our Swedish hosts for inviting us to this joint project and also for facilitating the conference.

One of the main tasks of the German Institute for Human Rights is to bring together human rights experts from universities, politics and civil society. This is why we have proposed to invite not only academics, but also representatives of the Swedish and German ministries of foreign affairs.[13] Today, our Institute's most notable contributions are two experts of the Committee on the Elimination of Discrimination against Women (CEDAW Committee) and the Human Rights Committee (HRC), both members of our advisory board. First there is Hanna Beate Schöpp-Schilling who has been an international fighter for women's rights for over 14 years. Following this seminar she will return to Berlin and there with her expertise lead a group to work on the newly established CEDAW Committee inquiry procedure. Secondly, there is Eckart Klein, who recently chaired a most interesting conference on human rights customary law in Potsdam in which I had the honour to participate.

Both of our advisory members – as well as the other experts invited to this conference – have longtime experience in the practice of 'their' human rights treaty monitoring bodies and have a lot to offer to the debate over the role of reservations.

---

* The Conference took place on 6–7 December 2002 in Lund, Sweden.

** Presiding judge at the Berlin administrative court, first director of the German Institute for Human Rights (2002/2003).

[13] For the List of Participants, see Annex 2.

PERCY MACLEAN

There is a book by Liesbeth Lijnzaad whose title in itself displays the dilemma: 'Reservations to UN Human Rights Treaties – Ratify and Ruin?' The question is: Do reservations really reap a benefit to the people in so far as they enable their governments to ratify the treaty without renouncing their 'national interests', thus promoting cultural relativism? Or will the human rights treaties – which in fact have the character of international constitutions – in the long run be bogged down by thousands of exceptions?

My priority as the director of a national human rights institution is, in any event, to fight against these reservations by convincing my government and other governments of the fact that human rights are universal and that every country should be proud of achieving what is the internationally accepted standard. It is truly a shame, for instance, that 65 out of the 192 States that ratified the *Convention on the Rights of the Child* (CRC) had reservations. Not only do reservations limit the protection provided for by the treaty in question, they also might lead to confusion regarding the obligations agreed to by the State. My own government, for example, declares that it would be of no difference to them at all to retract their reservations against the CRC, but they don't do it. So my question is: Why?

Another negative consequence to the protection of human rights are reservations contrary to the object and purpose of the treaties. These reservations are generally regarded as impermissible, as stated in Article 19(c) of the *Vienna Convention on the Law of Treaties*. Unfortunately, the legal consequences of this inadmissibility of reservations (leading to their severability or seeing them as null and void *ab initio*) are widely unclear as is the competence of the different treaty bodies and other signatory States to formulate decisions or objections to that effect.

During this conference we should exchange our views and experiences. While maintaining great focus on international law, the utmost protection of human rights for all should be the aim, taking into account the concerns and interests of the individual States.

Perhaps this will result in the development of lobbying strategies to approach our respective governments and persuade them to retract their reservations.

RESERVATIONS TO HUMAN RIGHTS TREATIES – SETTING THE STAGE: WISHFUL THINKING OR PROSPECTS FOR DEVELOPMENT

*Göran Melander**

In spite of the fact that all human rights are universal, several States upon ratification or accession to a human rights treaty have included reservations, whereupon they have intended to modify their obligations, following the convention. In a way a reservation to such a treaty is an expression of what sometimes are viewed as cultural diversities. Sweden, for instance, has submitted a reservation to Article 20 of the *International Covenant on Civil and Political Rights*, which prohibits propaganda for war. In the view of the Swedish Government and Parliament, freedom of the press is more important than prohibiting any propaganda for war. The freedom of the press is indeed a deep-rooted right in Swedish society. Other Contracting parties have not met the reservation with any objection, from which it may be concluded, that this reservation is acceptable.

Other reservations to human rights treaties have a more sweeping character. The Kingdom of Bahrain, for instance, has made a reservation to Articles 2 and 16 of the *Convention on the Elimination of All Forms of Discrimination against Women* (CEDAW) 'in order to ensure its implementation within the bounds of the provision of the Islamic Shariah'. That reservation has been met with several objections, one of them by the Government of Denmark, which stated: 'the reservation to articles 2 and 16 with reference to the provisions of Islamic Sharia is of unlimited scope and undefined character. Consequently, the Government of Denmark considers the said reservations as being incompatible with the object and purpose of the Convention and accordingly inadmissible and without effect under international law' Denmark did, however, not preclude the entry into force of the Convention in its entirety between Bahrain and Denmark.

The issue of reservations to human rights treaties has raised the legal effect of such reservations to the forefront. Reservations are only permissible provided such reservations are not incompatible with the purpose and object

* Professor Emeritus, Faculty of Law, Lund University; Chairman of the Board of the Raoul Wallenberg Institute and the Member of the CEDAW Committee.

of the Convention. The question then arises, who is competent to decide, whether or not a reservation is compatible or incompatible.

A human rights treaty is a treaty, concluded between States. Accordingly, it seems logical that the 1969 *Vienna Convention on the Law of Treaties* should comply, from which follows that the issue under consideration can only be decided by other Contracting parties, as is prescribed for in Articles 19–23.

A clear reservation clause can rarely be found in the most important human rights treaties. Article 19(c) is applicable: the reservation is not permissible if it is contrary to the object and purpose of the Convention and the same applies according to Article 20 of the *Convention on the Elimination of All Forms of Racial Discrimination* and Article 28 of the CEDAW. It is the other Contracting parties, which are competent to decide the issue of object and purpose. They are entitled to object to the reservation and they may also add, that the Convention will not enter into force between the reserving State and the objecting State.

The bilateral relation between a State, which has made a reservation and another State party, which has not objected to the reservation is clear: the Convention as revised by the reserving State is applicable in their mutual relations. The bilateral relation between the reserving State and a State which has objected and declared that the Convention will not enter into force between the two States is equally clear: mutually the Convention is not in force between the two States. The third alternative is the relation between the reserving State and the State, which has objected but without any declaration of non-entry into force of the Convention. The only logical solution is, that in that bilateral relation, the Convention in the version of the reserving State is applicable. It could be added that it is irrelevant in this context if a reservation is specific or is of a sweeping character.

It has been argued, that the *Vienna Convention on the Law of Treaties* should not be applicable with respect to human rights treaties. The argument goes that such Conventions belong to a particular regime, as they for the most part protect individuals within the jurisdiction of the State, which has ratified the Convention. The view exists that the treaty body, established in accordance with the provisions of the relevant treaty, should decide the issue of 'object and purpose'. The motive behind this argument is that the treaty body is most suitable to determine the validity of the reservation, as it has the best understanding of the treaty in question and is responsible for the interpretation of the treaty.

It seems, however, that this opinion is wishful thinking more than anything else. It is not likely that the Contracting parties will accept such a view. It seems as if this proposal is based upon a desire to enlarge the mandate of the treaty bodies to include relevant rules of international customary law.

It may very well be that even if a State has made a reservation to a particular treaty, the State may nevertheless be bound by a particular rule in accordance with the treaty but based upon international customary law. It seems as if the treaty body is then tempted to monitor that particular rule, not because the State is bound to respect that rule by virtue of the Convention, but because it is a rule of international customary law. However, the mandate of a treaty body is clearly limited to the Convention, according to which it has been established and the treaty body cannot exceed its mandate without amending the Convention.

It has been argued, that the CEDAW Committee is entitled to monitor not only the Convention but also the *Beijing Platform for Action* and the *Beijing + 5 Final Document*. It is a disputed question, if the Committee in fact has been given such a power. In so far as the two final documents only mean an interpretation of the Convention, the Committee can be guided by these documents. However, should the two Documents clearly deviate from the Convention, such a view may mean an enlargement of the Convention and an interpretation of the Convention, which is too wide.

It seems accurate to conclude that the issue of reservations and the legal effect of them have to be interpreted in line with the *Vienna Convention on the Law of Treaties*. This is at least what States in most cases consider, as also a human rights treaty is a treaty between States. Upon giving its consent to be bound by a Convention, States must know what obligations they undertake, in particular as in most cases they are not entitled to denounce the Conventions.

PART I. ELEMENTS OF PRACTICE OF HUMAN RIGHTS MONITORING BODIES

RESERVATIONS TO THE CONVENTION ON THE ELIMINATION OF ALL FORMS OF DISCRIMINATION AGAINST WOMEN: AN UNRESOLVED ISSUE OR (NO) NEW DEVELOPMENTS?

Hanna Beate Schöpp-Schilling[*]

TABLE OF CONTENTS

1. THE CONVENTION AND ITS OPTIONAL PROTOCOL

The *Convention on the Elimination of All Forms of Discrimination against Women* (CEDAW) was adopted in December 1979 and came into force in September 1981. The Convention is the most important international human rights instrument for women. It combines three approaches: a non-discrimination approach, a protective approach (maternity protection based on biological grounds), and a corrective approach (application of temporary special measures defined as not being discriminatory). The goal is to achieve

[*] Dr. Phil.; Consultant; Member of the UN Committee on the Elimination of All Forms of Discrimination of Women (CEDAW) since 1989.

de jure as well as *de facto*, or substantive equality for women, 'irrespective of their marital status', in comparison with men. The Convention covers 'all' forms of discrimination and, while specifically naming the 'political, economic, social, cultural, civil' fields, it also goes beyond these by adding 'or any other field', thus allowing for a wide interpretation. Although the norms of non-discrimination on the basis of sex and the equal right of men and women to the enjoyment of their human rights are also contained in the *Universal Declaration on Human Rights* (UDHR) and in the two *International Covenants on Civil and Political* and *on Economic, Social and Cultural Rights* (ICCPR, ICESCR), CEDAW spells them out in a more detailed way. Thus, the Convention lists the many facets of women's equality with men in the private sphere in marriage and family relations (Article 16) which, as the Committee on the Elimination of Discrimination against Women (CEDAW Committee) made clear in its *General Recommendation No. 21*, is of special relevance in that it overcomes the traditional neglect of the worth of women's work in this sphere as well as in that it stipulates that there can be no justification for applying different or discriminatory legal standards to that sphere as compared to those which are applied to the public sphere. Article 5(a) is of particular importance, too. It obliges States parties to modify the 'social and cultural patterns of conduct of men and women' with a view of eliminating prejudices, concepts of alleged superiority or inferiority of either of the sexes and of 'stereotyped roles for men and women'. Article 5(a) thereby implicitly also recognizes the concept of discrimination based on gender with regard to the socially constructed roles ascribed to women and men in public and private life, in addition to the concept of discrimination based on sex.

In addition to State actors and according to Article 2(e) the Convention covers private actors ('any person, organization or enterprise'). It obliges States parties to respect, protect, promote and fulfil women's rights to non-discrimination and equality in the enjoyment of their human rights. Within this framework of obligations States parties must, wherever appropriate under each article, eliminate discriminatory legislation and adopt enabling legislation, advance women's equality through programs and other measures and challenge, modify or eliminate the cultural assumptions which impede women's progress towards formal and substantive equality.[14] State parties, according to Article 2 of the Convention, must act 'without delay' since the norm of non-discrimination does not allow for progressive realization. In addition, they must ensure the 'practical realization' of the principle of

[14] I am indebted to Rikki Holtmaat for this differentiation.

equality, which implies that results must be achieved. These results may be of a quantitative and/or qualitative nature regarding women's representation and participation at all levels of education and employment and in public and political life as well as regarding resource allocation for them in order to achieve and sustain their substantive equality with men in the enjoyment of their human rights. Temporary special measures are permitted according to Article 4(1) and are deemed appropriate and necessary by the Committee in order to achieve such substantive equality. In addition, substantive equality must be achieved for all groups of women, including those suffering from multiple discrimination due to, *inter alia*, race, ethnic identity, class, religious belief, age, and disability.

The Convention mandates the monitoring of its implementation by States parties through a reporting procedure (Article 18). A Committee of twenty-three independent experts, who represent different legal systems and regions of the world, is charged with the examination of States parties' reports (*inter alia*, Article 17). In October 1999, two new monitoring procedures for the CEDAW Committee – a communication and an inquiry procedure – were added to the Convention through the adoption of an Optional Protocol by the General Assembly of the United Nations.[15] This Protocol came into force in December 2000.

[15] A complaint procedure had already been proposed during the process of formulating the Convention since 1973 by Canada, the Netherlands and Sweden, in 1976 by Belgium, and again, in 1977 by the Netherlands. However, States were not ready at the time to include this procedure in the Convention. The idea was raised again in the 1991. It gained momentum through the *Vienna Declaration and Programme of Action* adopted at the 1993 World Conference on Human Rights in Vienna and through *Suggestion 5* of the CEDAW Committee in 1994. Later that year, the Economic and Social Council asked the Commission on the Status of Women to examine, in co-operation with the Committee, the feasibility of introducing the right of petition through the preparation of an optional protocol to CEDAW. In the fall of 1994, an independent expert meeting took place, convened by a non-governmental organization, in co-operation with the Maastricht Centre for Human Rights at the University of Limburg in the Netherlands. A draft text resulted from that meeting, which was also attended by CEDAW Committee members. Based on this draft, the CEDAW Committee adopted *Suggestion No. 7* in 1995, which described the elements that an optional protocol to the Convention should contain. In July 1995, the Economic and Social Council in its Resolution 1995/29 requested the Commission on the Status of Women to establish an open-ended working group on this issue. It also requested the Secretary General to invite Governments, inter-governmental organizations, and non-governmental organizations to submit their views. The *Beijing Declaration* and *Platform for*

While it had been one of the goals, stipulated in the *Beijing Platform for Action*, to achieve universal ratification of the Convention by the year 2000, it was not reached. Ratification stood at 175 at the end of 2003. This makes the Convention the second most ratified of the now seven human rights treaties of the United Nations, but also one with many reservations. Ratification of the Optional Protocol stood at 59 in January 2004.

2. THE ISSUE OF RESERVATIONS

It has been said and often repeated, that the 'question of reservations has been one of the most controversial subjects of contemporary international law'.[16] It has also been pointed out with regard to CEDAW, that reservations to this Convention raise not only a number of legal problems which may be inherent in the system of the *Vienna Convention on the Law of Treaties* (VCLT), but also many political, economic, moral and social issues.

The Convention itself does allow for reservations as described in Article 19 of the *Vienna Convention on the Law of Treaties*. The history of formulating the two respective articles (Article 28 and Article 29) of the Convention, which cover the issue of reservations is well described in the *travaux préparatoires* and commented upon by several scholars.[17] Suffice it to underline that the discussion took place within the framework of the 'universality-integrity dilemma'. At the time, some delegations of the Member States of the United Nations in the respective working group of the Commission on the Status of Women even thought it unnecessary to formulate and adopt any articles on this issue at all, since their thinking 'clearly operated on the assumption that the Vienna Convention provided adequate solutions' for this dilemma. I agree with Lijnzaad (and others) that

---

Action of September 1995 requested support for the process initiated by the Commission on the Status of Women. Thus, the process of formulating such a protocol began, and the text was negotiated in record time between 1996 and 1999. For documents of this process, see Division for the Advancement of Women, *The Convention on the Elimination of All Forms of Discrimination Against Women. The Optional Protocol: Text and Materials* (United Nations, New York, 2000).

[16] S. S. Ali, *Gender and Human Rights in Islam and International Law. Equal Before Allah, Unequal Before Man?* (Kluwer Law International, The Hague/London/Boston, 2000), p. 240.

[17] R. Cook, 'Reservations to the Convention of All Forms of Discrimination Against Women' 30 *Virginia Journal of International Law* (1990) pp. 643–716, here pp. 673–678; also L. Lijnzaad, *Reservations to Human Rights Treaties: Ratify and Ruin?* (Martinus Nijhoff, Dordrecht, 1995), p. 300.

'the history of the Women's Convention has proved them to have been wrong.'[18]

Article 28 (1) of the Convention notes that the Secretary-General of the United Nations 'shall receive and circulate to all States the text of the reservations made by States at the time of ratification or accession'.

Article 28(2) states in a language stronger than in the *Vienna Convention on the Law of Treaties* that a 'reservation incompatible with the object and purpose of the present Convention shall not be permitted'.[19]

Article 28(3) allows for the withdrawal of reservations and describes the procedure for this withdrawal.

Article 29(1) allows a) for a dispute between two or more States parties concerning the interpretation or application of the Convention, and b) if the dispute cannot be settled, for a submission of that dispute to arbitration at the request of one of them, and c) if the States parties cannot agree on the organization of the arbitration within six months, for referring the dispute by any one of the States parties to the International Court of Justice.

Article 29(2) allows for a reservation by a State party to Article 29(1) at the time of signature or ratification of the Convention or accession thereto, and stipulates that other States parties are not bound by that paragraph with regard to the reserving State party.

Article 29(3) allows for the withdrawal of the reservation made according to article 29(2) and describes the procedure for doing so.

There is no provision in the Convention stating that a reservation must be explicitly accepted by the other States parties as formulated in Article 20(1) of the VCLT, nor is there a provision determining the meaning of 'incompatibility' as Article 20 of the *International Convention on the Elimination of All Forms of Racial Discrimination* (ICERD) does.[20]

States parties entered reservations to the Convention from the very beginning of the ratification or accession process in the form of general

---

[18] Lijnzaad, *supra*, note 4.

[19] VCLT uses the formulation of 'may not be formulated'. Clark interprets this fact as giving grounds for 'concluding that a one-tier test of admissibility was intended to operate under the Convention,' i.e. that an incompatible and therefore impermissible reservation cannot be accepted by other States parties. B. Clark, 'The Vienna Convention Reservations Regime and the Convention on Discrimination Against Women' 85 *American Journal of International Law* (1991) pp. 281–321, here p. 307.

[20] Art. 20 of the ICERD states that a reservation shall be considered 'incompatible' or 'inhibitive' if 'at least two thirds of the States Parties /sic/ to this Convention' object to it.'

declarations and reservations and as explicit reservations to various substantive articles and to the procedural Article 29(1). The Committee has been concerned about reservations almost since its inception. Already in 1990, Cook characterized the Convention as 'among the most heavily reserved of international human rights conventions', describing and analysing the 'paradox' that the Convention, while on its way of gaining almost universal application, was being jeopardized in its integrity.[21] Other commentators either echoed or modified this opinion over the years.

Since then, some States parties withdrew their substantive reservations due to changes in their legal and/or political and social context. The motivation behind such changes has many sources. In some cases States, when ratifying the Convention, clearly recognize that their domestic legislation is not in conformity with the Convention. There does, however, exist the political will to change this legislation as soon as possible and to withdraw the reservation when the new legislation is in place. In other instances, the interaction between CEDAW Committee members and the respective State party in the monitoring process of discussing States parties' reports and/or the influence of that process on the lobbying activities of national non-governmental organizations, may have contributed to such changes in domestic legislation and to the subsequent withdrawal of reservations. In the case of Germany, a court verdict by the European Court of Justice played a decisive role, which led to a change in the *German Basic Law* and to the withdrawal of the respective reservation. Mayer claims that political considerations determine both the formulation and the withdrawal of reservations allegedly based on Islam.[22]

Despite the withdrawal of reservations too many, however, remain, and newly ratifying States have been entering more. In the eyes of scholars and objecting States parties most of the general reservations as well as those to substantive articles must be seen as going against 'the object and purpose' of the Convention. The combination of reservations both to substantive articles and to the article on dispute negotiation raises particular concern, since the door for any dispute resolution between two or more States parties is closed. On the other hand, one should not overestimate this issue, since such a

[21] Cook, *supra*, note 4, p. 644.

[22] A. F. Mayer, 'Religious Reservations to the Convention on the Elimination of all Forms of Discrimination against Women: What Do They Really Mean?', in C.W. Howland (ed.) *Religious Fundamentalisms and the Human Rights of Women* (Palgrave, New York, 2001), pp. 105–116, here pp. 109–110.

dispute resolution has never been used so far, even when it would have been legally possible.

The Optional Protocol to the CEDAW is unique among existing UN human rights petition instruments in that it does not allow for any reservations according to its article 17.[23] Article 17 was made possible by the 'opt-out clause' of Article 10(1) of the Optional Protocol. This provision allows for a declaration, to be made at the time of signature or ratification, regarding the non-recognition of the competence of the Committee to pursue the inquiry procedure under Articles 8 and 9. Article 10(2) opens the possibility of withdrawing that declaration and describes the respective procedure.

Currently, the *travaux préparatoires* of the Optional Protocol to CEDAW are incomplete. However, a collection of documents, put together by the Division of the Advancement of Women, gives insight into the discussion regarding Articles 10 and 17.[24] These documents also have relevance for the question of reservations to the Convention. Some key points of the discussion highlight both aspects: In its *Suggestion No. 7* (1995) the CEDAW Committee had drawn up a list of 'elements' for an optional protocol. In element 28 it had stated that no 'State-to-State communication procedure should be included and no reservations permitted'.[25] While *Suggestion No. 7* and its element 28 seem to have been welcomed by a number of delegations, other delegations feared that a prohibition of reservations might impede ratification of the future instrument. In addition, some delegations clearly enunciated their opinion at different points of the negotiation process that no reservations to the Convention itself could be made through an optional protocol. Some even expressed hope that the Committee would have to consider the issue of reservations to the Convention in its future work under an optional protocol and that this might promote the withdrawal of some reservations. Conflicting opinions were also voiced as to who has the power to decide on whether reservations to the Convention go against its object and purpose, i.e. the Committee or the States parties.[26]

---

[23] First Optional Protocol to the ICCPR, Articles 20 and 22 of the CAT, Article 14 of the ICERD, and Article 77 of the MWC, *supra*, p. 110, para. 3 and p. 114, para. 31.

[24] *Supra*, note 2.

[25] *Ibid.*, p. 35, para. 28.

[26] 'Delegations considered that ratification of the optional protocol would leave substantive reservations to the Convention unaffected, without prejudice to the

3. PURPOSE OF THIS ARTICLE

Soon after the Convention came into force, the issue of reservations became a matter of debate for the CEDAW Committee, for States parties and for scholars. Lijnzaad's chapter on CEDAW, while developing her analysis of the then existing reservations which differs in some points from that of others scholars who preceded her, summarizes this discussion up to December 1992.[27] Chinkin followed up on Lijnzaad by discussing developments up until 1994.[28] Others continued the discussion by focussing on the reservations by States parties with a predominantly Muslim population covering developments ultimately until 1998.[29] In general, these scholars pursue a more or less similar pattern of discussion. Building on each other's work they usually characterize the Convention and describe and discuss the nature of the various reservations. They then evaluate various responses by different actors, i.e. by the Committee itself in its discussion of States parties' reports and in its other pronouncements; by chairpersons of all human rights treaty bodies in the respective reports of their meetings; by States parties in voicing objections; and States parties in discussing the issue in the various organs and fora of the United Nations, including UN World Conferences in the 1990's. They also show how and in what way they influenced each other.

The purpose of my paper is to build on and to continue this discussion, and to do so explicitly from a Committee member's point of view. Thus, I

---

permissibility of a reservation and its compatibility with the Convention and with international treaty law . . . Thus, it was observed that it would be up to the Committee to examine the compatibility of such reservations with the convention, and, consequently, the admissibility of a communication.' 'summary of exchange of views on elements as contained in suggestion 7 held in the open-ended working group in 1996', *ibid.*, p. 60, para. 22.

[27] *Supra*, note 4, pp. 298–370. Lijnzaad builds on Clark and Cook.

[28] C. Chinkin, 'Reservations and Objections to the Convention on the Elimination of All Forms of Discrimination against Women', in J.P. Gardner (ed.) *Human Rights as General Norms and a State's Right to Opt Out* (The B.I. I.C.L., London, 1997), pp. 64–84.

[29] J. Connors, 'The Women's Convention in the Muslim World' in *supra* note 15, pp. 85–103, covers developments until 1994/5; Mayer, *supra* note 9, until 1997; Ali, *supra* note 3 until 1998 as does Helbling in G. Helbling, *Das völkerrechtliche Verbot der Geschlechterdiskriminierung in einem plurikulturellen Kontext* (Schulthess, Zürich, 2001).

will be looking at the impact of the Committee's decisions, general recommendations, suggestions, statements and reporting guidelines on

- the formulation of reservations by States which ratified the Convention after 1994,
- the reporting practice of some reserving States parties after 1997,
- the Committee's discussion of these reports and formulation of Concluding Comments.

I will also touch upon the question of how the issue of reservations may affect the future work of the Committee under its *Optional Protocol.*

Within this context, the following questions will also be commented upon:

- what is the 'object and purpose' of the Convention, which are its core provisions, and which reservations go against its 'object and purpose,'
- to what extent is the implementation of CEDAW permitted to be gradual and, if so, what is the time-frame for such a concept of progressive implementation and how does this relate to the issue of reservations,
- who should decide whether a reservation is against the 'object and purpose' of the Convention,
- has the Committee been sufficiently active on the issue of reservations or can it do more and if so, what?

4. STATUS OF RESERVATIONS IN 2003

At the end of 1992 Lijnzaad records 120 States parties to the Convention, of which 81 had ratified without reservations and 27 had entered reservations to 'substantive provisions or other declarations'. Reservations to Article 29(1) had been entered by 23 States parties; in her analysis, however, Lijnzaad does not deal with these reservations.[30] By January 2004, there were 175 States parties to the Convention. The document on Multilateral Treaties deposited with the Secretary-General, dated 5 February 2002, which includes a list of declarations and reservations, counts 55 States parties expressing substantive reservations and/or declarations and/or reservations only to Article 29(1). Of these 55 States parties only ten had entered a reservation to Article 29(1), while 22 had combined this reservation with reservations to

[30] *Supra* note 4, p. 304.

substantive articles.[31] Since 2002, of the newly ratifying States, Bahrain and the Syrian Arab Republic entered both substantive reservations as well as one to Article 29(1), raising the number of reserving States parties to 57.

There are 17 remaining Member States of the United Nations who have not ratified the Convention.[32] Of these, 7 are States with a predominantly Muslim population and/or with Islam as the declared State religion.. If ratification by the remaining Muslim States should occur, one can probably expect, based upon the experiences of most other States parties with a predominantly Muslim population, both substantive and procedural reservations (though not all States with a predominantly Muslim population entered reservations).[33] Thus, while it was rightly pointed out by Chinkin and Ali that the issue of reservation should not be identified as being a Muslim problem, it may become one in the future.

5. EFFORTS BY THE CEDAW COMMITTEE WITH REGARD TO RESERVATIONS UNTIL 1993

While there is no need to repeat the full discussion of the Committee's efforts on reservations covered by scholars up to 1998, I will, nevertheless highlight the salient points in the development of the Committee's point of view from my own perspective as a Committee member and add some comments. By the end of 1993 the Committee had reacted to the issue of reservations in various ways, i.e. through its constructive dialogue, two general recommendations, one suggestion and decisions.

5.1. Constructive Dialogue and Decision No. 4

Members had regularly commented on this issue during the 'constructive dialogue' with reserving States parties' delegations. Although some members had made clear and strong statements as to the permissibility of reservations[34], the Committee on the whole had been more cautious in its

---

[31] <www.unhchr.ch/html/menu3/b/treaty9-asp.htm>.

[32] These States are: Somalia, Sudan, Brunei Darussalam, Islamic Republic of Iran, Oman, Qatar, United Arab Emirates. The other States are: Swaziland, Kiribati, Marshall Islands, Federated States of Micronesia, Nauru, Palau, Tonga, Monaco, United States of America, and Holy See.

[33] Djibouti and Afghanistan did not enter any reservations, Indonesia only to Article 29 (1).

[34] The Swedish member, Mr. Nordenfeldt, in 1984, in discussing the initial report of Egypt 'was particularly concerned by the reservations entered with respect to article

pronouncements on the issue, partly due to a legal opinion it had obtained in 1984 from the Treaty Section of the Office of Legal Affairs of the United Nations Secretariat. The question had been as to who had the power to determine whether a reservation was compatible with the object and purpose of the Convention. The two-fold reply had been that the Secretary General 'does not have the power to interpret the Convention' and that 'the functions of the Committee do not appear to include a determination of the incompatibility of reservations, although reservations undoubtedly affect the application of the Convention and the Committee might have to comment thereon in its reports in this context'.[35] The Committee had also addressed the issue indirectly through *Decision No. 4* (1987) in which it had asked 'the United Nations system as a whole . . . to promote or undertake studies on the status of women under Islamic law and customs . . . taking into consideration the principle of *El Ijtihad* in Islam'.[36] This request, which had followed the Committee's discussion of the report of Bangladesh, had created great controversy in the Economic and Social Council. It had never been implemented, though the Committee had repeated its question in 1988 by pointing to the usefulness of such material given the many references to Islamic law by States parties when entering reservations.[37]

5.2. General Recommendations No 4 and 20 and Suggestion No. 4

The Committee has also adopted two general recommendations, i.e. *General Recommendations No. 4* (1987) and *20* (1992) , and one suggestion, *Suggestion No. 4* (1993) , on the issue of reservations. In order to understand why it took the Committee five years to formulate an opinion on the important issue of reservations to the Convention in a general recommendation, it has to be recalled that the impact of the 'Cold War' also played a role in the Committee's work despite the fact that its experts were

---

2 of the Convention, which was the very heart of that instrument. A related matter was the reservation about article 16, which touched on another fundamental aspect of the equality of the sexes, namely, marriage and family relations'. *See* 'summary Records of the Third Session of the Committee on the Elimination of Discrimination against Women', in United Nations, *The Work of CEDAW: Reports of the Committee on the Elimination of Discrimination against Women* (New York, 1989), vol. I, 1982-1985, p. 356.

[35] United Nations, *Ways and means of expediting the work of the Committee. Report of the Secretariat*, CEDAW/C/2001/II/4 (30 May 2001), Annex VI, pp. 33–34.

[36] *Supra* note 21, p. 296.

[37] Connors, *supra* note 16, p. 99.

supposed to be independent. From its second session in 1983 until its fifth session in 1986, the Committee was unable to formulate any general recommendations at all because of a disagreement among its members on the meaning and mandate of Article 21. Committee members from socialist countries had opposed the implementation of the mandate as outlined in Article 21, i.e. that the 'Committee . . . may make suggestions and general recommendations based on the examination of reports and information received by States Parties /sic/', because they were of the opinion that the Committee 'had no power to interpret the Convention'. In their opinion, it was only the States parties who had the responsibility to do so. The issue was resolved after the Treaty Section of the Office of Legal Affairs of the United Nations Secretariat advised the Committee that, on the basis of Article 21 of the Convention, it did, in fact, have the mandate to formulate such general recommendations.[38]

It is important to note the precise language of *General Recommendation No. 4* in which the Committee welcomed the decision of States parties to consider the issue of reservations at its next meeting in 1988, because it was concerned about the 'significant number of reservations that *appeared* to be incompatible with the object and purpose of the Convention'. Thus, it clearly followed the opinion of the Office of Legal Affairs by not making a definite and analytical statement on the issue of incompatibility.[39] However, the Committee also suggested to respective States parties to 'reconsider such reservations with a view to withdrawing them'.[40] It continued to engage States parties on this issue during its subsequent constructive dialogues and to make statements of a more general nature.

---

[38] E. Evatt, 'Finding a Voice for Women's Rights: the Early Years of CEDAW', 34 *The George Washington International Law Review* (2002) no. 3, pp. 515–553, here pp. 535–539.

[39] The original draft formulation of that recommendation had even been less forceful in that it had not even used the language of the Convention: 'the Committee expressed concern in relation to the significant number of reservations made to different substantial articles of the Convention affecting, subsequently, the goals and principles of the Convention'. *See* 'summary Records of the 102nd meeting on 10 April 1987', in United Nations, *The Work of CEDAW: Reports of the Committee on the Elimination of Discrimination Against Women* (New York, 1990), vol. II, 1986-1987, p. 482, para. 16. (Emphasis added).

[40] Raoul Wallenberg Institute, *General Comments or Recommendations Adopted by Human Rights Treaty Bodies: The Committee on the Elimination of Discrimination against Women* (Lund, 2001, 2nd edition) Vol. IV, p. 7.

General Recommendation No. 20 (1992) is very carefully phrased considering the hostile discussions on the issue of reservations to CEDAW by States parties to the Convention and by Member States of the United Nations in the various bodies of the United Nations between 1987 and 1988. The General Recommendation refers to the decision of States parties at their fourth meeting, although that decision had been of a very general nature and had not solved any problems. Again, it is addressed to States parties, asking them to consider the issue of reservations to CEDAW in connection with their preparations for the World Conference on Human Rights. It is important in that it makes a link between a respective State party's reservations to CEDAW and to other human rights treaties, thus not only implicitly challenging the consistency of reserving States, but also implicitly strengthening the very nature of the Convention as a human rights instrument. *General Recommendation No. 20* expresses concern about the 'validity and the legal effect' of reservations to CEDAW 'in the context of reservations to other human rights treaties' and asks – not explicitly to withdraw them – but to 'reconsider' them 'with a view to strengthening the implementation of all human rights treaties'. It also recommends that States parties consider 'introducing a procedure on reservations to the Convention comparable with that of other human rights treaties'.[41] Lijnzaad calls this recommendation a 'remarkable document,' and positively emphasizes the Committee's 'integrated approach,' though she criticizes the Committee's procedural recommendation. She does not think that adequate procedures to deal 'with (supposedly) incompatible reservations have been designed' so far. She notes that States definitely did not like to see a procedure for CEDAW comparable to Article 20 of ICERD, as had been suggested by Sweden earlier.[42] The Summary Records of the Committee's 198th meeting, however, clearly show, that it is exactly this procedure that some members had had in mind.[43]

In its discussion of this recommendation the Committee raised the issue of doing a comparative analysis of reservations to CEDAW and reservations to other human rights instruments at some future time. In addition, it asked its chairperson to utilize her presence in the preparatory meeting for the World Conference on Human Rights to place the 'global issue of reservations to human rights conventions' on the agenda, noting that

[41] *Ibid.*, p. 41.
[42] *Supra* note 4, p. 336.
[43] CEDAW/C/SR.1998 (30 January 1992) pp. 2–3, paras. 1–6. Lijnzaad differs on this issue from Clark, who had also proposed this same meaning to the debate.

CEDAW 'had the highest number of reservations of all the international human rights treaties', and that most of the reservations 'were worded so generally that it was difficult to determine what was being reserved and what impact the reservation would have on the obligations . . . assumed by the reserving countries'.[44] Again, it is important to note that the Committee did not seem to see a role for itself apart from bringing the issue to the attention of the States parties.

In its 12th session in early 1993 the Committee considered its final contribution to the World Conference on Human Rights by adopting *Suggestion No. 4* which, in discussing *inter alia* the issue of reservations, builds on *General Recommendation No. 20* but states its message more analytically. The Committee reiterated its concern with the 'large number and scope of the reservations' and its opinion that some of these reservations appear to be questionable concerning their compatibility with the object and purpose of the Convention. It recommended to States parties to review the consistency of reservations to CEDAW with those made to other human rights conventions, to review 'the need for and the desirability' of withdrawing them, to keep the number and scope at a minimum and to make them 'as specific as possible' and – in a somewhat cautious wording 'give full consideration to lodging objections to reservations entered by other States parties whenever such action is appropriate'.[45]

In addition, the Committee took action in response to *Resolution 1992/93* of the Sub-Commission on Prevention of Discrimination and Protection of Minorities on the desirability of obtaining an advisory opinion on the validity and legal effect of reservations to CEDAW, by generally endorsing this notion and pointing out its particular concern that it wanted 'to have an opinion that might assist Governments to reconsider their reservations with a view to withdrawing them.'[46] However, upon the suggestion of its member and former chairperson it did not want to do this alone[47], but decided to 'support steps taken in common with other human

[44] *Report of the Committee on the Elimination of Discrimination Against Women (Eleventh Session)*, A/47/38 (24 June 1992), p. 106, para. 469.

[45] *Report of the Committee on the Elimination of Discrimination against Women (Twelfth Session)* A/48/38, p. 7, para. 4.

[46] *Ibid.*, p. 10, para. 4.

[47] Ms. Tallawy from Egypt noted that the General Assembly would be more inclined to consider the idea of requesting an opinion from the ICJ, if that request came from all the treaty bodies. *See* 'summary Record of the 211th meeting', CEDAW/C/SR.211, p. 11, para. 55. This had also been discussed at the Fourth Meeting of Persons Chairing the Human Rights Treaty Bodies. *Ibid.*, p. 8, para. 40.

rights treaty bodies to seek an advisory opinion from the International Court of Justice' that would clarify the issue and assist States parties 'in their ratification and implementation of those international instruments'.[48] The notion that the Sub-commission on the Prevention of Discrimination and Protection of Minorities 'should be authorized to prepare an analytical study of questions of incompatibility arising out of such reservations', was, however, not taken up by the CEDAW Committee.[49] The request for an advisory opinion never materialized, nor did the Committee ever follow up on it.

The World Conference on Human Rights proved to be a breakthrough for women's rights as human rights. In the *Vienna Declaration* and *Programme of Action* of June 1993 Member States of the United Nations reaffirmed that the 'human rights of women and the girl-child are an inalienable, integral and indivisible part of universal human rights'.[50] Both documents also contain recommendations regarding the issue of reservations to human rights instruments in general as well as to CEDAW in particular, i.e. by asking to limit the number of reservations as far as possible, or, if they were deemed unavoidable to formulate them 'precisely and narrowly as possible', to ensure their compatibility with the object and purpose of the relevant instrument and to 'regularly review any reservations with a view to withdrawing them'.[51] The paradox of universality vs. integrity is implicitly recognized when the United Nations is being asked to encourage the goal of CEDAW's universal ratification, while 'States are urged to withdraw reservations that are contrary to the object and purpose of the Convention or which are otherwise incompatible with international law treaty'.[52] The document, however, neither clearly points to who should be responsible for deciding on the compatibility of reservations to CEDAW nor to what the criteria should be. The recommendation that ways and means of 'addressing the particularly large number of reservations to the Convention should be encouraged' does not specify any actor, and the Committee is mentioned

---

[48] *Supra* note 32, p. 10, para. 5.

[49] *Supra* note 34, pp. 8–9, para. 43.

[50] *World Conference on Human Rights: The Vienna Declaration and Programme for Action June 1993* (United Nations, New York, 1993), pp. 33–34, para. 18. The document also condemns gender-based violence, urges the adoption of the draft declaration on violence against women by the General Assembly and recommends the examination of the possibility of introducing an optional protocol to CEDAW.

[51] *Ibid.*, p. 45, para. 5.

[52] *Ibid.*, p. 55, para. 39.

only '*inter alia'* as being recommended to 'continue its review of reservations to the Convention'.[53] Thus, while the Committee's efforts – supported by State and non-governmental actors – had proven successful in bringing the issue onto the agenda and into the final documents of the World Conference on Human Rights, the issue in its many ramifications remained unresolved.

6. EFFORTS BY THE CEDAW COMMITTEE WITH REGARD TO RESERVATIONS AFTER 1993

In its 13th session in 1994, the Committee built on the success of the World Conference on Human Rights by including the issue of reservations in a new general recommendation, by deciding on a number of steps which were recommended to be taken by different actors, by amending its reporting guidelines, by making a number of decisions and further requests, and by formulating a contribution to celebrate the 50th anniversary of the UDHR.

6.1. General Recommendation No. 21

In *General Recommendation No. 21* on Articles 9 (nationality), 15 (equality before the law) and 16 (non-discrimination and equality in marriage and family relations) the Committee addressed the issue of reservations to these articles in seven paragraphs. The Committee embedded its discussion of these articles in a web of references to other articles of the Convention, thus underlining implicitly the interdependence of all articles.[54] It noted with 'alarm' the sheer number of reservations; the combination of reservations to Articles 16 and 2, based on cultural and religious beliefs or customs, which seemed to nullify any hope for change; and the persistence and re-emergence of patriarchal family structures, old values and traditions due to 'fundamentalist or other extremist views or economic hardships'. In consistency with Articles 2, 3, and 24 it '*requires* that all States parties *gradually* progress to a stage where . . . each country will withdraw its

[53] *Ibid.* The *Beijing Declaration* and *Platform for Action* of the Fourth World Conference on Women echoes these recommendations. *See Report of the Fourth World Conference on Women*, A/CONF.177/20/Rev.1, p. 93, para. 230(c).

[54] *Report of the Committee on the Elimination of Discrimination against Women (Thirteenth Session)* A/49/38, pp. 1–9. In addition to the Articles 9, 15 and 16 to which *General Recommendation No. 21* addresses itself, references were made to Articles 1, 2, 3, 5(a) and 5(b), 10(h), 11(a) and 24 as well as implicitly to Articles 12 and 14. Reference was also made to *General Recommendation No. 19.*

reservation, in particular to articles 9, 15, 16 of the Convention'. It spelled out the need to discourage notions and customs as to the inequality of women in the home and to change religious or private law. In addition, the Committee noted the contradiction inherent in the fact that, although some States parties did not enter reservations to these respective articles, their laws, 'based on norms, customs and socio-cultural practices' nevertheless discriminate against women in the family. The Committee found it difficult 'to evaluate and understand the status of women' in these countries and requested States parties to analyse this situation on the basis of Articles 1 and 2 and change it.[55] The Committee also referred to the fact that all societies assign inferior roles to women which result in 'principles of justice and equality contained particular in article 16 and also in articles 2, 5 and 24 of the Convention . . . being violated'.[56] It requested reserving States parties to report on whether their laws comply with these articles and if not, explain their religious and private laws or customs which impede the realization of the Convention as well as on progress for the removal of reservations to Articles 9, 15 and 16 including the introduction of measures 'directed at encouraging full compliance'.[57] Although the Committee, again, did not yet make a clear statement as to which reservations contradict the object and purpose of the Convention, it did strongly highlight the core importance of a number of its articles.

6.2. Decision on Steps to be Undertaken

The Committee also built on the recommendations of the World Conference on Human Rights by adopting a number of steps to be implemented by States parties, the Secretary-General, the Secretariat and by the Committee itself. These steps are as follows: the Committee

- underlined the 'seriousness' with which it considered the problem of reservations and requested 'that this concern be conveyed to the seventh meeting of States parties',
- requested that 'a special letter be sent by the Secretary-General to those States parties that have entered substantive reservations to the Convention drawing their attention to the Committee's concern',
- recommended that the program of advisory services of both the Division for the Advancement of Women and the Centre for Human

[55] *Ibid.*, pp. 8-9, paras. 41–47. (Emphasis added).
[56] *Ibid.*, p. 4, para. 12.
[57] *Ibid.*, p. 9, para. 48.

Rights 'provide, on request, advice . . . on the withdrawal of reservations',

- requested the Secretariat to bring the Committee's concern about reservations to the Commission on the Status of Women, the Commission on Human Rights and to the other human rights treaty bodies,
- requested the Secretariat to include an indication of reservations to other human rights treaties in the analysis of a State party's report which it regularly submits to the Committee at each session,
- decided to include in its Concluding Comments to a State party's report a section reflecting the Committee's view on the reservations of that respective State party.[58]

Finally, the Committee noted that some States parties enter objections to those reservations of other States parties, which they think to be incompatible with the object and purpose of the Convention; the Committee therefore encouraged the objecting States parties to 'to enter into a dialogue on a bilateral basis . . . with a view to finding a solution'.[59]

The implementation of this impressive slate of tasks cannot be followed up in detail at this point, since the emphasis is on the work of the Committee. Suffice it to say, that a letter was sent by the Secretary-General, but most of the replies are no longer in the archives of the Division of the Advancement of Women due to limitations in space.[60] The Secretariat regularly provides information to the Committee on reservations of a State party to other human rights treaties. The Committee never received any information on whether a bilateral dialogue had been started between an objecting and a reserving State party nor did it receive information on whether any advisory services have ever been requested by reserving States parties or by States deliberating ratification of the Convention with reservations.

---

[58] Following this decision the Committee changed its strategy several times as to which sections of the Concluding Comments should include references to reservations. Today, the issue of reservations is referred to in the 'introduction' section and in the section 'concerns and recommendations'.

[59] *Supra* note 41, pp. 12–14, paras. 1–4 and 6–11.

[60] Personal Communication by the Secretary to the Committee on 16 December 2003.

6.3. New Reporting Guidelines

The Committee also amended its guidelines for initial and periodic reports by requesting that a reserving State party should

- include information on its substantive reservations in each of its reports,
- indicate why it considered a respective reservation to be necessary,
- indicate whether reservations entered or not entered to the same rights contained in other human rights treaty bodies are consistent with those entered to CEDAW,
- indicate the precise effect of a respective reservation in terms of national law and policy,
- indicate plans to limit the effect of the respective reservation as well as plans for withdrawal, and whenever possible, specify a time-table for withdrawal, and
- make a particular effort, when having entered reservations to Articles 2 and 3 or reservations that do not refer to a specific article, to report on the effect and interpretation of such reservations.

Within the context of these guidelines the Committee, in its clearest statement so far, pointed out that it considered both the reservations to Articles 2 and 3 and those that do not refer to a specific article 'to be incompatible with the object and purpose of the present Convention'.[61]

6.4. Further Decisions

At the 15th session of the Committee (January 1996), the CEDAW Committee's member, who acted as liaison person to the HRC, drew the attention of the Committee to the fact that the Human Rights Committee had adopted *General Comment No. 24* on the issue of reservations, which she thought should be of considerable interest to the CEDAW Committee due to that treaty body's position that this Committee itself was entitled to make a statement on the compatibility question. She voiced her opinion that the

---

[61] *Supra* note 41, p. 13, para. 5. The complete amended guidelines are contained in the *Report of the Committee on the Elimination of Discrimination against Women (Fourteenth Session)*, A/50/38, pp. 126–128, the part on reservations is on pp. 127–128, para. 8. To formulate new guidelines had also been recommended by Lijnzaad.

Committee might also consider adopting a new general recommendation.[62] Subsequently, the Committee requested a detailed report from the Division on the Advancement of Women in order 'to facilitate a discussion on reservations to the Convention'. The report was to have four parts including a 'review of what United Nations conferences have said about reservations to the Convention;' a 'review of comments made by women's human rights non-governmental organizations;' a 'qualitative comparison of reservations to the Convention with those to other treaties;' and an 'analysis of States parties' reservations that are contrary to the object and purpose of the Convention or which are otherwise incompatible with international treaty law'.[63]

This report was delivered to the Committee for its 16th Session in early 1997. It contained all the information requested as well as a description of the pattern of reservations to the Convention, including those phrased in a rather general way and those entered to specific articles of the Convention. It listed the responses by States parties, by the Committee itself, by scholars and non-governmental organizations, and by other human rights treaty bodies and the International Law Commission (ILC). It referred to the relevant sections in the *Beijing Declaration* and *Platform for Action.* It also summarized *General Comment No. 24* of the HRC and stressed the fact that both this Committee and the ILC 'suggest an active role for human rights treaty bodies to determine whether reservations are contrary to the object and purpose of the treaty under consideration'. The report underlined that 'although the number and reach of the reservations to the Convention are second only to those for the *Convention on the Rights of the Child*, more reservations to it have been removed than in the case of any other human rights treaty'. It laid out various options to be implemented by the Committee in its future work, some of which reiterated previous decisions by the Committee. The report also asked the Committee to consider co-ordinated strategies with the Secretariat and others to run seminars,

---

[62] The wording in the Summary Records of that meeting, i.e. 'had considered adopting a general comment on the issue of reservations' is misleading, since the Human Rights Committee had adopted *General Comment No. 24* on reservations already in November 1994. CEDAW/C/SR.287 (22 January 1996), pp.11–12, para. 67.

[63] *Report of the Committee on the Elimination of Discrimination against Women (Fifteenth Session)*, A/51/38, p. 42, para. 346.

briefings, and consultations, or have studies conducted by non-governmental organizations.[64]

The document was discussed in a working group of the Committee, and, based on the report of that group, the Committee adopted a few decisions as to how it would deal with the issue of reservations in its working methods.[65] It also discussed the necessity of convening a number of international or regional seminars which should deal, *inter alia*, with the issue of reservations and in *Suggestion No. 16/1* it looked to the budget of the Centre for Human Rights for technical and advisory services to make this possible.[66] The new *General Recommendation No. 23* on Articles 7 (political and public life) and 8 (international level) also contained a recommendation to States parties regarding their required reporting on reservations which basically reiterates the Committee's guidelines.[67]

---

[64] United Nations, *Reservations to the Convention on the Elimination of All Forms of Discrimination against Women: Report by the Secretariat*, CEDAW/C/1997 (12 November 1996) p. 10, para. 27, p. 11, para. 29, pp. 11–14, paras. 28–37. The other options included to strictly monitor the Committee's *General Recommendation No. 20* and its amended guidelines, to emphasize, where appropriate, the issue of reservations in the constructive dialogue, and in particular the possible inconsistencies in a respective State party's behaviour, to encourage States parties to object to those reservations which are perceived to be contrary to the object and purpose of the Convention and to draw up a new general recommendation taking into account the work by the HRC and the ILC.

[65] *Report of the Committee on the Elimination of Discrimination against Women (Sixteenth Session)* A/52/38/Rev.1., p. 47, para. 357. At this point the Committee decided that the issue of reservations should be covered in the section on 'factors and difficulties' of its Concluding Comments and that the Secretariat should include the text of any reservation to CEDAW as well as the text of reservations to other human rights treaties, information on modifications and withdrawals and on objections by other States parties in its 'analysis report' of respective States parties' reports to the Committee. *Ibid.,* p. 49, para. 368.

[66] *Ibid.,* p. 50, para. 374, also pp.1–2.

[67] 'states parties should explain the reason for, and effect of, any reservations' to these articles; they should indicate 'where the reservations reflect traditional, customary or stereotyped attitudes towards women's roles in society'; they should indicate steps being taken to change these attitudes, should keep 'the necessity for such reservations under close review' and report on 'a timetable for their removal'. *General Recommendation No. 23* was adopted in the Committee's 16th session, but was included in its edited form in the report of its 17th session. *Report of the Committee on the Elimination of All Forms of Discrimination against Women (Seventeenth Session)*, A/52/38/Rev.1, pp. 61–70, here p. 69, para. 44.

6.5. Contribution to the 50th Anniversary of the UDHR

In its 17th session in the summer of 1997 the Committee decided that its contribution to the 50th anniversary of the UDHR in 1998 and the five-year review of the *Vienna Declaration* and *Program of Action* should be a statement on reservations, 'particularly in the context of article 2 of the Convention'. It designated one member to submit a first draft for discussion at the eighteenth session. All available material should be used in making the statement.[68]

A draft statement was circulated among Committee members in the Committee's 18th session (1998), and the final statement, which relates to both Articles 2 and 16, was adopted in the Committee's 19th session in the summer of the same year. The statement contains five major sections, including subsections on 'impermissible reservations,' 'impact of reservations,' and the 'role of the Committee'.[69] It refers to previous statements made by the Committee, i.e. *General Recommendations Nos. 20* and *21*.[70] It bases its arguments on pronouncements made at both the World Conference on Human Rights and the Fourth World Conference on Women and on statements of concern by other human rights treaty bodies, the ILC, some Member States of the United Nations, scholars and non-governmental organizations. The most salient points of the statement, which appear in different sections of the text, include the following: the Committee

- reaffirmed its mandate as expressed in the *Vienna Declaration* and *Platform of Action* Paragraph 39 to 'continue its review of reservations,' and it points to its practice of routinely expressing concern about reservations in its Concluding Comments;

---

[68] *Ibid.*, p. 128.

[69] *Report of the Committee on the Elimination of All Forms of Discrimination against Women (Nineteenth Session)* A/53/38/Rev.1, pp. 47–50. The five major sections are: Introduction, Background, Reservations to the Convention, Role of the Committee and Conclusion.

[70] It is interesting to note, that the Committee refers to *General Recommendation No. 20* as a text in which it '*inter alia*, . . . sought to resolve the problem of impermissible reservations'. This is a notion that is not supported by *General Recommendation 20* unless the request for a 'procedure on reservations . . . comparable with that of other human rights treaties' can be understood as an intended solution. This request, however, was never taken up again by the Committee. *Ibid.*, p. 48, para. 11.

- considered Articles 2 and 16 'to be core provisions of the Convention,' and explicitly 'holds the view that Article 2 is central to the objects /sic/ and purpose of the Convention'; and,
- recognized that the Convention does not prohibit reservations on the one hand, but reiterated the Convention's principle as contained in Article 28(2) that reservations which 'challenge the central principles of the Convention are contrary to the provisions of the Convention and to general international law';
- remained 'convinced that reservations to article 16, whether lodged for national, traditional, religious or cultural reasons, are incompatible with the Convention and therefore impermissible and should be reviewed and modified or withdrawn';
- analysed the impact of reservations to Articles 2 and 16 as perpetuating 'the myth of women's inferiority' and reinforcing 'the inequalities in the lives of millions of women throughout the world' in 'every sphere of their lives'; argued that reservations to Articles 2 and 16 would put women on an unequal footing with men when competing, in particular, for 'such fundamental rights as equality of income, access to education, housing and health care, and equality of rights and responsibilities within the family; and noted the connection of Article 2 with Article 7(b), although without explicitly mentioning it, by referring to reservations to Article 2 which aim 'to protect rights of succession to the throne and to chiefly and other traditional titles,' a practice it had already condemned in its *General Recommendation No. 23*;
- quoted paragraphs from its *General Recommendation No. 21*, asking for gradual withdrawal of reservations to Articles 9, 15, and 16 in consistency with Articles 2, 3, and 24;
- concluded that neither the Committee's *General Recommendation No. 20* nor the recommendations in the *Vienna Declaration* and *Platform of Action* had resulted in a great number of reservations to Article 2 to be modified or withdrawn and reiterated the four options for removal of reservations as outlined by the Special Rapporteur appointed by the ILC;
- appreciated the practice of objections as conducted by some States parties which have an 'empowering effect . . . for women in the State party' and 'acknowledges the view of the Special Rapporteur . . . that objections are not only a means of exerting pressure on reserving States, but also serve as a useful guide for the assessment of the permissibility of a reservation by the Committee itself';

- reaffirmed its responsibilities regarding reservations by discussing them during the constructive dialogue with States parties and by 'routinely expressing concern at the entry of reservations to articles 2 and 16 or the failure of States parties to withdraw or modify them' in its Concluding Comments; and,
- while it noted the opinion of the Special Rapporteur 'that control of the permissibility of reservations is the primary responsibility of the States parties,' nevertheless wished 'to draw to the attention of States parties its grave concern at the number and extent of impermissible reservations' and at the lack of compliance with the general principles of international law by reserving States parties when confronted with objections to their reservations as being impermissible and calls upon a re-examination of 'States' self-imposed limitation to the full compliance with all the principles of the Convention'.[71]

Lack of documentation makes it difficult to assess the nature and extent of the discussion that took place in the Committee, or, for that matter, in its working groups.[72] The lengthy quotation from the statement, however, makes it clear that the Committee had moved to its most articulate positioning on the issue of impermissibility of particular reservations since its inception. While the Committee in this statement explicitly focused on Articles 2 and 16, which it had already highlighted in its *General Recommendation No. 21*, it also highlighted the Convention's overall objective as to ending 'discrimination against women and to achieve *de jure* and *de facto* equality for them'.[73] It further underlined the interdependence of the Convention's articles, when discussing the impact of impermissible reservations entered to Article 2, by connecting this article to at least five other articles of the Convention, though it did not name them specifically.[74]

---

[71] *Ibid.* The quotes are taken from p. 49, para. 22; p. 47 para. 6 and p. 49, para. 16; p. 47, para. 8; p. 49, para. 17; p. 49, para. 15 and p. 48, para. 10; p. 48, para. 12; p. 48, para. 11 and p. 49, paras. 18 and 19; p. 49, paras. 20 and 21; p. 49, para. 23; pp. 49–50, paras. 24 and 25.

[72] Starting in 1997, the Committee has no longer been receiving any Summary Records of its meetings.

[73] *Supra* note 56, p. 48, para. 10.

[74] In its statement the Committee implicitly referred to Article 7(b) by mentioning succession to the throne and to other chiefly and traditional titles; to Articles 11.1(d) (equal renumeration), 13.1(a) (right to equal family benefits) and (b) (bank loans,

Through these references, taken together with the main message of the statement as to the impermissibility of reservations to Articles 2 and 16 and the various pronouncements in previous statements to other articles of the Convention, it may be argued that the Committee moved, perhaps unwittingly and certainly not explicitly, to a position from which it might consider *all* reservations to substantive articles to be incompatible with the object and purpose of the Convention and thus impermissible. This interpretation, however, is certainly mine and has not yet been discussed and confirmed by the Committee.

From today's point of view, it is surprising that the CEDAW Committee has never explicitly referred to *General Comment No. 24* of the Human Rights Committee, though the Committee must have been aware of it as has been described. Despite this, the CEDAW Committee's statement is implicitly in line with this general comment when pronouncing reservations to Article 2 of the Convention to be impermissible, which parallels the Human Rights Committee's point of view with regards to reservations to Article 2 of the ICCPR. And by stating which reservations to the Convention are clearly impermissible, the CEDAW Committee also echoes the Human Rights Committee's position that it 'necessarily falls to the Committee to determine whether a specific reservation is compatible with the object and purpose of the Covenant'.[75] However, it would have been important for the CEDAW Committee to comment on the fact that the Human Rights Committee did not include the norm of non-discrimination on the basis of sex in its list of peremptory norms, to which any reservations would be considered incompatible with the object and purpose of the Covenant, a point which is also noted by Ali.[76] While scholars differ in their evaluation of the norm of non-discrimination on the basis of sex as a norm of *jus cogens*, the Committee has never found time so far to address this important issue.[77] The CEDAW Committee also neglected to explicitly refer to the Human Rights Committee's opinion on the role of this treaty body in

---

mortgages, other forms of financial credit) and 14.2(c) (social security programs), (e) (economic opportunities), (g) (agricultural credits and loans, market facilities, appropriate technology, land agrarian reform) by referring to equality of income; to Article 10 by referring to access to education; to Article 14.2(h) by referring to housing and to Article 12 by referring to health care.

[75] Raoul Wallenberg Institute, *General Comments or Recommendations adopted by United Nations Human Rights Treaty Bodies. Human Rights Committee* (Lund, 2000, 3rd edition) Vol. I, pp. 77–86, here p. 85, para. 18.

[76] *Supra* note 3, p. 245.

[77] Helbling, *supra* note 16, pp.220–224.

determining the incompatibility of reservations, though through its pronouncements on the various articles cited above it does assume that role and distinctly sets itself apart from the opinion of the ILC Special Rapporteur.

6.6. Other Responses

The Committee continued to be occupied with the issue of reservations outside of its constructive dialogue with reserving State parties. Its statement on reservations was discussed in the General Assembly, and in the Committee's 20th session in January 1999 it was informed of *GA Resolution 53/119* in which universal ratification of the Convention, 'full compliance by States parties with their obligations under the Convention,' withdrawal or limitation of reservations as well as 'due consideration' to the Committee's statement of reservations of the previous year was emphasized.[78] The Chairperson also noted modifications and withdrawals of reservations by some States parties.[79] A response to the preliminary report by the Special Rapporteur on reservations of the ILC resulted in the Committee's request, that its Chairperson should provide both the Special Rapporteur and the expert of the Sub-Commission on Prevention of Discrimination and Protection of Minorities, who had been asked to do a study on reservations, with an outline of the Committee's work and concerns.[80] The Committee also adopted *General Recommendation No. 24* on Article 12. Since no reservations have been entered to Article 12 of the Convention, this recommendation does not contain a reference to this issue, although the Committee's 1998 statement makes a reference to health in connection with reservations to Article 2, and a consideration of its *General Recommendation No. 19* and of its own statements regarding reservations to Articles 9 and 16 might have led to an identification of barriers for women in the implementation of Article 12 resulting from these reservations.

The issue re-emerged in the context of statements made to the Committee at its 23rd session in June 2000, which referred to requests and commitments as to the review and subsequent withdrawal of reservations that had been expressed at the 44th session of the Commission on the Status

[78] *Report of the Committee on the Elimination of Discrimination against Women (Twentieth Session)* A/54/38/Rev. 1, p. 8, para. 11.
[79] *Ibid.*, p.11, para. 34.
[80] *Ibid.*, pp. 40–41, para. 421.

of Women and in the 23rd Special Session of the General Assembly.[81] However, no further discussion ensued.

At its 24th session in 2001, the Committee requested the Secretariat to prepare an analysis of the approach to reservations, within the context of considering reports and communications of other human rights treaty bodies. This report was to be discussed by the Committee at its next session. The contribution of the Committee to the preparatory process for the World Conference against Racism, Racial Discrimination, Xenophobia and Related Intolerance contained a reference to the need for the removal of reservations.[82]

Though the requested report was delivered by the Division to the Committee,[83] the Committee's reports of its 25th and the 26th sessions do not indicate any discussion of it. This may have been the result of time constraints, since the Committee prepared a number of contributions to the Special Session on Children of the General Assembly, a statement in support and solidarity of Afghan women and contributions to other UN world conferences, none of which, however, contain any references to reservations.[84] The reformulation of the Committee's reporting guidelines, which were adopted in June 2002 at the Committee's 27th session, reiterate the criteria for reporting on reservations by the respective State parties as adopted in 1994.[85]

7. EVALUATION OF STATES PARTIES' AND THE COMMITTEE'S PRACTICE SINCE 1995

Having outlined the Committee's evolving position on the issue of reservations to the Convention as formulated in various formal and non-formal decisions, general recommendations, suggestions, other statements and reporting guidelines, questions on their impact on reserving States

[81] *Report of the Committee on the Elimination of Discrimination against Women, (Twenty-third Session)* A/55/38, p. 50, paras. 7, 8, 10 and p. 52, paras. 24 and 26.
[82] *Report of the Committee on the Elimination of Discrimination against Women (Twenty-fourth Session)* A/56/38, p. 37, para. 363 and p. 41, para. 385.
[83] *Supra* note 22, pp. 7–14, paras. 20–56.
[84] *Report of the Committee on the Elimination of Discrimination against Women (Twenty-fifth Session)* A/56/38, pp. 83–84, paras. 379–391, and *Report of the Committee on the Elimination of Discrimination against Women (Twenty-sixth Session), ibid.*, pp. 68–72,-71, paras. 417–436.
[85] *Report of the Committee on the Elimination of Discrimination against Women (Twenty-seventh Session)* A/57/38, p.137, para. C 2.

parties and on the Committee's work remain to be asked, i.e. to what extent did the Committee's pronouncements have an effect

- on newly ratifying States parties after 1993, who entered reservations,
- on reserving States parties' reporting after 1996 and
- on the Committee's constructive dialogue with these States parties since that period, including its Concluding Comments?

While the nature of reservations to the Convention and responses by various actors have been discussed by a number of commentators, covering reserving States parties in general until 1994 and reserving States parties with a predominantly Muslim population until 1998,[86] these particular questions have either not been covered at all or not in detail, nor have developments since 1998 been covered.

An analysis of the reservations formulated by newly ratifying States since 1994 is disappointing, since many of these States parties do not pay attention to the criteria set out by the Committee and others. They continue to enter either very general reservations or reservations to specific substantive articles, both of which, according to the opinions of the Committee as well as of objecting States parties, go against the object and purpose of the Convention.[87]

Starting with 1994, Kuwait ratified the Convention with reservations to substantive Articles 7(a), 9(2), and 16(f) in September of that year. From 1995 to January 2004 another 15 States ratified with general or specific reservations, combining them often, as Kuwait, with the procedural reservation to Article 29(1).[88] These States are Algeria (1996), Bahrain (2002), Democratic People's Republic of Korea (2001), Fiji (1995), Lebanon (1997), Lesotho (1995), Liechtenstein (1995), Malaysia (1995), Mauritania (2001), Niger (1999), Pakistan (1996), Saudi Arabia (2000), Singapore (1995) Switzerland (1997) and Syrian Arab Republic (2003).

Of these, Lesotho, Liechtenstein, Malaysia, Mauritania, Pakistan and Saudi Arabia either referred to their Constitution and/or Islamic *Shari'a* Law as prevailing over the Convention without mentioning any specific articles of the Convention to which their reservations would apply. Thus, they did not follow the recommendation to formulate their reservations as specific as

[86] Ali, *supra* note 3; Mayer, *supra* note 9; Connors and Helbling, *supra* note 16.

[87] All of the newly ratifying reserving States parties were objected to except Fiji, Liechtenstein and Switzerland.

[88] Fiji, Liechtenstein and Switzerland did not enter reservations to Article 29(1).

possible. According to the Committee's and some objecting States parties' position on unspecific reservations, these reservations must be considered incompatible with the object and purpose of the Convention and thus impermissible.

Some of these States parties, in addition, entered specific reservations to substantive articles, i.e. Lesotho to Article 2, Liechtenstein to Article 9(2), Malaysia to Articles 2(f), 5(a), 7(b), 9 and 16, and Saudi Arabia to Article 9(2). Liechtenstein withdrew its reservation to Article 9(2) in 1998; Malaysia also withdrew some of its reservations in 1998, i.e. 2(f), 9(1), 16(b), 16(d), 16(e), 16(h), thereby indirectly specifying the remaining ones. Again, according to the Committee's and objecting States parties' stated position, these are incompatible with the object and purpose of the Convention.

The remaining States parties entered their reservations to specific articles. Some did so without any explanations at all (Democratic People's Republic of Korea, Fiji, Lebanon, Syrian Arab Republic), others referred to Islamic *Shari'a* law (Syrian Arab Republic, Bahrain, Kuwait) and to specific national legislation (Algeria, Kuwait, Switzerland, Singapore) or to religious and personal laws (Singapore). Singapore based its reasoning on the multi-racial and multi-religious character of its population. Interestingly, Niger, with a large Muslim population, did not refer to Islamic *Shari'a* law, but explained its specific reservations to particular articles with the existing cultural and social customs and practices, which can be 'modified only by the passage of time and the evolution of society and cannot, therefore, be abolished by an act of authority'.[89] Fiji, which had not given any explanations for its reservations, withdrew them completely in 2000.

In general, the pattern of reservations of the seven States parties with a predominantly Muslim population, based on either Islamic *Shari'a* Law, their Constitutions or domestic laws, or all of these, is the usual one of other such States parties, and has been discussed, *inter alia*, by Connors and, in even more depth, by Ali.[90] A unique reservation, however, was entered by Kuwait, to Article 7(a), since it does not allow its female adult population to vote. Only six out of these sixteen new States parties submitted reports so far, all of which have been discussed by the Committee at this point.

A somewhat more positive picture as to the adherence to the Committee's 'resolutions' emerges if one looks at States parties' reports which were submitted after 1996, including some of those States parties who ratified only since 1994. An analysis of 21 reserving States parties' initial

[89] *Supra*, note 18, p. 14.
[90] *Supra*, note 16 and note 3 in particular chapter VII, pp. 238–285.

and periodic reports which were discussed by the Committee from its 16th session in 1997 to its 30th session in January 2004 shows that the majority of these States parties followed the Committee's reporting guidelines in that they referred to their reservations in their reports and explained the necessity, as they saw it, for entering them.[91] The Committee itself always addressed the issue either in its oral or written questions, thus prompting the majority of the States parties in their responses to go into more detail as to their plans for any legal changes that would allow for the withdrawal of some or all reservations. Some of the reporting States parties had already withdrawn some or all of their reservations before coming to the Committee (Austria, Belgium, Fiji, Liechtenstein, Thailand), and Turkey fulfilled its plans for withdrawal subsequently. It seems that the question of consistency regarding reservations to CEDAW and to other human rights treaty bodies was touched upon only in the case of Tunisia.

It is interesting to compare the argumentation of some of the States parties with a predominantly Muslim population, as presented in their reports or their responses, to questions by the Committee, i.e. Algeria, Egypt, Iraq and Tunisia, as to the necessity for having reservations and to their plans for withdrawal. Although Tunisia seems to be first in place among these countries in having made decisive progress in reforming its Constitution and a number of its domestic laws pertaining to sections of Articles 9, 15, 16 and 29, the State party never even mentioned the issue of reservations in its report nor any plans for their withdrawal. Egypt, on the other hand, heralded its partial reform of the Family Law as representing a 'significant turning point and a major step forward towards the withdrawal' of its reservation to Article 16.[92] Algeria attempted a balancing act to satisfy both the progressive and conservative parts of its population. It clearly acknowledged

---

[91] The analysis does not cover all reports by reserving States parties which were discussed by the Committee between 1997 and 2004 nor does it include reports which were discussed in 1995 and 1996, because it is highly improbable that the latter were written after the publication of the new reporting guidelines. The States parties analysed are Algeria, Austria, Belgium, Egypt, Fiji, France, India, Iraq, Ireland, Jordan, Kuwait, Liechtenstein, Luxembourg, Maldives, Morocco, New Zealand, Singapore, Thailand, Tunisia, Turkey and the United Kingdom of Great Britain and Northern Ireland. Of the 16 new States parties with reservations since 1994, only 6 submitted reports so far, including Switzerland, which was not analysed.

[92] *Responses to the list of issues and questions for consideration of the third and combined fourth and fifth periodic reports*, CEDAW/PSWG/2001/I/CRP.2/Add.3 (23 October 2000), p. 4.

the 'dichotomy' in the legal status of its women, and cited those provisions of the Family Code that go against the Convention, but characterized the Code 'both in its form and in certain rulings that have been based on it, as a attempt to restrict the role of Islamic law'. It saw the need for 'a reinterpretation of the role of religion in society', which, however, would take time. It professed to a gradual approach for introducing gender non-discrimination and equality, while 'ensuring that there is no backsliding with respect to the personal status of women' and placed the ratification of the Convention with reservations in this context. Despite the objections by other States parties it declared, however, that these reservations 'do not question the essence of the Convention' and that they would be removed, as gradual changes would progress.[93] Iraq argued that its reservations served to ensure compliance with the Convention. It explained its reservations to Article 9 as a consequence of preserving family unity and to Article 16 as a consequence of following Islamic law as the 'peremptory norm in this field', though, in its opinion, a 'review of Iraqi legislation in the relevant area nevertheless shows that it is essentially in compliance with the spirit of article 16'.[94] In its response to the written questions of the Committee it ruled 'out the possibility of withdrawing its reservations'. In a somewhat startling argument, it referred to the Committee's *General Recommendation No. 20*, the *Beijing Platform for Action* and its reasons for making them, i.e. to ensure compliance with the Convention.[95] Morocco, which, in its initial report, had given a lengthy interpretation of women's status according to Islam, which 'made a distinction between men and women only when it is dictated by considerations relating to the nature of each of the sexes, their responsibilities in life and what is most suited to them . . . ', attempted, similarly to Algeria, a balancing act in its responses to the questions posed by the Committee to its second report.[96] It described its attempt to combine the attachment to eternal values defining the identity of its people with the universality of human rights, i.e. keeping the Moroccan general legal system while wanting to move towards legal improvements for its women. Kuwait

[93] *Initial reports of States parties: Algeria.* CEDAW/C/DZA/1 (1September 1998) pp. 10–11.
[94] *Second and third reports of States parties: The Republic of Iraq.* CEDAW/C/IRQ/2-3 (19 October 1998) pp. 11, 25.
[95] 'Response to the list of issues and questions for consideration of the combined second and third periodic reports: Iraq', CEDAW/PSWG/2000/II/CRP.2/Add.2, p.7.
[96] *Initial reports of the States parties: Morocco.* CEDAW/C/MOR/1 (3 November 1994) p. 4.

reported on its attempts (and on some of the results) to change domestic laws on which its reservations were based. These attempts, however, had not been successful in the case of giving women the right to vote, though a future second attempt was announced. Unfortunately, the Committee has never had enough time to probe into the details of these descriptions and justifications as well as the impact the legal situation in these countries has on the lives of women. But, even if the Committee was able to find more time, the issue would still remain very complex. Ali rightly points out that the 'multiplicity of norms affecting women's human rights in Muslim jurisdictions', i.e. 'constitutional/statute law, Islamic law and customary norms,' makes it 'extremely difficult to sketch with any degree of accuracy the fine details of' what she calls 'operative Islamic law' as it concerns women.[97]

8. CONCLUDING COMMENTS OF THE CEDAW COMMITTEE

An analysis of the Committee's Concluding Comments since 1995 clearly shows that the Committee conscientiously, though not always consistently, has been following its own 'resolutions' on the issue of reservations when discussing the reports of reserving and non-reserving States parties in the constructive dialogue and when formulating its evaluation in its Concluding Comments. Firstly, the Committee almost always in its discussion of initial or combined initial and periodic reports of States parties as well as in its subsequent Concluding Comments noted and/or welcomed the fact, when no reservations had been entered. Secondly, it commended the intention for review and/or withdrawal as well as the actual withdrawal of some or all of the reservations. Thirdly, it always expressed concern about existing or remaining reservations and either recommended or even urged a review and withdrawal of them in a general fashion or pointed concretely to desirable changes in specific laws that could subsequently result in a removal of such reservations. Several times, in the case of States parties with predominantly Muslim populations, who had entered reservations to the same articles, i.e. Articles 2 and/or 16 by either referring to their Constitutions, domestic laws or *Shari'a* law, it stated that these reservations either were contrary to the object and purpose of the Convention (Morocco), or, by referring to its statement from its 19th session in 1998, declared these articles as being central to the object and purpose (Egypt, Iraq, Kuwait). In addition, in the case of Kuwait, it also voiced its 'belief' that the reservation to Article 7(a)

[97] Ali, *supra* note 3, pp. 187–188.

was contrary to the object and purpose of the Convention. However, it did not follow a consistent pattern in making such statements in the case of Algeria or with regard to Tunisia's general declaration.[98] Nor did it use the same language when asking for withdrawal of reservations to these articles. Fourthly, the Committee also clearly identified State parties who, despite having entered no reservations, have not moved forward in eliminating existing discriminatory laws. It asked them to speed up their legal reform process in order to comply with the obligations of the Convention and encouraged them, in some cases, to compare their legislation with respective non-discriminatory legislation in other countries. Fifthly, some of the Nordic countries (Finland, Norway, Sweden), the Netherlands, and most recently, the Federal Republic of Germany, have been commended for their objections to reservations as being against the object and purpose of the Convention. This, however, has neither been done in a consistent manner nor have other States parties, who have also been objecting to reservations over the years, ever received this recognition and praise.

---

[98] The reasons for these inconsistencies may have been based on a conscientious evaluation of the factual legal situation in the respective countries, on political considerations of the Committee or on mere oversight by the Committee. There is never enough time in the Committee to discuss Concluding Comments in detail nor to compare them with previous comments to other States parties with comparable situations and to evaluate them in that context. Also, since there is not enough institutional memory in the Committee to be aware of previous pronouncements. Thus, I tend to see the main reason for these inconsistencies in the last criteria, though a thorough study exploring this issue and based on Ali, *supra* note 3, may come to a different conclusion. Unfortunately, I was not able to analyse Bangladesh's explanations in its fourth periodic report which, together with the third periodic report, was discussed by the Committee at its 17th session in 1997. However, in its Concluding Comments the Committee used yet another version of dealing with a reserving State party with a predominantly Muslim population. It commended Bangladesh for the withdrawal of reservations to Articles 13(a) and 16(1)(f), which Bangladesh had done in 1997, and 'commended the initiative of the Government in leading the way for other countries with similar reservations to also consider lifting their reservations'. In expressing concern over the remaining reservations to Articles 2 and 16(1)(a) the Committee noted 'that it regards article 2 as a fundamental and core provision of the Convention, while article 16 is critical to the full enjoyment by women of their rights.' It recommended to Bangladesh to comply with its Constitution and the Convention, review and 'eventually' withdraw its remaining reservations. *Supra*, note 52, pp. 119–121, paras. 424, 433, 449.

9. CONCLUSIONS

Although the Committee stopped addressing the issue of reservations to the Convention in new statements in a more general fashion in 1998 and has not dealt with the issue since asking for a report from the Division on the Advancement of Women on the practice of other human rights treaty bodies in 2000, it has continued its practice in addressing States parties' reservations, on the basis of its decisions, suggestions, general recommendations, statements and reporting guidelines, when entering into a constructive dialogue with these States parties and when formulating its Concluding Comments. It has done so in a consistent manner by referring to the issue as such and by continuously reiterating its request for the withdrawal of such reservations. However, in light of the Committee's position, which, as has been shown, evolved over time, as to which reservations are contrary to the object and purpose of the Convention and whether it is in within its mandate to clearly state this fact, there are inconsistencies in the contents of its Concluding Comments.

On the part of States parties themselves, several things must be noted. On the one hand, some newly ratifying States have neither heeded the Convention provisions nor the Committee's request that reservations should not go against the object and purpose, be consistent with reservations by these States parties to other human rights instruments and be as precise as possible. Some of these States parties have not even fulfilled their reporting obligations, thus having avoided not only a discussion of the topic but also any progress for the legal and *de facto* status of their women on the basis of a constructive dialogue with the Committee. On the other hand, some progress can be identified with other new States parties, in that most of their reservations are fairly precise and are being explained, even though these explanations may not be acceptable and do not solve the problem of the impermissibility of these reservations.

The issue of consistency of reserving States parties has not received sufficient attention. Because of this, it is difficult to evaluate, despite the stipulations of the World Conference on Human Rights that women's rights are human rights and that all human rights are indivisible and interdependent, whether or not CEDAW is still considered by some reserving States parties as being of lesser status than other human rights treaties because of the Convention's 'cultural' sensitivity.[99] This would also

[99] Clark, *supra* note 6, p. 286. Clark also analyses the consistency in the behaviour of the then existing reserving and objecting States parties.

entail that discrimination on the basis of sex and gender is still deemed as being of less importance than discrimination on the basis of race or religion, a fact which has been noted by scholars previously.[100]

On the other hand, a number of reservations have been withdrawn since 1994 and others, especially from States parties in the so-called Western region, are under review and, according to these States parties, legal change continues to progress so that their future withdrawal is possible and likely. If this happens, those States parties with a predominantly Muslim population, whose general declarations and reservations to Articles 2, 7, 9(2), 15(4), and all or part of Article 16 have been declared impermissible by the Committee (as well as by a few States parties), will remain as the only reserving States parties. While it does have to be acknowledged that a few States parties with a predominantly Muslim population did withdraw some of their reservations and that some of them never entered reservations at all, the issue of reservations consequently may become a predominantly Muslim issue in the future. This hypothesis rests on the experience that, so far, some reserving States parties have explicitly expressed their unwillingness to review and withdraw their reservations as well as on the fact that others, despite of having introduced positive changes in their domestic laws for women, seem to keep their reservations for political reasons. Given the negative history of the Committee's request for a study on Islam as well as the internal and external pressures States with a predominantly Muslim population experience in the world's current demographic, economic and political situation, an easy or quick solution to eliminate these reservations is not in sight. The reservations may not always be motivated by only religious considerations, as a number of commentators have pointed out. On the other hand, there is no doubt, that the status of women is at the centre of the agenda of political Islamists, as Ali underlines, who want to restore indigenous customs and laws of the past for women. While this is also true of the political agendas of fundamentalist groups in other religions, I concur with her and others in their psychological explanation of this phenomenon, which they offer for Islamic 'Revivalists,' but which I would like to apply to all such groups, i.e. the 'psychological need to maintain a minimal sense of identity in a confusing and shifting reality'.[101]

Nevertheless, it may be advisable for the Committee to renew its efforts in addressing the issue of reservations in a more legal way through a new general recommendation, especially in view of the work done for the ILC

[100] *Inter alia,* Chinkin, *supra* note 15, pp. 83–84.
[101] Ali, *supra* note 3, p. 186, where Ali refers to other commentators.

and the Sub-Commission on the Promotion and Protection of Human Rights in the last couple of years as well as in view of the Committee's future work under the Optional Protocol.[102] While so far, the Committee in its work under the communication and inquiry procedure, has not yet been confronted with an alleged violation of an article of the Convention, to which a reservation had been entered, this may happen in the near future, and the Committee will have to find a position on this issue and also take note of and discuss the practice of the Human Rights Committee in that regard. Such a general recommendation should also take up and decide on the issue of so-called 'core' articles. While acknowledging its various previous statements, which single out specific articles as central, the Committee should, nevertheless, in my opinion, end the discussion of so-called 'core'-articles[103] and clearly express a comprehensive understanding of the Convention's objective, by pointing explicitly to all articles and their interdependence, for achieving the elimination of all forms of discrimination against women and *de jure* and *de facto* equality for them in the enjoyment of their human rights. The issue of a time-frame for States parties' implementation of the Convention should also be addressed in this recommendation. The Committee will have to strongly underline States parties' obligation to undertake steps for eliminating discrimination without delay and will have to find a position for determining the criteria of a time-span, which allows for a more 'gradual implementation' as to the 'practical realization' of the principle of equality (Article 2) in the form of substantive results which indeed due to structural reasons and cultural norms and stereotypes will not be achieved immediately. The recommendation should also contain explicit encouragement of States parties to object to reservations in greater numbers and to do so in a consistent way, though the latter no doubt entails still unresolved questions of international law.[104]

In addition, the previous decision to have studies and seminars organized to come to a better understanding of the Convention and of Islamic *Shari'a* law in its complex manifestations in various States parties and especially in view of the many different existing interpretations regarding conflicts

---

[102] Except for Bangladesh, who still reserves Articles 2 and 16(1)(c) and which opted out of the inquiry procedure, none of the reserving States parties with a predominantly Muslim population has ratified the *Optional Protocol* so far.

[103] *Inter alia*, Cook and Lijnzaad, *supra* note 4.

[104] See Clark on her early analysis of the inconsistency in States parties' behaviour as regards both aspects and of her discussion on the one- and two-tier system of permissibility and acceptability. *Supra* note 6.

between *Shari'a* law and the Convention, should be pursued further as should be an analytical study on the issue of consistency of reservations by reserving States parties. Whether or not the idea of seeking an advisory opinion of the ICJ should be reiterated, needs careful analysis of the theoretical reasoning of scholars, UN bodies, human rights treaty bodies and others actors as well as a thorough and detailed analysis of practical developments in the handling of reservations by treaty bodies in the last decade.

Whatever the reasons may be for a State to ratify CEDAW–whether it may be, according to McBride, 'a genuine sign of its good intentions and not a cynical act of propaganda'[105] or the result of pressure with regard to international standing and acceptance– the result may not be, that it is done with reservations which go against both the Convention and international law in general and serve to perpetuate women's inferior status indefinitely. While the CEDAW Committee's many efforts on the issue of reservations since its inception must be acknowledged, the Committee, despite its lack of working time, must find ways, together with other actors, to continue and strengthen these efforts both in a theoretical and practical manner in order to have justice done to all women whose governments have ratified the Convention.

105 J. McBride, 'Reservations and the Capacity to Implement Human Rights', in Gardner, *supra* note 15, p. 124.

RESERVATIONS BY STATES UNDER THE INTERNATIONAL COVENANT ON CIVIL AND POLITICAL RIGHTS AND ITS OPTIONAL PROTOCOLS, AND THE PRACTICE OF THE HUMAN RIGHTS COMMITTEE

Martin Scheinin[*]

CONTENTS

1. INTRODUCTION

In 1994 the Human Rights Committee, the treaty body acting under the *International Covenant on Civil and Political Rights* (ICCPR),[106] adopted its *General Comment No. 24* (52)[107] on issues related to reservations made to the Covenant or its two Optional Protocols.[108] The General Comment did not break new ground as to the regime on reservations under human rights treaties but it certainly made explicit some of the tensions that existed between the *Vienna Convention on the Law of Treaties* (Vienna Convention)[109] and the approach taken to reservations under human rights treaties. The General Comment triggered off critical comments by certain

---

[*] Professor of Constitutional and International Law, Åbo Akademi University, Member, Human Rights Committee (1997–2004).

[106] UNTS, vol. 999, p. 171.

[107] UN doc. HRI/GEN/1/Rev.5 p. 150.

[108] UNTS, vol. 999, p. 171; UN doc. A/RES/44/128.

[109] UNTS, vol. 1155, p.331.

States,[110] and still after ten years it still remains an important background factor for the ongoing work of the International Law Commission (ILC) under the theme of reservations to multilateral treaties.[111]

This short essay is not a commentary of *General Comment No. 24*. Rather, the author aims at an overview of the present approach of the Human Rights Committee in respect of reservations by States. Within that context, *General Comment No. 24* and its relationship with the Vienna Convention regime is also addressed.

2. HUMAN RIGHTS TREATIES AND THE VIENNA CONVENTION REGIME

General Comment No. 24 includes two fundamental elements of a human rights approach to reservations that are in tension with the Vienna Convention regime: (a) A human rights treaty body, established for the purpose of interpreting the treaty and monitoring the compliance by States with its provisions has the competence to address the permissibility of reservations made under the treaty in question;[112] (b) The usual (but not automatic) consequence of an impermissible reservation will be its severability, i.e. the State in question is considered bound by the treaty but without the benefit of its reservation.[113]

These two dimensions of a human rights treaty approach to reservations are at least seemingly at variance from the provisions of the Vienna Convention. Article 19 of the Vienna Convention shows that reservations to multilateral treaties are permissible, within certain limits, and Articles 20 and 21 establish the regime of objections to reservations, through which other States may control each others' reservations. The consequences of applying the Vienna Convention regime would be, again at least seemingly, that *the reserving State always wins*: either its reservation is accepted by other States through their decision not to object, or the other States' objections will determine whether the reserving State is not at all a party to the treaty or is a party with the modification that the provision to which a reservation was made is not applicable in the relationship between the

---

[110] *See Annual Report 1995 of the Human Rights Committee*, A/50/40 vol. I pp. 126–134 (the United States and the United Kingdom); *Annual Report 1996 of the Human Rights Committee*, A/51/40 vol. I pp. 104–106 (France).

[111] *Report of the International Law Commission, Fifty-fifth session* (5 May-6 June and 7 July-8 August 2003), A/58/10, Chapter VIII.

[112] *See*, paragraph 18 of *General Comment No. 24* (*supra*, note 2).

[113] *Ibid.*

reserving State and the objecting State. In no case would the reserving State be bound by the treaty beyond its own consent. Leaving it for other States to react through objections to reservations, and the limited range of legal consequences of such objections appear to leave no room for the two central elements of a human rights approach to reservations.

Neither one of the two central dimensions of a human rights approach to reservations is an innovation by the Human Rights Committee. Reference can be made to the *Belilos,*[114] *Loizidou*[115] and *Ilascu*[116] cases before the European Court of Human Rights. These cases also express the two central elements of a human rights approach to reservations.

3. CAN THE TWO APPROACHES BE RECONCILED?

Despite of what has been said above, there is no need to assert that there would be a 'conflict' between the rules of the Vienna Convention and a human rights treaty approach to reservations. Instead, there are several ways to resolve the apparent contradictions between the two regimes.

Firstly, a legal positivist could note that under its own terms the Vienna Convention has no retroactive effect: Article 4 is explicit in that the Vienna Convention applies only to treaties which are concluded by States after the entry into force of the Vienna Convention with regard to such States. The Vienna Convention entered into force in 1980, i.e. subsequent to the entry into force of the ICCPR and its (first) *Optional Protocol* in respect of many of their States parties. This kind of a formalistic approach would be clearly unsatisfactory in order to harmonize the two regimes, as it would make the rules related to reservations under one and the same human rights treaty depend on the time of entry into force of that treaty in respect of a specific State. Furthermore, it would ignore the fact that the Vienna Convention as a

[114] *Belilos* v. *Switzerland,* Judgment of 29 April 1988, European Court of Human Rights, in particular para. 49–51 and 58–60.

[115] *Loizidou* v. *Turkey,* Judgment on preliminary objections, European Court of Human Rights, 23 February 1995, in particular paras. 76–79 and 93–98.

[116] Admissibility decision by a Grand Chamber of the European Court of Human Rights, 4 July 2001, Application no. 48787/99 by Ilie Ilascu, Alexandru Lesco, Andrei Ivantoc and Tudor Petrov-Popa against Moldova and the Russian Federation. The Court concluded that a 'declaration' by Moldova could be equated with a reservation within the meaning of Article 57 of the *European Convention on Human Rights* and was deemed invalid. For more on the practice of the European Court of Human Rights, *see* article by J. Polakiewicz in this book below – ed.

whole and also the wording of Article 4 itself imply that the Convention reflects applicable rules of customary international law.[117]

Secondly, and accepting that the Vienna Convention reflects rules of customary international law, one should be conscious of this double nature of the Convention both as a set of positive rules and as a reflection of customary international law. As a consequence one should not read individual provisions of the Vienna Convention in a legal positivist fashion. In a holistic reading of the Vienna Convention it becomes quite clear that many of its provisions are written to reflect the operation of a multilateral treaty between States in issues where States act in their own interest in respect of other States, where there are no third parties with their own rights or obligations involved and where the treaty does not establish an independent international mechanism for its application and interpretation. This perspective is reflected already in Article 1 of the Convention.[118] A careful reading of the Vienna Convention shows that room is left for the operation of modified rules in respect of treaties that do not correspond to this presumed ideal type of a multilateral treaty. In the section on reservations reference can be made to Article 20, paragraph 3:

> 'When a treaty is a constituent instrument of an international organization and unless it otherwise provides, a reservation requires the acceptance of the competent organ of that organization.'

A legal positivist might argue that this provision is, as such, applicable to human rights treaties that have a life of their own compared to the intergovernmental organization that once upon a time adopted the text of the treaty for ratification by States and which establish an independent ('competent') organ to monitor States' compliance with the treaty. Hence, the ICCPR and its two Optional Protocols would together qualify as a constituent instrument of an international organization, and any reservation would require the acceptance of the Human Rights Committee.

A less positivist position, preferred by the present author, is that Article 20, paragraph 3, reflects a more general principle according to which

[117] 'Without prejudice to the application of any rules set forth in the present Convention *to which treaties would be subject under international law independently of the Convention*, the Convention applies only to treaties which are concluded by States after the entry into force of the present Convention with regard to such States.' (emphasis added).

[118] 'The present Convention applies to treaties between States.'

Articles 20 and 21 of the Vienna Convention are not fully identical with corresponding norms of customary international law and not automatically applicable in respect of multilateral treaties that are concluded between States for the protection of third parties, and which subject States to monitoring by an international court or an independent expert body as to their compliance with the treaty.

A third way to reconcile a human rights treaty approach with the Vienna Convention regime would be based on the observation that the Vienna Convention does not at all regulate the consequences of *impermissible* reservations. Instead, it first sets out the rules for the permissibility of reservations by States (Article 19) and then moves to regulate the reactions by other States to such permissible reservations (Article 20) and the legal effect of permissible reservations (Article 21).[119] A legal positivist would conclude that reservations that are contrary to the object and purpose (Article 19) of a human rights treaty are simply prohibited by the Vienna Convention. A person looking beyond positivism would then move to a holistic reading of the Vienna Convention, trying to understand it as a reflection of norms of customary international law and leaving room for solutions emanating from international and State practice as to the consequences of impermissible reservations.

The above discussion hopefully shows that there is plenty of room for efforts to reconcile the Vienna Convention regime and a human rights treaty approach to reservations. In order to be successful such efforts must give due recognition to the practice of regional human rights courts and of global-level human rights treaty bodies. A view, according to which the rules of the Vienna Convention are 'crystal clear' and leave it merely to other States to accept or object to reservations by States, is plainly erroneous.

4. RESERVATIONS IN THE PRACTICE OF THE HUMAN RIGHTS COMMITTEE

4.1. The Consideration of Government Reports

General Comment No. 24 was adopted some six months before the consideration of the initial report by the United States of America. The

[119] Specifically, attention is drawn to Paragraph 1 of Article 21, making it clear that the provision relates to reservations that have been made '*in accordance with articles 19*, 20 and 23' (emphasis added), i.e. permissible reservations.

number and far-reaching nature of reservations and declarations by the US[120] came therefore to be the first test for the practical application of the Committee's approach as presented in the General Comment. The reservations and declarations indeed had an important role in the Committee's consideration of the report[121] and in the Concluding Observations adopted at the end of the exercise.[122] While in respect of many of the declarations made by the US upon ratification the Committee could conclude with a positive statement that they would not lead to departing from Covenant obligations,[123] the Committee was highly critical in certain remaining issues:

> 'The Committee regrets the extent of the State party's reservations, declarations and understandings to the Covenant. It believes that, taken together, they intended to ensure that the United States has accepted only what is already the law of the United States. The Committee is also particularly concerned at reservations to article 6, paragraph 5, and article 7 of the Covenant, which it believes to be incompatible with the object and purpose of the Covenant.'[124]

While the Committee here followed its General Comment in assessing the permissibility of reservations under the object and purpose test

---

[120] United Nations Treaty Collection.

[121] CCPR/C/SR.1401-1402 and SR.1405-1406. The last one of these summary records includes a statement by the Committee's chairpersons on the issue of reservations to the ICCPR.

[122] CCPR/C/79/Add.50; reproduced in the *Annual Report of the Human Rights Committee* 1995, A/50/40, as paras. 266–304.

[123] *See*, paras. 275–277 of the Concluding Observations (as renumbered in the Annual Report).

[124] *Ibid.*, para. 279. The two reservations referred to as particular matters of concern read as follows: '(2) That the United States reserves the right, subject to its Constitutional constraints, to impose capital punishment on any person (other than a pregnant woman) duly convicted under existing or future laws permitting the imposition of capital punishment, including such punishment for crimes committed by persons below eighteen years of age.' and '(3) That the United States considers itself bound by article 7 to the extent that "cruel, inhuman or degrading treatment or punishment" means the cruel and unusual treatment or punishment prohibited by the Fifth, Eighth, and/or Fourteenth Amendments to the Constitution of the United States'.

corresponding to article 19 of the Vienna Convention, to the degree of declaring some of them to be incompatible with the object and purpose of the Covenant, it did not refer to the consequence of severability, i.e. the United States being bound by Articles 6 and 7 without the benefit of its reservations. Instead, the Committee invited the State party to reconsider its reservations.[125]

The conclusion of severability has been drawn by the Committee in the consideration of a government report at least on one occasion. In July 2000, the Committee was confronted with an 'interpretive declaration' by Kuwait that appeared to deviate from the basic Covenant principles of non-discrimination (Article 2) and equality between men and women (Article 3):

> 'Interpretative declaration regarding article 2, paragraph 1, and article 3:
>
> Although the Government of Kuwait endorses the worthy principles embodied in these two articles as consistent with the provisions of the Kuwait Constitution in general and of its article 29 in particular, the rights to which the articles refer must be exercised within the limits set by Kuwaiti law.'[126]

In its Concluding Observations on Kuwait's initial report, the Committee was quite clear in its pronouncement that such a general 'declaration' is impermissible as a reservation and without legal effect, resulting in the State party being bound by the Covenant without the benefit of the reservation or declaration. However, the State party was nevertheless invited to withdraw its reservations and declarations:

> '5. The Committee, referring to its General Comment No. 24 on reservations, notes that the "interpretative declarations" of the State party regarding article 2, paragraph 1, article 3, and article 23, as well as the 'reservations' concerning article 25 (b) of the Covenant raise the serious issue of their compatibility with the object

[125] Para. 292: 'The Committee recommends that the State party review its reservations, declarations and understandings with a view to withdrawing them, in particular reservations to article 6, paragraph 5, and article 7 of the Covenant.'
[126] United Nations Treaty Collection.

> and purpose of the Covenant. In particular, the Committee notes that articles 2 and 3 of the Covenant constitute core rights and overarching principles of international law that cannot be subject to "limits set by Kuwaiti law". Such broad and general limitations would undermine the object and purpose of the entire Covenant.
>
> 6. The Committee finds that the interpretative declaration regarding articles 2 and 3 contravenes the State party's essential obligations under the Covenant and is therefore without legal effect and does not affect the powers of the Committee. The State party is urged to withdraw formally both the interpretative declarations and the reservations.'[127]

The request to withdraw all reservations is by no means exceptional in the reporting procedure and does not mean that the Committee would have held that all declarations and reservations by Kuwait would be impermissible. Paragraph 6 of the Concluding Observations, quoted above, includes a legal finding of the impermissibility and severability of the interpretive declaration on Articles 2 and 3, and a policy-oriented call for the State party to withdraw this declaration as well as other, possibly permissible, reservations.

5. THE CASE OF KENNEDY V. TRINIDAD AND TOBAGO

The most important instance where the Human Rights Committee has applied its approach to reservations is the individual communication by *Rawle Kennedy* v. *Trinidad and Tobago.*[128] Subsequent to a ruling by the Judicial Committee of the Privy Council that keeping a person under the sentence of death for more than five years constituted inhuman or degrading punishment or treatment, and had the consequence of outlawing any later

---

[127] CCPR/CO/69/KWT, reproduced in the *Annual Report of the Human Rights Committee* 2000, A/55/40, paras. 452–497. For the summary records on the consideration of the report, *see* CCPR/C/SR.1851-1854.

[128] *Rawle Kennedy* v. *Trinidad and Tobago*, Communication No 845/1999, admissibility decision of 2 November 1999, CCPR/C/67/D/845/1999. In its final views, adopted on 26 March 2002, CCPR/C/74/D/845/1998, the Committee found violations of Articles 6, Paragraph 1, 7, 9, Paragraph 3, 10, Paragraph 1, 14, Paragraphs 3(c) and 5, and 14, Paragraphs 1 and 3(d), the latter in conjunction with Article 2, Paragraph 3, of the Covenant.

execution,[129] Trinidad and Tobago denounced the Optional Protocol and immediately reacceded with a reservation according to which the right of individual complaint did not apply to persons sentenced to death.[130] After the reaccession had entered into force, a communication was submitted on behalf of Mr Rawle Kennedy, a person under the sentence of death. With reference to its *General Comment No. 24* the Committee affirmed its competence, as the treaty body to the *International Covenant on Civil and Political Rights* and its Optional Protocols, to interpret and determine the validity of reservations made to these treaties.[131] Thereafter, the Committee moved to a recognition of the object and purpose test for determining the permissibility of a reservation[132] and, again with reference to *General Comment No. 24*, to its assessment that the reservation was impermissible:

> '6.7 The present reservation, which was entered after the publication of General Comment No. 24, does not purport to exclude the competence of the Committee under the Optional Protocol with regard to any specific provision of the Covenant, but rather to the entire Covenant for one particular group of complainants, namely prisoners under sentence of death. This does not, however, make it compatible with the object and purpose of the Optional Protocol. On the contrary, the Committee cannot accept a reservation which singles out a certain group of individuals for lesser procedural protection than that which is enjoyed by the rest of the population. In the view of the Committee, this constitutes a discrimination which runs counter to some of the basic principles embodied in the Covenant and its Protocols, and for this reason the reservation cannot be deemed compatible with the object and purpose of the

---

129 *Pratt and Morgan* v. *the Attorney General for Jamaica*, 2 A.C. 1, 1994.

130 'Trinidad and Tobago re-accedes to the Optional Protocol to the International Covenant on Civil and Political Rights with a Reservation to article 1 thereof to the effect that the Human Rights Committee shall not be competent to receive and consider communications relating to any prisoner who is under sentence of death in respect of any matter relating to his prosecution, his detention, his trial, his conviction, his sentence or the carrying out of the death sentence on him and any matter connected therewith.' *See* United Nations Treaty Collection.

131 Paragraph 6.4 of the admissibility decision (*supra*, note 23).

132 *Ibid.*, paragraph 6.5.

> Optional Protocol. The consequence is that the Committee is not precluded from considering the present communication under the Optional Protocol.'

One may legitimately pose the question whether the Committee went too far in applying the consequence of severability in this particular case. Did not the conduct by the State party, through its denunciation and immediate reaccession with a reservation, make clear that Trinidad and Tobago wanted to be a party to the Optional Protocol only as conditioned by the reservation? Hence, the Committee could perhaps have concluded that the communication by an individual awaiting execution was inadmissible *ratione personae*, as Trinidad and Tobago, despite of its reaccession, in the Committee's view was not a party! This line of reasoning was offered by five members of the Committee who in a forcefully argued dissenting opinion came to the conclusion that the communication, indeed, should have been declared inadmissible.[133]

The author of this essay voted with the majority in declaring the case admissible and has not changed his position. It is true that the majority view was not thoroughly reasoned and that the particular issue of severability was plainly declared as a consequence of the impermissibility of the reservation, without legal arguments. Kennedy is not the only case by the Human Rights Committee where a dissenting opinion is more complete in its argumentation than the majority view. One may, as a general explanation for this phenomenon, refer to the fact that Committee views often represent the common denominator between differing lines of reasoning that nevertheless come to the same result. In controversial cases they are formulated in the course of a meeting between eighteen individual experts, often by deleting what is controversial in the reasoning. Members, who have been a part of a process towards consensus, or at least a majority view, are often reluctant to

---

[133] Admissibility decision in Kennedy (*supra*, note 23), individual dissenting opinion by Nisuke Ando, Prafulachandra N. Bhagwati, Eckart Klein and David Kretzmer There is no need here to give a full account of the dissenters' argumentation. Nevertheless, it should be made clear that their position was not primarily based on the idea of Trinidad and Tobago not being a party to the Optional Protocol. Rather, the minority was of the view that the reservation in question was a permissible one: 'If a State party is free either to accept or not accept an international monitoring mechanism, it is difficult to see why it should not be free to accept this mechanism only with regard to some rights or situations, provided the treaty itself does not exclude this possibility. All or nothing is not a reasonable maxim in human rights law.' More on this point *see* article by E. Klein below in this book – ed.

reopen the resulting consensus in the form of a concurring individual opinion.[134] Dissenters, in turn, have several weeks after the decision to work on their individual opinion.

It remains the opinion of the present author that the Human Rights Committee was *right* in applying the consequence of severability in the Kennedy case, after having found the State party's reservation impermissible. The rights of individuals as beneficiaries of a human rights treaty should govern the application of a human rights treaty by the monitoring body of such a treaty. Therefore, it is not for the treaty body to refuse to treat a State as a party to the treaty, as long as the State itself has not drawn the conclusion of not being a party.

Does this lead us to the position that severability is not only the normal consequence of an impermissible reservation but an *automatic* consequence? Not necessarily. There might be situations where a reservations is simply declared impermissible, without the treaty body needing to express a position as to whether the treaty continues to apply but the State party should nevertheless withdraw its reservation, or whether the reservation is indeed severed, or whether there is a way to interpret the reservation in a way that helps to avoid its impermissible application. In particular in the reporting procedure it will relatively often be possible to choose the first option, with an expectation that the continuous nature of the system of periodic reporting will lead to the State party withdrawing or amending its reservation.[135]

6. OTHER INDIVIDUAL CASES UNDER THE OPTIONAL PROTOCOL

The nature and modalities of the procedure for individual complaints is such as to often require a definitive decision as to whether an impermissible reservation is severable, as a part of the admissibility decision. However, one should not exclude the possibility of taking a case-by-case approach in order

---

[134] In the Kennedy case, Louis Henkin did append a concurring individual opinion. However, even he chose just to distance himself from the laconic reasoning in the majority view, instead of explaining his own reasons why he came to the conclusion of admissibility.

[135] The general issue of the possibility of States to amend their reservations after the ratification and entry into force of a treaty will not be discussed here. For the purposes of the present analysis, it suffices to treat such an amendment as a partial withdrawal of the original impermissible reservation.

to avoid a final determination by first exhausting the possibilities of interpretation. Two examples help to illustrate this.

In the case of *Francis Hopu and Tepoaitu Bessert* v. *France* the Human Rights Committee was confronted with a 'declaration' by France that under the terms of *General Comment No. 24* could have been considered an impermissible reservation.[136] As the reservation issue arose in the context of an individual case, a determination of its permissibility and severability might appear as unavoidable as a part of the admissibility decision. However, the majority of the Committee decided to treat the reservation as a permissible one,[137] despite language in *General Comment No. 24* that would have spoken for a different conclusion.[138] This approach resulted from the existence of earlier cases where the same reservation had, prior to the adoption of *General Comment No. 24*, been accepted by the Committee by declaring inadmissible individual cases covered by the declaration or reservation.[139] This approach by the majority indicates that earlier case law has stronger effect as precedent for the Committee's work than pronouncements in general comments. In the context of the present article, however, attention is drawn to a partly dissenting opinion by five members, including the current author. These members sought to resolve the tension between the pronouncement in *General Comment No. 24* and earlier case law by interpreting the reservation so that it had no effect in the

[136] 'In the light of article 2 of the Constitution of the French Republic, the French Government declares that article 27 is not applicable so far as the Republic is concerned.' *See* United Nations Treaty Collection.

[137] *Francis Hopu and Tepoaitu Bessert* v. *France*, Communication No. 549/1993, CCPR/C/60/D/549/1993/Rev.1, paragraph 4.3.

[138] *General Comment No. 24* (*supra*, note 2), paragraph 8: 'a State may not reserve the right . . . to deny to minorities the right to enjoy their own culture, profess their own religion or use their own language'.

[139] *See, for example*, *T.K.* v. *France*, Communication No. 220/1987, CCPR/C/37/D/220/1987 (1989), paragraph 8.6: 'In the present case, the statement entered by the French Government upon accession to the Covenant is clear: it seeks to exclude the application of article 27 to France and emphasizes this conclusion semantically with the words "is not applicable". The statement's intent is unequivocal and thus must be given preclusionary effect in spite of the terminology used. Furthermore, the State party's submission of 15 January 1989 also speaks of a French "reservation" in respect of article 27. Accordingly, the Committee considers that it is not competent to consider complaints directed against France concerning alleged violations of article 27 of the Covenant.' In her individual opinion Rosalyn Higgins held that the declaration by France did not operate as a reservation.

circumstances of the new case.[140] The dissenting opinion was formulated in a way which leaves it open whether this conclusion is based on the severability of the reservation or a textual interpretation of the reservation itself.

Likewise, in *Mümtaz Karakurt* v. *Austria*,[141] two members resorted in a partly dissenting opinion to the interpretation of a reservation instead of plainly applying the reservation. The case concerned the exclusion of non-EEA citizens from the elections of workers' councils. Austria had when ratifying the Covenant entered a reservation according to which:

> 'Article 26 is understood to mean that it does not exclude different treatment of Austrian nationals and aliens, as is also permissible under article 1, paragraph 2, of the International Convention on the Elimination of All Forms of Racial Discrimination.'[142]

The majority accepted this declaration as a reservation, preventing the Committee from examining whether there was discrimination between (certain categories of) foreigners and Austrian nationals.[143] Nevertheless, a violation of Article 26 was found because of discrimination between different categories of foreigners.[144] The minority, in turn, interpreted the reservation as only meaning that distinctions between nationals and foreigners will not be considered to constitute (indirect) discrimination on account of race or ethnicity, whereas it did not preclude the Human Rights Committee from examining whether a distinction based on nationality is as

---

[140] *Francis Hopu and Tepoaitu Bessert* v. *France* (*supra,* note 32), partly dissenting opinion by Elizabeth Evatt, Cecilia Medina Quiroga, Fausto Pocar, Martin Scheinin and Maxwell Yalden: 'Whatever the legal relevance of the declaration made by France in relation to the applicability of article 27 may be in relation to the territory of metropolitan France, we do not consider the justification given in said declaration to be of relevance in relation to overseas territories under French sovereignty.'

[141] *Mümtaz Karakurt* v. *Austria*, Communication No. 965/2000, CCPR/C/74/D/965/2000 (2002).

[142] Quoted in *ibid.*, paragraph 2. The relevant provision of the CERD reads: 'This Convention shall not apply to distinctions, exclusions, restrictions or preferences made by a State Party to this Convention between citizens and non-citizens.' *See also* United Nations Treaty Collection.

[143] *Ibid.*, paragraph 7.5.

[144] *Ibid.*, paragraph 8.4.

such a form of direct discrimination prohibited by Article 26 of the Covenant.[145]

These examples illustrate that although it would, in the author's view, not be proper for a human rights body to declare that a ratifying State is not a party to a human rights treaty because of the unacceptable nature of its reservation, the severability of a reservation is nevertheless not the only available option when the Committee is confronted with a reservation that is, or *might be* if interpreted in a certain way, incompatible with the object and purpose of the treaty.

7. ARE RESERVATIONS APPLIED EX OFFICIO?

If reservations require interpretation before their application or, alternatively, severance, it will be very difficult for the Human Rights Committee to determine the effect of a reservation in a concrete case without hearing the arguments of the parties in the case as to what is the meaning of the reservation in the circumstances of the case. This speaks strongly against *ex officio* application of reservations and in favour of an approach where a State party must both invoke its reservation and explain its effect in the circumstances of a case, before the Committee can apply a reservation. Indeed, such an approach was confirmed in 2002 as the correct one by the Human Rights Committee in the case of *Manuel Wackenheim* v. *France*.[146]

Prior to *Wackenheim*, there were some instances when a reservation was relied upon by the Committee in declaring cases inadmissible without even transmitting the communication to the State party concerned. This was done in the cases of *A.M.* v. *Denmark* (1982)[147] and *C.L.D.* v. *France* (1991),[148] both based on a so-called Special Rapporteur's Draft on inadmissibility.[149]

---

[145] *Ibid.*, partly dissenting opinion by Nigel Rodley and Martin Scheinin.

[146] *Manuel Wackenheim* v. *France*, Communication No. 854/1999, CCPR/C/75/D/854/1999 (2002), paragraph 6.2: 'Although France has entered a reservation to article 5, paragraph 2 (a) [of the Optional Protocol], the Committee notes that it has not invoked that reservation which does not, therefore, impede consideration of the communication by the Committee.'

[147] *A.M.* v. *Denmark*, Communication No. 121/1982, CCPR/C/16/D/121/1982, para. 5.

[148] *C.L.D.* v. *France*, Communication No. 439/1990, CCPR/C/43/D/439/1990, para. 4.3.

[149] This expression refers to a possibility of the Committee's Special Rapporteur on New Communications deciding, already at the time of registration, that instead of being transmitted to the State party concerned a communication will be brought to the Committee plenary with a recommendation of declaring it inadmissible without

However, in recent years and definitely after *Wackenheim*, the practice of the Committee has been not to use in decisions on admissibility the existence of a reservation as a ground for inadmissibility, unless the State party has invoked its reservation.

8. THE RESERVATION BY SPAIN IN THE ISSUE OF 'SAME MATTER'

One of the most difficult issues with which the Human Rights Committee repeatedly has been confronted with is a reservation by Spain to Article 5, paragraph 2(a) of the Optional Protocol. In its English translation the reservation does not appear to differ from reservations by many other European States, aimed at precluding the subsequent consideration of a case by the Human Rights Committee after it has been concluded under the complaints procedure of the *European Convention of Human Rights*:

> 'The Spanish Government accedes to the Optional Protocol to the International Covenant on Civil and Political Rights, on the understanding that the provisions of article 5, paragraph 2, of that Protocol mean that the Human Rights Committee shall not consider any communication from an individual unless it has ascertained that the same matter has not been or is not being examined under another procedure of international investigation or settlement.'[150]

What is specific in the Spanish reservation is that although its English translation uses the verb 'to examine', similarly to the English text of the provision of the Optional Protocol, the Spanish language original version of the reservation corresponds to the authentic Spanish text of the Optional Protocol that uses the verb '*sometido*' which could be understood as 'to submit'. A comparison with other authentic language versions of the Optional Protocol and with the drafting history of the instrument show that the Spanish text of Article 5, paragraph 2(a) of the Optional Protocol includes a clear translation error. Consequently, the Human Rights

---

transmittal to the State party. It is the practice of the Committee to use this procedure only when the ground for inadmissibility constitutes an objective obstacle to admissibility and does not depend on whether the State party contests admissibility.

[150] United Nations Treaty Collection. *See also*, reservations to the same provision by, *inter alia*, Germany, France, Denmark, Italy, etc.

Committee already in 1978 decided to follow the other authentic languages in its interpretation of the provision.[151]

However, this does not settle the matter of the correct interpretation of the reservation by Spain, entered upon ratification in 1985, i.e. later in time than the Committee's decision to ignore the Spanish version in the interpretation of the provision. One way to read the Spanish reservation is to see it as a way to preserve the integrity of the Spanish language version of the Optional Protocol by entering as a reservation what perhaps originally was a translation error.

Every time the Spanish reservation is relevant in an individual case, the Human Rights Committee is in great difficulties, not the least because of the different language versions of the Optional Protocol and of the text of the reservation that members have in front of them differ in substance and all what is said in Spanish is translated into other languages and vice versa.

For the purposes of this article, it suffices to emphasize that the experiences with the Spanish reservation also bear witness of the fact that a reservation cannot be applied without first engaging in a process of interpretation. One of the latest cases where the Spanish reservation was discussed is *Joseph Semey* v. *Spain* where the dilemma was solved, for the purposes of the particular case, by applying the *Wackenheim* approach of not basing inadmissibility on a reservation unless a State party explicitly invokes its reservation:

> '8.3 Pursuant to article 5, paragraph 2 (a), of the Optional Protocol, before considering a communication the Committee must ascertain that the same matter is not being examined under another procedure of international investigation or settlement. The Committee is aware that there is a discrepancy between the Spanish text of article 5, paragraph 2 (a), and the English and French versions which goes beyond a mere translation error and reveals fundamental differences in substance. This discrepancy was discussed by the members of the Committee at its fourth session in New York on 19 July 1978 (CCPR/C/SR.88). Therefore, bearing in mind the decision taken on the matter in 1978, the Committee reiterates that the term "sometido" in the Spanish version should be interpreted in the light of the other versions, i.e. that it should be understood as

[151] CCPR/C/SR.88.

> meaning "is being examined" by another procedure of international investigation or settlement. On the basis of this interpretation, the Committee considers that the case of Joseph Semey is not being examined by the European Court. The Committee also notes that the State party has not invoked its reservation to article 5, paragraph 2 (a), of the Optional Protocol. Consequently, there is no obstacle to the communication's admissibility in this respect.'[152]

In another recently decided case, *Luis Pascual Estevill* v. *Spain*, in which Spain explicitly invoked its reservation, the existence of another ground for inadmissibility helped the Committee to avoid a final determination of whether the Spanish reservation precludes admissibility under the Optional Protocol due to mere submission of the same matter to the procedure under the *European Convention on Human Rights*.[153]

9. CONCLUSION

As was emphasized in *General Comment No. 24*, human rights treaties are not a web of inter-State exchanges of mutual obligations because they concern the endowment of individuals with rights.[154] From the specific nature of human rights treaties as treaties with third-party beneficiaries and as treaties monitored and interpreted by a human rights court or other independent expert body, emerges a need to reflect critically upon the rules of the *Vienna Convention on the Law of Treaties* before a mechanic application of its provisions. The two central elements of a human rights treaty approach to reservations by States are the competence of the respective monitoring body to address the permissibility of reservations and the possible consequence of the severability of the reservation. In the view of

---

[152] *Joseph Semey* v. *Spain*, Communication No. 986/2001, CCPR/C/78/D/986/2001 (2003).

[153] *Luis Pascual Estevill* v. *Spain*, Communication No. 1004/2001, CCPR/C/77/D/1004/2001 (2003), para. 6.3.

[154] *General Comment No. 24* (*supra*, note 2), para. 17.

the present author these elements are not necessarily in contradiction with the Vienna Convention but can be reconciled with the Vienna Convention regime.

A COMMENT ON THE ISSUE OF RESERVATIONS TO THE PROVISIONS OF THE COVENANT REPRESENTING (PEREMPTORY) RULES OF GENERAL INTERNATIONAL LAW

Eckart Klein[*]

I.

The following remarks do not address the full range of issues connected with the problem of reservations entered by States when signing, ratifying or acceding to a human rights treaty. They will only focus on a statement of the Human Rights Committee contained in *General Comment No. 24 (1994)* on 'Issues relating to reservations made upon ratification or accession to the Covenant or the Optional Protocols thereto, or in relation to declarations under article 41 of the Covenant'.[155] Paragraph 8 of this General Comment reads:

> 'Reservations that offend peremptory norms would not be compatible with the object and purpose of the Covenant. Although treaties that are mere exchanges of obligations between States allow them to reserve *inter se* application of rules of general international law, it is otherwise in human rights treaties, which are for the benefit of persons within their jurisdiction. Accordingly, provisions in the Covenant that represent customary international law (and *a fortiori* when they have the character of peremptory norms) may not be the subject of reservations. Accordingly, a State may not reserve the right to engage in slavery, to torture, to subject persons to cruel, inhuman or degrading treatment or punishment, to arbitrarily deprive persons of their lives, to arbitrarily arrest and detain persons, to deny freedom of thought, conscience and religion, to presume a person guilty

[*] Dr. iur., Professor for Constitutional Law, Public International Law and European Law, Director of the Human Rights Centre, University of Potsdam, Member of the UN Human Rights Committee 1995–2002.

[155] *See* UN Doc. HRI/GEN/1/Rev. 5 (26 April 2001), p. 150. The Covenant does not contain a provision regarding the admissibility or inadmissibility of reservations.

> unless he proves his innocence, to execute pregnant women or children, to permit the advocacy of national, racial or religious hatred, to deny to persons of marriageable age the right to marry, or to deny to minorities the right to enjoy their own culture, profess their own religion, or use their own language. And while reservations to particular clauses of article 14 may be acceptable, a general reservation to the right to a fair trial would not be.'

II.

1. This quotation carries two different legal messages, apart from the examples given. The first message is that reservations cannot be entered regarding Covenant rights that represent customary international law. The second message entails an *a fortiori* conclusion from the first one: Covenant rights that have the character of peremptory norms may not be the subject of reservations. In both cases reservations would be incompatible with the object and purpose of the treaty. While the Committee believes that the provisions of the 1969 *Vienna Convention on the Law of Treaties* (VCLT) regarding the role of State objections in relation to reservations are inappropriate to address the problem of reservations to human rights treaties (*General Comment No. 24* paragraph 17), it accepts the object and purpose test provided for by this Convention (Article 19), as far as no specific treaty rules concerning the reservation issue exist.

2. One may wonder why, on the basis of this test, the Committee did not adopt the view that reservations to Covenant rights are, generally and without exception, inadmissible. In fact, the Committee expresses the opinion that '[i]n an instrument which articulates very many civil and political rights, each of the many articles, and indeed their interplay, secures the objectives of the Covenant' (paragraph 7). How, then, is it possible to distinguish between the rights enshrined in the Covenant, and to accept reservations in some cases? No criterion is available for making any convincing distinction. One could think of the different importance of rights as a basis for distinction, but the Committee correctly considers that 'there is no hierarchy of importance of rights under the Covenant' (paragraph 10).[156]

[156] For the general question of a hierarchy of norms in international law *cf.* P. Weil, 'Towards Relative Normativity in International Law?' 77 *American Journal of International Law* (1983), p. 413; E. Klein, 'Preferred Freedoms-Doktrin und deutsches Verfassungsrecht', in E. Klein (ed.), *Grundrechte, soziale Ordnung und*

However, looking at State practice it very soon becomes clear that no consensus on a general prohibition of reservations to human rights guarantees under a treaty has been established. While some human rights treaties exclude the possibility of reservations[157], others openly accept them.[158] It would be difficult to develop a general rule of prohibition from this basis. The Committee therefore shows a realistic view by not excluding reservations in general, and its practice also indicates that it has accepted reservations to provisions of the Covenant[159].

3. However, according to the Committee the admissibility to enter reservations is excluded if the provisions concerned represent 'rules of general international law'. Let us assume for a moment that human rights norms may be identified representing rules of general international law but not having the character of peremptory norms – an assumption which cannot easily be verified but is implicit in the Committee's argument – then the conclusion drawn by the Committee is rather astonishing. If a rule of general international law is not of a peremptory nature, it is, consequently, *jus dispositivum* and may always be modified among the parties to a treaty[160], of course not relating to third States; here the binding force of the general rule will remain unchanged.[161] It is true that the Human Rights Committee has attributed specific objective effects to the provisions of the Covenant,

---

Verfassungsgerichtsbarkeit, Festschrift für Ernst Benda, (Heidelberg, C.F. Müller, 1995) p. 135, 150 *et seq.*

[157] *E.g.*, the 1987 *European Convention for the Prevention of Torture and Inhuman or Degrading Treatment or Punishment*, ETS No. 126.

[158] *E.g.*, Article 57 of the 1950 *Convention for the Protection of Human Rights and Fundamental Freedoms*, ETS No. 5. The jurisprudence of the European Court for Human Rights is rather restrictive, *see e.g.*, Judgement of 29 April 1988, *Belilos* v. *Switzerland*, No. 10328/83 Ser. A 132, and Decision of 4 July 2001, *Ilascu* v. *Moldovia and Russian Federation*, No. 48787/99, <//hudoc.echr.coe.int>; Hudoc reference: REF 00006431. Further for the debate on this point, *see* article by J. Polakiewicz in this book below – ed.

[159] *E.g., T.K.* v. *France* (No. 220/1987), Decision of 8 November 1989, paras. 8.5 – 8.6, UN Doc. A/45/40/II (1990) Annex X A, p. 118. At the time of the adoption of *General Comment No. 24 (1994)*, 46 States of the 127 parties to the Covenant had entered 150 reservations.

[160] *See* Article 53 VCLT.

[161] *See* C. Grabenwarter, 'Probleme paralleler Rechtsverbürgungen durch Vertrag und Gewohnheitsrecht', in E. Klein (ed.), *Menschenrechtsschutz durch Gewohnheitsrecht*, (Berlin, Berliner Wissenschafts-Verlag, 2003) p. 147, 154 *et seq.*

resulting in the survival of Covenant rights or obligations in case of State succession[162] and in the denial of the possibility to denounce the Covenant or to withdraw from it.[163] While this is a progressive, but well reasoned step towards the protection of human rights, it would not be reasonable to argue that the States parties have lost the power to reframe the Covenant system, concerning its substantive as well as its procedural provisions (always under the assumption that no peremptory rule is involved). States parties may shape the rights enshrined in the Covenant in a different way than they are framed now and may strengthen, but also weaken or abolish the Human Rights Committee as a monitoring body. When States, therefore, may modify human rights guarantees *inter se*, it is not convincing at all to argue that reservations are excluded when other States parties accept them expressly or implicitly.

4. Let us now turn to Covenant rights which represent peremptory norms. Concerning peremptory norms (*jus cogens*) we know that from such norms no derogation is permitted and that a treaty if conflicting with such norms is void or becomes void (Articles 53, 64 of the VCLT).

The Human Rights Committee maintains that '[r]eservations that offend peremptory norms would not be compatible with the object and purpose of the Covenant' (paragraph 8 cl. 1). This statement is not clear at all, because it mixes up a peremptory norm of general international law with a rule created by a treaty heaving the same substance as the peremptory norm. The substantial identity, however, does not turn the treaty rule itself in a peremptory norm.

It is generally recognized that a rule set forth in a treaty may develop into a customary rule of international law[164] and, likewise, that a rule set forth in a treaty may exactly reflect a pre-existing customary rule of international law. In both cases we have to distinguish, though substantially identical, two different norms – a treaty provision and a rule of general international law having a peremptory norm character or not. The two norms exist side by side and do not mingle but preserve their own legal nature[165].

[162] *See* UN Doc. CCPR/C/SR.1178/Add. 1; CCPR/C/SR.1200-1202.

[163] *See* UN Doc. CCPR/C/SR.1178/Add. 1; CCPR/C/SR.1200-1202.

[164] *See* Article 38 of the VCLT; K. Doehring, 'Gewohnheitsrechtsbildung aus Menschenrechtsverträgen', in E. Klein (ed.), *Menschenrechtsschutz durch Gewohnheitsrecht*, (Berlin, Berliner Wissenschafts-Verlag, 2003) p. 67 *et seq*.

[165] *Cf. Military and Paramilitary Activities In and Against Nicaragua*, Judgement of 27 June 1986, *ICJ Reports*, 1986, p. 14, 95 (para. 178): '. . . even if two norms belonging to two sources of international law appear identical in content, and even if the States in question are bound by these rules both on the level of treaty-law and

If this is true the conclusion is not convincing that reservations which offend peremptory norms would not be compatible with the object and purpose of the treaty only because it is not permissible to derogate from peremptory norms unilaterally or by agreement with other States. A reservation to the treaty norm can never have the legal effect of weakening the peremptory norm as such. The peremptory norm is unassailable by unilateral or joint acts. The obligation arising from this norm remains completely unaffected. Therefore a State declaring a reservation to an identical treaty norm cannot absolve itself from the respective obligation rooted in general international law.

If this is correct what is then the sense of entering a reservation to a corresponding treaty norm? The purpose cannot be to exclude or modify the substance of the obligation (this is not possible because it is a peremptory norm), but to exclude the monitoring system established by the treaty with regard to this treaty provision. Of course, no State may liberate itself from the prohibition of torture being a peremptory norm of general international law. A reservation to Article 6 of the ICCPR would not have this effect either, but would (merely) restrict the powers of the Committee to monitor the compliance of a State party with this obligation. The substantial obligation remains untouched.

One might argue that the object and purpose of the Covenant is less to give human rights an additional foundation in treaty law, but rather to establish a monitoring system for these rights. If this is true, what in fact seems to be convincing, the decisive argument would be that any weakening of the Committee's competencies would be incompatible with the object and purpose of the Covenant and therefore inadmissible. The consequence would be that no reservation to any human rights guarantee under the Covenant would be admissible, because it always would have the corresponding effect of restricting the Committee's monitoring competences vis-à-vis the reserving State. This conclusion, however, would amount to a result that is certainly not supported by State and Committee practice: We know that the possibility to enter reservations is by no means totally excluded.[166]

---

that of customary international law, these norms retain a separate existence'; *see also* A. Watts, 'The International Court and the Continuing Customary Law of Treaties', in N. Ando *et al.* (eds.), *Liber Amicorum Judge Shigeru Oda*, (The Hague, Martinus Nijhoff, 2002) Vol. 1, p. 251, 261.

[166] *See supra* note 5.

Nevertheless, two lines of argumentation are available that might permit us to concur in the results found by the Committee. First, one could say that the combination of two arguments – the peremptory nature of individual human rights norms and the purpose to secure their protection by a specific treaty mechanism – establishes the object and purpose of the human rights treaty in question, here the Covenant, and that therefore reservations to such a treaty-based human rights norm violate this object and purpose. Second, one could argue that a treaty provision reflecting a peremptory norm of general international law adopts the nature of a peremptory norm, without losing its character as a treaty provision. I could not completely rule out such a possibility, but it would be necessary to establish this view in a more systematic way than it is possible in this context. I should only add that Article 53 of the VCLT seems to restrict the existence of peremptory norms to the framework of general international law. Be it as it may, at least the reasoning given for the statements contained in Paragraph 8 of *General Comment No. 24 (1994)* is not very convincing.

III.

There remains another issue that would deserve to be dealt with very thoroughly. The Committee takes the view that an inadmissible reservation is without legal effect. The Committee concludes that 'such a reservation will generally be severable, in the sense that the Covenant will be operative for the reserving party without benefit of the reservation' [167]. I am not convinced by this statement either. I have expressed my own view on this matter in the joint dissenting opinion in the *Rawle Kennedy* v. *Trinidad and*

[167] *General Comment No. 24 (1994)*, para. 18.

Tobago case[168], and I have nothing to add. I still think that the Committee went too far in applying its opinion expressed in the General Comment.[169]

---

[168] *See* dissenting opinion of Committee members Ando, Bhagwati, Klein and Kretzmer, CCPR/C/67/D/845/1999.

[169] C. Tomuschat, *Human Rights. Between Idealism and Realism* (Oxford University Press, 2003) p. 162, pointing to the fact that Trinidad and Tobago, in reaction to the Committee's decision took the opportunity to denounce the Optional Protocol: 'It is clear that the overzealous attitude of the HRC has done more harm than good to the course of human rights.'

APPROACHES TO RESERVATIONS BY THE COMMITTEE ON THE ELIMINATION OF RACIAL DISCRIMINATION

*Morten Kjærum**

CONTENTS

1. THE PROVISIONS ON RESERVATIONS IN THE INTERNATIONAL CONVENTION ON THE ELIMINATION OF ALL FORMS OF RACIAL DISCRIMINATION

The *International Convention on the Elimination of All Forms of Racial Discrimination* (ICERD) lays down its own set of rules applicable to reservations. Thus, Article 20 contains rules on the making of reservations, their withdrawal and the duties of the Secretary General for the United Nations, acting as the depository of the Convention, as well as rules on the permissibility of reservations. These rules differ in some respects from the regime subsequently laid down in the 1969 *Vienna Convention on the Law of Treaties*.[170]

The first paragraph of Article 20 deals with the procedural aspects of making reservations. It follows that the Secretary General shall receive and circulate to all States, which are or may become parties to the Convention, reservations made by States at the time of ratification or accession. Any State, which objects to the reservation, shall, within a period of 90 days from the date of the said communication, notify the Secretary General that it does

---

* Director, Danish Institute for Human Rights and member of the Committee on the Elimination of Racial Discrimination. I want to thank Mette Undall-Behrend for assistance in making this article.

170 *Vienna Convention on the Law of Treaties*, 23 May 1969, entry into force 27 January 1980. (ICERD of 21 December 1965, entry into force 4 January 1969).

not accept it.[171] This paragraph sets a very strict time limit for States to object to reservations, compared to the limit of twelve months laid down in the Vienna regime.[172]

The third paragraph of Article 20 simply states that reservations may be withdrawn at any time by notification to the Secretary General, and that such notification shall take effect on the date in which it is received.[173]

The second paragraph of Article 20 deals with the permissibility of reservations, and it can thus be considered the core of Article 20. It states that reservations, which are incompatible with the object and purpose of the Convention, are prohibited as are reservations inhibiting the operation of any of the bodies established by the Convention.[174] Paragraph 2 also lays down the procedure to determine whether a reservation should be considered incompatible or inhibitive. It states that a reservation shall be considered incompatible or inhibitive if at least two thirds of the States parties to the convention object to it.

The ICERD provisions on reservations are similar to the Vienna regime as for the substantial rule of compatibility of reservations with the object and purpose of a treaty,[175] whereas they differ when it comes to the procedure of determining the compatibility. Under the Vienna regime each State party decides itself whether it will object to the reservation and whether it wants this objection to have the effect that the treaty does not enter into force between the two States in question. However, the objecting state cannot prevent the reserving State from becoming a party to the convention if at least one other State accepts the reservation. In that case, the convention will enter into force between the reserving and the 'accepting' States.

---

[171] ICERD, Article 20.1: 'The Secretary-General of the United Nations shall receive and circulate to all States which are or may become Parties to this Convention reservations made by the States at the time of ratification or accession. Any State which objects to the reservation shall, within a period of ninety days from the date of the said communication, notify the Secretary-General that it does not accept it.'

[172] VCLT, Article 20.5.

[173] ICERD, Article 20.3: 'Reservations may be withdrawn at any time by notification to this effect addressed to the Secretary-General. Such notification shall take effect on the date on which it is received.'

[174] ICERD, Article 20.2: 'A reservation incompatible with the object and purpose of this Convention shall not be permitted, nor shall a reservation the effect of which would inhibit the operation of any of the bodies established by this Convention, be allowed. A reservation shall be considered incompatible or inhibitive if at least two-thirds of the States Parties to this Convention object to it.'

[175] VCLT Article 19.c.

By contrast, ICERD leaves it to the States parties *collectively* to decide on the compatibility of the reservation. If two thirds of the States parties object to a reservation, the reservation is not permitted. Article 20 does not explicitly state the legal effect of this, which is probably the reason why three States have made declarations stating that they interpret Article 20 as meaning that if a reservation is not accepted, the State making the reservation does not become a party to the Convention.[176] This collective method also applies in the case of objections to reservations inhibiting the operation of any of the bodies established by the Convention, that is the Committee on the Elimination of Racial Discrimination (CERD) established according to Article 8 and the ad hoc Conciliation Commission, which can be set up under Article 12. The Vienna regime does not contain a corresponding rule.

Thus, in case of objections to either of the two kinds of reservations entered in relation to ICERD, it is for the States parties to do the interpretation and determination as well as – if necessary – to take action. However, since 169 States are parties to the Convention,[177] 113 States would have to object to stop a reservation. This must be considered highly unlikely and, in fact, no reservation has ever been stopped. Obviously, Article 20 only deals with reservations, not with interpretative declarations, which are not entered with the intention to exclude or modify the obligations of the state party in question. Such declarations do not have any legal effect on the obligations of States parties.[178]

2. RESERVATIONS AND DECLARATIONS TO THE ICERD

Declarations and reservations to the ICERD can be divided into different groups.

The majority of the declarations and reservations do not concern the material provisions. A number of them are statements dealing with the non-recognition of Israel,[179] Taiwan[180] and the regime in Rhodesia.[181] Further, 12

[176] Fiji, Tonga, United Kingdom.

[177] Source: <www.unhchr.ch>, 14.11.03.

[178] The Convention was ratified by Turkey on September 2002 and by Thailand on January 2003. Both States made general interpretative declarations. Other State parties have objected to these declarations as they amount to reservation.

[179] Bahrain, Iraq, Kuwait, Libya, Syria, United Arab Emirates, Yemen.

[180] China.

[181] United Kingdom.

States[182] have stated that Article 17 (and 18) are discriminatory because signature and accession should be open to all States, and four States[183] have made declarations that Article 15, which reaffirms the right of petition for the inhabitants of Trust and Non-Self-Governing Territories to which *GA Resolution 1514(XV)* applies, is discriminatory because it provides for a petition procedure only relating to dependent territories and not to States without such territories.

A considerable group of 23 States hold reservations concerning the jurisdiction of the International Court of Justice provided for in Article 22.[184] There are, however, no reservations concerning the operation of any of the two bodies established by the Convention – CERD and the Ad Hoc Conciliation Commission. Another group of States[185] have restricted their acceptance of the Committee's power to receive individual communications to cases not previously dealt with by another international body of investigation or settlement. However, these restrictions are not reservations to the Convention as such, but limited acceptances of the – optional – individual communications procedure laid down in Article 14. The remaining reservations and declarations deal with the material provisions.

Some of the reservations[186] are general in scope, saying that the national constitutions guarantee the fundamental rights and freedoms and that the acceptance of the Convention does not imply acceptance of obligations going beyond the rights and freedoms provided by the constitutions.[187] One State[188] has made a general reservation that it will implement the provisions of the Convention, provided these do not conflict with the precepts of the Islamic *Shariah*. A number of objections were made to this reservation whereas there were no objections made with respect to the first group.[189]

---

[182] Afghanistan, Belarus, Bulgaria, Cuba, Hungary, Mongolia, Poland, Romania, Russian Federation, Ukraine, Vietnam, Yemen.

[183] Fiji, France, Tonga, United Kingdom.

[184] Currently Bahrain, China, Cuba, Egypt, India, Indonesia, Iraq, Israel, Kuwait, Lebanon, Libya, Madagascar, Morocco, Mozambique, Nepal, Rwanda, Saudi Arabia, Syria, Thailand, Turkey, United States of America, Vietnam, Yemen.

[185] Denmark, Finland, Germany, Iceland, Ireland, Italy, Malta, Norway, Portugal, Slovenia, Sweden, Former Yugoslav Republic of Macedonia.

[186] Antigua & Barbuda, Bahamas, Barbados, Guyana, Jamaica, Papua New Guinea.

[187] Thailand made a similar statement in a General Interpretative Declaration. Other State parties have objected to this declaration as it amounts to a reservation.

[188] Saudi Arabia.

[189] Seven States – Austria, Finland, Germany, Netherlands, Norway, Spain and Sweden.

The rest of the reservations and declarations are attached to specific articles, the biggest group concerning Article 4. This article may be considered the most controversial provision because it is trying to strike the right balance between the condemnation and prevention of racist propaganda and the freedom of expression and association. Article 4 obliges States to adopt measures such as to declare punishable all dissemination of ideas based on racial superiority or hatred, prohibit organisations promoting racial discrimination, and not permit promotion of racial discrimination by public institutions. However, states must at the same time give due regard to the principles laid down in the *Universal Declaration on Human Rights* and the rights expressly mentioned in Article 5 of the ICERD.

Some States have made reservations that they will enact legislation according to Article 4 only in so far they may consider it necessary for the attainment of the object in Article 4.[190] Their fulfilment of the ICERD obligations are thus made dependant upon national legislative considerations. Another group of States have made declarations indicating that they intend to interpret Article 4 with due regard to other human rights, thus stressing the fact that the obligations in Article 4 can easily collide with, in particular, the freedom of expression and association.[191] Of the remaining few States, one[192] indicated that the application of Article 4(a) and (b) is subject to the national constitution, another[193] that the freedom of speech, expression and association is extensively protected by domestic legislation (the constitution and the laws) and that no obligation is accepted to restrict those rights, while the last one[194] indicated that it could not at the time of ratification fully apply Article 4, but that it sought to do so at the first suitable moment. (However, after 27 years, this still has not happened.)

A reservation to Article 1 is formulated by one State to the effect that the Commonwealth Immigration Acts of 1962 and 1968 and the implementation thereof do not represent racial discrimination as defined in Article 1.[195] Further, a reservation to Article 1 in connection with Articles 2(1)(c) and (d) and Articles 3 and 5, has been formulated by the one State to the effect that

---

[190] Antigua & Barbuda, Bahamas, Barbados, Fiji, Malta, Nepal, Papua New Guinea, Thailand, Tonga, United Kingdom.

[191] Austria, Belgium, France, Ireland, Italy, Monaco, Switzerland.

[192] Japan.

[193] United States of America.

[194] Australia.

[195] United Kingdom.

the State party does not accept an obligation to enact legislation on discrimination with respect to private conduct.[196]

Article 2 deals with the obligation to take measures in order to eliminate racial discrimination. Two States have made reservations to Article 2 in the sense that they reserve their right to apply their own regulation on the access of foreigners to the labour market.[197] Further, two States have made reservations covering Articles 2, 3 and 5, paragraphs (c), (d)(v), (e)(v), and paragraphs (d)(v), respectively.[198] Article 3 concerns the condemnation of apartheid, whereas Article 5 contains a non-exhaustive list of human rights that should be enjoyed on the basis of equality. Paragraph (c) concerns political rights, in particular the right to participate in elections, to vote and to stand for election. Paragraph (d)(v) concerns the right to own property, and paragraph (e)(v) concerns the right to education. One State[199] has made a reservation not to be bound by paragraph (c) and (d)(iv, vi, and vii), the latter covering the right to marriage and choice of spouse, the right to inherit, and the right to freedom of thought, conscience and religion.[200]

Finally, seven States have made reservations or declarations to Article 6, which is dealing with the question of remedies. Two States indicate that the question of remedies against acts of racial discrimination is governed by ordinary law.[201] Thus, these States cannot be requested to establish special remedies and special rules for such cases. Another five States have stated that the obligation in Article 6 to provide effective remedies contains an obligation to provide for either reparation or satisfaction.[202]

3. ROLE OF THE CERD

The Convention does not expressly confer any power on CERD to decide on the compatibility of reservations. In 1976, the United Nations Office of Legal Affairs has – answering a question from the Committee – stated that:

---

196 United States.

197 Monaco, Switzerland.

198 Fiji, Tonga.

199 The then Yemen Arab Republic.

200 Objections were raised by Australia, Belgium, Canada, Denmark, Finland, France, Germany, Italy, Mexico, Netherlands, New Zealand, Norway, Sweden and United Kingdom (14 States).

201 France, Italy.

202 Fiji, Malta, Nepal, Tonga and United Kingdom.

> 'The Committee is not a representative organ of the States parties (which alone have general competence with regard to the implementation of the Convention). When a reservation has been accepted at the conclusion of the procedure expressly provided for by the Convention (article 20), a decision – even a unanimous decision – by the Committee that such a reservation is unacceptable could not have any legal effect.'[203]

Members of the Committee took note of this answer and agreed, at its 393rd meeting on 5 April 1978, that the Committee must take the reservations made by States parties at the time of ratification or accession into account since it has no authority to do otherwise.[204]

However, over the years, other human rights bodies have taken a different approach. Most significantly, in 1994, the Human Rights Committee adopted *General Comment No. 24*, which deals with issues relating to reservations.[205] The Committee finds in short that the Vienna regime is inappropriate to address the problem of reservations in relation to human rights treaties, and that it is not safe to assume that the absence of objections means that the States parties find a specific reservation acceptable. Therefore, it necessarily falls to the Committee to determine whether a specific reservation is compatible with the object and purpose of the Covenant. The Committee finds that the compatibility must be established objectively, and that the Committee itself is particularly well placed to perform this task. The Human Rights Committee further concludes that the normal consequence of an unacceptable reservation (presumably meaning so decided by the Committee) is not that the Covenant will not be in effect for the reserving party, but rather that the reservation will be severable, in the sense that that Covenant will be operative for the reserving party without the benefit of the reservation.[206]

In the report of their session of February 1998,[207] the Chairpersons of the human rights treaty bodies expressed their support for the approach taken by the Human Rights Committee. They expressed the view that the capacity of

203 UN Juridical Yearbook 1976, pp. 219–221.
204 Report of CERD to GA, A/33/18, paras. 371–176.
205 The *International Covenant on Civil and Political Rights* does not contain specific rules on reservations.
206 Paras. 17 and 18.
207 A/53/125.

a monitoring body to perform its function of determining the scope of the provisions of the relevant convention cannot be performed effectively if it is precluded from exercising a similar function in relation to reservations. No specific mentioning is made of the ICERD regime.

The question of reservations has been touched upon in the *Durban Declaration*, paragraph 75, which urges States to withdraw reservations contrary to the object and purpose of ICERD and to consider withdrawing other reservations. This may be seen as meaning that a reservation does not necessarily comply with the object and purpose of the Convention even though the States parties have accepted it.

In a preliminary opinion of CERD from March 2003[208], CERD underscores that ICERD in principle is following the Vienna regime concerning reservations, from the point of view of the normative level, maintaining the requirement of compatibility with the object and purpose of the Convention as the criterion of admissibility of reservations. Furthermore, the note states that the question of reservations is essentially a matter for States, underlining, *inter alia*, that even though human rights treaties are different from traditional reciprocal treaties, they are still treaties, with the consequences resulting from the law of treaties, and reservations are an integral part of a State's content to become a party to a treaty.

The opinion recognises that it would be within the mandate of the treaty body to take a view on the compatibility of a reservation, to comment thereon and even to include in the concluding observations suggestions and recommendations to the State in relation to the reservation such as changing or withdrawing it. Thus, the Committee can promote, as it has done, the complete implementation of the Convention. The opinion states that this method of dialogue is much more profitable than opening a legal struggle with the reserving States and insisting that their reservations have no legal effect.

CERD has not had the opportunity to deal with reservations in its handling of individual complaints. However, in dealing with State party reports, the Committee often faces this issue. The States parties themselves seem only rarely to explicitly invoke reservations as a reason for not complying with the provisions of the Convention. An example of this, though, is Japan's comments on the concluding observations of April 2001 where Japan states 'there are sufficient domestic laws to secure fulfilment of

208 *Preliminary Opinion of the Committee for the Elimination of Racial Discrimination on the issue of reservations to treaties on human rights.* CERD/C/62/Misc. 20/Rev.3: 13 March 2003.

the obligations under the Convention *with the above reservation*' (emphasis added).[209]

Older as well as recent summary records concerning the States parties holding material reservations show that members of the Committee regularly question States parties about their reservations and declarations and comment thereon. A wide range of issues is covered, such as the implementation and application of the provisions in question, recent developments and considerations, the scope of the reservation and whether it is actually redundant. They also include questions on the object and purpose of the reservations and the precision of the reservations, and members have stated their opinion that certain reservations and the policies, which they reflect, were unacceptable.

When considering the report of Switzerland in 1998, the Swiss reservation concerning foreigners' access to the labour market was discussed. In this connection, a member of the Committee stressed that the Swiss rules which were covered by the reservation, were 'indeed contrary to the object and purpose of the Convention'.[210] Other examples are the reports of United Kingdom and Fiji. When the former was discussed in 1997, one member stated that such fundamental principles as those covered by Article 4 could not (as it was the case) be subject to reservations, and that the Committee should indeed discuss the question of admissibility of reservations on the basic principles of the Convention.[211] As for the latter, which was discussed in 1996, a member stated that the State party's reservations were incompatible with the goal and purpose of the Convention, but noted that at the time no objections were made to them.[212]

On the other hand, when considering the report of Fiji in 2002, a member stated that there was, of course, provision for reservations, but that this need not prevent the Committee from discussing those reservations as it had done in other cases.[213] Along the same lines was a statement made during the consideration of the report of the United Kingdom and Northern Ireland in 2000, according to which it was the State party's sovereign right to issue reservations, whereas it was only fitting for the Committee to

---

[209] A/56/18, Annex VIIA.

[210] CERD/C/SR.1248 (van Boven).

[211] CERD/C/SR.1188 (Rechetov). This war repeated at the examination in August 2003.

[212] CERD/C/SR.1165 (Diaconu).

[213] CERD/C/61/CO/5 (Thornberry).

express its regret and to insist that the Government should accept all the obligations under Article 4.[214]

The Committee has in general been dealing with the implementation of the ICERD provisions covered by declarations and reservations, and the reserving States have in fact to a greater or lesser extent provided information thereon. In its concluding observations, however, the Committee usually confines itself to recommend giving full effect to the provisions of the ICERD, and to express concern about and recommend the withdrawal of reservations. This is the case for instance in the examples of Switzerland,[215] Yemen[216] and Nepal.[217] However, a recent example where the Committee

[214] CERD/C/SR.1420 (Diaconu).

[215] CERD/C/60/CO/14: 'Noting that the former "three-circle" immigration policy of Switzerland which classified foreigners according to categories of national origin and capacity for integration was abandoned and replaced by a binary admissions system and in view of the dialogue held with the Swiss delegation in this respect, the Committee invites the State party to consider if the reservation to article 2 (1) (a) of the Convention is still necessary or may be withdrawn.'

[216] CERD/C/61/CO/10: 'While noting that the State Party has provided information under article 5 of the Convention despite the reservations previously submitted, the Committee invites the State party to continue to provide specific information on how this article is implemented and to consider formally withdrawing those reservations.'

has gone further is the concluding observations mentioned before concerning Japan in 2001. The Committee noted Japan's reservation and expressed concern that such an interpretation as contained in the reservation was in conflict with Japan's obligations under Article 4.[218] The response from the Japanese government addressed only the substantial issues and not the question of the competence of CERD to raise the issue of the reservation.[219]

The approach of CERD is unclear since the opinion is only preliminary. However, the preliminary opinion is somewhat more cautious than the approach announced by the Human Rights Committee, though the compatibility of reservations is indeed discussed in the Committee.

---

[217] A/55/18: 'In view of the State party's reservations on articles 4 and 6 of the Convention, the Committee remains concerned that the full implementation of those provisions may not be ensured, and therefore, reiterates its previous recommendation to the State party to consider withdrawing its reservation.'

[218] CERD/C/304/Add.114.

[219] Comments (summary) of the Japanese Government on the Concluding Observations of the CERD on its initial and 2nd periodic reports: Japan. 10/08/2001. A/56/18,AnnexVIIA. (Concluding Observations/Comments)

THE CONVENTION AGAINST TORTURE AND OTHER CRUEL, INHUMAN OR DEGRADING TREATMENT OR PUNISHMENT – LIMITATIONS, RESTRICTIONS AND RESERVATIONS

Bent Sørensen and Paul Dalton***

TABLE OF CONTENTS

1. INTRODUCTION

From around 1750 and onwards an increasing number of national legal codes included a prohibition of torture. In 1874 Victor Hugo went so far as to claim that 'torture has ceased to exist'.[220]

---

* Professor of Law, MD, DMSc. Former member of both the UN Committee against Torture (1988 – 1995) and the Council of Europe Committee for the Prevention of Torture (1987 – 1997).
** BA, LLB.

[220] E. Peters, *TORTURE, Expanded Edition* (University of Pennsylvania Press, Philadelphia, 1996) p. 5.

Between the two world wars, however, totalitarian regimes were established, and they used torture systematically, in order to stay in power. Since the end of the Second World War there has been increasing focus on the problem of torture. This is reflected in the response of the international community, which has addressed the issue of torture in a series of declarations and conventions over the past 50 years.

Article 5 of the *Universal Declaration on Human Rights* (UDHR), adopted on 10 December 1948,[221] says that:

> 'No one shall be subjected to torture or to other cruel, inhuman or degrading treatment or punishment.'

This formulation has been used ever since all over the world, with the one exception, that the Council of Europe omitted the word 'cruel' in the relevant provision prohibiting torture in the *European Convention for the Protection of Human Rights and Fundamental Freedoms* (*European Convention on Human Rights*, ECHR).[222] The phrase 'torture or other cruel, inhuman or degrading treatment or punishment' has demonstrated its sustainability – as has the problem of torture.

In all regional and international organisations the issue of torture has been taken very seriously; it has been regarded as one of the worst of all violations of human rights, often resulting in severe sequelae for both the individual and the society.

As mentioned above, Article 3 of the *European Convention on Human Rights*[223] uses the same formulation as Article 5 of the UDHR,[224] with the omission of the word 'cruel'. It is note-worthy that Article 3 is mentioned in Article 15 of the ECHR as being one of the rights in respect of which no derogation is permitted, state of emergency or other crisis affecting the life of the State notwithstanding. A similar non-derogability provision has been included in the 1966 *International Covenant on Civil and Political Rights*

---

221 Text of the Universal Declaration of Human Rights, in *Human Rights. A compilation of International Instruments* (United Nations, New York and Geneva, 2002) Vo. 1, pp. 1–6.

222 Text of the European Convention for the Protection of Human Rights and Fundamental Freedoms available at <www.conventions.coe.int>.

223 *Ibid.*

224 *Supra* note 2.

(ICCPR).[225] Article 7 of the ICCPR prohibits torture and, by virtue of Article 4, the prohibition is subject to no derogation.

Thus, the international community considers the prohibition of torture to be of fundamental importance – the prohibition is understood to be absolute; no derogation from this rule is permitted in international law. Where reservations have been made by States parties to the 1984 UN *Convention against Torture and Other Cruel, Inhuman or Degrading Treatment or Punishment* (CAT, the Convention),[226] they must therefore be carefully considered to ensure that they are not in conflict with the absolute nature of the prohibition.

2. LIMITATIONS

2.1. The Title

One way of reading the provisions of the Convention, particularly in view of Article 16, would be to consider the Convention as two separate but interrelated parts:

i) 'The Convention Against Torture' – i.e., those provisions that relate specifically to torture; and
ii) 'The Convention against – other Cruel, Inhuman or Degrading Treatment or Punishment'; those (smaller number) of provisions that relate to the various forms of prohibited ill treatment.

Articles 10, 11, 12 and 13 are common to both, as stated in Article 16, whereas the remaining substantive articles, numbers 1–9, 14 and 15, apply exclusively to the prohibition of torture.

Regarding the other forms of prohibited ill treatment, Article 16 obliges States parties to:

> '. . . undertake to prevent in any territory under its jurisdiction other acts of cruel, inhuman or degrading

---

225 Text of the International Covenant on Civil and Political Rights, in *Human Rights. A compilation of International Instruments* (United Nations, New York and Geneva, 2002) Vol.1, pp. 17–33.

226 Text of the Convention against Torture and Other Cruel, Inhuman or Degrading Treatment or Punishment, in *Human Rights. A compilation of International Instruments* (United Nations, New York and Geneva, 2002) Vol. 1, pp. 315–326.

> treatment or punishment which do not amount to torture as defined in article 1 . . .'

Furthermore, States parties are obliged to:

- educate (Article 10),
- review (Article 11),
- investigate (Article 12) and
- secure the right of victims of ill treatment to make a complaint, to have their case investigated effectively and to enjoy protection, along with witnesses, from possible further harm or reprisal. (Article 13).

However, in contrast with torture, which is defined in Article 1 of the CAT, there is no definition of the phrase 'cruel, inhuman or degrading treatment or punishment' to be found in the Convention (or, for that matter, in any other international or regional human rights instrument). The prohibition of torture also has special status in the Convention as regards the following key provisions:

(I) Articles 2, paragraph 1, and 2, paragraph 2, are an absolute demand to States parties to prevent acts of torture.

(II) Article 2, paragraph 3, which states that an order from a superior cannot be used as an excuse.

(III) Article 3 prohibits the *refoulement* of persons to their home country where there are reasonable grounds to believe that they will be subjected to torture.

(IV) Article 4 obliges States to ensure that all suspected torturers are brought to justice. There is no room for the exercise of discretion in the prosecution of the crime of torture.

(V) Articles 5–8 oblige States to establish and exercise jurisdiction over all persons believed to have committed acts of torture. Torture is a crime of universal jurisdiction; that is, the crime need not have been committed in the territory of the State where the prosecution takes place, and neither the alleged victim nor the alleged perpetrator need be a national of the State concerned.

(VI) Article 9 obliges States parties to the Convention to co-operate with each other in the investigation and prosecution of alleged perpetrators.

(VII) Article 14 obliges States parties to ensure that victims of torture obtain redress, compensation and rehabilitation.
(VIII) Article 15 states that confessions obtained by the use of torture may not be used as evidence in court proceedings, except against the person alleged to have performed the act of torture.

Thus, as reflected in the title of the Convention itself, there is a clear distinction made between acts of torture and other forms of prohibited ill treatment in the Convention. The formal and practical consequences of an act being determined to be torture are quite far-reaching, not least for the victim of a violation. In contrast to the absolute nature of the prohibition of torture, and the rather detailed provision describing the machinery for the establishment of jurisdiction over the crime of torture, Article 16, and those other articles that apply *mutatis mutandis* to cruel, inhuman and degrading treatment or punishment are, nevertheless, different leaving a choice as to their implementation to the States parties.

2.2. The Definition of Torture

Article 1, paragraph 1, of the Convention reads as follows:

> 'For the purposes of this Convention, the term "torture" means any act by which SEVERE PAIN OR SUFFERING, WHETHER PHYSICAL OR MENTAL, is INTENTIONALLY inflicted on a person for such PURPOSES as obtaining from him or a third person information or a confession, punishing him for an act he or a third person has committed or is suspected of having committed, or intimidating or coercing him or a third person, or for any reason based on discrimination of any kind, when such pain or suffering is inflicted by or at the instigation of or with the consent or acquiescence of A PUBLIC OFFICIAL or other person acting in an official capacity. It does not include pain or suffering arising from, inherent in or incidental to lawful sanctions' (Capital lettering added by the authors).

It is of importance to note that the Convention was adopted 10 December 1984 by the General Assembly of the United Nations by consensus vote. The use of torture is by now recognized as a rule of customary international law.

The fact that it was adopted by consensus is an element of evidence of the existence of such a rule.

The content and necessity of the last sentence in the Article 1 definition, '[i]t does not include pain or suffering arising from, inherent in or incidental to lawful sanctions' can be viewed as a limitation and as a general, universal restriction to the scope of the Convention. Why were these words added to the definition? The answer lies in the fact that if this limitation had not been included, the Convention might not have been adopted by the General Assembly at all, and would certainly not have been adopted by consensus. One of the most difficult issues to resolve during the drafting process was how to distinguish the unlawful act of torture, a crime which according to the Convention is committed exclusively 'by, or at the instigation of or with the consent or acquiescence of a public official' from forms of punishment arising from lawful punishments, also administered by public officials, which might by their very nature entail some degree of pain or suffering. The ensuing compromise has created problems in the prevention and prosecution of cases of torture, particularly in countries where punishments widely considered by the international community to be 'torturous' are condoned by the penal code of the State in question. But leaving aside this issue, it is of paramount importance that the term torture has been legally defined in the Convention, as this provides the basis for unlocking the possibilities for action against torturers or on behalf of victims of torture that are contained within the operative provisions of the Convention.

In order for an act to amount to torture, as per the definition in Article 1, four conditions must be fulfilled which are capitalised in the version of the definition cited above.

(1) The act must cause 'severe pain or suffering, whether physical or mental.'

For a medical doctors it is rather easy (and it should be also for lay-men) to distinguish between 'severe' and 'not severe'. From a medical point of view it is really a question of common sense.

(2) The act must have been performed 'intentionally'.

The word intentionally is crucial. Many may have realized the fact that the sequelae of torture can with good reasons be characterized as 'a disease'. The fact that torture is performed 'intentionally' (and even with a purpose) makes it quite unique amongst diseases, in that it is the only disease made by man that exists. Furthermore, the requirement of intention, the '*mens rea*' of the crime of torture, is the principal distinguishing feature between torture and those other forms of cruel, inhuman or degrading treatment or punishment. Thus torture can not be considered as 'top of the list' of ill-treatment, (despite the fact that torture is the worst violation of human rights), starting from degrading over inhuman etc. to torture. No; torture is something completely different.

(3) The act shall be performed for 'a purpose'.

Article 1 lists a number of purposes, but the result is a very old problem. Either a list shall be exhaustive (and that can be very difficult), or it should be made clear that the list is only indicative, by the use of a word such as 'including', so as not to exclude purposes that may not have been considered by the drafters. One example of this problem can be found in the communication to CAT 202/2002.[227]

(4) The act shall be performed by 'a public official . . .'.

This requirement certainly has a restricting effect on the applicability and the scope of the Convention. Acts of torture committed by non-State actors fall outside the Convention, and States cannot be held responsible for them, unless it can be shown that a causal link exists, of the kind described in the words of Article 1 itself. In case of a civil war, it is only the governmental troops that can torture not the other side. In spite of the fact that the actual acts and methods are very often identical.

The understanding of the concepts of the Convention and especially their differences may be important for the purposes of ensuring that States parties entering into reservations do not do that contrary the absolute nature of, at least, some obligations.

---

[227] The communication deals with the problems related to imprisonment in ISOLATION of remand prisoners. The authors state that some of these cases could be labelled as torture, as defined in Article 1 of the Convention. In the observations from the State party it is claimed that 'isolation' do not fit in any of the listed 'purposes' and consequently the case cannot be classified as torture. Observations from the State party (Denmark) to CAT 202/2002.

3. Reservations

Articles 20 and 28, Article 30, Articles 21 and 22 of the Convention provide for different possibilities for the States parties to enter into reservations.

3.1. Article 20: 'The Committee against the State'

Article 20, paragraph 1, reads as follows:

> 'If the Committee receives reliable information which appears to it to contain well-founded indications that torture is being systematically practised in the territory of a State Party, the Committee shall invite that State Party to co-operate in the examination of the information and to this end to submit observations with regard to the information concerned.'

The key elements that need to be established before an investigation is triggered are the following: 'reliable information', 'well founded indications', and 'torture is being systematically practised.'

If these conditions are fulfilled, the CAT Committee 'shall invite the State Party to co-operate in the examination of the information'. Such an examination may lead to an in-country visit by the Committee, but, once again, this can only take place with the co-operation of the State concerned. All in all a potentially forceful article – which no doubt explains the existence of Article 28 in the Convention, which, quite unusually for a human rights convention, specifically raises the possibility that States may make a reservation in respect of Article 20 'at the time of ratification'. While reservations to Article 20 (or to any other provision of the Convention) may be subsequently withdrawn, the phrase 'at the time of ratification' appears to exclude the possibility of States parties making a reservation to Article 20 post-ratification; i.e., it is possible to change a 'no' to a 'yes', but it is impossible to change a 'yes' to a 'no'

By 16 May 2003, Article 20 was in force with respect to all States except the following: Afghanistan, China, Equatorial Guinea, Israel, Kuwait, Morocco, Saudi Arabia and Ukraine.[228]

The number of actions that have been taken under Article 20 are also very limited, just five reports have been published:

---

[228] *Report of the Committee against Torture,* A/58/44, Annex II. On Ukraine refer to section 'C. Reservations due to Procedures'.

- Turkey (1993)[229]
- Egypt (1995)[230]
- Peru (2001)[231]
- Sri Lanka (2002)[232]
- Mexico (2003)[233]

The making of a reservation to Article 20 prevents the CAT Committee from exercising one of its potentially most effective powers in relation to that State party. Nevertheless, it should be noted that less than 10 per cent of States parties (8 out of 134) have chosen to do so.

3.2. Article 30: 'Disputes between States'

Article 30, paragraphs 1–3, read as follows:

> '1. Any dispute between two or more State Parties concerning the interpretation or application of this Convention which cannot be settled through negotiation shall, at the request of one of them, be submitted to arbitration. If within 6 months from the date of the request for arbitration the Parties are unable to agree on the organisation of the arbitration, any one of those Parties may refer the dispute to the International Court of Justice by request in conformity with the Statute of the Court.
>
> 2. Each State may, at the time of signature or ratification of this Convention or accession thereto, declare that it does not consider itself bound by paragraph 1 of this article. The other States Parties shall not be bound by paragraph 1 of this article with respect to any State Party having made such a reservation.
>
> 3. Any State Party, having made a reservation in accordance with paragraph 2 of this article may at any time withdraw

229 'Turkey 1993'. *Report of the Committee against Torture*, A 48/44, add. 1.

230 'Egypt 1995'. *Report of the Committee against Torture*, A 51/44, para. 180–222.

231 'Peru 2001'. *Report of the Committee against Torture*, A 56/44, para. 144–193.

232 'Sri Lanka 2002'. *Report of the Committee against Torture*, A 57/44, para. 123–195.

233 Mexico Special Report (CAT/C1 75) 26 May 2003.

> this reservation by notification to the Secretary-General of the United Nations.'

As is the case with Article 20, Article 30, paragraph 2, explicitly flags the possibility of a State making a reservation to Article 30, paragraph 1, while Article 30, paragraph 3, gives the possibility of a State to withdraw its reservation. Once again, whereas an initial 'no' to the operation of Article 30 can later be changed to a 'yes', the text appears to rule out the possibility of changing a 'yes' to a 'no'.

Rather few State parties have made reservations to the operation of Article 30, paragraph 1, and of those that have, four have subsequently withdrawn their reservation. 13 States parties to the Convention have a current reservation to Article 30. These are:

China, Cuba, France, Ghana, Israel, Kuwait, Monaco, Panama, Poland, Saudi Arabia, South Africa, Turkey, and the United States.

The provisions in Article 30 have never been invoked.

3.3. Reservations not Specific to Individual Articles

In the past the German Democratic Republic (DDR) had made some reservations, which received numerous objections by other State parties. However since the DDR no longer exists, these will not be commented upon.

Upon ratification Qatar made the reservation in relation to Article 2 whereby it did not accept 'any interpretation of the provisions of the Convention, that is incompatible with the precepts of Islamic law and the Islamic religion'. Four State parties reacted, finding 'the reservation to be of general nature', ' incompatible with the object and purpose of the Convention' and 'raising doubts as to the commitment of Qatar to fulfil her obligations under the Convention'.

Upon the ratification of the CAT, the US submitted a long list of reservations, understandings and declarations. Some of these understandings (interpretations) of the wording in the Convention could be considered to be reservations. Several States parties expressed their opinion on some of these statements. The Netherlands commented that 'reservation made regarding Article 16 of (the Convention) to be incompatible with the object and purpose of the Convention'. Finland commented that 'general reference to national law without specifying its contents . . . may cast doubts about the commitment . . . to fulfil its obligations under the Convention'. Sweden objected to reservations entered by the United States of America with regard to Articles 7 and 16 and stated that:

> 'It is the view of the Government of Sweden that the understandings expressed by the United States of America do not relieve the United States of America as a party to the Convention from the responsibility to fulfil the obligations undertaken therein.'[234]

3.4. 'Individual' Reservations and Clarifications

(1) Examples of reservations from States parties – Article by Article.[235]

Article 1

Botswana declared that the definition of torture should be the same as the definition found in the Botswanian Constitution, section 7. Denmark in a note of 4 October 2001 'objects' to this reservation.

Luxembourg and the Netherlands both remarked regarding Article 1 that 'lawful sanctions' must be understood as those sanctions that ought to be lawful both in national and in international law. No State party has made comments to this.

Article 2, paragraph 3

Chile at the time of ratification (1988) of the CAT made reservations, among others to Article 2, paragraph 3, concerning so-called 'due obedience'.

This resulted in many protests – 20 State parties which is a very high number, in particular considering the limited number of State parties that had at that time ratified the Convention. These States declared that this reservation was 'incompatible with the objects and purposes of the convention'.

In a note, received by the Secretary-General of the UN on 7 September 1990, Chile withdrew this reservation and also the reservations regarding Article 3 and it furthermore accepted the provisions of Article 20.

---

[234] Available at <www.unhchr.ch/html/menu2/6/cat/treaties/convention-reserv.htm> (accessed on 19 March 2004).
[235] *See* United Nations Treaty Collection. Declarations and Reservations, available at <www.unhchr.ch/html/menu3/b/treaty12_asp.htm>.

Article 14

Bangladesh made the following declaration: 'The Government of the People's Republic of Bangladesh will apply Article 14, paragraph 1, in consonance with the existing laws and legislation in the country'.

Germany commented that this was 'a reservation of a general nature' and Germany as well as the Netherlands considered the reservation to be a limitation of the provisions in the Convention.

New Zealand reserved the rights to award compensation to torture victims . . .'only at the discretion of the Attorney-General of New Zealand'. No State parties commented on this reservation.

4. DECLARATIONS

4.1 Articles 21 and 22

The 'no' to Articles 20 and 30 require a negative attitude from the State party at the time of ratification. Furthermore: a 'no' can be changed to a 'yes', but not the other way around. Actually an almost opposite rule exists regarding Articles 21 and 22.

In paragraph 1 of both articles, it is stated that 'A State Party to this Convention may *at any time* declare under this article, that it recognizes the competence of the Committee . . .' (emphasis added). In the last paragraph (1d of Article 21 and paragraph 8 of Article 22) it is stated '[a] declaration may be withdrawn *at any time* by notification to the Secretary-General . . .' (emphasis added). Thus a 'no' can be changed to a 'yes', and a 'yes' can be changed to a 'no'.

One would have expected that this freedom in the declarations regarding Articles 21 and 22 would have lead to many declarations in favour. This has not been the case.

There are further limitations on the scope of application of Articles 21 and 22. Two conditions must to be fulfilled in order to invoke the provisions of Articles 21 and 22:

(i) the State Party shall declare in favour of the articles
(ii) 'Such declarations shall be deposited by the State Parties with the Secretary-General of the United Nations . . .'.

For example, Ukraine by ratification on 11 May 1998, declared in favour of Articles 21 and 22. However the declarations have not been deposited with the Secretary-General of the United Nations.

In the conclusions and recommendations of the 4th report on Ukraine to the Committee against Torture, in November 2001, the Committee took note of this, and recommended that Ukraine deposit the declarations. In September 2003, the declarations were finally duly deposited.

4.2. Article 21 – STATE against STATE

The content of Article 21 is that the committee is given the competence to 'receive and consider communications to the effect that a State Party claims that another State party is not fulfilling its obligations under this Convention'.

52 State parties have ratified both Article 21 and 22; four State parties only Article 21: Japan, Uganda, UK and US.

In 15 years of the existence of the Convention Article 21 has never been invoked – and probably never will be.

4.3. Article 22 - the INDIVIDUAL against the STATE

The content of Article 22 is 'the competence of the Committee to receive and consider communications from, or on behalf of individuals subject to its jurisdiction who claim to be the victims of a violation by a State Party of the provisions of the Convention.'

In addition to the 52 State parties, who have also ratified Article 21, three State parties have only declared in favour of Article 22: Azerbaijan, Mauritius and Serbia and Montenegro. Thus, 55 State parties have accepted the competence of the Committee to deal with individual complaints.

The geographical distribution is rather interesting:

	Western and Eastern European States[236]	Africa	Latin America + Caribbean	Asia
No. of State Parties	37	10	8	0

The number of communications to the Committee under Article 22 is more than 220. Most of them deal with alleged breaches of Article 3 of the Convention.

5. CONCLUSIONS

The Title of the Convention and the definition of torture in Article 1 contain some limitations with consequences for the work against torture and other cruel, inhuman or degrading treatment or punishment, in particular for the latter. The Convention contains a very detailed definition of 'torture', and this has proved to be of great importance for the work of the Committee against Torture. As the International Criminal Tribunal for the Former Yugoslavia has held in a series of cases, there is now general acceptance world-wide of the main elements contained in the Article 1 definition.[237] By contrast, the non-inclusion of a definition of the phrase 'other cruel, inhuman or degrading treatment or punishment' has created some challenges, and it has been necessary to look to the work of the European Committee for the Prevention of Torture and Inhumane or Degrading Treatment or Punishment (CPT), regional and national courts, the writings of the UN Special Rapporteur on Torture and other experts in this field to understand the scope of the phrase and the distinctions between the forms of ill treatment described.[238] However, the lack of definition in the Convention has not created problems in the work of the Committee.

Furthermore the States parties, when ratifying, are offered the possibility to make reservations (Articles 20 and 30). The inclusion of this flexibility

[236] Cyprus is counted as belonging to the group of Western Countries; it will be member of the EU from 2004.
[237] *Prosecutor* v. *Anto Furundzija*, Case No. IT-95-17/1, 10 December 1998, para. 160–61, <www.un.org/icty/cases/jugemindex-e.htm>.
[238] From the Report of the Special Rapporteur on Torture to the 53rd session of the Commission on Human Rights, Report E/CN.4/1997/7, <www.unhchr.ch>.

within the provisions has no doubt, in our opinion, made it more attractive for some States to ratify the Convention who might otherwise have been reluctant to do so. The right to make declarations in favour of State party and individual communications to the Committee against Torture (Articles 21 and 22 respectively) is a matter for State parties to decide. In this regard, we note that no country from the Asian region has yet made a declaration in favour of Article 22.

It is the opinion of the authors that the Convention is very clear and balanced. It provides State parties with a number of built in possibilities, beyond the simple act of ratification: to make two specific reservations (explicitly flagged in the text of the Convention) or to 'opt in' to two procedures empowering the Committee against Torture to receive and consider communications. This could explain the relatively small number of 'individual reservations' that have been made by States parties, of which only a few have been considered by other participating States parties to be 'incompatible with the object and purpose of the Convention' or ' to be of a general nature'.

Two State parties, Luxembourg and the Netherlands, have made comments which seem to enlarge the provisions of the Convention. The comments are with respect to the last sentence in Article 1, paragraph 1 regarding 'pain or suffering arising only from, inherent in or incidental to lawful sanctions'. Both countries have made the comment that 'lawful sanctions' must be understood as lawful both in national and international law, and no country has opposed or even referred to these comments. Furthermore Nigel Rodley, in his former capacity as Special Rapporteur on Torture, has explained the limits of the 'lawful sanctions' exception as being 'those criminal sanctions that are widely recognized as being legitimate by the international community'. In our opinion a more in-depth analysis and discussion of this issue is merited.

COLLECTIVE RESPONSIBILITY AND RESERVATIONS IN A COMMON EUROPEAN HUMAN RIGHTS AREA

*Jörg Polakiewicz**

TABLE OF CONTENTS

1. INTRODUCTION

The question of reservations to human rights treaties has been the subject of much debate in international law.[239] Concern has been expressed that

* Deputy Head of the Council of Europe's Legal Advice Department and lecturer at the Europainstitut of the University of Saarbrücken. The article reflects the author's personal views only. I am very grateful for comments by Prof. P.-H. Imbert, Director General of Human Rights at the Council of Europe.

[239] B. Simma, 'Reservations to Human Rights Treaties – Some Recent Developments', in G. Hafner et al. (eds), *Liber Amicorum Professor Seidl-Hohenveldern – in honour of his 80th birthday* (1998), pp. 659–682; J. P. Gardner (ed.), *Human Rights as General Norms and a State's Right to Opt Out: Reservations and Objections to Human Rights Conventions* (1997); C. Redgwell, 'Reservations to

widespread participation is often only achieved at the expense of the integrity of the treaties in question, which is increasingly impaired by sweeping reservations. A growing number of, in particular, European States object regularly to inadmissible reservations, linking such non-acceptance with express declarations as to the legal consequences of their objections.[240] The consequences specified in the declarations vary, ranging from the view that the reserving State will not be regarded as a party to the treaty in question to a kind of 'severance' or 'severability' approach. According to this approach, the inadmissible reservation is considered null and void, leaving both the reserving State's consent to be bound and the original treaty rule unaffected.

Within the Council of Europe, the Ad Hoc Committee of Legal Advisers on Public International Law (CAHDI), which brings together the Legal Advisers to the Foreign Ministries of all member States, has examined the question of reservations to multilateral treaties.[241] The CAHDI prepared a study on 'Practical Issues regarding Reservations to International Treaties'[242] and Recommendation No. (99) 13 on responses to inadmissible reservations to international treaties[243], which the Committee of Ministers adopted in 1999. The recommendation contains model response clauses to reservations that give rise to doubts as to their admissibility.

Treaties and Human Rights Committee General Comment No. 24 (52)', 46 *International and Comparative Law Quarterly* (ICLQ) (1997) p. 390; E. Lijnzaad, *Reservations to UN-Human Rights Treaties. Ratify and Ruin?* (1995); T. Giegerich, 'Vorbehalte zu Menschenrechtsabkommen: Zulässigkeit, Gültigkeit und Prüfungskompetenz von Vertragsgremien', 55 *Heidelberg Journal of International Law* (1995) p. 713; W. A. Schabas, 'Reservations to Human Rights Treaties: Time for Innovation and Reform', 32 *Canadian Yearbook of International Law* 39 (1994); in particular on Council of Europe practice S. Åkermark, 'Reservation Clauses in Treaties concluded within the Council of Europe', 48 *ICLQ* (1999) p. 479.

240 Simma, *ibid.*, pp. 664–669.

241 Franz Cede, 'European Responses to Questionable Reservations' in Konrad Ginther *et al.* (eds.), *Development and Developing International and European Law: Essays in Honour of Konrad Ginther on the Occasion of his 65th Birthday* (Peter Lang Publishing, Frankfurt, 1999) pp. 21–34; S. Åkermark, 'Reservations: Breaking New Ground in the Council of Europe', 24 *European Law Review* (Eur. L. Rev.) (1999) p. 499; *see also* the statement made before the CAHDI in 1998 by P.-H. Imbert, document DI-S-RIT (98) 9/CAHDI (98) 23.

242 Appendix 4 to the decision relating to CAHDI's work adopted by the Committee of Ministers on 3 May 2000 at the 708th meeting of Ministers' Deputies.

243 Adopted by the Committee of Ministers on 18 May 1999 at the 670th meeting of Ministers' Deputies.

In 1998, the CAHDI started a regular screening process of reservations to international treaties acting as a 'European observatory of reservations to multilateral treaties of significant importance to the international community and of reactions by Council of Europe Member States.' Its purpose is to exchange views on outstanding reservations and declarations and possibly to arrive at common responses to statements that are considered inadmissible. The screening process is not restricted to treaties of universal scope, but includes also conventions concluded in the regional context of the Council of Europe. Although it was clear from the outset that the concern about inadmissible reservations to human rights instruments constituted the primary motivation for the establishment of the said observation procedure, the first exchanges of views on current lists of reservations quickly revealed that reservations created difficulties in other areas of international law as well. The screening process now also includes treaties concerning the protection of the environment or counter-terrorism treaties. In numerous instances, common evaluations have emerged, leading to a certain measure of harmonization of State practice in the European regional context. CAHDI's activities have also contributed to the work of the International Law Commission in this field. They are evidence for the growing concern about the integrity of international commitments not only in the field of human rights.

2. RESERVATIONS TO THE EUROPEAN CONVENTION ON HUMAN RIGHTS IN PRACTICE

2.1. State Practice

The *European Convention on Human Rights* (ECHR) and its *Protocols* have given rise to an important number of reservations and interpretative declarations.[244] The provisions which have attracted most reservations are

[244] Apart from the relevant passages of general comments to the Convention, *see* in particular 'The European Convention on Human Rights and Reservations' (with contributions by F. Horn and F. Schurmann), Council of Europe doc. H (96) 18 (December 1996); J. Polakiewicz, *Treaty-making in the Council of Europe* (Council of Europe Publishing, Strasbourg, 1999), pp. 104–117; G. Cohen-Jonathan, 'Les réserves dans les traités institutionnels relatifs aux droits de l'homme. Nouveaux aspects européens et internationaux', *Revue générale de droit international public* (RGDIP) (1996) p. 915; I. Cameron and F. Horn, 'Reservations to the European Convention on Human Rights: The Belilos Case', 33 *German Yearbook of International Law* (1990) p. 69; R. St. J. MacDonald, 'Reservations under the

the right to liberty and security (Article 5 of the ECHR), the right to a fair trial (Article 6 of the ECHR), the protection of property (Article 1 of *Protocol No. 1* to the ECHR) and the right to education (Article 2 of *Protocol No. 1* to the ECHR). The European Court of Human Rights has acknowledged that the nature and scope of such reservations may influence the interpretation of the Convention's provisions.[245]

Many reservations made with respect to Article 5 of the ECHR have the purpose of safeguarding the imposition of disciplinary penalties resulting in a deprivation of liberty against members of the national armed forces (Armenia, Azerbaijan, Czech Republic, France, Lithuania, Portugal, Romania, Russian Federation, Slovakia, Spain, Ukraine). Moldova stated that Article 5 must not result in the removal of the possibility of enforcing criminal sentences in the form of non-custodial forced labour and administrative sentences of the same nature. Austria reserved the right to apply its laws on the deprivation of liberty ordered by administrative organs subject to only limited review by the Administrative Court or the Constitutional Court.

A number of States were not prepared to respect the full extent of the fair trial guarantees contained in Article 6 of the ECHR. Austria declared that it will apply Article 6 without prejudice to Article 90 of its *Federal Constitution Law*. Croatia stated that it will not be in a position to 'guarantee the right to a public hearing before the Administrative Court in cases in which it decides on the legality of individual acts of administrative authorities' on account of Article 34 § 1 of the *Law on Administrative Disputes*. Estonia declared that it cannot ensure the right to a public hearing as far as certain proceedings at the appellate court level (*Ringkonnakohtus*) are concerned, which may be decided through written procedure. Ireland declared that it does not interpret Article 6 § 3 (c) as 'requiring the provision of free legal assistance to any wider extent than is now provided in Ireland.' Malta interpreted the presumption of innocence (Article 6 § 2) in the sense that it 'does not preclude any particular law from imposing upon any person charged under such law the burden of proving particular facts.' Azerbaijan, the Czech Republic, France and Slovakia reserved the right not to apply

---

European Convention on Human Rights', 21 RBDI (1988) p. 429; J. A. Frowein, 'Reservations to the European Convention on Human Rights', in F. Matscher and H. Petzold (eds.), *Protecting Human Rights. The European Dimension* (Heymanns, Köln, 1988) p. 193.

[245] In its Memorial in the case of *Kjeldsen and Others* v. *Denmark*, the Commission referred to reservations to the provisions there in question as 'useful guides to interpretation', Publications of the Eur. Court H.R., Series B no. 21, 44–45 (§ 154).

Article 6 in disciplinary proceedings against members of their armed forces. Serbia and Montenegro entered reservations in respect of Articles 5 and 6 of the ECHR regarding certain aspects of the penal procedure, the procedure concerning minor offences before magistrates' courts and the publicity of hearings before administrative courts.

Concerning *Protocol No. 1* to the ECHR, many States made reservations regarding the protection of property (Article 1). With respect to Article 2 (the right to education), a number of States made statements to the effect that this provision must not result in an obligation to finance religious or philosophical education.

In the case of *Protocol No. 4* to the ECHR reservations were made with respect to Article 3 prohibiting the expulsion of nationals and Article 4 prohibiting the collective expulsion of aliens. Cyprus for example declared that it refuses to apply the provisions of Article 4 to aliens unlawfully present.

Given its restricted scope, it is surprising that *Protocol No. 7* to the ECHR had been the subject of such a high number of reservations. Several States formally restricted the application of the right of appeal in criminal matters (Article 2) and the right not to be tried or punished twice (Article 4) to what their national laws on these matters already provide.[246] Furthermore, certain countries entered reservations in respect of Article 5 on equality between spouses, concerning the transmission of the patronymic name.[247] Reservations of this type run counter to the very essence of what the Convention is about. Instead of reforming their national laws to comply with the Convention's minimum standards, the States in question apply the rights and freedoms only to the extent that they are already safeguarded by their national legislation. Such a practice is all the more surprising given the fact that these rights are also guaranteed by the *International Covenant on Political and Civil Rights*.

Many of the States that have recently joined the Council of Europe have limited the temporal validity of their reservations. When Lithuania ratified the Convention in 1995, it made a reservation with regard to Article 5 § 3 of the ECHR in order to safeguard the application of Article 104 of the *Code of Criminal Procedure* of the Republic of Lithuania (amended version No. I-551, 19 July 1994) which provides that a decision to detain in custody any persons suspected of having committed a crime may also, by decision of a

[246] Austria, Denmark, France, Germany and Italy.
[247] France, Luxembourg and Switzerland.

prosecutor, be so detained. It was expressly stated that '[t]his reservation shall be effective for one year after the Convention comes into force in respect of the Republic of Lithuania'.[248] Albania made reservations to the right to free elections (Article 3 of *Protocol No. 1* to the ECHR) for a period of five years from the date of deposit of the instrument of ratification on 2 October 1996.[249] Ukraine ratified the Convention in 1997 and formulated reservations to Article 5 § 1 of the ECHR concerning the detention of a person and the arrest warrant issued by the public prosecutor as well as to Article 8 of the ECHR concerning warrants for arrest and search warrants issued by the public prosecutor. Each time it was expressly stated that '[s]uch reservations will be in force until the appropriate amendments to the *Criminal Procedure Code of Ukraine* have been made or until the adoption of the new *Criminal Procedure Code of Ukraine*, but not later than 28 July 2001'.[250] Moldova ratified the Convention in 1997 and made a reservation to Article 4 of the ECHR 'with a view to retaining the possibility of enforcing criminal sentences in the form of non-custodial forced labour, as provided for in Article 27 of the *Criminal Code*, and also administrative sentences in the form of forced labour, as provided for in Article 30 of the *Code of Administrative Offences*'. Moldova also formulated a reservation to Article 5 § 3 of the ECHR, 'with a view to extending the validity of an arrest warrant issued by the public prosecutor as set out in Article 25 of the *Constitution of the Republic of Moldova*, Article 78 of the *Code of Criminal Procedure* and Article 25 of *Law No. 902-XII* on the Prokuratura of the Republic of Moldova of 29 January 1992'. The validity of the reservations was limited to one year and six months respectively. The instrument of ratification deposited by Russia on 5 May 1998 contained reservations with regard to Paragraphs 3 and 4 of Article 5 of the ECHR which were designed to safeguard the application of procedures of arrest and detention under the *Disciplinary Code of the Armed Forces* and the 1960 *RFSR Code of Criminal Procedure* (Articles 89, 90, 92, 96, 96^1, 96^2, 97, 101 and 122). The mentioned provisions of the *Code of Criminal Procedure* regulate the

[248] Reservation contained in the instrument of ratification deposited on 20 June 1995 – Or. Engl. The reservation expired on 21 June 1996 (*cf.* letter from the Permanent Representative of Lithuania, dated 19 July 1996, registered at the Secretariat General on 22 July 1996 – Or. Engl. – notification JJ3634C of 30 July 1996).

[249] Reservation contained in the instrument of ratification, deposited on 2 October 1996 – Or. Engl.

[250] Reservations contained in the instrument of ratification, deposited on 11 September 1997 – Or. Ukr./Engl.

reasons for preventive detention and detention pending trial, the arrested person's right to be informed as well as the delays for and modalities of review by the prosecutor and the courts. Arrests for administrative offences are not covered by the reservation. Without indicating a precise time limit, Russia declared that 'the period of validity of these reservations shall be the period required to introduce amendments to the Russian federal legislation which will completely eliminate the incompatibilities between the said provisions and the provisions of the Convention'.[251]

This practice can be explained by the fact that the countries in question were carrying out wide-ranging reforms of their administrative and judicial system. When ratifying the Convention, the reform process was not yet fully accomplished and some of the old legislation was still on the statute books. It was therefore necessary to safeguard its application until the necessary reforms had been fully implemented. Under these circumstances, the temporal limitation of the reservations' validity was encouraged by the Secretariat since it underlined the willingness of the countries concerned to bring their legislation into line with the requirements of the Convention. Acting as depositary, the Secretary General took the view that the reservations whose validity had been limited precisely in time lapsed automatically at the indicated date even in the absence of any explicit withdrawal.[252] In the case of *Ječius* v. *Lithuania*, the Strasbourg Court confirmed that a State cannot be held responsible for acts or omissions prior to the expiry of the reservation.[253]

Within the context of the *European Convention on Human Rights*, States have rarely objected to reservations. In 1979, the United Kingdom[254], Germany[255] and France[256] reacted to the reservation made by Portugal to the protection of property rights contained in Article 1 of the *Protocol to the ECHR*.[257] By making these reservations, Portugal intended to exclude the

---

[251] Reservations contained in the instrument of ratification deposited on 5 May 1998 – Or. Rus./Eng./Fr.

[252] *E.g.*, the reservations by Lithuania, Moldova and Ukraine, but not the reservation by the Russian Federation.

[253] *Ječius* v. *Lithuania* (application no. 34578/97), judgment of 31 July 2001, §§ 81–86.

[254] Notification JJ698C of 8 March 1979.

[255] Notification JJ771C of 31 July 1979.

[256] Notification JJ831C of 12 December 1979.

[257] A letter from the Permanent Representative of Portugal, dated 8 November 1978 and handed to the Secretary General at the time of deposit of the instrument of

sweeping expropriation and nationalisation measures that had been adopted in the wake of the Carnations revolution from any challenge before the European Commission and Court of Human Rights. Fearing adverse consequences for their investments in Portugal, the reacting States did not formally object to the reservation, but rather made declarations to the effect that it could not affect the general principles of international law which required the payment of prompt, adequate and effective compensation in respect of the expropriation of foreign property. Following constitutional and legislative amendments, Portugal withdrew these reservations in 1987.[258]

In 1987, when Turkey recognised for the first time the competence of the European Commission of Human Rights to receive individual petitions, it made this acceptance subject to a number of 'conditions'.[259] Until 1998, the

---

ratification, on 9 November 1978, contained *inter alia* the following reservation: 'Article 1 of the Protocol will be applied subject to Article 82 of the Constitution of the Portuguese Republic, which provides that expropriations of large landowners, big property owners and entrepreneurs or shareholders may be subject to no compensation under the conditions to be laid down by the law.
Article 82 of the Constitution reads as follows:
1. The law shall determine the methods and forms of intervention, nationalisation and socialisation of the means of production and criteria for fixing compensation.
2. The law may stipulate that expropriations of large landowners, big property owners and entrepreneurs or shareholders shall not be subject to any compensation whatsoever.'

[258] Reservations withdrawn by letter from the Permanent Representative of Portugal, registered at the Secretariat General on 11 May 1987 – Or. Fr.

[259] 'The Government of Turkey, acting pursuant to Article 25 (1) of the Convention for the Protection of Human Rights and Fundamental Freedoms hereby declares to accept the competence of the European Commission of Human Rights to receive petitions according to Article 25 of the Convention subject to the following:
(i) the recognition of the right of petition extends only to allegations concerning acts or omissions of public authorities in Turkey performed within the boundaries of the territory to which the Constitution of the Republic of Turkey is applicable ;
(ii) the circumstances and conditions under which Turkey, by virtue of Article 15 of the Convention, derogates from her obligations under the Convention in special circumstances must be interpreted, for the purpose of the competence attributed to the Commission under this declaration, in the light of Articles 119 to 122 of the Turkish Constitution;
(iii) the competence attributed to the Commission under this declaration shall not comprise matters regarding the legal status of military personnel and in particular, the system of discipline in the armed forces ;

ratification of the Convention in itself did not entail automatic acceptance of the competence of the two supervisory organs established under the original Convention. Parties had to make separate declarations recognising the competence of the Commission to receive individual petitions (former Article 25 of the ECHR) and the jurisdiction of the Court to deal with all matters concerning the interpretation and application of the Convention (former Article 46 of the ECHR). Following the entry into force of *Protocol No. 11* to the ECHR on 1 November 1998, the Court and Commission have been replaced by a single permanent Court in Strasbourg.[260] Acceptance of the new Court's jurisdiction is automatic, at least as far as the 'main' national territory is concerned (Article 34 of the ECHR as amended by *Protocol No. 11*). As far as territories for whose international relations a State is responsible are concerned, States still have an option to accept the new Court's jurisdiction or not (Article 56 § 4 of the ECHR as amended by *Protocol No. 11*).

In a letter to which the declaration was attached, the Director of Legal Affairs, acting on behalf of the Secretary General, emphasised that '[a]t the time this declaration was deposited, I drew the Turkish authorities' attention to the fact that this notification made pursuant to Article 25 § 3 of the Convention in no way prejudges the legal questions which might arise

---

(iv) for the purpose of the competence attributed to the Commission under this declaration, the notion of "a democratic society" in paragraphs 2 of Articles 8, 9, 10 and 11 of the Convention must be understood in conformity with the principles laid down in the Turkish Constitution and in particular its Preamble and its Article 13 ;
(v) for the purpose of the competence attributed to the Commission under the present declaration, Articles 33, 52 and 135 of the Constitution must be understood as being in conformity with Article 10 and 11 of the Convention.
This declaration extends to allegations made in respect of facts, including judgments which are based on such facts which have occurred subsequent to the date of deposit of the present declaration. This declaration is valid for three years from the date of deposit with the Secretary General of the Council of Europe', Annex to notification JJ1939C, dated 29 January 1987.

[260] *Protocol No. 11* to the *Convention for the Protection of Human Rights and Fundamental Freedoms, Restructuring the Control Machinery Established Thereby* (ETS 155, 1994). *See* A. Drzemczewski and J. Meyer-Ladewig, 'Principal characteristics of the new ECHR control mechanism, as established by Protocol No. 11, signed on 11 May 1994', 14 *Human Rights Law Journal* (HRLJ) (1994) p. 81; A. Drzemczewski, 'A major overhaul of the European Human Rights Convention control mechanism: Protocol No. 11', in *Collected Courses of the Academy of European Law* 1995, Vol. IV (1997), pp. 121–244.

concerning the validity of the said declaration'.[261] This disclaimer was clearly intended to alert the other parties to the possibility that the restrictions may be invalid. Turkey protested against these comments and invoked the depositary practice of the United Nations where no comments on the substance of statements are made.[262] Following the notification, Greece objected to the Turkish declaration, and Sweden, Luxembourg, Denmark, Norway and Belgium reserved their position as to its legal validity.[263]

In 1990, Turkey also recognised the jurisdiction of the European Court of Human Rights, specifying that its declaration 'relates to the exercise of jurisdiction within the meaning of Article 1 of the Convention, performed within the boundaries of the national territory of the Republic of Turkey, and provided further that such matters have previously been examined by the Commission within the power conferred upon it by Turkey'.[264] When notifying this declaration, it was again pointed out that the notification was without prejudice to the legal questions that might arise concerning the validity of the declaration. In a letter of 31 May 1990, Greece objected to the restrictions contained in the Turkish declaration.[265]

2.2. Depositary Practice

The exercise of depositary functions by the Secretary General of the Council of Europe with regard to the *European Convention on Human Rights* must take into account the special features of the Convention.[266] Answering a State's request for clarification about a reservation entered by France in respect of Article 15 of the ECHR, the Director of Legal Affairs observed in a letter dated 23 June 1975:

> 'The European Convention on Human Rights having instituted specific procedures and organs for the quasi-judicial and judicial supervision of its application, any

---

[261] Notification JJ147, dated 29 January 1987.

[262] Letter dated 13 March 1987 by the Permanent Representative of Turkey to the Council of Europe, notification JJ1950C of 17 March 1987.

[263] The facts are summarised in *Case of Loizidou* v. *Turkey (Preliminary Objections)*, judgment of 23 March 1995, Series A no. 310, §§ 15–29.

[264] Notification JJ2339C of 24 January 1990.

[265] *Case of Loizidou* v. *Turkey (Preliminary Objections)*, judgment of 23 March 1995, Series A no. 310, §§ 27–29.

[266] Article 59 of the ECHR; *see* Polakiewicz, *supra* note 6, pp. 90 *et seq.*, in particular pp. 104–105.

> questions concerning the scope and admissibility of a reservation relating to one of its provisions may, if appropriate, be raised and settled by the same organs.'[267]

In its capacity as depositary, the Secretary General refrains from any act or declaration that could interfere with the exercise of the functions of the Convention's supervisory organs. However, even with respect to the *European Convention on Human Rights*, the Secretary General must ensure that reservations conform to the applicable clauses, in particular Articles 56 and 57 of the ECHR. In order to do this, the Treaty Office evaluates the legal nature of a statement independently, if necessary after having consulted the State concerned and determines whether it constitutes a proper reservation or only an interpretative declaration. This evaluation is based on the definition contained in the *Vienna Conventions* which restates established customary international law.[268] The phrasing or title given by the State formulating the declaration provides an important indication of the desired objective. This is the case, in particular, when several unilateral declarations are formulated in respect of a single treaty, some of which are designated as reservations and others as interpretative declarations.[269]

If the terms of a reservation are unclear or ambiguous or if the legal nature of a statement is doubtful, the Treaty Office will informally consult the State concerned, usually via the Permanent Representation. A certain number of States, before expressing their consent to be bound, have informally consulted the Treaty Office with respect to the compatibility of envisaged reservations with the ECHR, in particular following the enlargement of the Council of Europe since 1989. Possible reservations to the ECHR and its protocols are sometimes also discussed prior to ratification

[267] Translation by P.-H. Imbert, 'Reservations and Human Rights Conventions', 6 *Human Rights Review* 28 (1981) (p. 60, note 99).

[268] Based on the definitions of the term 'reservation' contained in each of the three *Vienna Conventions* of 1969, 1978 and 1986, the ILC established the following composite text in 1998: '"Reservation" means a unilateral statement, however phrased or named, made by a State or an international organization when signing, ratifying, formally confirming, accepting, approving or acceding to a treaty or by a State when making a notification of succession to a treaty, whereby the State or organization purports to exclude or to modify the legal effect of certain provisions of the treaty in their application to that State or to that international organization.'

[269] Compare A. Pellet, 'Third report on reservations to treaties', UN Doc. A/CN.4/491/Add.4 (1998), § 298.

during so-called 'compatibility exercises' when experts study the law and practices of candidate countries in order to identify possible contradictions between the domestic law and the requirements of the Convention.[270] Though not legally binding for the States concerned, the opinions given by the Secretariat have provided useful guidance and have usually been followed in practice.

2.3. The Approach of the European Commission and Court of Human Rights

Under traditional international law, as reflected in the *Vienna Convention on the Law of Treaties* (Vienna Convention, VCLT), it is up to each State party individually to decide both about the admissibility of a reservation and about the consequences to be attached to reservations which that State considers inadmissible.[271] The formulation of numerous reservations may therefore lead to the fragmentation of a coherent multilateral agreement into bilateral treaties of variable content. The original agreement remains only in force among those States that have become parties without any reservations. As between reserving and accepting or objecting States, different regimes prevail, the exact scope of which is determined in each case by the nature and scope of reservations and objections made by the parties.

The *European Convention on Human Rights* differs from this system in that it has set up judicial organs to control its implementation by the States parties. The Commission and the Court were given the mandate to 'ensure the observance of the engagements undertaken by the High Contracting Parties' (Article 19 of the ECHR). Following a very cautious approach in its early practice, the European Commission of Human Rights examined the admissibility of a statement made upon ratification for the first time in 1982.[272] In the *Temeltasch* case, it decided that a 'declaration' made by Switzerland amounted in fact to a reservation, which was then measured against former Article 64 (now Article 57) of the ECHR and found to be valid.[273]

---

270 *See* A. Drzemczewski, 'Ensuring Compatibility of Domestic Law with the European Convention on Human Rights prior to Ratification: The Hungarian Model', 16 *HRLJ* (1996) p. 241.

271 *See* Articles 19 to 23 of the *Vienna Convention on the Law of Treaties*.

272 Frowein, *supra* note 6, p. 196.

273 *Temeltasch* v. *Switzerland* (application no. 9116/80), Commission's report of 5 May 1982, DR 31, p. 120 (§ 49). *See* the excellent comment by P.-H. Imbert, 'Reservations to the European Convention on Human Rights before the Strasbourg Commission, The Temeltasch Case', 33 *ICLQ* (1984)pp. 558–595.

Six years later the European Court of Human Rights followed the Commission and vindicated the competence to judge the validity of reservations. In its famous *Belilos* judgment of 29 April 1988, the Court made no reference to the *Vienna Convention on the Law of Treaties* or customary international law in general. The Swiss Government had invoked the twelve months tacit acceptance rule of Article 20 § 5 of the VCLT arguing that the contested declaration had been tacitly accepted since neither the Secretary General as depositary nor the other parties to the Convention had raised any objections to it. The Strasbourg Court rejected this argument, stating simply that '[t]he silence of the depositary and the Contracting States does not relieve the Convention institutions of the power to make their own assessment'.[274] In the light of the arguments put forward both by the respondent government and the Commission, the decision of the Court to distance itself from the rules of traditional international law in this field seems to have been deliberate. The Court held that the reservation (formulated by Switzerland as an 'interpretative declaration') was invalid and of no effect. Switzerland was held to be bound by the Convention irrespective of the validity of its declaration.[275]

It was probably no coincidence that this judgment came at a time when virtually all parties had accepted the competence of the Commission and the jurisdiction of the Court under the former Articles 25 and 46 of the ECHR. The Convention rights and freedoms benefit from a collective enforcement guarantee through an independent judicial organ to which the individuals have direct access. In order to be effective, this judicial control must extend to the control of reservations. Otherwise, States could evade their responsibilities under the Convention. Article 57 of the ECHR would loose much of its legal effect if the Court had no jurisdiction to control its application. It is therefore not surprising that reservations to the Convention have come under strict scrutiny in Strasbourg. If a State does not invoke a reservation during the proceedings, the Court will not be inclined to consider it *ex officio*.[276]

Following the entry into force of *Protocol No. 11* to the ECHR on 1 November 1998, the new permanent Court, has confirmed and further

---

[274] *Belilos* judgment of 29 April 1988, Series A no. 132, § 47.

[275] *Belilos* judgment of 29 April 1988, Series A no. 132, § 60. *See* the excellent comment by S. Marks, 'Reservations Unhinged: The Belilos Case before the European Court of Human Rights', 39 *ICLQ* (1990) pp. 300–327.

[276] *See Öktan* v. *France*, judgment of 2 July 2002, § 51 (application no. 33402/96).

developed the 'Strasbourg approach' with regard to reservations. In *Slivenko and Others* v. *Latvia*, it held:

> 'It follows from the text of Article 57 § 1 of the Convention, read in conjunction with Article 1, that ratification of the Convention by a State presupposes that any law then in force in its territory should be in conformity with the Convention. If that should not be the case, the State concerned has the possibility of entering a reservation in respect of the specific provisions of the Convention (or Protocols) with which it cannot fully comply by reason of the continued existence of the law in question. Reservations of a general character, in particular those which do not specify the relevant provisions of the national law or fail to indicate the Convention articles that might be affected by the application of those provisions, are not however permitted. The Court always retains the power to examine whether or not a purported reservation has been validly made in conformity with the requirements of Article 57; if the reservation is found to be valid, the Court will be barred from examining the conformity of the reserved legal provisions with the Convention articles in relation to which the reservation has been made.'[277]

3. THE STRUCTURE AND LIMITS OF ARTICLE 57 OF THE ECHR

Article 57 (former Article 64) of the ECHR[278] regulates the right to make reservations as follows:

> '1 Any State may, when signing this Convention or when depositing its instrument of ratification, make a reservation in respect of any particular provision of the Convention to

[277] *Tatjana Slivenko and Others* v. *Latvia*, judgment of 31 January 2002, § 46, ECHR, (application no. 48321/99) *See also Ječius* v. *Lithuania*, judgment of 31 July 2001, § 81, (application no. 34578/97); *Eisenstecken* v. *Austria*, judgment of 3 October 2000, §§ 24–30, ECHR (application no. 29477/95).

[278] *Protocol No. 11* to the ECHR (ETS 155, 1994) which entered into force on 1 November 1998 did not amend this provision, but only modified the numbering of this article.

> the extent that any law then in force in its territory is not in conformity with the provision. Reservations of a general character shall not be permitted under this article.
>
> 2 Any reservation made under this article shall contain a brief statement of the law concerned.'

The *European Convention on Establishment* (ETS 19, 1955, Article 26) and the *Convention on Human Rights and Biomedicine* (ETS 164, 1997, Article 36) contain identically worded provisions concerning reservations.

Article 57 of the ECHR applies not only with regard to the Convention itself, but also with regard to certain protocols thereto which contain additional rights (*Protocols Nos. 1, 4, 7* and *12* to the ECHR). *Protocols Nos. 6* (ETS 114, 1983) and *13* (ETS 187, 2002) concerning the abolition of the death penalty explicitly prohibit the making of any reservations.

3.1. The Scope of Admissible Reservations

Compliance with Article 57 § 1 of the ECHR requires precision and clarity.[279] Reservations must be made 'in respect of a particular provision of the Convention' and '[r]eservations of a general character shall not be permitted' (Article 57 § 1 of the ECHR). According to the definition given by the Commission in the *Temeltasch* case and recently reaffirmed by the Grand Chamber of the Court in the *Ilaşcu* case, a reservation is of a general character 'if it does not refer to a specific provision of the Convention or if it is worded in such a way that its scope cannot be defined'.[280] In the *Belilos* case, the Court used slightly different language, holding that 'by "reservation of a general character" . . . is meant in particular a reservation couched in terms that are too vague or broad for it to be possible to determine their exact meaning and scope'.[281]

Any reservation must refer to a domestic law that is not in conformity with the Convention's provision to which the reservation is made. The domestic legislation should be identified by referring to particular provisions of a law. Rather than indicating to what extent they intend to derogate from

279 *Belilos* judgment of 29 April 1988, Series A no. 132, § 55.
280 *Temeltasch* v. *Switzerland* (application no. 9116/80), Commission's report of 5 May 1982, DR 31, p. 147 (§ 84); *Ilaşcu and Others* v. *Moldova and the Russian Federation*, admissibility decision of 4 July 2001, ECHR (application no. 48787/99) p. 20.
281 *Belilos* judgment, *ibid.*, § 56.

the Convention's provisions, most of the States that have recently ratified indicated simply which provisions of their national legislation they want to 'insulate' from adverse findings by the European Court of Human Rights. This practice does not appear to be objectionable. In fact, by referring to precise provisions of a domestic law, the scope of the reservations is clearly circumscribed. Sweeping references to the constitution or entire codes are not allowed because they would make it impossible to determine whether the statement amounts to a general reservation, which is not permitted under the Convention.

The law in force at time of the ratification of the Convention may of course be modified. Any subsequent amendments would be covered by the initial reservation, provided that the new legislation is not to a larger extent incompatible with the Convention than the one that was initially protected by the reservation. For the sake of legal certainty, any subsequent amendments of the domestic legislation in question should be notified to the Secretary General of the Council of Europe. In principle, such amendments should permit a partial withdrawal of the initial reservation.[282]

Mere amendments must be distinguished from new legislation which would not be covered by the initial reservation even if it concerns the same

[282] A good example is the following declaration contained in a letter of 28 May 1986 from the Permanent Representative of Spain: 'At the time of deposit of the instrument of ratification of the Convention for the Protection of Human Rights and Fundamental Freedoms, on 29 September 1979, Spain formulated a reservation to Articles 5 and 6 to the extent to which those Articles might be incompatible with the provisions of the Code of Military Justice – Chapter XV of Part II and Chapter XXIV of Part III – concerning the disciplinary regime of the Armed Forces.

I have the honour to inform you, for communication to the Parties to the Convention, that these provisions [i.e. Chapter XV of Part II and Chapter XXIV of Part III of the Spanish Code of Military Justice] have been replaced by Basic Law 12/1985 of 27 November - Chapter II of Part III and Chapters II, III and IV of Part IV – concerning the disciplinary regime of the Armed Forces, which will enter into force on 1 June 1986.

The new legislation amends the former provisions by reducing the duration of the sanctions imposing deprivation of liberty which can be applied without judicial intervention by increasing the guarantees of persons during the preliminary investigation.

Spain confirms nevertheless its reservation to Articles 5 and 6 to the extent to which those articles might be incompatible with the provisions of Basic Law 12/1985 of 27 November – Chapter II of Part III and Chapters II, III and IV of Part IV – concerning the disciplinary regime of the Armed Forces, which will enter into force on 1 June 1986.'

subject matter. In the case of *Fischer* v. *Austria* the Strasbourg Court had to examine whether the refusal of the Administrative Court to hold a public hearing was in conformity with Article 6 of the ECHR.[283] The legislation in question was an amendment to the *Administrative Court Act* that had been adopted in 1982. The Austrian Government argued that this legislation was covered by Austria's reservation to Article 6 of the ECHR, which had been formulated in 1958,[284] because the 1982 amendment was – from a teleological point of view – identical to the corresponding provisions then in force. The Court rejected this argument arguing that the 1982 amendment had in fact broadened the Administrative Court's power to refuse to hold a public hearing. In 1958, the grounds for such a refusal related to cases in which formal or procedural matters were an issue as well as those where a ruling favourable to the appellant to quash an administrative decision were to be made. The ground added in 1982 made it possible for the first time to refuse an oral hearing on grounds pertaining to the merits of the cases, in instances where the appeal failed to be dismissed.[285]

The Strasbourg Court has not yet had any opportunity to decide whether a reservation, though being clearly circumscribed as to its scope, could also be inadmissible due to the fundamental character of the Convention provision from which derogation is sought. Reservations to human rights norms, which form part of jus cogens, would certainly be invalid.[286] According to Article 53 of the 1969 *Vienna Convention on the Law on Treaties*, a *jus cogens* norm is 'accepted and recognized by the international community of States as a whole as a norm from which no derogation is

---

[283] *Fischer* v. *Austria*, Strasbourg Court, judgment of 26 April 1994, Series A no. 312.

[284] 'The provisions of Article 6 of the Convention shall be so applied that there shall be no prejudice to the principles governing public court hearings laid down in Article 90 of the 1929 version of the Federal Constitution Law', reservation contained in the instrument of ratification, deposited on 3 September 1958.

[285] *Fischer* v. *Austria*, *ibid.*, § 41. The Court adopted a similar reasoning in the cases of *Stallinger and Kuso* v. *Austria*, judgment of 23 April 1997, *Reports of Judgments and Decisions* 1997 II, 679 (§ 48) and *Pauger* v. *Austria*, judgment of 28 May 1997, *Reports of Judgments and Decisions* 1997-III, 895 (§ 53).

[286] *See* Concurring Opinion of Judge De Meyer to the *Belilos* judgment of 29 April 1988, Series A no. 132; Schabas, *supra* note 1, pp. 937–938.

permitted'. The Human Rights Committee provided as examples the prohibition of torture and of arbitrary deprivation of liberty.[287]

In addition, certain reservations, though not affecting peremptory norms of international law, might not pass the 'object and purpose' test of Article 19 of the *Vienna Convention*, even if they are formulated in conformity with the formal requirements of Article 57 of the ECHR. Nothing prevents the Court from applying this test, which has its roots in international law as much as in the Convention.[288] In this respect, it is probably not appropriate to establish an automatic correlation between non-derogable rights and incompatibility, an approach that was also rejected by the Human Rights Committee with regard to the ICCPR.[289] The Committee concluded that '[w]hile there is not automatic correlation between reservations to non-derogable provisions, and reservations which offend against the object and purpose of the Covenant, a State has a heavy onus to justify such reservations'.[290]

Regarding the *European Convention on Human Rights,* the 'object and purpose' test must be applied taking into account the exact scope of the reservation and its impact on the application of the Convention as a whole. In this respect not only the non-derogable rights under Article 15 § 2, but also certain other rights, such as the non-retroactivity of penal law (Article 7) or the right to free elections (Article 3 of *Protocol No. 1* to the ECHR) are of paramount importance. 'Democracy is without doubt a fundamental feature of the European public order'[291], which is apparent both from the preamble of the Convention and the systematic reference to a 'democratic society' in the clauses allowing for restrictions of the rights guaranteed in Articles 8, 9, 10 and 11. In each case, it will be decisive whether only some limited

[287] 'General Comment on issues relating to reservations made upon ratification or accession to the Covenant or the Optional Protocols thereto, or in relation to declarations under article 41 of the Covenant', UN Doc. CCPR/C/21/Rev.1/Add. 6, adopted by the Committee at its 1382nd meeting (52nd session) on 2 November 1994, reproduced in *HRLJ* 15 (1995), 464 (§ 10).

[288] MacDonald, *supra* note 6, p. 438.

[289] Imbert, *supra* note 29, 6 *Human Rights Review* (1981) pp. 31–32; Schabas, *supra* note 1, pp. 49–53.

[290] *General Comment No. 24 (52)*, *supra* note 49, § 10.

[291] Case of the *United Communist Party of Turkey and Others* v. *Turkey*, judgment of 30 January 1998, Reports of Judgments and Decisions 1998-I, 21 (§ 45). *See* also Case of the *Socialist Party and Others* v. *Turkey*, judgment of 25 May 1998, Reports of Judgments and Decisions 1998-III, 1252 (§ 29).

aspects of a certain right or the right as such are covered by the reservation.[292]

3.2. Brief Statement of the Law

According to the Strasbourg Court, the requirement of a brief statement of the law both constitutes an evidential factor and contributes to legal certainty.[293] The purpose of Article 57 § 2 is to make it visible, both for the other parties and the Court, that a reservation is not of a 'general character', if it relates to a 'law then in force' and does not go beyond the provisions expressly excluded by the reserving State. Although it cannot change the scope of a reservation, it may clarify it.[294] The other parties, the Court and any other interested party are put in a position to acquaint themselves with the relevant domestic law.

Departing from a less demanding approach of the Commission[295], the Court stressed in the *Belilos* case that the 'brief statement' was not 'a purely formal requirement but a condition of substance' whose omission 'cannot be justified even by important practical difficulties'.[296] In subsequent cases, the Court invalidated a number of reservations simply because they had not been accompanied by a 'brief statement' of the law (or the laws) concerned.[297]

However, in the *Chorherr* case, the Court adopted a more lenient approach with regard to an Austrian reservation to Article 5 of the ECHR.[298]

---

[292] *See mutatis mutandis* the Advisory Opinion of the Inter-American Court of Human Rights no. OC 3/83 of 8 September 1983, 23 *International Legal Materials* (ILM) (1984) 320 (§ 61).

[293] *Belilos* judgment of 29 April 1988, Series A no. 132, § 59.

[294] Imbert, *supra* note 35, 33 *ICLQ* (1984) pp. 576–578.

[295] In *Temeltasch* v. *Switzerland* (application no. 9116/80), Commission's report of 5 May 1982, DR 31, p. 120, the Commission had considered that the failure to attach a statement of the relevant legislation was 'not decisive', because the rule in Article 6 § 3 (e) of the ECHR was a clear rule with a well determined scope (§ 91).

[296] *Belilos* judgment of 29 April 1988, Series A no. 132, § 59.

[297] *Weber* judgment of 22 May 1990, Series A no. 177, § 38; *Gradinger* v. *Austria*, judgment of 23 October 1995, Series A no. 328-C, § 51.

[298] The Austrian reservation contained in the instrument of ratification which was deposited on 3 September 1958, reads as follows: 'The provisions of Article 5 of the Convention shall be so applied that there shall be no interference with the measures for the deprivation of liberty prescribed in the laws on administrative procedure, BGBl no. 172/1950, subject to review by the Administrative Court or the Constitutional Court as provided for in the Austrian Federal Constitution.'

The Court considered it sufficient that reference had been made to the relevant number of the Austrian *Official Gazette*. The 'reference to the Federal Gazette – preceded moreover by an indication of the subject-matter of the relevant provisions – makes it possible for everyone to identify the precise laws concerned and to obtain any information regarding them'.[299] The Court's approach in this case was not entirely convincing.[300] The said reference in the *Official Gazette* refers in fact to four rather voluminous pieces of legislation (the *Code of Administrative Procedure*, the *Code of Administrative Offences*, the *Act on the Implementation of Administrative Measures* and the *Introductory Provisions to the Administrative Procedures Act*). The reservation does not specify exactly which provisions might be incompatible with Article 5 of the ECHR. If a reservation refers to entire codes or to a large number of provisions, it will be important to indicate precisely which aspects of the legislation are not compatible with which Convention provision. The Court's reluctance to invalidate the reservation in question might have been prompted by the fact that Commission had previously applied it in a number of cases without questioning its legality.[301]

In the case of *Eisenstecken* v. *Austria*, the new permanent Court took the opportunity to dissipate any doubts with respect to the requirements of Article 57 § 2 of the ECHR. It invalidated Austria's reservation in respect to Article 6 of the ECHR, which had been considered valid and applicable in cases that had been decided before *Belilos*[302], on purely formal grounds:

> 'The Court notes that the reservation in issue does not contain a "brief statement" of the law which is said not to conform to Article 6 of the Convention. From the wording of the reservation it might be inferred that Austria intended to exclude from the scope of Article 6 all proceedings in civil and criminal matters before ordinary courts – and even all kinds of other quasi-judicial bodies – in so far as particular laws allowed for non-public hearings. However, a reservation which merely refers to a permissive, non-exhaustive, provision of the Constitution and which does not

[299] *Chorherr* v. *Austria*, judgment of 25 August 1993, Series A no. 226-B, § 21.
[300] Dissenting Opinion by judge Valticos, *ibid.*; Horn, *supra* note 6, pp. 11–12.
[301] *See e.g.*, decisions on admissibility of 29 August 1959 (Application 473/59); 15 December 1961 (Application 1047/61); 7 April 1967 (Application 2431/65), 14 December 1970 (Application 3923/69) and 29 March 1971 (Application 4002/69).
[302] *See* the *Ettl and Others* judgment of 23 April 1987, Series A no. 117, § 42; *Ringeisen* judgment of 16 July 1971, Series A no. 13, § 98.

> refer to, or mention, those specific provisions of the Austrian legal order which exclude public hearings, does not "afford to a sufficient degree a guarantee . . . that [it] does not go beyond the provision expressly excluded' by Austria" (see the Gradinger judgment cited above, p. 65, § 51, and the Chorherr judgment cited above, pp. 34-35, § 20). Accordingly, the reservation does not satisfy the requirements of Article 57 § 2 of the Convention.
>
> This conclusion is a sufficient basis for finding the reservation invalid, without it being necessary to examine further whether there has been compliance with the other requirements of Article 57.'[303]

3.3. The Relevant Time for the Making of Reservations

In accordance with Article 57 § 1 of the ECHR, reservations must be made 'when signing this Convention or when depositing its instrument of ratification'. Reservations made upon signature subject to ratification must be formally confirmed by the reserving State when expressing its consent to be bound by the treaty (Article 23 § 2 of the 1969 *Vienna Convention on the Law of Treaties*). Strict observance of these requirements is consistent Council of Europe practice, not only with respect to the *European Convention on Human Rights*, but generally with regard to all Council of Europe treaties. Accepting the belated formulation of reservations may create a dangerous precedent, which could be invoked by other States in order to formulate new reservations or to widen the scope of existing ones. Such a practice would jeopardise legal certainty and impair the uniform implementation of European treaties. It would also run counter to the efforts by the Parliamentary Assembly and the Committee of Ministers to reduce the number of reservations.[304]

Exceptions may only be justified by the fact that a certain reservation or declaration had been formulated by the competent national authority

[303] *Eisenstecken* v. *Austria*, judgment of 3 October 2000, §§ 29–30, ECHR (application no. 29477/95).

[304] *See* Parliamentary Assembly's Recommendation 1223 (1993) and the Reply adopted by the Committee of Ministers on 17 February 1994 at the 508th meeting of the Ministers' Deputies.

(parliament or government) before ratification, but that due to administrative oversight it had forgotten to communicate the text when depositing the instrument of ratification or accession. There are no such examples regarding the *European Convention on Human Rights*, but one can refer to the reservation made by Greece in 1988 to the *European Convention on the Suppression of Terrorism* (ETS 90, 1977)[305] or to certain declarations made in 1997 by Portugal with regard to the *European Convention on Mutual Assistance in Criminal Matters* (ETS 30, 1959).[306]

4. CONSEQUENCES OF INVALIDITY AS DETERMINED BY THE STRASBOURG COURT

The *Vienna Convention* is not particularly clear with regard to the consequences of inadmissible reservations.[307] Due to the general inertia of States, the tacit acceptance clause (Article 20 § 5 of the VCLT) has in practice lead to the result that even States that have formulated inadmissible reservations become parties to multilateral treaties. Even in the case of a formal objection by one State against the reservation made by another State,

[305] Reservation contained in a letter from the Permanent Representative of Greece, dated 5 September 1988, registered at the Secretariat General on 6 September 1988. The letter explained that Parliamentary approval had been subject to a reservation which had not been mentioned in the instrument of ratification which had been deposited on 4 August 1988. The reservation read as follows:

'In pursuance of Article 13 of the European Convention on the Suppression of Terrorism, Greece declares that it reserves the right, in accordance with paragraph 1 of the same article, to refuse extradition for any of the offences listed in Article 1 of the Convention if the person suspected of having committed the offence is being prosecuted for his or her action in favour of freedom.'

[306] Declarations contained in a letter from the Permanent Representative of Portugal, dated 3 April 1997, registered at the Secretariat General on 4 April 1997, following the letter of the Permanent Representative of Portugal, dated 19 December 1996, registered at the Secretariat General on 2 January 1997. The letter explained that the declarations contained in the Decree of the President of the Republic and the Assembly Resolution had not been mentioned in the instrument of ratification which had been deposited on 27 September 1994.

[307] As Sir Ian Sinclair concluded, the *Vienna Convention* 'leaves unanswered a whole series of questions . . . particularly questions concerning the distinction . . . between permissible and impermissible reservations'. *See* Sir Ian Sinclair, *The Vienna Convention on the Law of Treaties* (second edition 1984), p. 77.

the *Vienna Convention* foresees that neither the reservation nor the original treaty provision can be applied.[308]

The flexible system of the *Vienna Convention* is intended to balance conflicting State interests in treaties which establish a set of reciprocal rights and obligations. As in a private law contract, the reservation is treated as a sort of offer, which may be accepted in whole or in part by the other parties.[309] This reservations regime is not particularly well suited for human rights treaties that operate mainly 'internally' by setting minimum standards for the protection of individuals to which domestic legislation must conform.[310] Human rights treaties do not operate within bilateral relationships that can be modified on the basis of reciprocity. Their obligations are essentially 'objective' rather than 'subjective' and 'mutual' in nature.

In its *Belilos* judgment, the Strasbourg Court departed from the traditional rules of the *Vienna Convention on the Law of Treaties* as far as the consequences of impermissible reservations were concerned. Declaring Switzerland's reservation null and void, it left this State's consent to be bound by the Convention unaffected.[311] In *Belilos*, the Court's conclusion was facilitated by the fact that Switzerland's counsel had admitted during the hearing that his country would regard itself bound by the Convention irrespective of the declaration's validity. There was no such admission from Turkey in cases, where both the Commission and subsequently the Court held that certain restrictive 'conditions' made with respect to the recognition of the Commission's competence to receive individual petitions and the Court's jurisdiction under former Articles 25 and 46 of the ECHR were invalid. Rather than rendering the State's consent null and void in its entirety, the Court nullified only the inadmissible restrictions and left Turkey's consent to be bound unaffected.

---

308 Article 21 § 3 of the *Vienna Convention* provides: 'When a State objecting to a reservation has not opposed the entry into force of the treaty between itself and the reserving State, the provisions to which the reservations relates do not apply as between the two States to the extent of the reservations.'

309 This parallel was drawn by Schabas, *supra* note 1, p. 64.

310 Simma, *supra* note 1, p. 663; Horn, *supra* note 6, p. 16.

311 *Belilos* judgment of 29 April 1988, Series A no. 132, § 60; *Case of Loizidou* v. *Turkey (Preliminary Objections)*, judgment of 23 March 1995, Series A no. 310, §§ 90–98.

Only this 'severance' or 'severability doctrine'[312] is consistent with the character of the Convention as 'a constitutional instrument of European public order (*ordre public*) for the protection of individual beings'.[313] Where States have accepted human rights obligations subject to the compulsory jurisdiction of an international court, there are compelling reasons to apply the general principle *ut res magis valeat quam pereat*.[314] This approach has the obvious advantage that a State remains bound by the Convention in its entirety even subsequent to the determination that the reservations which it had initially formulated are invalid. Despite some initial controversy both within Switzerland and in legal doctrine, the principles developed by the Convention's supervisory organs have by now become routine jurisprudence.[315] They have been accepted by all States parties to the Convention.

5. MODIFICATION OF RESERVATIONS MADE UPON RATIFICATION

Occasionally, it has been considered whether existing reservations may be modified at a later stage.[316] Here the same reasoning as in the case of belated reservations applies. In line with the *Vienna Convention on the Law of Treaties*, Article 57 of the ECHR allows States to make reservations no later than upon ratification and only with respect to legislation then in force. Reservations may of course be withdrawn, either wholly or partially, and a modification limiting the scope of the original reservation may be interpreted as a 'partial withdrawal'. However, States are foreclosed from any subsequent modification that would extend the scope of the reservation made upon ratification. Allowing such modifications *a posteriori* would be

312 Simma, *supra* note 1, p. 670.

313 Loizidou case (Preliminary Objections), §§ 75 and 93.

314 *Chrysostomos and Others* v. *Turkey* (applications nos. 15299, 15300 and 15318/89), admissibility decision of 4 March 1991, *HRLJ* 12 (1990), p. 113, § 47; Schabas, *supra* note 1, p. 74.

315 L. Wildhaber, 'Rund um Belilos. Die schweizerischen Vorbehalte und auslegenden Erklärungen zur Europäischen Menschenrechtskonvention im Verlaufe der Zeit und im Lichte der Rechtsprechung', in *Kleinstaat und Menschenrechte. Festgabe für Gerhard Batliner zum 65. Geburtstag* (1993), p. 325 (particularly 331 *et seq*).

316 Judge Valticos proposed that States should be given an opportunity to rectify reservations which have been invalidated by the European Court of Human Rights, Dissenting Opinion to the case of *Chorherr* v. *Austria*, judgment of 25 August 1993, Series A no. 226-B, 42; *see* also Schabas, *supra* note 1, pp. 76–79.

contrary to the letter and spirit of the Convention and create a dangerous precedent jeopardising legal certainty.

Theoretically, the modification of existing reservations may be achieved by denouncing the treaty in question and ratify it again, this time with the modified reservations. Such a step was indeed considered in Switzerland following the *Belilos* judgment and in the United Kingdom. In January 2003, the British Prime Minister held out the prospect of Britain withdrawing from some of its obligations under the Convention if measures taken to curb the flow of asylum seekers did not produce the expected results.[317] The objective was apparently to circumvent Article 3 of the ECHR, which prohibits a State from returning a person to a place where he or she is likely to face ill treatment, irrespective of whether the person is a danger to the removing State.[318] However, in the end both countries refrained from denouncing the Convention.

Apart from the fact that the *European Convention on Human Rights* belongs to a limited number of treaties, adherence to which constitutes a prerequisite for membership in the Council of Europe, such an approach would be contrary to the letter and spirit of the Convention. The restrictions on reservations would have little effect if States were allowed to circumvent them by denouncing the Convention. Article 57 of the ECHR does not allow reservations with respect to future legislation. The provision is based on the idea that Convention standards can only be reinforced over time, by withdrawing reservations. Subsequent derogations are only possible in time of emergency or war, within the strict limits of Article 15 of the ECHR, which does not allow derogations from Articles 2, 3, 4 § 1 and 7 of the ECHR. Emphasising the special features of the Convention, which is based on the idea of integration, the Swiss Federal Court considered that it is not permitted to use the power of denunciation as a device to introduce new reservations. Such a procedure would not only be contrary to Article 57 of the ECHR, but would also constitute an abuse of rights.[319]

---

[317] Tony Blair spoke on the BBC1 'Frost Programme' on 26 January 2003, *see* 'The Guardian' of 6 February 2003. Similar proposals had also been floated by the Conservative Party.

[318] *Chahal* v. *UK*, judgment of 15 November 1996, (1996) (application no. 22414/93) 23 *European Human Rights Reports* 413.

[319] Swiss Federal Court, judgment of 17 December 1992, ATF 118 Ia 473. *See* J.-F. Flauss, 'Le contentieux de la validité des réserves à la C.E.D.H. devant le Tribunal fédéral suisse: Requiem pour la déclaration interprétative relative à l'article 6 § 1', (1993) *Revue universelle des droits de l'homme* 297.

6. OTHER STATEMENTS

6.1. Interpretative Declarations

Reservations have to be distinguished from interpretative declarations.[320] States resort to interpretative declarations in order to make their understanding or interpretation of a treaty or a particular provision thereof known. Such declarations may be prompted by uncertainty as to the existence of a conflict between domestic legislation and the treaty obligations. A distinction is sometimes drawn between simple and conditional or qualified interpretative declarations.[321] Simple interpretative declarations are mere clarifications of the State's position which may be given up once a certain interpretation has been authoritatively established by common agreement between the parties or by an international tribunal.

Within the context of the *European Convention on Human Rights*, several States made interpretative declarations regarding the right to education (Article 2 of *Protocol No. 1* to the ECHR). States are in principle free to make such declarations at the time of signature or ratification. The limits and conditions formulated in Article 57 of the ECHR do not apply to them.

An interpretative declaration may also constitute an absolute condition for the State's consent to be bound by the treaty. Such conditional interpretative declarations can be considered as 'dormant' reservations, which reveal their true nature only once a different interpretation has been agreed upon as the correct one. In order to establish the legal nature of a statement, the Court considers its substantive content, not the title given to it or the intention of the reserving State in making it.[322]

---

320 F. Horn, *Reservations and Interpretative Declarations to Multilateral Treaties* (Kluwer, The Hague, 1988), p. 229 *et seq*.; A. Pellet, 'Third report on reservations to treaties', UN Doc. A/CN.4/491/Add.4 (1998), §§ 236 *et seq*.; *Anglo-French Continental Shelf* arbitration, decision of 30 June 1977, 18 *ILM* (1979) 397 = RIAA XVIII, 3; *see also* the comment by P.-H. Imbert, 'La question des réserves dans la décision arbitrale du 30 juin 1977 relative à la délimitation du plateau continental entre la République française et le Royaume-Uni de Grande-Bretagne et l'Irlande du Nord', 24 *Annuaire français de droit international* (1978) pp. 29–58.

321 Horn, *ibid*., p. 238 *et seq*. and pp. 325–337.

322 *Belilos* judgment of 29 April 1988, Series A no. 132, § 49; *Temeltasch* v. *Switzerland* (application no. 9116/80), Commission's report of 5 May 1982, DR 31, p. 120 (§ 73); *Ilaşcu and Others* v. *Moldova and the Russian Federation* (application no. 48787/99), admissibility decision of 4 July 2001, p. 20.

When ratifying the *European Convention on Human Rights* in 1974, the Swiss Government had made the following 'interpretative declaration':

> 'The Swiss Federal Council declares that it interprets the guarantee of free legal assistance and the free assistance of an interpreter, in Article 6, paragraph 3.c and e of the Convention, as not permanently absolving the beneficiary from payment of the resulting costs.'[323]

In 1978 the European Court of Human Rights adopted precisely the interpretation that had been rejected by Switzerland. In the *Luedicke, Belkacem and Koç* case, it held in 1978 that Article 6 § 3 (e) of the ECHR absolved the accused permanently and without any conditions from the payment of costs for interpretation.[324] When the European Commission of Human Rights had to examine the Swiss 'declaration' in 1982, it came to the conclusion that, having regard to the terms used and the preparatory work, it amounted in fact to a reservation.[325]

6.2. Territorial Declarations

Article 56 of the ECHR enables a State to extend the application of the Convention 'to all or any of the territories for whose international relations it is responsible'.[326] This provision has almost exclusively been used by the Netherlands and the United Kingdom with respect to their overseas territories. However, the British practice shows that territories falling within the ambit of Article 56 may also be situated in Europe.[327] Denmark has occasionally declared that certain additional protocols shall, until further notice, not apply to the Faeroe Islands and Greenland.[328] Most of these

---

[323] Declaration contained in the instrument of ratification, deposited on 28 November 1974 – Or. Fr.
[324] *Luedicke, Belkacem and Koç* judgment of 28 November 1978, Series A no. 29.
[325] *Temeltasch* v. *Switzerland* (application no. 9116/80), Commission's report of 5 May 1982, DR 31, p. 120 (§ 49).
[326] *See* the excellent commentary by M. Wood in L.-E. Pettiti, E. Decaux and P.-H. Imbert (eds.), *La Convention européenne des Droits de l'Homme* (Economica, Paris, 1995), pp. 915–921.
[327] *See Gillow* judgment of 24 November 1986, Series A no. 109, § 62.
[328] *E.g.*, with respect to *Protocols Nos. 7* and *13* of the ECHR, updated information can be found at <http://conventions.coe.int>, under 'search on reservations and declarations'.

declarations have eventually been withdrawn. The initial exclusion of the territories in question can be explained by the fact that ratification of a treaty by Denmark does not automatically apply to these territories. Before extending its application, the Danish authorities must seek the approval from the competent self-governing bodies in these territories.[329]

States are, however, not entitled to exclude portions of their national territory from the application of the Convention. The Strasbourg Court held that neither the spirit nor the terms of Article 56 permit an interpretation that would allow a restriction of the scope of the term 'jurisdiction' within the meaning of Article 1 to only part of the national territory.[330] It is against this background that several declarations concerning the application of the Convention to territories, which due to secessionist developments or occupation are no longer under the control of central government, must be examined.

The Republic of Moldova, for example, declared in 1997 that 'it will be unable to guarantee compliance with the provisions of the Convention in respect of omissions and acts committed by the organs of the self-proclaimed Trans-Dniester republic within the territory actually controlled by such organs, until the conflict in the region is finally settled'.[331] Contrary to the second, third and fourth statements contained in the instrument of ratification, which explicitly referred to former Article 64 of the Convention, the declaration in question did not mention any particular provision of the Convention.

Georgia submitted similar declarations when ratifying *Protocols Nos. 1* and *12* to the ECHR in 2002, declaring that

---

[329] On the complex constitutional situation of Denmark, *see* A. Olafsson, 'A note on the Faroe Islands – Home Rule case', in European Commission for Democracy Through Law, *Local self-government, territorial integrity and protection of minorities* (Council of Europe Publishing, Strasbourg, 1996), pp. 103–111; B. Dahl, T. Melchior, L. Adams and D. Tamm (eds.), *Danish Law in a European Perspective* (Gad Jura, Copenhagen, 1996) pp. 85–87; H. W. Poulsen, 'Faroese Home Rule: some considerations regarding its place in constitutional and international law', in G. Alfredsson and P. Macalister-Smith (eds.), *The Living Law of Nations. Essays in memory of Atle Grahl-Madsen* (Engel, Kehl, 1996), p. 287, in particular pp. 296–297.

[330] *Ilaşcu and Others* v. *Moldova and the Russian Federation* (application no. 48787/99), admissibility decision of 4 July 2001, p. 20.

[331] Declaration contained in the instrument of ratification, deposited on 12 September 1997 and was intended to concern Article 1 of the Convention.

> 'due to the existing situation in Abkhazia and Tskhinvali region, Georgian authorities are unable to undertake commitments concerning the respect and protection of the provisions of the Convention and its Additional Protocols on these territories. Georgia therefore declines its responsibility for violations of the provisions of the Protocol by the organs of self-proclaimed illegal forces on the territories of Abkhazia and Tskhinvali region until the possibility of realization of the full jurisdiction of Georgia is restored over these territories.'[332]

Although this declaration also refers to the application of the Convention, Georgia has not formally entered a declaration limiting the application of the Convention itself. In 2002, Azerbaijan also deposited a similar declaration excluding the application of the provisions of the Convention in the territories of Nagorno-Karabakh. While including a schematic map of the territories occupied by Armenia, no reference is made to any particular provisions of the Convention.

The scope and legal effects of statements of this kind, which the three countries in question also made with respect to other Council of Europe treaties, are disputed. In its draft guidelines on reservations to treaties, the International Law Commission has taken the view that 'a unilateral statement by which a state purports to exclude the application of the treaty or some of its provisions to a territory to which that treaty would be applicable in the absence of such a statement constitutes a reservation'.[333] According to this view, the statement made by Georgia with respect to the *European Convention for the Prevention of Torture* would be inadmissible, because the

[332] Declaration contained in the instrument of ratification of *Protocol No. 1* to the ECHR deposited on 7 June 2002 and declaration contained in the instrument of ratification of *Protocol No. 12* to the ECHR, deposited on 15 June 2001.

[333] 'Consolidated text of all draft guidelines adopted by the Commission or proposed by the Special Rapporteur', UN doc. A/CN.4/526/Add. 1 of 16 May 2002, point 1.1.3. In light of the *Ilaşcu* decision, the Special Rapporteur on Reservations, Mr. Alain Pellet, concluded however that 'insofar as the Court refers exclusively to the specific provisions of Article 57 of the European Convention, it might be excessive to draw overly categorical conclusions'. *See* 'Eighth Report on Reservations', UN doc. A/CN.4/535, § 25.

Convention prohibits explicitly the making of any reservations (Article 21).[334]

In the Case of *Ilaşcu and Others* v. *Moldova and the Russian Federation*[335], the European Court of Human Rights had to examine the statement made by Moldova with respect to the Transdniestria region.[336] Several Moldovan nationals who had been sentenced to death or to terms of imprisonment by the 'Supreme Court of the Moldovan Republic of Transdniestria' (MRT) had introduced the application against the Russian Federation and the Republic of Moldova. Arguing that Articles 56 and 57 of the ECHR could be applied together, the Moldovan Government maintained that its statement had to be interpreted as a reservation.

According to the Moldovan Government, the reservation should be interpreted as a negative declaration under former Article 25 of the ECHR and, from 1 November 1998 onwards, under Article 34 of the ECHR, in the sense that Moldova did not recognise the Court's jurisdiction in respect of individual applications directed against the Republic of Moldova concerning acts and omissions by the organs of the 'MRT' on the territory actually controlled by those organs. The government admitted that the reservation did not concern a specific law, but argued that the lack of any actual control over the breakaway territory was a situation of objective fact that was not capable of being governed by a law. Lastly, the reservation in question was not of a general character as it was worded clearly and was of definite scope, namely the territory of Transdniestria. Relying on Article 29 of the *Vienna Convention on the Law of Treaties*, the government argued that Article 56 of the ECHR should be interpreted broadly. While conceding that this provision had been designed to allow the extension of the Convention's application to a territory for whose international relations it was responsible, the government pointed out that the Court was confronted for the first time with a situation like the present one, in which a State agreed to be bound by the Convention although *de facto* part of its territory was not under its control. The applicants on the other hand submitted that Moldova's declaration was a reservation of a general character, which did not satisfy the conditions of Article 57 of the ECHR.

---

[334] 'No reservation may be made in respect of the provisions of this Convention.'

[335] Application No. 48787/99, admissibility decision of 4 July 2001.

[336] When depositing its instrument of ratification on 12 September 1997, Moldova declared 'that it will be unable to guarantee compliance with the provisions of the Convention in respect of omissions and acts committed by the organs of the self-proclaimed Trans-Dniester republic within the territory actually controlled by such organs, until the conflict in the region is finally settled'.

The Grand Chamber started its consideration of Moldova's objection with the observation that the country 'had ratified the Convention with effect throughout the whole of its territory'. Recalling the definition of reservations of a general character given by the Commission in the *Temeltasch* case, the Grand Chamber noted that 'Moldova's declaration does not refer to any particular provision of the Convention' and that it 'does not refer to a specific law in force in Moldova'. The Grand Chamber rejected Moldova's argument that the declaration could be based on Article 57 read together with Article 56 of the ECHR, because 'neither the spirit nor the terms of Article 56, which provides for extending the Convention's application to territories other than the metropolitan territories of the High Contracting Parties, could permit of a negative interpretation in the sense of restricting the scope of the term "jurisdiction" within the meaning of Article 1 to only part of the territory'. The Grand Chamber therefore concluded that 'the aforementioned declaration cannot be equated with a reservation within the meaning of the Convention, so that it must be deemed invalid'.

A careful reading of the decision in the *Ilaşcu* case suggests that the declaration was only found to be invalid as a reservation within the meaning of Article 57 alone or even taken together with Article 56 of the Convention. The decision of the Grand Chamber is wholly consistent with the Court's earlier case law, which seeks to avoid any loopholes or gaps, whether in space or time, which would deprive persons of the effective protection of the Convention. Indeed, neither the relatively precise wording nor the spirit of the provisions in question lend themselves to an extensive interpretation, which would allow States to restrict unilaterally the scope of 'jurisdiction' in the sense of Article 1 of the ECHR.

On the other hand, it does not seem that the Grand Chamber intended to prejudge the validity of the Moldovan declaration as a general statement on the territorial application of the Convention. To what extent Moldovan authorities exercise jurisdiction on the territory of Transdnistria is a factual question, which the Court must address when dealing with the merits of the case. The Court will have to examine carefully in each case whether the defendant government exercises jurisdiction within the meaning of Article 1 of the ECHR on the territory in question. In 2003, the Court did indeed send a fact-finding mission to Transdniestria in order to enable it to make a ruling on the question of state responsibility for alleged human rights violations on this territory.

Despite some differences, the statements by Azerbaijan, Georgia and Moldova should not be seen as reservations in the sense of the *Vienna*

Conventions, but as declarations relating to a factual situation in the territories concerned. Their main purpose was to inform the other parties of a situation, which made it impossible for the countries in question to guarantee compliance with their treaty commitments in territories over which they exercise no effective control. The statements cannot absolve the countries of all responsibility regarding events occurring on these territories. They remain doubtlessly responsible in so far as they exercise 'jurisdiction' in the sense of Article 1 of the ECHR, for example as a consequence of military action against the separatist movements. But it may even been argued that they have a positive obligation to take reasonable steps not resulting in an unbearable or excessive burden to ensure their sovereignty over the territories in order to secure the rights and freedoms set forth in the Convention.[337]

6.3. Conditions Contained in Declarations Recognising the Competence of the Commission and the Jurisdiction of the Court

When recognising the competence of the Commission and the jurisdiction of the Court for the first time in 1987 and 1990 respectively, Turkey attached a number of conditions to its declarations under former Articles 25 and 46 of the ECHR.[338] In legal doctrine, such restrictions of the right of individual petition have sometimes been assimilated to 'reservations' in the sense of Article 2 (d) of the *Vienna Convention on the Law of Treaties*.[339] This was not the view taken by Turkey. In a letter dated 26 June 1987, Turkey's Permanent Representative to the Council of Europe emphasised that the restrictions contained in the Turkish declaration under Article 25 of the ECHR 'cannot be considered as "reservations" in the sense of international treaty law'. They 'do not purport to modify or to exclude any of the legal provisions of the Convention', but only 'to define and limit the granting of additional power and authority which Turkey as contracting State has on its own volition bestowed upon the Commission'.[340]

---

[337] This was the position of the intervening Romanian government in the *Ilaşcu* case, *ibid.*, p. 18.

[338] The Turkish declarations are reproduced in footnotes 21 *et seq.* above.

[339] W. Kälin, 'Die Vorbehalte der Türkei zu ihrer Erklärung gemäß Art. 25 EMRK', (1987) *Europäische Grundrechte Zeitschrift* (EuGRZ) p. 421 (424); C. Rumpf, 'Die Anerkennung des Individualbeschwerderechts gemäß Art. 25 EMRK durch die Türkei', (1987) 47 *Heidelberg Journal of International Law* 778 (pp. 790–791).

[340] Notification JJ1989C of 1 July 1987.

The 'conditions' differ from reservations in the sense that they do not purport to qualify the scope of existing treaty obligations, but the acceptance of additional undertakings. Since they refer to the functioning of the Convention's control mechanism, they do not have a purely conventional character. For similar reasons, the substantive, territorial and temporal restrictions which some States attached to their acceptance of the jurisdiction of the International Court of Justice under the optional clause in Article 36 of the *Statute of the ICJ* are not considered to constitute 'reservations' in the sense of Article 2 (d) of the VCLT.[341]

In the case of *Loizidou* v. *Turkey*, the Strasbourg Court applied the principles developed in the *Belilos* case with respect to reservations to the Turkish declarations. Without clearly determining the legal nature of the 'conditions', it came to the conclusion that all restrictions except those *ratione temporis* were invalid and severable,[342] thereby confirming earlier findings of the Commission.[343] Rather than rendering the State's consent null and void in its entirety, it nullified only the inadmissible restrictions and left Turkey's acceptance unaffected.

In its judgment, the Court examined the validity of the 'conditions' primarily with respect to Articles 25 and 46, and referred only subsidiarily to the provision on reservations (then Article 64 of the ECHR). The Court invoked the wording of Articles 25 and 46, which does not provide for any restrictions of the kind made by Turkey, and is consistent with the practice of other parties. Before Turkey, no other State party had made its acceptance of the competence of the Convention's supervisory bodies subject to any restrictions other than temporal ones.[344] The Court rejected the argument that States were able to attach restrictions to their acceptance of the jurisdiction

[341] J. Crawford, 'The Legal Effect of Automatic Reservations to the Jurisdiction of the International Court', 50 British Yearbook of International Law (BYIL), (1979) 63 (77).

[342] *Loizidou* v. *Turkey (Preliminary Objections)*, judgment of 23 March 1995, Series A no. 310, §§ 65–98.

[343] *Chrysostomos and Others* v. *Turkey* (applications nos. 15299, 15300 and 15318/89), admissibility decision of 4 March 1991, *HRLJ* 12 (1990), p. 113.

[344] In *Kjeldsen and Others* v. *Denmark*, Denmark had initially argued that its recognition of the Court's jurisdiction was limited to cases brought by other States. The Commission, which had referred the case to the Court, took the view that this limitation was invalid. The Court did not have to decide the matter because Denmark accepted the jurisdiction *ad hoc*, *see* the judgment of 7 December 1976, Series A no. 23, pp. 5 *et seq*.

of the International Court of Justice under the optional clause in Article 36 of the *Statute of the ICJ*. The Court reaffirmed the special character of the Convention as 'a constitutional instrument of European public order (*ordre public*) for the protection of individual beings' and its mission 'to ensure the observance of the engagements undertaken by the High Contracting Parties' (Article 19 of the ECHR).[345] This special character 'militates in favour of severance of the impugned clauses since it is by this technique that the rights and freedoms set out in the Convention may be ensured in all areas falling within Turkey's "jurisdiction" within the meaning of Article 1 of the Convention'.[346]

In 1996, Turkey renewed its declarations under former Articles 25[347] and 46[348] of the ECHR with more limited conditions, which did not provoke any

---

[345] *Loizidou* case (Preliminary Objections), §§ 75 and 93.

[346] *Loizidou* case (Preliminary Objections), § 96.

[347] 'The Government of the Republic of Turkey, acting pursuant to Article 25 of the Convention for the Protection of Human Rights and Fundamental Freedoms, hereby declares to accept the competence of the European Commission of Human Rights, to receive petitions which raise allegations concerning acts taken under the jurisdiction of the Republic of Turkey.

This Declaration shall be extended to petitions in relation to anything done or omitted by a Turkish authority outside the national territory of Turkey, having due regard to local, factual and legal circumstances and provided that the Turkish authority concerned had exercised Turkish jurisdiction only and not jurisdiction shared with or exercised by an international or any other state authority.

In the event that the Commission, when interpreting any of the rights or obligations of the Convention, takes into consideration other international treaties or conventions as a supplementary means of interpretation, the Government of Turkey assumes that due regard will be given to the intrinsic conditions contained in each of these treaties or conventions with respect to the delimitation of the relevant substantive and territorial scope of the application.

This Declaration extends to petitions made in respect of facts, including judgments based on such facts which have occurred subsequent to January 28, 1987. Any petition previously registered by the Commission in reliance on the previous Declaration made by Turkey pursuant to Article 25 shall be deemed to have been made on the basis of the present Declaration.

This Declaration, replacing that of January 28, 1987, is valid until January 31, 1998 and may be renewed', Annex I to notification JJ3504C, dated 15 January 1996. The declaration was renewed in 1998 (notification JJ4001C of 18 February 1998).

[348] 'The Government of the Republic of Turkey, acting pursuant to Article 46 of the Convention for the Protection of Human Rights and Fundamental Freedoms, hereby recognizes as compulsory *ipso facto* and without special agreement the jurisdiction

reactions from either the depositary or other parties. The absence of any reaction should not be interpreted as tacit approval of the new Turkish declarations. It could rather be seen as an implicit recognition of the European Court of Human Rights' competence to deal with the legality of the declarations. Finally, following the entry into force of *Protocol No. 11* to the ECHR on 1 November 1998[349], the Court and Commission have been replaced by a single permanent Court in Strasbourg whose jurisdiction extends automatically to all parties.[350]

---

of the European Court of Human Rights in all matters concerning the interpretation and the application of the Convention.

This Declaration shall be extended to acts of jurisdiction exercised by a Turkish authority outside the national territory of Turkey, having due regard to local, factual and legal circumstances and provided that the Turkish authority concerned had exercised Turkish jurisdiction only and not jurisdiction shared with, or exercised by an international or any other state authority.

In the event that the Court, when interpreting any of the rights or obligations of the Convention, takes into consideration other international treaties or conventions as a supplementary means of interpretation, the Government of Turkey assumes that due regard will be given to the intrinsic conditions contained in each of these treaties or conventions with respect to the delimitation of the relevant substantive and territorial scope of the application.

This Declaration is made on condition of reciprocity including reciprocity of obligations assumed under the Convention. It extends to all matters raised in respect of facts, including judgments which are based on such facts which have occurred subsequent to January 22, 1990.

Any case pending before the Commission at the time of effectiveness of this Declaration and filed pursuant to the former Declaration made by Turkey pursuant to Article 25 shall be deemed to have been made on the basis of the present Declaration.

This Declaration, replacing that of January 22, 1990, is valid until January 31, 1998 and may be renewed', Annex II to notification JJ3504C, dated 15 January 1996. The declaration was renewed in 1998 until the entry into force of Protocol No. 11 (notification JJ4001C of 18 February 1998).

349 *Protocol No. 11* to the *Convention for the Protection of Human Rights and Fundamental Freedoms, Restructuring the Control Machinery Established Thereby* (ETS 155, 1994).

350 *See* Articles 34 and 56 § 4 of the ECHR as amended by *Protocol No. 11*.

7. CONCLUSIONS

Already in 1998, the former Vice-President of the Commission, Prof. Jochen Abr. Frowein, found a certain antinomy in the application of the traditional international law institution of reservations to human rights treaties.[351] While being necessary to achieve widespread participation, the sovereign right to make reservations runs counter to the aim of the Convention 'to achieve greater unity in the maintenance and further realization of human rights'. Reservations create inequalities between States, as some of them are obliged to respect the Convention in full, whereas others benefit from certain exceptions. States ratifying the Convention today can formulate their reservations taking into account fifty years of case-law, placing them clearly in a privileged position compared to those that ratified at an early stage. In the highly integrated legal order of the Convention, where the Strasbourg Court is gradually assuming the role of a European constitutional court, the traditional freedom of States to unilaterally modify their obligations through the formulation of reservations appears now as somehow anachronistic. An increasing number of Council of Europe member States are members of the European Union, where the *EU Charter of Fundamental Rights* does not provide for any reservations or derogations. Many provisions of this Charter are based on the corresponding provisions of the *European Convention on Human Rights*, sometimes going even beyond the Convention standards.

In accordance with Article 57 of the ECHR, reservations to the Conventions and its Protocols should be limited to precisely defined legislation in force at the time of ratification. They should be seen as a purely temporary measure, giving the reserving State the opportunity to bring its legislation 'within a reasonable time' in full conformity with the Convention. The Parliamentary Assembly continues to urge that reservations 'should not be of a permanent nature and should be confined to the period required to bring the legislation in question into conformity with the Convention'.[352] State authorities should regularly review all reservations made with a view to withdrawing those that are no longer necessary.

Against this background, recent State practice of formulating and withdrawing reservations to the Convention has on the whole been rather encouraging. Many of the countries that have joined the Council of Europe since 1989, ratified the Convention while implementing wide-ranging social

[351] Frowein, *supra* note 6, p. 193.

[352] Parliamentary Assembly Doc. 10136, 13 April 2004, para. 7; in this sense also Giegerich, *supra* note 1, pp. 751–752.

and political reforms. The countries in question formulated nevertheless only relatively few reservations, generally of restricted scope and sometimes clearly limited in time. Assistance by the Council of Europe Secretariat, through 'compatibility exercises', legislative expertise and legal advice by the Treaty Office, has been instrumental in this context. The practice of informal consultations on the admissibility of draft reservations should be encouraged.

The innovative practice of the Strasbourg organs with respect to reservations was unparalleled in international law.[353] It has been facilitated by certain special features of the Convention, which, in the words of the Court, constitutes 'a constitutional instrument of European public order (*ordre public*) for the protection of individual beings'.[354] Article 57 of the ECHR lays down binding criteria for validity of reservations that are self-contained and suitable for judicial examination. The application of Article 57 of the ECHR leaves little room for individual State action and the 'general rules of international law' as embodied in the *Vienna Convention on the Law of Treaties*. The parties undertake to ensure the enjoyment of the individual rights and freedoms set forth in the Convention to everyone within their jurisdiction. This essentially non-reciprocal nature of the obligations excludes almost completely the scope for unilateral State action. In the Convention's highly integrated legal order, general rules of international law can only have a complementary role, applying to instances where the Convention is silent.[355] The Strasbourg Court had to extend its jurisdiction to the admissibility and legal effects of reservations and interpretative declarations restricting as far as possible their scope and, where possible, eliminate them. Otherwise the Convention's collective enforcement guarantee would be largely ineffective.

When preparing new human rights instruments, drafters should be mindful of the words of Lord McNair who spoke of an 'imperative

---

[353] A similar position has subsequently been adopted by the Human Rights Committee which was established under the *UN Covenant on Civil and Political Rights*, *see General Comment No. 24 (52)*, *supra* note 49. The Committee's position was, however, opposed by several Parties to the Covenant, including Council of Europe member States such as France and the United Kingdom.

[354] *Loizidou* v. *Turkey (Preliminary Objections)*, judgment of 23.3.1995, Series A no. 310, § 75. *See also* the admissibility decision of the Commission, applications 15299, 15300 and 15318/89 – *Chrysostomos and Others* v. *Turkey* (4 March 1991), *HRLJ* 12 (1990), 113 (121).

[355] MacDonald, *supra* note 6, p. 438.

necessity' to formulate regimes on reservations specific to each treaty.[356] The same concern was expressed by the Parliamentary Assembly in *Recommendation 1223* (1993), which suggested the inclusion in each convention of 'a clause specifying the conditions under which States may make reservations'. In certain cases, it may be justified to have 'sunset' reservation clauses, which contain precise time limits for the validity of reservations.[357] Following the expiry of the agreed period, the reservations made upon ratification will disappear unless explicitly renewed. In addition to having appropriate reservation clauses, the concepts and guarantees to be included in new instruments must be carefully drafted.[358] In many instances, the making of reservations is prompted by the desire to uphold the application of certain provisions of national law against international human rights standards whose exact meaning had not been completely clarified during the negotiations.

---

[356] A. McNair, *The Law of Treaties* (Claredon, Oxford, 1961), p. 170.
[357] *See* the CAHDI document 'Practical Issues regarding Reservations to International Treaties', *supra* note 4, point I (1).
[358] *See e.g.*, some of the reservations and declarations made with respect to some of the provisions of *Protocol No. 7* to the ECHR.

DECLARATIONS TO THE COUNCIL OF EUROPE FRAMEWORK CONVENTION FOR THE PROTECTION OF NATIONAL MINORITIES: PRACTICE OF THE ADVISORY COMMITTEE

Rainer Hofmann[*]

TABLE OF CONTENTS

1. INTRODUCTION

The Council of Europe *Framework Convention for the Protection of National Minorities* (Framework Convention, FCNM)[359] entered into force on 1 February 1998 subsequent to its ratification by twelve Council of Europe Member States. As of 1 October 2003, it has been in force for 35 of the 45 Member States; within a very short period of time, it had thus become one of the Council of Europe's human rights instruments with the highest rate of membership.[360] This means that, as of 1 October 2003, seven Council

[*] Professor Dr.; Director, Walther-Schücking-Institute for International Law, University of Kiel, Germany; President of the Advisory Committee under the Council of Europe Framework Convention for the Protection of National Minorities. The following views, however, are solely those of the author.

[359] E.T.S. No. 157 (hereinafter 'Framework Convention').

[360] These were: Albania (entry into force on 1 January 2000), Armenia (1 November 1998), Austria (1 July 1998), Azerbaijan (1 October 2000), Bosnia and Herzegovina (1 June 2000), Bulgaria (1 September 1999), Croatia (1 February 1998), Cyprus (1 February 1998), Czech Republic (1 April 1998), Denmark (1 February 1998), Estonia (1 February 1998), Finland (1 February 1998), Germany (1 February 1998), Hungary (1 February 1998), Ireland (1 September 1999), Italy (1 March 1998), Liechtenstein (1 March 1998), Lithuania (1 July 2000), Malta (1 June 1998), Moldova (1 February 1998), Norway (1 July 1999), Poland (1 April 2001), Romania

of Europe Member States had signed but not yet ratified the Framework Convention[361] whereas three Member States had not yet taken any step in order to become legally bound by this treaty.[362]

When the Framework Convention entered into force, much criticism was levelled both because of its textual vagueness and the weakness of the implementation procedures.[363] Today, with the end of the first cycle of monitoring approaching, it seems justified to give a positive assessment of the monitoring activities so far carried out by the two organs involved. The first being the Council of Europe Committee of Ministers which, as the politically responsible body, adopts Resolutions consisting of Conclusions and Recommendations concerning the implementation of the principles set out in the Framework Convention into the domestic legal order of the respective States parties. The second is the Advisory Committee, which, using strictly legal criteria, adopts country-specific opinions the contents of which is usually reflected in the above-mentioned Resolutions of the Committee of Ministers.[364]

(1 February 1998), Russian Federation (1 December 1998), San Marino (1 February 1998), Serbia and Montenegro (1 September 2001), Slovak Republic (1 February 1998), Slovenia (1 July 1998), Spain (1 February 1998), Sweden (1 August 2000), Switzerland (1 February 1999), Former Yugolav Republic of Macedonia (1 February 1998), Ukraine (1 May 1998), and United Kingdom (1 May 1998).

[361] These were Belgium (signature on 31 July 2001), Georgia (22 September 2000), Greece (22 September 1997), Iceland (1 February 1995), Latvia (11 May 1995) and the Netherlands (1 February 1995).

[362] These were Andorra, France, and Turkey.

[363] *See e.g.*, G. Alfredsson, 'A Frame with an Incomplete Painting: Comparison of the Framework Convention for the Protection of National Minorities with International Standards for Monitoring Procedures' 7 *International Journal on Minority and Group Rights* (2000) p. 291; and G. Gilbert, 'Minority Rights under the Council of Europe', in P. Cumper and S. Wheatley (eds.), *Minority Rights in the 'New' Europe* (The Hague, 1999) p. 53; for a reply to Alfredsson *see* F. Steketee, 'The Framework Convention: A Piece of Art or a Tool for Action ?' 8 *International Journal on Minority and Group Rights* (2001) p. 1.

[364] For extensive reports on results of the monitoring process under the Framework Convention, *see* R. Hofmann, 'Review of the Monitoring Process of the Council of Europe Framework Convention for the Protection of National Minorities', 1 *European Yearbook of Minority Issues* (2001/2) p. 435; and R. Hofmann, 'Review of the Monitoring Process of the Council of Europe Framework Convention for the Protection of National Minorities', 2 *European Yearbook of Minority Issues* (2003) (forthcoming).

DECLARATIONS TO THE COUNCIL OF EUROPE FRAMEWORK CONVENTION FOR THE PROTECTION OF NATIONAL MINORITIES

As of 1 October 2003, the Advisory Committee had received 33 State reports[365] on which it had adopted 28 opinions of which 25 were in the public domain subsequent either to the communication of the government concerned relating to the publication of the opinion before the adoption of the Committee of Ministers Resolutions, or to the adoption of such Resolutions.[366] Based upon these opinions and the corresponding State comments, the Committee of Ministers had adopted 20 Resolutions consisting of Conclusions and Recommendations.[367]

As concerns the substantive aspects of the monitoring activities of the Advisory Committee, the issue of the personal scope of application of the Framework Convention was – and still is – of particular significance. More

---

365 These were – in chronological order – San Marino, Cyprus, Finland, Liechtenstein, Croatia, Czech Republic, Italy, Slovak Republic, Denmark, Hungary, Romania, United Kingdom, Malta, Ukraine (all in 1999), Germany, Russian Federation, Moldova, Austria, Slovenia, Spain (all in 2000), Norway, Switzerland, Sweden, Armenia, Albania, Lithuania, Ireland (all in 2001), Azerbaijan, Poland, Serbia and Montenegro (all in 2002), Bulgaria, and Former Yugoslav Republic of Macedonia (both in 2003); the full text of these state reports is available at <www.coe.int/T/e/human_rights/minorities>.

366 In 2000, the Advisory Committee had adopted opinions on Denmark, Finland, Hungary, Slovak Republic (all on 22 September 2000), and on Liechtenstein, Malta, and San Marino (all on 30 November 2000); in 2001 on Croatia, Cyprus, Czech Republic, Romania (all on 6 April 2001), Estonia, Italy (both on 14 September 2001), and on the United Kingdom (on 30 November 2001); in 2002 on Germany, Moldova, Ukraine (all on 1 March 2002), Armenia, Austria (both on 156 May 2002), Albania, Norway, the Russian Federation, and Slovenia (all on 12 September 2002); and in 2003 – so far – on Lithuania, Sweden, Switzerland (all on 20 February 2003), Azerbaijan and Ireland (both on 22 May 2003). As of 1 October 2003, only the opinions on Azerbaijan, Ireland, and Slovenia were not yet in the public domain; the full text of the publicly accessible opinion and state comments is available *at* <www.coe.int/T/e/human_rights/minorities>.

367 In 2001, the Committee of Ministers had adopted Resolutions on Denmark, Finland (both on 31 October 2001), Hungary, Slovak Republic (both on 21 November 2001), Liechtenstein, Malta and San Marino (all on 27 November 2001); in 2002, on Croatia, Czech Republic (both on 6 February 2002), Cyprus (21 February 2002), Romania (13 March 2002), Estonia, United Kingdom (both on 13 June 2002) and Italy (on 3 July 2002); and in 2003 – so far – on Armenia, Germany, Moldova (all on 15 January 2003), Ukraine (5 February 2003) and the Russian Federation (on 10 July 2003); the full text of all these Resolutions is available *at* <www.coe.int/T/e/human_rights/minorities>.

specifically, it forced the Advisory Committee to develop an approach as to the declarations on the personal scope of application of the Framework Convention made by some States parties upon its signature or ratification. This issue, thus, also raised the more general question as to whether such declarations had to be considered as binding upon the Advisory Committee (and – eventually – the Committee of Ministers) or whether they were subject to the scrutiny of the monitoring bodies.

2. THE LEGAL EFFECTS OF STATES PARTIES DECLARATIONS ON THE PERSONAL SCOPE OF APPLICATION OF THE FRAMEWORK CONVENTION

In order to evaluate the legal effects of such declarations on the personal scope of application of the Framework Convention, it seems appropriate to first give an overview of the pertinent practice of the Advisory Committee which, as will be shown, considers itself to be legally entitled to monitor that such declarations do not lead to results which would be incompatible with the Framework Convention. Then, it is important to describe the reaction of State governments as expressed in their comments on the respective opinions and, finally, the position taken by the Committee of Ministers in its Resolutions.

2.1. The Practice of the Advisory Committee

At the outset, it must be recalled that the drafters of the Framework Convention did not agreed on a definition of the term *national minority* and, thus, failed to provide the monitoring bodies with a clear indication as to the personal scope of application of the Framework Convention. While this situation reflects the actual state of international law, which is characterized by the absence of a generally accepted definition of that term, it prompted several States to add *declarations* to their instruments of ratification.[368] These usually limit the applicability *ratione personae* to such groups as are commonly referred to as 'old' or 'traditional' minorities, i.e. those who have long-lasting ties with the territory on which they live and are nationals of the State of which that territory is a part.[369] Thus, they wished to exclude, in

---

368 *See* F. Capotorti and R. Hofmann, 'Minorities', in R. Bernhardt (ed.), *Encyclopedia of Public International Law*, (Aalphen a.d.Rhijn, 1997) Vol. III, p. 410.

369 *See e.g.*, the declarations made by Austria (limiting the applicability of the Framework Convention to those groups coming within the scope of application of

particular, 'new' minorities from the personal scope of application of the Framework Convention.

Such declarations raise, from a theoretical point of view, several questions, namely as to their legal nature, i.e. whether they are indeed to be considered as *declarations*, or whether they should rather be regarded as *interpretative declarations*, or even as – disguised – reservations. The latter assessment, in turn, would call into question their compatibility with the object and purpose of the Framework Convention if they were to exclude members of a group, which is generally recognised as a national minority, from the applicability of the Framework Convention, as well as to their legal effect, namely whether they are to be considered as binding upon the Advisory Committee and the Committee of Ministers, in the conduct of their monitoring activities.[370] This issue was further complicated by the fact that several States parties indicated in their State reports the groups which they considered as being covered by the Framework Convention: Some States referred only to 'old' minorities, whereas others opted for a broad and inclusive approach making the Framework Convention applicable also to 'new' minorities.

As regards the issue of declarations, the Advisory Committee, after considerable internal deliberation, decided to make use of the flexibility inherent in the wording of the Framework Convention and adopted, at least with respect to the first cycle of its monitoring activities, a pragmatic and flexible approach. It should be stressed that this approach has been followed

---

the *Volksgruppengesetz*), Denmark (restricting the applicability of the Framework Convention to the German-speaking minority in Southern Jutland), Germany (identifying Danes, Sorbians, Frisians and Sinti and Roma of German citizenship as being covered by the Framework Convention), Slovenia (indicating that the Framework Convention would be applied to Italians, Hungarians, and the Roma), Sweden (identifying Sami, Swedish Finns, Tornedalers, Roma, and Jews as national minorities in Sweden), and the Former Yugoslav Republic of Macedonia (where the Framework Convention would be applied to Albanians, Turks, Vlachs, Roma, and Serbs).

[370] For a thorough discussion of these complex issues, *see* J. A. Frowein and R.Bank, 'The Effect of Member States' Declarations Defining "National Minorities" upon Signature or Ratification of the Council of Europe Framework Convention for the Protection of National Minorities', 59 *Zeitschrift für ausländisches öffentliches Recht und Völkerrecht* (1999) p. 649.

also in those opinions that were adopted after 1 June 2002, i.e. by the Advisory Committee in its new personal composition.[371]

In this respect, the Advisory Committee developed the following practice. It sets out by underlining that, in the absence of a definition of the term 'national minority' in the Framework Convention itself, the governments of the States parties must examine the personal scope of application to be given to the Framework Convention within their respective countries. The position of each government is, therefore, deemed to be the outcome of this examination. The Advisory Committee would then continue by noting that, on the one hand, States parties have a margin of appreciation in this respect in order to take the specific circumstances prevailing in their countries into account, and that, on the other hand, this margin of appreciation must be exercised in accordance with general principles of international law and the fundamental principles set out in Article 3 of the FCNM. The Advisory Committee stresses, in particular, that the implementation of the Framework Convention should not be a source of arbitrary or unjustified distinctions. For this reason, the Advisory Committee considers that it is part of its duty to examine the personal scope of application given to the implementation of the Framework Convention in order to verify that no such arbitrary or unjustified distinctions have been made. Furthermore, it considers that it must verify the proper application of the fundamental principles set out in Article 3 of the FCNM.[372] This

---

[371] It might be noted that on 31 May 2002, pursuant to Rule 16 of Committee of Ministers Resolution (91)10 of 17 September 1997 which contains fundamental provisions on the monitoring arrangements under Articles 24 to 26 FCNM, the term of office of nine of the original ordinary members of the Advisory Committee expired. By virtue of the above-mentioned Rule, they were replaced by nine persons who, at that time, served as additional members.

[372] *See e.g.* paras. 17–22 of the opinion on Albania (where the Advisory Committee came to the finding that, given the historic presence of *Egyptians* in Albania, their *a priori* exclusion from the personal scope of application of the Framework Convention was not compatible with the Framework Convention); *see* para. 20 of the opinion on Armenia; paras. 12–20 of the opinion on Austria (where the Advisory Committee encourages the Austrian authorities to continue to examine the issue of the existence of a Polish minority in consultation with the representatives of the Polish community; according to the Austrian government, only the following groups are considered to meet the conditions set out in Article 1(2) of the *Law on Ethnic Groups* (*Volksgruppengesetz*) and therefore recognised as national minorities: The Croat minority in Burgenland, the Slovene minority, the Hungarian minority, the Czech minority; the Slovak minority, and the Roma minority); paras. 14–17 of the

approach of the Advisory Committee well reflects its general position to avoid unnecessary confrontation with governments and to rather seek to engage in a constructive dialogue with a view to settling any disagreement as to the interpretation of the Framework Convention.

Therefore, the Advisory Committee, if met with a situation where it considered that the Framework Convention could, in addition to the groups identified by the government, also be applicable to other groups, limited itself to call upon the competent authorities to examine the issue in consultation with those concerned. The Advisory Committee clearly stated,

---

opinion on Croatia; paras. 15–16 of the opinion on Cyprus; paras. 14–15 of the opinion on the Czech Republic; paras 13–15 of the opinion on Denmark (where the Advisory Committee came to the finding that persons belonging to groups with long historic ties to Denmark such as the Faeroese, Greenlanders, Roma and Germans outside their area of settlement in Southern Jutland could not *a priori* be excluded from the personal scope of application of the Framework Convention); paras. 14–16 of the opinion on Estonia; paras. 12–13 of the opinion on Finland; paras. 13–15 of the opinion on Germany; paras. 11–13 of the opinion on Hungary; paras. 13–15 of the opinion on Italy; paras. 10–12 of the opinion on Liechtenstein; paras. 15–17 of the opinion on Lithuania; paras. 10–12 of the opinion on Malta; paras. 17–26 of the opinion on Moldova; paras. 15–18 of the opinion on Norway; paras. 10–11 of the opinion on San Marino; paras. 14–18 of the opinion on Romania (where the Advisory Committee came to the finding that Romania should favourably consider the extension of the applicability of the Framework Convention to persons stating that they are members of the Csango community and should explore this question in consultation with the representatives of the Csangos); paras. 17–21 of the opinion on the Russian Federation; paras. 13–19 of the opinion on Sweden (where the Advisory Committee considered that the issue as to whether inhabitants of the regions of Gotland and Scania might be considered as members of a national minority protected under the Framework Convention should be addressed through dialogue between the authorities and those concerned); paras. 16–23 of the opinion on Switzerland (where the Advisory Committee noted, *inter alia*, that the issues resulting from the application of the principle of territoriality should be addressed by the Swiss authorities); paras. 13–16 of the opinion on Ukraine (where the Advisory Committee expects that the results of the 2001 census will provide a basis for an improved dialogue between persons belonging to so-called *sub-ethnic groups of the Ukrainian people* – such as *e.g.* Rusyns – and the authorities, covering also issues pertaining to the implementation of the Framework Convention); and paras. 11–16 of the opinion on the United Kingdom (where the Advisory Committee noted that a number of persons living in Cornwall consider themselves to be a national minority within the scope of the Framework Convention, a view which is not shared by the British government).

in only two of the 25 opinions so far publicly accessible, that the position taken by the government was not compatible with the Framework Convention since it excluded *a priori* certain groups from the application *ratione personae* of the Framework Convention. And even in the presence of such an – extremely rare – finding the Advisory Committee called upon the respective government to examine, in consultation with those concerned, the issue of the applicability of the Framework Convention.[373]

As regards the issue of the potential applicability of the Framework Convention to persons also belonging to 'new' minorities, the Advisory Committee developed the following practice: It notes that some of the provisions of the Framework Convention – such as Article 11(3) with its explicit reference to areas traditionally inhabited by persons belonging to a national minority – would obviously be applicable only to 'old' minorities. In contrast thereto, it is clear that Article 6 of the FCNM applies to 'all persons living on the territory' of a given State party and, thus, also to persons belonging to 'new' minorities.[374] Furthermore, it seems indeed possible to argue that also other provisions, such as Articles 3, 5, 7 and 8 of the FCNM could, at least in certain circumstances, be applicable also to persons belonging to 'new' minorities.

Based upon this analysis, the Advisory Committee opted, again, for a flexible approach. As concerns persons belonging to groups other than those determined by the respective government to be covered by the Framework Convention, this approach makes it possible to consider the inclusion of persons belonging to such groups in the application of the Framework Convention on an article-by-article basis. As a result thereof, the Advisory Committee expressed its opinion that the competent State authorities should consider this issue in consultation with those concerned – again an example of the general position of the Advisory Committee to foster and support constructive dialogue.[375] It must be stressed, however, that the Advisory

---

[373] *See* para. 22 of the opinion on Albania (as concerns the *Egyptians*); and paras. 18–22 of the opinion on Denmark (concerning Faeroese in mainland Denmark, Germans outside Southern Jutland, Greenlanders in mainland Denmark, and Roma).

[374] *See* paras. 35 of the opinion on Austria; paras. 37–40 of the opinion on Germany; and para. 40 of the opinion on Italy.

[375] *See* para. 23 of the opinion on Albania; para. 21 of the opinion on Armenia; para. 20 of the opinion on Austria; para. 17 of the opinion on Croatia; para. 22 of the opinion on Cyprus; para. 23 of the opinion on the Czech Republic; para. 24 of the opinion on Denmark; para. 18 of the opinion on Estonia; para. 18 of the opinion on Finland; paras. 17–18 of the opinion on Germany; para. 14 of the opinion on

Committee clearly favours an inclusive approach as concerns the personal applicability of the Framework Convention as witnessed by several statements in which it either welcomes such an inclusive approach by a government[376] or supports developments towards the *de facto* implementation of such an approach.[377]

To sum up, it is important to note that the Advisory Committee established a clear practice as regards the legal effects of designations by governments, made either in a formal declaration given upon signature or ratification of the Framework Convention, or in the respective State report: The Advisory Committee does not consider itself bound by such designations but rather perceives them as the outcome of the examination by the respective government as to the personal scope of application of the Framework Convention in the country concerned. The position thus taken by the government is, however, subject to the monitoring of the Advisory Committee applying both principles of international law and the fundamental principles set out in Article 3 of the FCNM; this means, in particular, that the domestic application of the Framework Convention must not result in arbitrary or unjustified distinctions. Thus, it must be emphasized that the Advisory Committee considers itself to have the competence to examine any such designation of the personal application of the Framework Convention as to its compatibility with this treaty.

Having said that it is equally important to stress that the Advisory Committee concluded only in two instances that the position taken by a government was not compatible with Article 3 of the FCNM – and even then it called upon the governments concerned to examine the issue through dialogue with the groups thus excluded from the application of the

---

Hungary; para. 17 of the opinion on Italy; para. 13 of the opinion on Liechtenstein; para. 27 of the opinion on Lithuania; para. 14 of the opinion on Malta; para. 27 of the opinion on Moldova; para. 20 of the opinion on Norway; para. 22 of the opinion on the Russian Federation; para. 20 of the opinion on Sweden; para. 27 of the opinion on Switzerland; para. 18 of the opinion on Ukraine; and para. 17 of the opinion on the United Kingdom.

376 *See e.g.*, para. 16 of the opinion on Sweden; and para. 14 of the opinion on the United Kingdom.

377 *See e.g.*, para. 17 of the opinion on Croatia; para. 17 of the opinion on Estonia. para. 20 of the opinion on Norway; and para. 21 of the opinion on the Russian Federation.

Framework Convention.[378] The same appeal was made in all other instances where the Advisory Committee did not find the designation made by the respective governments to be incompatible with the principles set out in the Framework Convention but only considered that certain additional groups might be included in the application of the Framework Convention and, therefore, called upon the authorities concerned to discuss the issue with the respective groups.[379]

2.2. The Reaction of the Governments

In line with the monitoring mechanism established under the Framework Convention, all governments are entitled to comment upon the respective opinions of the Advisory Committee before the Committee of Ministers embarks upon its deliberations with a view to adopt its Resolutions. For the purposes of this paper it seems justified to focus on the comments of the governments of States parties with respect to which the Advisory Committee considered that the governmental position as to the personal application of the Framework Convention was either not compatible therewith or raised doubts as to its compatibility.[380]

All governments, with the exception of Austria and Sweden, submitted comments with regard to the pertinent proposal made by the Advisory Committee to engage in a dialogue with the groups concerned as to their possible inclusion into the personal scope of application of the Framework Convention: The Romanian government explained that the *Csangos* will be considered as a distinct ethnic-national group in the next census; the government of Ukraine declared that, according to Ukrainian scientists, the *Rusyns* were part of the Ukrainian nation and did not constitute a national minority; the British government stressed that, while it did not deny the *Cornish* people the right to maintain and promote their culture, this did not necessarily imply their recognition as a group to which the Framework Convention was to be applied.

---

378 *See* paras. 22 and 120 of the opinion on Albania; and paras. 18–23 and 39 of the opinion on Denmark.

379 *See* para. 19 of the opinion on Austria; para. 18 of the opinion on Romania; para. 19 of the opinion on Sweden; para. 16 of the opinion on Ukraine; and para. 16 of the opinion on the United Kingdom.

380 The full text of these comments is available *at* <www.coe.int/T/e/human_rights/minorities>.

The Albanian government defended its position that, in applying not only objective but also subjective criteria, the *Egyptians* have been integrated into the Albanian nation to such an extent that they cannot be considered a distinct national group and, thus, should not be recognised as a national minority in the sense of the Framework Convention. Also the Danish government, in quite an extensive comment, stressed its position that, in view of the Danish domestic legal order, the Framework Convention could not be applied in the Faeroer Islands and Greenland nor to Faeroese or Greenlanders in mainland Denmark; moreover, by virtue of Denmark's international obligations, the recognition of the German speaking minority as a national minority had to be limited to their area of settlement in Southern Jutland; and, finally, the Roma currently present in Denmark did not show the long historic ties with Denmark necessary in order to be considered as a national minority.

Two conclusions can be drawn from these comments:

- First, governments show considerable reluctance to follow the proposals of the Advisory Committee and to engage in a dialogue with representatives of those groups to which the governments do not wish to apply the Framework Convention. It is important to note, however, that in the two instances where the Advisory Committee found that the position of the respective governments was not compatible with the Framework Convention (Albania and Denmark), both governments made considerable efforts to explain and justify their respective position.

- Second – and, for the purpose of this paper, this conclusion is more important – no government has challenged the competence of the Advisory Committee to examine the position of a government concerning the personal scope of application of the Framework Convention as to its compatibility with the principles set out therein. So, it is important to emphasize that while governments might criticise the result of the pertinent scrutiny of the Advisory Committee, they do not challenge its legal powers to engage in such a scrutiny! It might be added that the same position is taken by governments as regards to calls by the Advisory Committee to discuss (through dialogue with those concerned) the application of the Framework Convention, on an article-by-article basis, also to other groups including, where appropriate, immigrants and refugees: Again, governments might dispute the appropriateness – or correctness – of this article-by-article approach, but they do not challenge the competence of the Advisory

Committee to examine the personal scope of application given to the Framework Convention by any government.[381]

2.3. The Position of the Committee of Ministers

As regards the position of the Committee of Ministers, it must be stressed, at the outset, that it has so far shown a very strong tendency to follow the draft conclusions and recommendations incorporated by the Advisory Committee into its opinions.[382] Since the Resolution on Albania has, as of 3 March 2004, not yet been adopted, the Resolution most relevant in this context is the one with respect to Denmark. This is the case because Albania and Denmark were the only countries so far that the Advisory Committee has proposed to the Committee of Ministers to include, in its Resolution, a reference to the issue of the personal scope of application of the Framework Convention. Insofar it must be stressed that the Committee of Ministers, notwithstanding the above-described, quite extensive comments made by the Danish government as concerns the personal scope of application of the Framework Convention in Denmark, concluded that 'the personal scope of application of the Framework Convention in Denmark merits further consideration by the Government of Denmark with those concerned'.[383]

As concerns all other Resolutions, it should be noted that the Committee of Ministers developed a clear practice to recommend that the respective State party takes appropriate account of the conclusions of the Committee of Ministers together with the various comments in the Advisory Committee's opinion. Furthermore it invites the respective government to continue the dialogue in progress with the Advisory Committee and to keep it regularly informed of the measures it has taken in response to the conclusions and recommendations of the Committee of Ministers.

Again, two conclusions might be drawn from the analysis of the Committee of Ministers' Resolutions:

- First, in the only truly relevant case so far dealt with in a Committee of Ministers Resolution, the one with respect to Denmark, the Committee of Ministers, notwithstanding the rather explicit statement of the Danish

---

[381] *See e.g.*, the comments of the German government of 19 July 2002 which vigorously defend the German position to apply the Framework Convention only to Danes, Sorbians, Frisians and Sinti and Roma of German citizenship, but do not challenge the right of the Advisory Committee to examine this position.

[382] *See* the pertinent analysis by R. Hofmann, *supra* note 7, p. 444 *et seq*.

[383] *See* Resolution ResCMN(2001)2 of 31 October 2001.

government, adopted a conclusion which clearly reflects the pertinent finding of the Advisory Committee.

- Second, and this is again of major importance, the Committee of Ministers, by recommending governments to take appropriate note of the various comments contained in the Advisory Committee's opinion, implicitly recognised the competence of the Advisory Committee to examine the position taken by governments as concerns the personal scope of application of the Framework Convention.

3. CONCLUDING REMARKS

By way of conclusion, it seems justified to state that, with the end of the first cycle of monitoring approaching, the Advisory Committee has an unchallenged competence to examine the position taken by a government, be it by a formal declaration made upon signature or ratification of the Framework Convention or by simply identifying the groups concerned, as regards the personal scope of application of the Framework Convention as to its compatibility with the principles set out therein. Thus, as regards this human rights treaty, an issue, which, as concerns other international human rights instruments, took many years to solve or is still awaiting a generally accepted solution, has been solved in a very short period of time. Obviously, this development was facilitated by the fact that, as far as Council of Europe human rights instruments are concerned, there seems to be unanimous acceptance of the competences of monitoring bodies to examine the compatibility of reservations, declarations or other acts defining – and, thereby, most frequently restricting – the geographical, personal, or temporal scope of application of such an instrument. Nonetheless, it is encouraging to see that, notwithstanding the often highly controversial character of the issue of minority rights protection in Europe, no State party to the Framework Convention has challenged the pertinent competence of the Advisory Committee. Finally, at least as far as Council of Europe Member States are concerned, there exists a sufficient amount of State practice which, supposedly, is also based upon a pertinent *opinio juris*; this again would mean that as far as Council of Europe human rights instruments are concerned, there is evidence for the existence of a norm of regional customary law empowering monitoring bodies under human rights instruments fully to examine reservations and other acts of States parties defining the scope of application of that instrument as to their compatibility with general principles of international law and the specific principles enshrined in the respective human rights instruments.

PART II. ELEMENTS OF A DOCTRINAL DEBATE

ON HUMAN RIGHTS TREATIES, CONTRACTUAL CONCEPTIONS AND RESERVATIONS

Jan Klabbers[*]

TABLE OF CONTENTS

1. INTRODUCTION

From the very moment the International Law Commission (ILC) took up the topic of the codification of the law of treaties, back in 1949, it has been concerned with and puzzled by the issue of reservations. The topic so occupied the minds of this highly visible college of international lawyers that the very first comment on the very first report presented by J.L. Brierly singled out an explicit reference to reservations and the many legal problems surrounding them that came from none other than Ivan Kerno, the UN's Assistant Secretary-General at the time.[384]

Kerno's interest was partly inspired by the then pending problems surrounding the Genocide Convention. As is well known, the conclusion of the Genocide Convention with its compulsory dispute settlement clause created a considerable political problem for the General Assembly. The General Assembly would, as Kerno's words already foreshadowed, later submit the matter to the International Court of Justice (ICJ), which would famously attempt to split the difference by opining that in case of a treaty

[*] Professor of International Law, University of Helsinki.

[384] At the International Law Commission's 49th meeting, in *Yearbook of the International Law Commission* (1950/I), p. 64.

being silent on reservations, reservations are permissible as long as they are compatible with the object and purpose of the treaty concerned.[385]

It would, however, be mistaken to explain Kerno's considerable interest merely in light of the *Genocide Convention*, for the notion of reservations has a much more fundamental importance in international law. On a higher level of abstraction, reservations carry the promise of reconciling the interests of individual States with those of the international community at large.[386] They suggest the Houdini-like trick of being able to bind the State without binding it.[387] Or perhaps it is more accurate to use the past tense: reservations used to carry the promise of reconciling conflicting interests, and they used to be considered as capable of performing Houdini-like tricks about being bound while remaining free.[388]

For, as has become clear in the years since the ICJ rendered its opinion on *Reservations to the Genocide Convention* and since the *Vienna Convention on the Law of Treaties* (*Vienna Convention*) entered into force, reservations are no longer deemed to be so useful. At best, they are often considered to be a necessary evil: necessary to attract States, but evil in their tendency to undo treaty regimes, especially regimes establishing human rights standards.[389] One prominent observer notes that 'the multitude of

[385] *See Reservations to the Convention on the Prevention and Punishment of the Crime of Genocide,* Advisory opinion, *ICJ Reports*, 1951, 15. The notion of object and purpose is itself fraught with ambiguities: *see* J. Klabbers, 'some Problems Regarding the Object and Purpose of Treaties', 8 *Finnish Yearbook of International Law* (1997) p. 138.

[386] As the ILC's fourth Special Rapporteur, Sir Humphrey Waldock, understood only too well. For him, the topic of reservations was among the main subjects on which the ILC 'could make a real contribution to the law of treaties'. *See* 653rd meeting, (1962/I) *Yearbook of International Law Commission* (YbILC) p. 159. Likewise, André Gros referred to the subject of reservations as 'the most important before the Commission', 656th meeting, in (1962/I) YbILC, p. 173.

[387] In much the same way as the unlikely phenomenon of non-legally binding agreements aims to reconcile commitment with non-commitment. On these, *see generally* J. Klabbers, *The Concept of Treaty in International Law* (Kluwer, The Hague, 1996).

[388] For a discussion of reservations as influenced by competing visions of international order, *see* J.K. Koh, 'Reservations to Multilateral Treaties: How International Legal Doctrine Reflects World Vision', 23 *Harvard International Law Journal* (1982) p. 71.

[389] For a subtle analysis using this mindset as a point of departure, *see* S. Marks, 'Three Regional Human Rights Treaties and their Experience of Reservations', in J.P. Gardner (ed.), *Human Rights as General Norms and a State's Right to Opt Out: Reservations and Objections to Human Rights Treaties* (British Institute of International and

reservations . . . has pushed human rights law into a crisis'[390]; the subtitle of a monograph published in the mid-1990s seriously suggested that reservations can 'ruin' a treaty regime[391], and more than once has the idea been proclaimed that somehow, the Vienna Convention's regime on reservations ought to be reconsidered, reworked and rethought.[392]

Since the mid-1990s, this is indeed what has happened and is happening. The ILC itself has re-opened the discussion by placing the topic of reservations back on its agenda.[393] Within the Council of Europe, the Ad Hoc Committee of Legal Advisers (CAHDI, after the abbreviation in French) has studied the topic and prepared recommendations, and the Council even harbours an observatory on reservations.[394] Reservations are also being studied, since 1998, in what used to be called the UN Subcommission on Prevention of Discrimination and Protection of Minorities (nowadays known as the Subcommission on the Promotion and

---

Comparative Law, London, 1997), p. 35. Less subtle is Y. Tyagi, 'The Conflict of Law and Policy on Reservations to Human Rights Treaties', 71 *British Yearbook of International Law* (BYIL) (2000) p. 181 who, having first observed that reservations 'fly in the face of the principle of universality of human rights' (p. 205), grudgingly concedes that 'human rights treaties will continue to have uncomfortable alliances with reservations.' (p. 256)

[390] *See* W.A. Schabas, 'Invalid Reservations to the International Covenant on Civil and Political Rights: Is the United States Still a Party?', 21 *Brooklyn Journal of International Law* (1995) p. 277, p. 315.

[391] *See* L. Lijnzaad, *Reservations to UN-Human Rights Treaties: Ratify and Ruin?* (Kluwer, Dordrecht, 1994). A more positive appraisal, emphasizing that reservations can facilitate the sharing of commitments between diverse states, is C.A. Bradley & J.L. Goldsmith, 'Treaties, Human Rights, and Conditional Consent', 149 *University of Pennsylvania Law Review* (2000) p. 399.

[392] *See e.g.*, D.N. Hylton, 'Default Breakdown: The Vienna Convention on the Law of Treaties' Inadequate Framework on Reservations', 27 *Vanderbilt Journal of Transnational Law* (1994) p.419. Others put their hopes on State practice developing in responsible ways. *See e.g.*, R. Kühner, *Vorbehalte zu multilateralen völkerrechtlichen Verträgen* (Springer, Berlin, 1986).

[393] Special Rapporteur Alain Pellet has, to date, submitted eight reports on the issue, on the basis of which the ILC has been drafting guidelines. The most recent documents include Pellet's 8th report (A/CN.4/535), and draft guidelines on withdrawal and modification of reservations (A/CN.4/L.630).

[394] For an overview of some aspects of Council of Europe practice, *see* S. Spiliopoulou Åkermark, 'Reservation Clauses in Treaties Concluded Within the Council of Europe', 48 *International and Comparative Law Quarterly* (ICLQ) (1999) p. 479.

Protection of Human Rights).[395] Various international tribunals and treaty organs have addressed the issue of reservations[396], and in particular the Nordic States have initiated a new practice when it comes to lodging objections to reservations.[397]

Yet, this flurry of activity notwithstanding, it would seem that nothing much of significance is changing. Thus, it is doubtful whether the Nordic practice or the CAHDI's recommendations have any significant and immediate legal effect[398], and the ILC's Special Rapporteur, Alain Pellet, has proved quite adamant in his insistence that the Vienna Convention's regime works reasonably well. One of its main assets, dixit Pellet, is that it leaves the parties to a treaty free to draw up any rules on reservations that they themselves see fit.[399] The Vienna Convention's regime acts merely as a normative safety net, so to speak: it is only activated when a treaty remains silent on reservations.

And even then, it is at least hypothetically possible (if not always practicable perhaps) that treaty partners, under the Vienna Convention's regime, respond *en bloc* to an undesirable reservation and refuse to enter into treaty relations with the reserving State. While perhaps difficult to organize, all it presupposes is that States actually agree on the despicable nature of the reservation concerned.[400]

---

[395] F. Hampson submitted her first report in 1999: E/CN.4/Sub.2/1999/28.

[396] The leading case is the decision of the European Court of Human Rights in *Belilos* v. *Switzerland*, decision of 29 April 1988, in 88 *International Law Reports* (*ILR*) p. 648. For a critical discussion, *see* I. Cameron & F. Horn, 'Reservations to the European Convention on Human Rights: The *Belilos* Case', 33 *German Yearbook of International Law* (1990) p. 69. This will be further discussed below, in section 6 of this paper.

[397] On the latter, *see* J. Klabbers, 'Accepting the Unacceptable: A New Nordic Approach to Reservations to Multilateral Treaties', 69 *Nordic Journal of International Law* (2000) p. 179.

[398] *Ibid.*

[399] *See* Alain Pellet, *First Report on the Law and Practice Relating to Reservations to Treaties* (A/CN.4/470), especially para. 169. Pellet's argument echoes Lord McNair, *The Law of Treaties* (Clarendon Press, Oxford, 1961), p. 169: '. . . the true solution of the difficulty which has arisen in connection with multipartite treaties lies not in the formulation of new rules of international law of general acceptance by States, but in insisting that the representatives of States when met together for the purpose of framing a certain treaty are themselves masters of the situation and must act as such.'

[400] *See e.g.*, R. Baratta, 'should Invalid Reservations to Human Rights Treaties Be Disregarded?', 11 *European Journal of International Law* (EJIL) (2000) p. 420. Schabas, *supra* note 7, p. 310, raises the possibility that the responses of a number of

ON HUMAN RIGHTS TREATIES, CONTRACTUAL CONCEPTIONS AND RESERVATIONS

The present paper does not purport to present the umpteenth solution to the problem of reservations. Indeed, with McNair and Pellet, the present writer does not consider there to be much reason to change things to begin with or, more accurately perhaps, to the extent that reservations pose a problem it is often a problem of diverging political views (often fundamental divergencies), which therewith calls for a solution by political means. The dubious premise underlying much writing on reservations, in particular with respect to human rights instruments, is the premise that law can somehow accomplish things on which agreement in the body politic is impossible to reach. Absent such agreement, the result could only be to force substantive rules on States reluctant to accept them, and that is rarely a good idea.

What follows starts with an exploration of the discussions within the ILC leading up to the creation of the Vienna Convention's regime.[401] This is not done with a view to establishing the drafters' intentions, or to figure out whether some policy option or other was explicitly excluded by the drafters, as is often the case with recourse to the *travaux préparatoires* to a treaty.[402] Instead, the idea is to highlight the intellectual problems which coloured the discussion and which, by remaining unresolved, still influence the discussion. After an initial sketch in Section 2, this will be done in two parts: section 3 of this paper will discuss much of the initial preparatory work, while section 4 will concentrate on the single most relevant and sustained discussion conducted within the ILC on the topic of reservations while drafting the Vienna Convention. This discussion took place during a handful of meetings of the Commission in 1962, and neatly highlights the elusive nature of the topic. And at the risk of stating the obvious: what follows is not a complete overview of the drafting history. Instead, it is an attempt to uncover recurring themes in the debates, not an attempt to discover some historical truth about reservations.[403]

European states to the US reservations to the *International Covenant on Civil and Political Rights* may have been orchestrated: those responses 'are worded in similar terms and suggest a considerable degree of cooperation.'

401 For a useful overview of the situation before the Vienna Convention, *see* J.M. Ruda, 'Reservations to Treaties' (1975/II) 146 *Recueil des Cours* (RdC) 95, esp. pp. 111–133.

402 *See* J. Klabbers, 'International Legal Histories: The Declining Importance of Travaux Préparatoires in Treaty Interpretation?', 50 *Netherlands International Law Review* (2003) p. 267.

403 The reader will find that the discussion sizzles out after 1962, and that I hardly address the Vienna Conference.

Sections 5 and 6 of this paper will aspire to make some sense of the ILC debates, whereas section 7 will contain some conclusions. As a further limitation, given the immense complexity of the topic, it is perhaps useful to underline that I am mainly interested in what might be deemed the two basic political questions surrounding reservations: when are they permitted? And what effects do objections to reservations have? I have looked at the ILC debates in order to trace the discussion on these two main questions, leaving a host of other questions undressed, precisely because those two form the heart of the matter: much of the debate about reservations is really a debate about objections and their effects.[404]

2. SOME IRONY

The main point to be developed in this paper will be the point that, as so much in the law of treaties, the discussion on reservation is coloured by a struggle between two competing conceptions of treaties generally, and reservations in particular. On the one hand, there is the vision of the treaty as a contractual arrangement, informed by such things as reciprocity and perhaps also consideration. The alternative conception is one which, on its face at least, shuns the contractual perspective. In this perspective, the contractual vision is either inaccurate or undesirable, and quite possibly both, as it is thought to fail to do justice to community concerns.

Much of the discussion on reservations, so I suggest, was (and is) conducted in terms of those two competing visions. Yet, that discussion is not helped much by the circumstance that neither of these two visions is terribly well developed. The contractual vision may realize that it misses an *ordre public* dimension but does not really know how to rectify this situation; and sadly, the *ordre public* vision itself does not really know how to insert community elements into the law of treaties either. As a result, the same themes keep coming back, often only thinly disguised as new themes: contract versus community becomes unanimity versus majority, which in turn becomes integrity versus universality, which in its turn becomes a discussion on the effects of objections to reservations; all of this is traceable to those two original positions.

---

[404] Thus, I do not discuss such issues as when reservations must be made, or how the *Vienna Convention* relates to regimes which do contain a few words on reservations. Occasionally though, where relevant a tangential issue is addressed: this relates, for instance, to the proper role in accepting reservations of organs of international organizations.

Still, I will argue that there is a sense in which both competing visions actually may complement and strengthen each other when it comes to reservations: the *ordre public* approach, so often thought to underlie in particular human rights instruments, may be well served by the introduction (or re-introduction, more accurately) of contractual notions.

One of the ways in which the two perspectives play out, in particular after the ICJ rendered its opinion on *Reservations to the Genocide Convention*, is in terms of a dichotomy between universality and integrity.[405] Thus, the political choice presented was to choose between either getting as many States as possible to ratify the treaty, or to prefer the idea that the treaty constitutes a coherent and balanced package which does not allow any interference.

This dichotomy, however intuitively plausible perhaps and however useful it may have been in order to come up with a decision regarding the Genocide Convention, has proved to be to some extent unfortunate. For all its merits, it is misleading in that it suggests that treaties are, somehow, absolute, almost God-given gospels which either have a natural universal appeal or are diluted by the forces of evil. The truth is, as so often, more subtle and much more complicated: whether a treaty attracts universal support depends on whether or not its terms are deemed acceptable to many, and this in turn depends on the existence of political agreement between the negotiating States. In the case of human rights treaties, it depends on fundamental agreement on basic values or, as the philosopher would say, on agreement on what constitutes the good life.[406]

Needless to say, such agreement is rare, and where it exists it often mainly exists in the abstract: we may *in abstracto* all agree that torture is a bad thing, but we are bound to disagree *in concreto* about what constitutes torture and about whether it may nonetheless be justified in extreme circumstances.[407]

---

[405] The leading monographs tend to be written with this dichotomy in mind. *See e.g.*, P.-H. Imbert, *Les réserves aux traités multilateraux* (Pedone, Paris, 1978); F. Horn, *Reservations and Interpretative Declarations to Multilateral Treaties* (North Holland, Amsterdam, 1988), and Lijnzaad, *supra* note 8. While Imbert chooses the side of universality, Horn and Lijnzaad are more inclined to take the side of integrity.

[406] And such agreement is not readily forthcoming. *See* A. McIntyre, *After Virtue: A Study in Moral Theory* (2d ed., Duckworth, London 1985).

[407] Useful here is J. Conroy, *Unspeakable Acts, Ordinary People: The Dynamics of Torture* (University of California Press, Berkeley, 2000).

Moreover, at first sight at any rate, the very notion of the integrity of a treaty is a curious notion to use in the context of human rights treaties, premised as it is (as so much of the law of treaties) precisely on the contractual conception of treaties (treaties are the result of a delicate, more or less reciprocal bargain between rational actors) that is so often deemed an unsuitable characterization of human rights treaties, both in the literature[408] and in the practice of treaty bodies.[409] Whatever motives States may be said to have to enter into human rights treaties[410], these do not often include such things as reciprocity. While we will see that a contractual perspective has some advantages, given the fact that such a perspective is often dismissed it is curious that the debate is cast in terms of universality versus integrity dichotomy.[411]

At any rate, the dichotomy between universality and integrity hardly convinced the first three rapporteurs on the law of treaties. Brierly, Lauterpacht and Fitzmaurice all were of the opinion that the classic rule that reservations must be accepted by unanimity still held good[412] – and a unanimity rule has no place for a universality versus integrity dilemma, as it automatically favours integrity without universality being of any concern.

There is a certain irony in the circumstance that the quest for universal acceptance, so often mentioned in connection with human rights treaties[413],

---

408 So, among many others, C. Redgwell, 'US Reservations to Human Rights Treaties: All for One and None for All?', in M. Byers and G. Nolte (eds.), *United States Hegemony and the Foundations of International Law* (CUP, Cambridge, 2003) p. 392, p. 410, conceptualizing human rights treaties as treaties 'whose normative obligations are owed nonreciprocally', and K. Korkelia, 'New Challenges to the Regime of Reservations under the International Covenant on Civil and Political Rights', 13 *EJIL* (2002) p. 437, esp. pp. 439–442.

409 *See* Section 6 below.

410 Moravcsik argues that human rights treaties find support because they allow political groups in new democracies to lock democracy into place. *See* A. Moravcsik, 'The Origins of Human Rights Regimes: Democratic Delegation in Postwar Europe', 54 *International Organization* (2000) p. 217.

411 For a general discussion, *see* E.W. Vierdag, 'some Remarks about Special Features of Human Rights Treaties', 25 *Netherlands Yearbook of International Law* (1994) p. 119.

412 So too, still in 1961, the work that was considered by many as having an almost treaty-like quality, McNair's *Law of Treaties*, *supra* note 16, p. 161.

413 The ICJ seemed to suggest, somewhat loosely perhaps, that universality was itself part of the object and purpose of the Genocide Convention. *See Reservations to the Genocide Convention*, *supra* note 2, p. 24: 'The object and purpose of the *Genocide Convention* imply that it was the intention . . . that as many States as possible should

has given rise to the dilution of the unanimity rule which would otherwise be so wonderfully compatible with the public order aspirations of human rights treaties. Instead, now, human rights treaties have to make do with curious rules on reservations which work best if treaties are regarded as contracts – precisely the perspective deemed unsuitable for human rights treaties.

3. UNANIMITY AND DIVISION

It was clear from the outset that much of the success of the drafting of the Vienna Convention would be dependent on whether or not the issue of reservations could be successfully tackled. In his first report on the law of treaties, Special Rapporteur J.L. Brierly already devoted an article to reservations. Brierly had no problem with reservations, provided they would be accepted unanimously by the other parties. His draft Article 10, paragraph 3, ran:

> 'The acceptance of a treaty subject to a reservation is ineffective unless or until every State or international organization whose consent is requisite to the effectiveness of that reservation has consented thereto.'[414]

The underlying theory, so Brierly affirmed at the start of the ILC's 53rd meeting[415], was that a reservation was to be considered as a part of the bargain between the parties, and would thus require the acceptance of all parties in order to become effective.[416] The rule of unanimous acceptance itself was, in Brierly's view, 'clear'[417]: 'a well-known rule of practice'[418], and the ILC itself seemed to be of the same opinion.[419]

Yet, this clarity notwithstanding, these early discussions within the ILC already highlighted a number of strands which would continue to run through discussions on reservations. One of those was whether reservations

---

participate.' The thought has later been echoed with respect to other treaties, such as the 1982 *Law of the Sea Convention*. *See* J.I. Charney, 'Entry Into Force of the 1982 Convention on the Law of the Sea', 35 *Virginia Journal of International Law* (1995) p. 381.

414 *See* J.L. Brierly, 'Report on the Law of Treaties', (1950/II) YbILC 222, p. 224.

415 ILC, 53rd meeting, (1950/I) YbILC, p. 90.

416 *See* Brierly I, *supra* note 31, p. 239.

417 *Ibid.*, p. 240.

418 *Ibid.*, p. 239.

419 ILC, 53rd meeting, (1950/I) YbILC, p 91. *See also* p. 92.

could be accepted tacitly, or whether acceptance would always have to be express. Another revolved around the question whose acceptance would be required: those of parties already applying a treaty regime, or also those of signatories or perhaps even negotiating States who themselves would not have any serious relationship with the treaty just yet?

In the end, most of these questions are traceable to two related points. The first of these is that the ILC seemed to think of treaties as being predominantly contractual in nature. Not only did Brierly specifically found his draft article on the eminently contractual notion of treaties being the result of bargains between States, telling is also that El-Khoury discussed tacit acceptance by enlisting an example from the contract law of his country (i.e., Syria).[420] And equally telling is that the ILC's Dutch member, Francois, reminded the Commission that reservations would have to be subject to reciprocity: typically a contractual notion, with which the Commission seemed largely in agreement.[421]

The second main point colouring these initial discussions is, that both Brierly and the ILC somehow were dimly aware that the contractual prism might have its limits – but without however doing much about it. In his first report, Brierly already pointed to the general inadmissibility of reservations to international labour conventions, despite the circumstance that the texts of those conventions remained silent on reservations.[422] He explained this by suggesting that the inadmissibility of making reservations followed from membership of the International Labour Organisation.[423] During the ILC's 53rd meeting, several of its members suggested likewise that somehow the question of reservations might be different when it came to treaties 'of a constitutional nature'.[424]

Half a year later, in November 1950, the General Assembly invited the ILC to have a more specific look at reservations to multilateral conventions, which prompted Brierly to devote a separate report to the topic[425], and prompted some other ILC members, Amado and Scelle, to put their thoughts

---

420 *Ibid.*, at 95.

421 *Ibid.*, p. 91.

422 Lauterpacht would later treat ILO Conventions as more or less typically contractual in nature (*see also* the discussion below, Section VI). *See* H. Lauterpacht, 'Report on the Law of Treaties', (1953/II) YbILC 90, p. 127.

423 Brierly I, *supra* note 31, p. 239.

424 So the Chairman of the meeting, Georges Scelle, as well as, to some extent, J.P.A. Francois. See 53rd meeting, (1950/I) YbILC, pp. 92 and 95 respectively.

425 *See* J.L. Brierly, 'Reservations to Multilateral Conventions', (1951/II) YbILC 1.

on paper as well.[426] Brierly, in his brief report, advocated that the Commission occupy itself with creating model clauses for insertion in treaties[427], having apparently become convinced of the impossibility of formulating a single rule which would be satisfactory in all cases.[428]

Gilberto Amado's memorandum was largely limited to extolling the virtues of the unanimous assent rule: for him, in particular with multilateral normative instruments (i.e. law-making treaties), it was of the utmost importance to safeguard the integrity of a treaty regime.[429] This was, so he seemed to suggest, a direct consequence of the sovereignty of States: States cannot be bound by obligations without their consent, so it follows that reservations require unanimous consent. He did, however, astutely note the existence of a contrary theory, equally based on sovereignty: reservations are themselves emanations of sovereignty and usually have only negative effects (i.e., they do not create obligations for others), so they would not require any acceptance to be effective.[430] Georges Scelle, arguably one of the intellectually more influential members of the ILC in those early days, also insisted on unanimous acceptance, but without highlighting any distinctions between law-making and contractual undertakings. By contrast, in a move which may, in retrospect, have done more harm than good, Scelle forcefully put forward the view that all treaties are, to some extent at least, legislative acts: in treaty-making, States legislate on behalf of the international community.[431]

The subsequent debate within the ILC was remarkably inconsequential, perhaps as a result of the circumstance that the ICJ had by now rendered its advisory opinion on *Reservations to the Genocide Convention*.[432] The ensuing debate was a curious mixture of discussions of broad principles (the

---

[426] (1951/II) YbILC, pp. 17 and 23, respectively.

[427] Brierly, *supra* note 42, p. 3. Annex E to his report contains a number of such model clauses.

[428] *Ibid.*, p. 4.

[429] Amado, *supra* note 43, esp. p. 21. He would later modify his views: see the report of the ILC's 651st meeting, (1962/I) YbILC, p. 140.

[430] Amado, *supra* note 43, p. 21.

[431] *See* Scelle's memorandum, *supra* note 43.

[432] Brierly's report was dated 6 April 1951; the Court delivered its opinion on 28 May 1951, and the ILC started to discuss the topic on 11 June 1951 (at its 100th meeting, very briefly), and continued doing so until 19 June 1951 (its 106th meeting): *See* (1951/I) YbILC. The memoranda by Amado and Scelle were written (or dated, at least) after the Court's opinion was delivered, but do not address it in any explicit fashion.

virtues of the Pan-American system from which the Court had drawn some inspiration were debated vis-à-vis those of the classic unanimity rule[433]) and detailed discussions on re-drafting the various paragraphs of Brierly's report, with Brierly himself in the chair.

Yet, one comment is noteworthy, and that is Yepes's disappointment with the ICJ opinion which, to his mind, was based on a misconception. The Court had based its opinion, so he claimed, on the idea (which was 'inadmissible', as he put it) that multilateral treaties are really a series of bilateral treaties, creating bilateral relations between the States.[434]

Unfortunately, Yepes did not expand on this idea, and even more unfortunate, the rest of the Commission failed to pick it up, yet Yepes's point already foreshadowed what would later become a fixture of the debate: whether multilateral treaties can always be recast as being creative of bundles of bilateral relationships, or whether a different conception is required.

While Brierly did still produce a report before the ILC's fourth session, largely dealing with the conclusion of treaties[435], he resigned in the interval between the third and fourth sessions. In August 1952, Hersch Lauterpacht was elected to replace Brierly as Special Rapporteur on the law of treaties. Lauterpacht approached the matter in an unorthodox manner: he produced a draft article which, so it seems, was meant to represent the *lex lata*, and no less than four alternative proposals, all *de lege ferenda.*[436] While Lauterpacht did base himself on the idea that there was something not quite right about States making reservations which would be 'sweeping, arbitrary, or destructive of the reasonably conceived purpose of the treaty and of the legitimate interests and expectation of the other parties'[437], nonetheless the remarkable thing about all his proposals *de lege ferenda* was that they concentrated exclusively on creating a procedure: none of them offered any substantive guidelines. Instead, Lauterpacht's *de lege ferenda* alternatives posit the idea that either a reservation stands if accepted by a two-thirds

---

433 Under the system in vogue in Latin America, broadly speaking, reservations would be permissible but could have limited effects, depending on acceptance or rejection.

434 101st meeting, (1951/I) YbILC, p. 160. Such treaties are sometimes referred to as 'bipolar': *see* A. Bleckmann, 'Zur Wandlung der Strukturen der Völkerrechtsverträge - Theorie des multipolären Vertrages', 34 *Archiv des Völkerrechts* (1996) p. 218.

435 J.L. Brierly, 'Third Report on the Law of Treaties', (1952/II) YbILC 50.

436 *See* Lauterpacht I, *supra* note 39, pp. 91–92: he explained that the rule of unanimity laid down in his draft article 'must be regarded as probably still representing the existing law' (p. 123).

437 *Ibid.*, p. 125.

majority of the treaty-partners[438], or if accepted by a treaty organ[439] or the ICJ in summary procedure.[440] After all, as he explained, if a State proposes to submit a reservation which would

> 'call seriously in question the good faith and sincerity of the State making the reservation then, it may be assumed, there will be found the requisite one-third of States who have finally accepted the treaty whether with reservations or not, who will object to the participation of that State in the treaty.'[441]

Lauterpacht was generally well aware of the highly political nature of reservations – and of the complexity of the topic.[442] Most importantly perhaps, Lauterpacht pointed out that reservations are more problematic with contractual undertakings than with treaties of a more normative character, and did so precisely by adopting a contractual perspective: with normative undertakings, no treaty partner is damaged or injured by a far-reaching reservation. Whereas with a contractual treaty, a reservation may disturb the balance of commitments between the parties, with normative treaties no such balance exists. The only thing worth looking out for, Lauterpacht pointed out echoing Sir Gerald Fitzmaurice[443], is that the reservation leaves something of the treaty intact.

With Lauterpacht having been called to higher office[444], he was replaced as Special Rapporteur by the same Sir Gerald Fitzmaurice. Sir Gerald, taking an apparent delight in abstraction and model-building, regarded the rules on reservations as part of what he termed the formal validity of treaties.

---

[438] Alternatives A and B.

[439] Alternative C.

[440] Alternative D.

[441] Lauterpacht I, *supra* note 39, pp. 127–128.

[442] 'The subject of reservations to multilateral treaties is one of unusual – in fact baffling – complexity and it would serve no useful purpose to simplify artificially an inherently complex problem.' *Ibid.*, p. 124.

[443] *Ibid.*, p. 128, referring to some of Fitzmaurice's scholarly writings. As if to underline their spiritual bond, Fitzmaurice later applauded Lauterpacht's sensible judicial position on reservations. *See* Sir G. Fitzmaurice, *The Law and Procedure of the International Court of Justice, volume II* (Grotius, Cambridge, 1986), p. 831.

[444] Lauterpacht's reports, incidentally, were never discussed within the ILC; the ILC was too busy doing other things, in particular finalizing the conventions on the law of the sea.

Curiously, the 'fundamental rule' contained in his first report on the law of treaties[445] was not all that fundamental really: it contained a definition, some words on the form of reservations, and laid down the presumption that if a treaty permits some reservations, then others are excluded, as well as a strict rule prohibiting the making of reservations with respect to dispute settlement[446], but that was it: the fundamental rule did not cover what to do with reservations when a treaty itself was silent on the issue.

This, instead, was covered in Article 39 of the first Fitzmaurice draft, and not surprisingly, like Lauterpacht, Fitzmaurice too ended up advocating a more or less procedural device without providing any substantive guidelines. A reservation would be perfectly feasible unless objected to; and if objections were maintained, the reserving State would not qualify as a party to the treaty concerned.[447] The sting, however, would be in the tail, and be firmly entrenched in the notion of reciprocity: an accepted reservation made by State A would allow not just A to derogate from the contemplated regime, but also all other treaty partners, to the extent of A's reservation and in relation to A.[448]

Again then, Fitzmaurice's draft relies exclusively on a contractual analogy, analyzing multilateral treaties (for this part of the draft dealt explicitly with multilateral treaties) as so many bundles of bilateral relations. And what is somewhat surprising is that it did so half a decade after the ICJ had rendered its advisory opinion on *Reservations to the Genocide Convention*. Fitzmaurice must have thought his bilateralized approach so obvious as not to dignify it with any explication. His commentary on the

---

[445] *See* G. Fitzmaurice, 'Report on the Law of Treaties', (1956/II) YbILC 104, draft Article 37.

[446] This in itself indicates how distanced he was from the ICJ's opinion (*supra* note 2), given the ICJ's conviction that dispute settlement clauses would not normally be considered as incompatible with a treaty's object and purpose, and thus be perfectly acceptable.

[447] Fitzmaurice I, *supra* note 62, draft Article 39. In his scholarly capacity, he wrote that the unanimity rule would be the 'least unsatisfactory' of the prevailing theories on reservations. *See* Sir G. Fitzmaurice, *The Law and Procedure of the International Court of Justice, volume I* (Grotius, Cambridge, 1986), p. 413.

[448] Fitzmaurice I, *supra* note 62, draft Article 40. This has found recognition in Article 21, paragraph 1(b) of the Vienna Convention which, however, is generally considered to have fairly little utility in case of human rights treaties. I am indebted to Varro Vooglaid and Rain Liivoja for intelligent discussion on this point.

effects of reservations merely states that he thought it 'useful to state these consequences, but they require no explanation.'[449]

Surprising as this may sound, it is not entirely impossible that Fitzmaurice had subconsciously excluded law-making conventions and conventions emanating from within international organizations. 'The practice of international organizations', so Fitzmaurice explained when introducing his first report to the ILC, 'was parliamentary rather diplomatic, and took place in circumstances quite different from those which governed relations between States'.[450] And a minute or two later he observed that a convention such as the *Universal Postal Convention*, 'although a treaty, was in a way a municipal law of the whole international community and, as an international construction, could not strictly be regarded as a treaty; being universal, it was something more'.[451] While there is no explicit reference to a purposeful omission of a group of treaties, it seems clear that law-making treaties were not Fitzmaurice's main concern.

Fitzmaurice's first report would only be discussed by the ILC in general terms, focusing on his overall approach. Consequently, not much of interest was said on the topic of reservations[452], except for the fact that Sir Gerald was provoked to pronounce his disapproval with the approach taken by the ICJ in *Reservations to the Genocide Convention.*[453] Such an approach, he opined, 'would, in general, be extremely difficult to apply'.[454] Moreover, and most problematically perhaps, it would introduce an element of unfairness by allowing States that were overruled during the negotiations 'to reintroduce for their own benefit points on which they had been overruled'.[455] And there was no particular need for this, so he continued, because such States are free not to join the regime.

---

[449] *Ibid.*, p. 127.

[450] 368th meeting, (1956/I) YbILC, p. 218.

[451] *Ibid.*, p. 218.

[452] Unless one counts Krylov's dig at Lauterpacht, who 'had simply been repeating matters with which all jurists had been fully familiar ever since the Peace of Campoformio.' 369th meeting, (1956/I) YbILC, p. 220.

[453] He did so in response to Zourek, *ibid.*, pp. 224–225.

[454] 370th meeting, (1956/I) YbILC, p. 227. The words echo the conclusion of the joint dissenting opinion of judges Guerrero, McNair, Read and Hsu Mo to *Reservations to the Genocide Convention*, *supra* note 2, p. 43 (noting that the object and purpose test is so difficult to apply that the General Assembly would not have passed it over in silence).

[455] 370th meeting, (1956/I) YbILC, p. 227.

While Fitzmaurice would write another four reports on the law of treaties, he would not seriously address the issue of reservations again, and after Fitzmaurice succeeded Lauterpacht at the International Court of Justice, the position of Special Rapporteur fell upon yet another Briton, Sir Humphrey Waldock.

Waldock, in his first report, departed from the procedural approach of his two immediate predecessors, and added an element of substance reminiscent of (if more laconically formulated than) the *Reservations to the Genocide Convention* opinion. In Waldock's draft Article 17, a reserving State 'shall have regard to the compatibility of the reservation with the object and purpose of the treaty'.[456] Waldock's draft Article 18 echoed, in paragraph 5, the reciprocity notion already developed by Fitzmaurice, while his draft Article 19 specified that an objection to a reservation would mean that the treaty would not enter into force as between the reserving and objecting States.[457]

Waldock's relaxed attitude and departure from the unanimity rule was inspired mainly, or so it would seem, by the conviction that generally reservations might lighten the burden of reserving States, but will not make international commitments more onerous for non-reserving States to live up to: 'The position of the non-reserving State is not made in any respect more onerous if the reserving State becomes a party to the treaty on a limited basis by reason of its observation.'[458]

Waldock expressed to have had 'a certain amount of hesitation'[459] about including a substantive criterion for the testing of reservations. After all, the notion of compatibility with a treaty's object and purpose had met with substantial criticism and would most often be extremely difficult to apply, as much would depend on how much a treaty provision represents a treaty's object and purpose, and how to decide on which provisions are considered to be material to achieve a treaty's object and purpose. Nonetheless, he did feel that the notion of object and purpose 'does express a valuable concept'[460], and thus decided to take it into consideration, but not in the objective (or quasi-objective) way advocated by the ICJ but in a more subjective rendition: States, when making a reservation, were to have regard to the object and purpose of the treaty. It would remain up to the treaty partners (or

---

456 *See* H. Waldock, 'First Report on the Law of Treaties', (1962/II) YbILC 27, p. 60.
457 *Ibid.*, p. 62.
458 *Ibid.*, p. 64.
459 *Ibid.*, p. 65.
460 *Ibid.*, p. 66.

prospective partners) to reject or accept the reservation, on the understanding that an objection would preempt treaty relations between reserving and objecting States. Still, this was as far as Waldock was willing to go: an objection would not prevent a reserving State from joining altogether, and the unanimity rule, still endorsed by Fitzmaurice, was therewith discarded.

So far then, the discussion seems premised on a number of related assumptions, not shared perhaps by all ILC members but nonetheless generating a sufficiently general consensus within the ILC. One of the assumptions colouring the debate was that treaties are mostly to be regarded as contractual in nature: they are the result of bargains between States, and classically operate by means of reciprocity.[461] Reservations, then, should themselves work reciprocally, so as not to upset the balance of the bargain. And while this may not be intuitively plausible with human rights conventions (or indeed other law-making conventions), Lauterpacht vividly demonstrated that here too a contractual perspective could be fruitfully applied.

The second generally shared (and related) assumption was that multilateral treaties can often be recast as bundles of bilateral treaties. This is the inevitable result of a contractual perspective, ultimately reducing all commitments to bargains between dyads of contracting States. The result is, obviously, that there is little place for treaties that cannot be reduced to bilateral sets, as some of the ILC's members, with admirable consistency, demonstrated when analyzing humanitarian instruments in terms of bargains and reciprocity.

The third assumption is one that grew during the discussions, in light of the ICJ's *Reservations to the Genocide Convention* opinion. Somehow, the impression took hold that treaty-making (at least where normative instruments are concerned) is a matter of balancing of the demands of universal participation with those of the integrity of the treaty. That this would come to the fore ought not be cause for surprise: when it became clear that the contractual framework could be used both to deny and to explain normative agreements; and when it became clear that the bundle of bilateral

---

461 Reciprocity, so political scientists would later discover, can be divided into specific (contractual) reciprocity, and diffuse reciprocity; the latter would possibly help explain law-making ventures. Yet, the distinction proves rather difficult to operationalize. *See* R.O. Keohane, 'Reciprocity in International Relations', reproduced in his *International Institutions and State Power: Essays in International Relations Theory* (Westview, Boulder CO, 1989), p. 132, and C. Rhodes, *Reciprocity, US Trade Policy, and the GATT Regime* (Cornell University Press, Ithaca, 1993).

sets approach both could and could not be applied to normative instruments, something had to give. Both basic assumptions appeared not to work, so slowly, almost unrecognizably, the discussion moved in a new direction: away from unanimity, towards an acceptance of some form of majority decision-making on the acceptability of reservations. But here a new dilemma presented itself: how to reconcile the demands of universality with those of integrity?

4. THE GREAT DEBATE

The discussion within the ILC, based on Sir Humphrey's first report in 1962, started slowly, so slowly that the Chairman felt compelled to make the observation that no one had asked the floor and had to call on members to speak.[462] Yet, once it got under way, it turned out to be the first and only sustained (and lengthy) discussion of reservations.

The overriding sentiment guiding this discussion was that indeed there was room for allowing reservations. This followed, so many of the ILC members opined, from the increased number of States and, more generally, the development of international relations or 'the present international state of affairs'.[463] Reservations, so ran the general opinion, should be permissible, not only for reasons of high politics perhaps but also so as to come to terms with democratic concerns. As De Luna put it:

> 'Reservations should be permissible in order to enable a legislature to protect itself from certain legal consequences of a treaty submitted to it by the Executive, instead of having to face the choice between accepting or rejecting the treaty in its entirety.'[464]

And Tabibi went one better, expressing his conviction that States often reserve their positions for constitutional reasons and that objecting States ought to take this into account. They should not make objections for political reasons: 'machinery should be devised to obviate such abuses'.[465]

---

462 651st meeting, (1962/I) YbILC, p. 140.
463 So Pal, 653rd meeting, (1962/I) YbILC, p. 154.
464 652nd meeting, (1962/I) YbILC, p. 147. De Luna made a similar point at the 654th meeting, stressing that one of the factors necessitating reservations was the evolution from absolute government to democratic government, which entailed that negotiators might agree to things without popular backing. (1962/I) YbILC, p. 167.
465 651st meeting, (1962/I) YbILC, p. 144.

By making such comments, De Luna and Tabibi aimed at depoliticizing, and hence defusing, a highly explosive topic. Reservations, so they suggested, were mostly the result of legal incongruities, with domestic legal systems not yet ready to accommodate international legal standards.[466] The same spirit of depoliticization is visible throughout the discussion, with ILC members often resorting to drafting comments and suggestions without coming to terms with underlying issues first. That is not to say that all comments were thus inspired; but it is to say that quite a few of them were, enough to warrant the conclusion that depoliticization functioned as one of the red threads of the discussion in the ILC in 1962, and it paved the way for the solution later presented by Tunkin in conjunction with Rosenne. And as such, this attempt at depoliticization is of course far from surprising, if only because the ILC sees it (or at least saw it) as its task to draft instruments, something which automatically entails the making of drafting suggestions, and because international lawyers generally have a tendency to try and depoliticize things.[467]

Clearly then, the unanimity rule was finally dead and buried after the 1962 discussions in the ILC, but the mechanics of some form of majority rule remained to be devised with any degree of cogency.[468] Some from the ILC's ranks once again brought forward a private law analogy[469]; others however, most forcefully perhaps Rosenne, pointed out that such analogy was really misplaced, as private law does not know the type of instrument analogous to the multilateral law-making treaty, containing both contractual and legislative elements.[470]

Perhaps the most principled critique of Waldock's position came from André Gros, who questioned Waldock's conviction that a reservation would not make the position of non-reserving States less attractive. To Gros, reservations were capable of causing 'grave prejudice to the signatory

[466] The present discussion echoes this in its far greater willingness to accept temporary reservations: reservations which are deemed to be withdrawn as soon as domestic law is put in order. For an example, *see* Redgwell, *supra* note 25, p. 403.
[467] A perhaps somewhat extreme example is U. Hingst, *Auswirkunger der Globalisierung auf das Recht der völkerrechtlichen Verträge* (Duncker & Humblot, Berlin, 2001).
[468] And would be picked up predominantly at the 654rd meeting, (1962/I) YbILC; *see* Section IV below.
[469] Most explicitly perhaps Bartos, 651st meeting, (1962/I) YBILC, p. 142.
[470] *Ibid.*, p. 144.

states'[471], and for that reason he would seem to prefer the integrity of a treaty over its apparent universal appeal. And in unequivocal terms he concluded:

> 'The only genuine rule in the matter was that, in the residual case where the treaty was silent on the subject of reservations, the consent of the parties was necessary for the reservation to have any effect. A state did not have the right to make reservations, only a right to request reservations . . .'[472]

Tsuruoka sided with Gros, at least to some extent, and echoed a point made earlier by Lauterpacht concerning normative conventions. Labour conventions, so Tsuruoka held, while normative in that they aim to create abstract rules of general application and thus seemingly not resulting in disadvantaged positions in case of reservations, nonetheless might end up hurting non-reserving States. After all, a reservation to a labour convention might mean more relaxed labour legislation domestically and therewith a stronger competitive position.[473]

In retrospect, perhaps the decisive moment (as far as creating an acceptable regime is concerned) occurred sometime midway through the ILC's 653rd meeting, between 11:00 and 11:30 on 29 May 1962. Responding to a hint dropped by Tunkin on the possible effects of objections to reservations[474], Rosenne made the useful point that practice, at least since the *Reservations to the Genocide Convention* opinion,

> 'indicated that states objecting to a reservation often refrained from drawing the conclusion that their objection meant refusal to enter into treaty relations with the reserving state.'[475]

This chimed nicely with Tunkin's observation, made a few minutes earlier, that reservations 'usually related to relatively unimportant provisions'[476], and eminently lent itself for further elaboration into an acceptable legal rule. For if it is indeed the case that reservations usually relate to relatively

---

[471] 652nd meeting, (1962/I) YbILC, p. 149.
[472] *Ibid.*, p. 150.
[473] *Ibid.*, p. 151.
[474] Tunkin had claimed that each state should be free to draw its own conclusions when objecting to a reservation; 653rd meeting, (1962/I) YbILC, p. 156.
[475] 653rd meeting, (1962/I) YbILC, p. 157.
[476] *Ibid.*, p. 156.

unimportant provisions, then little will be lost by allowing the reserving State to nonetheless become a treaty partner while maintaining its reservation. Even if the reservation as such would be difficult to accept, it would usually not be important enough to preclude treaty relations.

This possibility was, with impressive speed, picked up by Tunkin again who, also referring to practice (as Rosenne had done earlier) pointed out that 'there were few cases where reservations were of such a nature or so numerous as to impair the universal character of a multilateral treaty'.[477] And when the next speaker, Jiménez de Aréchaga, also expressed his support for the idea that States should have the possibility to enter into treaty relations despite being in disagreement on a reservation made by one of them, and De Luna a minute or two later made a drafting suggestion to that effect[478], the matter was all but clinched, with only Roberto Ago, ever the jurist looking for neat and airtight solutions, still expressing dissent.[479]

The Tunkin-Rosenne construction had one great advantage: it suggested that somehow the seemingly opposed values of universality and integrity could be reconciled. In practice, reservations would usually relate to minor matters. Hence, on this presumption, the thought that reservations could actually ever undermine a treaty regime comes close to being ludicrous: if they merely relate to minor matters, then treaties would well survive them. Indeed, even better, without sacrificing integrity, reservations would make it possible to achieve universality or something close to it, even in the absence of agreement on the good life, as they would allow States to safeguard their interests on those minor points yet join the regime. Hence, Rosenne and Tunkin struck a double chord: a tepid, potentially non-universal agreement could become universal without losing its integrity simply by allowing reservations. This wonderful construction showed the ILC how to make the best of a difficult situation, so much so that after this agreement on how to handle objections to reservations had emerged, the remainder of the discussion in the ILC, while still occupying a full meeting (the 654th) was

477 *Ibid.*, p. 157.

478 *Ibid.*, p. 160.

479 Ago pointed to the danger of letting individual states decide on the acceptance of reservations. He was skeptical of the possibility that future treaties would contain clauses on reservations, precisely because of the often serious political divisions between states. *Ibid.*, pp. 160–161.

decidedly lacklustre. Tunkin and Rosenne[480] had shown the Commission a way out; a thorny problem had been solved[481], or so it seemed, and what was left to discuss was the overall drafting of the regime.

The one thing the ILC failed to reach explicit agreement on was whether decisions relating to the acceptability of a reservation ought to be left to the individual partners, or ought to be entrusted to some form of collegiate decision-making. Some of the members maintained throughout that sovereign States ought not to be submitted to decision-making by the majority, whereas others insisted that leaving it to individual States would amount to giving them *carte blanche*: they could make the wildest reservations and yet possibly get away with it.

Here too, however, the Tunkin-Rosenne suggestion provided useful services, at least to the extent that it underlined that reservations usually relate to relatively unimportant matters.[482] If this were truly the case, then there would be little harm in leaving States the freedom to decide for themselves. Instead of setting up an elaborate and inherently controversial mechanism of majority decision-making in order to solve the trivial, it might be wiser to let States decide for themselves. At any rate, as El Erian reminded the Commission towards the end of its deliberations, if States really fear reservations which would jeopardize the integrity of a treaty, 'presumably the negotiating states would insert an express prohibition against reservations to specific provisions which they regarded as essential'.[483]

In the end, the Drafting Committee submitted a proposal (draft Article 18bis) characterized by great flexibility. Under the proposal, deciding on the acceptability of reservations would be left to the individual treaty partners,

[480] Tunkin immediately claimed authorship of the suggestion, but it would seem fair to say that without Rosenne's intervention, Tunkin's suggestion might not have been picked up; not even by Tunkin himself.

[481] Sir Humphrey, curiously, referred to this as 'a minor issue'. Either he must have been preoccupied by other matters, or he spoke with a sense of irony lost on the reporter. 654th meeting, (1962/I) YbILC, p. 162.

[482] Thus, Jiménez de Aréchaga pointed out that Argentina often made a perfunctory reservation with respect to sovereignty over the Falklands. Surely, this only was relevant to the United Kingdom, and the UK would be reluctant to accept a majority decision accepting the reservation. 653rd meeting, (1962/I) YbILC, p. 158.

[483] 654rd meeting, (1962/I) YbILC, p. 167.

whereas objections to reservations would not preclude the entry into force of the treaty between the reserving and objecting States.[484]

Interestingly, the discussion on draft Article 18bis hardly, if at all, touched upon the problems of how to accept reservations and what effect to give to objections. Instead, two other issues assumed prominence: the possible distinction between general (or universal) multilateral treaties and restricted multilateral treaties and the by now familiar question whether a reservation incompatible with object and purpose would automatically be invalidated, or whether it could nonetheless assume legal force through acceptance.[485]

The Commission would adopt draft Article 18bis, in slightly modified form, during its 667th meeting.[486] Briggs, Tsuruoka and Gros dissented on paragraph 2, dealing with the method of acceptance of reservations and the effect of objections, with Briggs opining that 'it reflected the reactionary view that a state had a unilateral right to choose the law by which it would be bound.'[487] This dissent, so Sir Humphrey promised, would find expression in the ILC's Commentary.[488]

Sir Humphrey's next two reports did not specifically address reservations, but his Fourth report contained the observations of governments on the draft articles adopted by the ILC on first reading.[489] While the familiar issues made an appearance, no new arguments were put forward, with one exception: some States were wondering whether it would be possible to object to reservations on grounds other than incompatibility with the treaty's object and purpose.[490] *Mutatis mutandis*, the same applies to the discussions during the 1965 meeting of the ILC: no new viewpoints were presented, and the general tone and tenor of the Special Rapporteur's draft was deemed acceptable.[491]

A year later, the ILC presented its draft articles, with commentary, to the General Assembly.[492] The ILC by now had clearly opted, in draft Articles 16

---

[484] The proposal was presented at the 663rd meeting, (1962/I) YbILC, p. 225, draft Article 18bis, Paragraph 2.

[485] *See* 664th meeting, (1962/I) YbILC, pp. 229-234.

[486] 667th meeting, (1962/I) YbILC, p. 253.

[487] *Ibid.*, p. 253.

[488] *Ibid.*, p. 253.

[489] *See* H. Waldock, 'Fourth Report on the Law of Treaties', (1965/II) YbILC 3.

[490] *See e.g.*, Denmark, (1965/II) YbILC, p. 46, as well as the United States, *ibid.*, p. 47.

[491] *See* the discussion reported in (1965/I) YbILC, 143-178.

[492] *See* (1966/II) YbILC 173.

and 17, for the system whereby treaty partners shall for themselves decide on the acceptability of reservations made by others.[493] Moreover, there was generally no need for unanimous acceptance of a reservation[494], and the legal effects of an objection were held to depend on the intentions of the objecting State. While draft Article 17 formulates a presumption that an objection shall preclude entry into force between reserving and objecting States, nonetheless this presumption may be rebutted: the objecting State is free to formulate a different intention. The Commission explained its choice on this point by reference to what it seemed to consider to be the normal practice:

> 'Although an objection to a reservation normally indicates a refusal to enter into treaty relations on the basis of the reservation, objections are sometimes made to reservations for reasons of principle or policy without the intention of precluding the entry into force of the treaty between the objecting and reserving States.'[495]

With some changes in the wording, draft Articles 16 and 17 survived the Vienna Conference on the Law of Treaties intact, and became Articles 19 and 20 of the Vienna Convention. There was but one substantive change made in Vienna: the presumption concerning the legal effect of an objection had been reversed. Following a Soviet Union proposal, the presumption came to be that an objection would not preclude entry into force, unless otherwise indicated.[496]

5. SIR HUMPHREY TO THE RESCUE

In its 1966 report, the ILC advertised its proposed system on reservations as a flexible system. Rhetorically, that was a smart move: the opposite, in normal parlance, of flexibility is rigidity, and few would wish to be accused of being rigid. Moreover, a certain measure of flexibility could do justice to

---

493 With the exception of reservations to treaties establishing international organizations. In such cases, acceptance by the appropriate organ of the organization is required. For a fine study, *see* M. Mendelson, 'Reservations to the Constitutions of International Organizations', 45 *BYIL* (1971) p. 137.

494 Except in those cases, thought to be few in number, where it would appear from the limited number of parties and the treaty's object and purpose that the treaty was meant to be accepted as a package: draft Article 17, Paragraph 2.

495 *See* (1966/II) YbILC, p. 207.

496 For a brief discussion, *see* Sir I. Sinclair, *The Vienna Convention on the Law of Treaties* (2d edn, Manchester University Press, Manchester, 1984), pp. 62–63.

the enormous demands placed on a system of reservations: aiming to bind States without pinning them down too severely. In this light, the one change made at the Vienna Conference (to reverse the presumption following objections) makes perfect sense: if flexibility is to be attained, then there is little point in insisting that normally, an objection would preclude entry into force of a treaty between reserving and objecting States. Such a presumption would do little to stimulate flexibility; instead, it would err on the side of rigidity.

A number of fundamental issues run through the entire debate conducted within the ILC, and keeps coming back in different forms and guises without ever being conclusively resolved; and the chronological focus of the previous section illustrates neatly that as soon as one issue disappears from the unwritten agenda (either because it is thought to have been settled, or some compromise is reached, or because it comes to be ignored), something else comes up.

Initially, the first three Special Rapporteurs still worked on the basis of acceptance of reservations by unanimity. Not only was this the classic rule (and it bears emphasizing that the ICJ had limited the scope of its novel opinion on *Reservations to the Genocide Convention* explicitly)[497], but it also had the advantage of avoiding much of the problems usually affiliated with reservations. A system insisting on unanimity does not have to bother, e.g., about the legal effect of an objection, or whether acceptance should be left to each and every individual partner. Indeed, it need not even bother, strictly speaking, about any criterion to measure acceptability with. Still, enough questions would remain, even in a system of unanimity: perhaps for this reason Brierly was happy to limit his ambition to drafting model clauses, and Fitzmaurice, basing himself on eminently contractual notions, was convinced that an accepted reservation should also work to the benefit of the treaty partners in their relations with the reserving State: even where acceptance was unanimous, the effect of accepted reservations would be subject to reciprocity.

The contractual analogy works as a red thread throughout the discussions, but does not always do so in the same way. Sometimes it occurs in the guise of a question into the nature of (some) multilateral agreements: are they bundles of bilateral relationships, or are they something beyond this, and more akin, as Fitzmaurice himself apparently believed, to municipal

[497] *See Reservations to the Genocide Convention*, *supra* note 2, p. 20 (observing that the questions asked are all limited to the Genocide Convention).

law? At other times, the discussion was a more straightforward one, debating the opposition between contractual and law-making treaties, but eventually without concluding anything.

Perhaps the great virtue of Waldock's approach is its moderation: he introduced what may, somewhat disrespectfully perhaps, be described as a 'cafeteria-model' of reservations. Having given up the idea of unanimity, he had to face all those questions his predecessors could ignore or circumvent, and managed to combine something substantive (but not very hard) in the form of the subjective notion that States when they make reservations be guided by the treaty's object and purpose, with some respect for reciprocity (again, without taking this very far), and a basic respect for sovereignty, reflected in the idea that objections would preclude the start of treaty relations between reserving and objecting States. Moreover, he aimed to defuse the issue by playing down the impact of reservations.

Indeed, perhaps the biggest drawback of Waldock's proposed solution was that it may have been too moderate. At any rate, it is noticeable that his soft criterion of taking object and purpose into account hardened considerably under the influence of discussions in the ILC, while his stand on objections was considerably softened in the ILC and even more during the Vienna Conference.

By the time the ILC came to discuss reservations in 1962, the general climate was such that reservations were considered to be good things; today's 'necessary evil' was actually welcomed in the name of the progressive development of international law. Where Waldock had already downplayed their impact, others followed suit, outlining that reservations are made with the greatest care and usually not so much for political reasons but for reasons connected with domestic legal concerns.

But not all ILC members were convinced that reservations were a good thing. Tsuruoka, Briggs to some extent, and in particular André Gros, who must have possessed great intellectual and moral capital[498], were not terribly keen on reservations, but again mainly because of their adoption of a contractual prism: reservations upset the bargain between States.

As the gulf seemed unbridgeable, the focus shifted away from the acceptability of reservations *per se* towards the question of how to handle objections to reservations, and here the joint Tunkin-Rosenne scheme worked wonders: recasting reservations as neither good nor bad, but

[498] He would later be appointed to the ICJ and had been involved with the Nuremberg trials in various positions. On his role with respect to the latter, *see generally* T. Taylor, *The Anatomy of the Nuremberg Trials* (Bloomsbury, London, 1993).

somehow often unimportant, and disrupting international intercourse as little as possible by proposing that one might both object yet have treaty relations, precisely because reservations are rarely important. One can, in other words, have one's cake and eat it too. Having settled this thorny issue, attention could shift yet again, with a procedural issue gaining prominence again: should reservations be accepted by States on their own, or should some form of collegiate acceptance be devised?

Yet, in the end, after a decade-and-a-half of reports and discussions, in the end the same fundamental questions arose again. The late discussion on the distinctions between general multilateral conventions and restricted multilateral conventions was, once again, a re-opening of the unanimity discussion albeit in a more limited fashion: the very point of identifying a restricted multilateral treaty is, after all, that such would warrant application of the unanimity rule. The belated question whether an incompatible reservations is invalid *ab initio* and need not even be assessed by treaty partners is, by the same token, an attempt to limit the possible working of reservations by means of escaping from contractual shackles. In addition, once the governments became involved, they immediately raised the question whether incompatibility with object and purpose would be the only criterion by which to measure the acceptability of reservations, and that, in turn, represents an ill-disguised return to the very question of the permissibility of reservations. But most of all, the contractual perspective kept (and keeps) recurring: Brierly's early draft was based on a conception of treaties as contracts, and the same conception would come back in virtually every discussion on reservations, guided by the ineradicable sentiment that reservations somehow end up upsetting the balance reached by the parties.

6. ISN'T THAT IRONIC?

While it would seem that the contractual perspective proved inescapable within the ILC discussions on reservations, the various bodies endowed with the task of monitoring State compliance with human rights treaties have done their best to cleanse the law of treaties (or at least the law on reservations) of its contractual premises.[499] The precise reason is not quite clear: perhaps the treaty bodies feel that to approach human rights conventions as the result of bargains between States for their mutual benefit

[499] For an argument that the contractual perspective is inappropriate to multilateral treaties generally, *see* Horn, *supra* note 22, esp. pp. 22–24.

is somehow too vulgar to do justice to the ideals often thought to be underlying the evolution of human rights law.[500] Or perhaps the natural inclination is to somehow associate human rights with constitutional discourse; historically and conceptually, this would seem to make some sense, albeit perhaps in unexpected ways.[501]

An early instance hereof was the decision of the European Commission of Human Rights in *Temeltasch* v. *Switzerland*.[502] Approvingly citing earlier decisions of the European Commission and European Court of Human Rights which themselves had seized upon the conception developed by the ICJ in *Reservations to the Genocide Convention*[503], the Commission recalled that the *European Convention on Human Rights* is of a 'specific nature'[504], and aimed to 'establish a common public order of the free democracies of Europe'.[505] Hence, the obligations laid down in the Convention 'are of an essentially objective character'.[506] Indeed, 'the Convention comprises more than mere reciprocal engagements between Contracting States. It creates over and above a network of mutual, bilateral undertakings, objective obligations which . . . benefit from collective enforcement.'[507] This has by now become the standard approach: the European Court has the power to decide on the permissibility of reservations made to the European

[500] On this evolution, *see* P.G. Lauren, *The Evolution of International Human Rights: Visions Seen* (University of Pennsylvania Press, Philadelphia, 1998).

[501] *See* J. Klabbers, 'Glorified Esperanto? Rethinking Human Rights', 13 *Finnish Yearbook of International Law* (2002) (forthcoming), which advocates a formal conception of human rights as facilitating political processes. A related approach focusing on constitutional law is J.H. Ely, *Democracy and Distrust: A Theory of Judicial Review* (Harvard University Press, Cambridge MA, 1980).

[502] Decision of 5 May 1982, in 88 *International Law Reports* (ILC) 619. On the perspective and practice of the European system, *see also* article by J. Polakiewicz earlier in this book. – ed.

[503] *See Reservations to the Genocide Convention, supra* note 2, p. 23: with respect to a treaty such as the Genocide Convention, so the ICJ opined, 'the contracting States do not have any interests of their own; they merely have, one and all, a common interest, namely, the accomplishment of those high purposes which are the *raison d'être* of the convention. Consequently, in a convention of this type one cannot speak of individual advantages or disadvantages to States, or of the maintenance of a perfect contractual balance between rights and duties.' [italics in original - JK]

[504] *Temeltasch, supra* note 119, para. 62.

[505] *Ibid.*, para. 63.

[506] *Ibid.*

[507] *Ibid.*, para. 64. Note that the language used strongly suggests that a contractual undertaking is (morally) inferior to a public order conception.

Convention[508], which it derives, in part, from a conception of human rights treaties as being normative, non-contractual, in conjunction with the provisions of the European Convention itself on reservations.[509]

The Human Rights Committee, for its part, used a similar approach when it claimed the power to decide on the permissibility of reservations to the *International Covenant on Civil and Political Rights*. In its *General Comment No. 24*, the Committee specified that human rights treaties,

> 'and the Covenant specifically, are not a web of inter-State exchanges of mutual obligations. They concern the endowment of individuals with rights. The principle of inter-State reciprocity has no place . . .'[510]

And confronted with the question whether the *American Convention on Human Rights* could enter into force despite some uncertainty about the legal effects of reservations made to it, the Inter-American Court of Human Rights, in much the same vein, stipulated that

> 'modern human rights treaties in general, and the American Convention in particular, are not multilateral treaties of the traditional type concluded to accomplish the reciprocal exchange of rights for the mutual benefit of the contracting States. Their object and purpose is the protection of the basic rights of individual human beings . . . In concluding these human rights treaties, the States can be deemed to

---

[508] *See* especially *Belilos* v. *Switzerland*, supra note 13, and *Loizidou* v. *Turkey*, judgment of 23 February 1995 (preliminary objections), esp. paras. 70–77.

[509] Often, decisions such as *Belilos* are cited as being generally applicable to reservations without investigating whether *Belilos*, being decided at least in part on the basis of Article 64 (now Article 57) of the European Convention, can be transposed to the Vienna Convention's regime. An example is J.A. Frowein, 'Reservations and the International Ordre Public', in J. Makarczyk (ed.), *Theory of International Law at the Threshold of the 21st Century: Essays in Honour of Krzysztof Skubiszewski* (Kluwer, The Hague 1996), p. 403. In *Belilos*, moreover, the circumstance that the Swiss government indicated to accept severance of the contested statement may have made the Court's life considerably easier; as mentioned, *e.g.*, by Baratta, *supra* note 17, p. 420.

[510] *General Comment No. 24*, para. 17, reproduced *e.g.* as appendix 1 in Gardner, *supra* note 6. For the debate on the HRC and its *General Comment No. 26*, *see also* earlier in this book articles by M. Scheinin and E. Klein. – ed.

> submit themselves to a legal order within which they, for the common good, assume various obligations, not in relation to other States, but toward all individuals within their jurisdiction.'[511]

Thus, the treaty bodies seemed to have clearly adopted the position, following the ICJ's lead, that when it comes to human rights treaties, a contractual perspective is no good. This implies, that a contractual perspective on reservations is ruled out as well. Reservations cannot plausibly be objected to on the ground of upsetting the contractual balance, because it is precisely the very existence of such a balance that is so vehemently denied. Thus, other methods have been devised to come to terms with reservations.

One is the position, popular in British scholarship[512], that an impermissible reservation is invalid to begin with and therewith would not require to be objected to. This has the advantage of ignoring the need for objections, but the drawback that the system thus envisaged does not work, for how else can it be determined that reservations are impermissible except by means of objections?

Another method, insisting on the severability of reservations from the instruments of ratifications containing them, is equally difficult to envisage in practice in the absence of an authoritative third party determination, and is moreover in at least one of its manifestations based on the unproven but rather crucial empirical claim that States use reservations as bargaining chips.[513]

The great, and painful, irony is that in their zeal to rid human rights treaties of all contractual associations, the human rights treaty bodies have themselves closed off the possibility for States to utilize the only, or at least most legitimate, source of objections to reservations: it is precisely (perhaps

---

[511] *Effect of Reservations on the Entry into Force of the American Convention (Articles 74 and 75)*, advisory opinion, Inter-American Court of Human Rights of 24 September 1982, in 67 ILR 558, para. 29.

[512] *See e.g.*, A. Aust, *Modern Treaty Law and Practice* (CUP, Cambridge, 2000), esp. pp. 117–118; D.W. Bowett, 'Reservations to Non-Restricted Multilateral Treaties', 48 *BYIL* (1976–77) p. 67, and C. Redgwell, 'Universality or Integrity? Some Reflections on Reservations to General Multilateral Treaties', 64 *BYIL* (1993) p. 245.

[513] *See* in particular R. Goodman, 'Human Rights Treaties, Invalid Reservations, and State Consent', 96 *American Journal of International Law* (AJIL) (2002) p. 531. Note, incidentally, how this aims to ground claims relating to purportedly non-contractual instruments on contractual premises.

exclusively) when bargained balances are upset that States may have a legitimate complaint against a reservation. Anything else will inevitably suffer from the problem that it will be inspired not by considerations of reciprocity or elementary fairness[514], but by different sets of values. Put concretely: an objection to a sweeping reservation aiming to let Islamic law prevail over international commitments is always vulnerable to the critique that the objecting State is keen to uphold different values while aiming to prevent the reserving State from organizing its society in the way it sees fit.[515] By the same token, objections against reservations shielding the death penalty are inspired by serious differences of opinion on the morality of the death penalty rather than, as the Vienna Convention prescribes, resulting from any in-depth investigations into the object and purpose of the treaty to which the reservation is made.

A contractual perspective on human rights treaties would prevent this clash of values from overshadowing anything else. The objecting State would be in the comfortable position of having something tangible, yet morally neutral, to refer to: the bargain. Here, the objecting State would not need to tap into value judgments and moral philosophy, and could therefore not easily be accused of aiming to impose its values on other societies.

To conceptualize human rights treaties as somehow contractual in nature is not even all that eccentric to begin with, although it may initially sound implausible in light of the various statements of the human rights treaty bodies. One of the reasons why there seems to be general agreement that reservations to conventions drafted within the International Labour Organisation are impossible resides in what is said to be the contractual nature of such conventions. As the ILO's Director-General explained to the League of Nations Secretariat in 1927, the very point of labour conventions is to make sure that international competition does not affect labour standards, which entails that such conventions must be uniformly applied.[516]

---

[514] Rawls quite appropriately saw a connection between reciprocity and fairness. *See* J. Rawls, *A Theory of Justice* (OUP, Oxford, 1973 (first published in 1972)).

[515] This is perhaps most clearly visible with reservations to provisions on incitement to hatred, which usually aim to protect free speech, and reservations to economic, social and cultural rights. For a brief suggestion along these lines, *see* M. Schmidt, 'Reservations to United Nations Human Rights Treaties - The Case of the Two Covenants', in Gardner (ed.), *supra* note 6, p. 20.

[516] The memorandum by the Director-General is summarized in the commentary to draft Article 13 in the 1935 Harvard Research on International Law, volume III: Law of Treaties, published as a supplement to (1935) 29 *AJIL*, esp. p. 844.

Put differently, labour conventions function so as to guarantee that competition between States is not intensified due to their being able to advertise lower standards than their neighbours; the possibility of making reservations would jeopardize this lofty goal, and therewith reservations are not acceptable.[517]

Several ILC members saw indeed fit to think of human rights instruments (in particular labour conventions) in contractual terms, with none other than Lauterpacht – whose human rights credentials are quite impeccable – leading the way. And in recent years, some authors have ascribed the economic success of the Asian tiger economies precisely to their relative disregard for human rights: being ruled in authoritarian fashion, those economies can (or could) afford to ignore special interest groups and the public at large; would not have to bother too much about labour conditions or adequate standards of living or freedom of assembly.[518] One need not be overly cynical to suspect that much of the popularity of the distinction between liberal and illiberal States (and the resulting outlawing of the illiberal States) owes something precisely to the competitive advantage that illiberal States would enjoy while liberal States are hard at work to realize human rights.[519]

7. BY WAY OF CONCLUSION

Reservations, as noted, are easiest to handle when considered in more or less contractual settings, because in those settings States can always find a value-neutral argument with which to object to a proposed reservation: in a contractual setting, reservations can simply be condemned for upsetting the balance of the bargain underlying the agreement.

When treaties are conceived as non-contractual, this becomes far more difficult, as inevitably the objecting State will have to rely on its own values to sustain the claim that someone else's reservation is impermissible; and

---

[517] Additionally, as reservations are the sole province of governments, they could potentially undo the contributions made by employer and employee representatives to labour conventions. *Ibid.*, p. 843.

[518] Such an argument is parsed by B.R. Barber, *Jihad vs. McWorld: Terrorism's Challenge to Democracy* (Corgi, London, 2003 (first published in 1995)), p. 348, note 3 (citing the economist Overholt).

[519] Petersmann, *e.g.*, acknowledges that human rights discourse can be used ('abused', as he has it) for protectionist purposes. *See* E.-U. Petersmann, 'Human Rights and the Law of the World Trade Organization', 37 *Journal of World Trade* (2003) p. 241, pp. 280–281.

where such claims need to resort to values, one automatically ends up in the realm of politics and may have to face the possibility that it is simply impossible (or at least implausible) to posit the superiority of one's own values over those of someone else.

That is not to say that a contractual perspective is thus always preferable; instead, there may be good reasons to prefer a public order approach, the one outlined by the various human rights treaty bodies, for such an approach at least carries the promise (even if delivery is not forthcoming just yet) of a better world.[520] The contractual perspective, in other words, sets limits on the human imagination and the power of ideals to become reality, and it is surely no coincidence that much of the ILC debates can be explained as an attempt to escape from the contractual perspective. But the normative public order approach has the inevitable drawback that it drags the issue of reservations into the cesspool that politics is so often perceived to be. Still, that may well be the price to pay: reservations find their origin mostly in different political opinions, and there is fairly little to be gained by pretending those differences do not exist or are somehow subordinate to a set of legal rules. The tragedy is that reservations can only be fought with a contractual perspective, while the contractual perspective itself fails to satisfy the sense of idealism and progress inextricably bound up with human rights

This also implies that the often-relied-on dilemma of universality versus integrity is, in part, a false dilemma. There is not really contradiction between the two, any more than there is a contradiction between apples and oranges. The choice is not between universality or integrity; instead, the choice is about whether to accept other people's values or not.

Like so many issues (interpretation comes to mind[521]), the very debate over reservations is really a continuation of the treaty negotiations once the treaty has been concluded.[522] Connors has astutely observed that many of the reservations to the *Convention on the Elimination of All Forms of Discrimination against Women* were entirely predictable. States failed to convince others during the negotiations, and thus end up doing the next best

---

[520] Moreover, the contractual perspective is of limited use in other contexts within the law of treaties. *See e.g.*, J. Klabbers, 'How to Defeat a Treaty's Object and Purpose Pending Entry into Force: Toward Manifest Intent', 34 *Vanderbilt Journal of Transnational Law* (2001) p. 283.

[521] *See* Klabbers, *supra* note 19.

[522] As Allott has sharply noted, a treaty is 'disagreement reduced to writing'. Small wonder then that discord does not stop when the ink has dried. *See* Ph. Allott, 'The Concept of International Law', 10 *EJIL* (1999) p. 31, p. 43.

thing: they submit a reservation on the topics on which they were outvoted during the negotiations.[523] In a world of sovereign States, there is fairly little by way of community interest to fall back on when judging the permissibility of such reservations[524], and in the end there is not all that much evil about protecting one's own position, unless that position itself is inherently evil: but whether that is the case is a matter of political judgment, not something for technical legal analysis.

[523] *See* J. Connors, 'The Women's Convention in the Muslim World', in Gardner, *supra* note 6, p. 85. Imbert, *supra* note 22, p. 390, makes a similar point, noting that reservations mark a defeat during negotiations.

[524] Thus, Craven astutely observes that we can hardly avoid thinking in contractual terms 'as a result of a palpable lack of epistemic access to 'collective interests' when utilizing a methodology that begins and ends with individual states.' *See* M. Craven, 'Legal Differentiation and the Concept of the Human Rights Treaty in International Law', 11 *EJIL* (2000) p. 489, pp. 505–506.

THE POTENTIALS OF THE VIENNA CONVENTION ON THE LAW OF TREATIES WITH RESPECT TO RESERVATIONS TO HUMAN RIGHTS TREATIES

*Anja Seibert-Fohr**

TABLE OF CONTENTS

1. INTRODUCTION

Reservations to human rights treaties have been a continuing matter of concern not only in legal writing but also in the practice of the international human rights treaty bodies.[525] The reason, apart from the nature of some

---

* Anja Seibert-Fohr, LL.M., S.J.D. cand., Senior Research Fellow at the Max Planck Institute for Comparative Public Law and International Law, Lecturer at Mannheim University Law School

[525] For the vast literature on this issue *see e.g.* F. Horn, *Reservations and Interpretative Declarations to Multilateral Treaties* (North-Holland, Amsterdam, 1988); J.A. Frowein, 'Reservations and the International Ordre Public', in J. Makarczyk, *Theory of International Law at the Threshold of the 21st Century, Festschrift für Skubiszewski* (Kluwer, The Hague, 1996), p. 403; T. Giegerich, 'Vorbehalte zu Menschenrechtsabkommen: Zulässigkeit, Gültigkeit und Prüfungskompetenz von Vertragsgremien', 55 *Zeitschrift für ausländisches öffentliches Recht und Völkerrecht* (ZaöRV) (1995) p. 713; J.P. Gardner (ed.), *Human Rights as General Norms and a State's Right to Opt out: Reservations and Objections to Human Rights Conventions* (British Institute of International and

reservations, is the considerable number of reservations. There are, for example, more than 150 reservations, declarations and understandings to the *International Covenant on Civil and Political Rights* (ICCPR).[526]

Reservations are intended to facilitate the ratification of treaties.[527] Provision is made for deviations so that the respective domestic system does not have to conform immediately to all standards set out by the conventions. Taking into account the great number of States parties to the universal human rights treaties the objective to facilitate ratification can be said to be achieved. There are, for example, 150 States parties to the *International Covenant on Civil and Political Rights*.[528] The flipside of this coin is that the great number of reservations has led to a fragmentation of the human rights instruments. Practice has evidenced a common reluctance of States parties to change domestic legislation in order to withdraw from reservations. Instead reservations and declarations are repeatedly used to perpetuate the domestic legal *status quo*.[529]

In the following it will be argued that although there is a need to allow for reservations to comprehensive human rights treaties the leeway given to States to formulate a reservation is limited. The analysis of the drafting history shows that the drafters of the ICCPR were aware of the pros and cons of making room for reservations. The decision not to include a provision on reservations was informed by the will to allow for broad ratification. The

---

Comparative Law, London, 1997); R. Baratta, 'should Invalid Reservations to Human Rights Treaties be Disregarded?', 11 *European Journal of International Law* (EJIL) (2000) p. 413. For the Human Rights Committee *see General Comment No. 24/52 on Reservations (1994)*, in UN Doc. HRI/GEN/1/Rev.6.

526 UN Doc. E/CN.4/Sub.2/2002/34, p. 10–34 (2002).

527 This was affirmed by the International Court of Justice in its *Advisory Opinion on Reservations to the Convention on the Prevention and Punishment of the Crime of Genocide* of 28 May 1951.

528 Office of the UN High Commissioner for Human Rights, Status of Ratifications of the Principal International Human Rights Treaties as of 10 October 2003, at <www.unhchr.ch/pdf/report.pdf>, 15 October 2003.

529 The Human Rights Committee in its General Comment on reservations criticized that '[r]eservations often reveal a tendency of States not to want to change a particular law'. *General Comment No. 24/52 on Reservations (1994)*, para. 12, in UN Doc. HRI/GEN/1/Rev.6. This statement was later put into question by the United States because the unwillingness to change domestic law was described as a motive for a large majority of the reservations made under the ICCPR. *See Observations by the United States of America on General Comment No. 24/52 relating to Reservations*, (1994–1995), HRC Report, in: GAOR, Suppl. No. 40, Doc. A/50/40, Vol. 1, 131, in: 16 *Human Rights Law Journal* (HRLJ) (1995) 422 *et seq.*

absence of such a provision, however, cannot be seen as evidence for an unfettered discretion of States in formulating reservations.[530] Reservations need to be carefully evaluated in order to preserve the overall integrity of the treaty system. The 1969 *Vienna Convention on the Law of Treaties* (*Vienna Convention*, VCTL) provides ample guidelines for this evaluation. This will be demonstrated with the example of reservations subjecting human rights treaties to domestic law. The object and purpose of the respective treaty is a major guiding principle in the evaluation of reservations. Though concerns have been raised whether the Vienna regime suits the exigencies of human rights treaties as a *sui generis* form of international law it will be shown that the *Vienna Convention* offers potentials with respect to reservations to human rights treaties which have not been fully realized so far.

2. LEARNING FROM THE DRAFTING HISTORY OF THE INTERNATIONAL COVENANT ON CIVIL AND POLITICAL RIGHTS

The issue whether reservations to human rights treaties should be allowed and to what extent is not new. Due to the controversy about reservations under the *Genocide Convention* which was the subject of an advisory opinion by the International Court of Justice[531] the UN General Assembly called on the Human Rights Commission to include a provision on reservations in the draft *International Covenant on Civil and Political Rights* at the time.[532] This led to a continuing controversy within the Human Rights Commission and the Third Committee of the General Assembly during the drafting of the ICCPR. The question whether reservations should be allowed was closely linked to the question whether the Covenant should be immediately binding or whether a system of progressive implementation should be applied.[533]

---

[530] *See General Comment No. 24/52 on Reservations (1994)*, para. 6, in: UN Doc. HRI/GEN/1/Rev.6.

[531] *Advisory Opinion on Reservations to the Convention on the Prevention and Punishment of the Crime of Genocide* of 28 May 1951, *I.C.J. Report*, 1951, p. 15. *See also* Pechota, in L. Henkin (ed.), *The International Bill of Rights* (Columbia Univ. Pr., New York, 1981), p. 32 (52).

[532] GA Res. 546 (VI) of 5 February 1952.

[533] The British representative argued in the Commission that the Covenant should be immediately applicable and open to reservations. On the contrary, the French

In order to prevent the formulation of reservations to the Covenant Chile and Uruguay proposed a provision excluding reservations.[534] They were afraid that reservations would undermine the universality of the Covenant and that States parties could avoid their responsibilities by formulating reservations.[535] Since human rights treaties were not bilateral in nature there was the risk of a great number of reservations. Reservations were deemed to be incompatible with the idea of inalienable human rights. Instead of making allowance for reservations a period of transition was proposed in which the States parties should make the necessary legal changes.[536]

Other members of the Commission, however, favoured an immediate applicability of the Covenant.[537] Since most domestic systems were not in accordance with its human rights standards it was deemed necessary to allow for reservations. This would secure a broad ratification of the Covenant. The right to formulate a reservation was characterized as growing out of State sovereignty and therefore as a recognized principle of international law.

It is important to note that both lines of argument were informed by the aim to have the most comprehensive (that is broad and universal) application possible for the standards set by the Covenant. The fact that most domestic standards were not in accordance with those of the Covenant required a compromise. The drafters were confronted with the choice between integrity and universality. The difference between the two positions was due to a difference in the evaluation of the effects of making allowance for reservations. Those who opposed reservations pointed to the selective process and were afraid of the potential great number of reservations. In order to make ratification possible they favoured a period of transition for the progressive implementation of the Covenant. On the contrary, those who advocated the permissibility of reservations ascertained that such a progressive implementation would undermine the validity of the standards. Making reservations to single articles was deemed to be the lesser evil.

---

representative favoured a progressive implementation due to the risks following from allowing reservations. UN Docs. E/CN.4/SR.328 (23.6.1952), p.12; E/CN.4/SR.329 (27.6.1952), p. 4 *et seq*.

[534] UN Doc. E/CN.4/L.354 (25.3.1954), in: ESCOR (XVIII), Suppl.7, p. 29, para. 273.

[535] UN Doc. E/2573 (E/CN.4/705) April 1954, in: ESCOR (XVIII), Suppl.7, p. 29, para. 274.

[536] UN Doc. (A/2929), 1.7.1955, in: GAOR (X), Annexes, Agenda item 28, part II, Ch.X, para. 27.

[537] UN Doc. E/2573 (E/CN.4/705) April 1954, in: ESCOR (XVIII), Suppl.7, p. 30, para. 276.

The permissibility of reservations was finally determined with the decision in the Third Committee of the General Assembly that the Covenant should be immediately binding on States parties upon ratification. This required the possibility of making reservations. However, no agreement could be reached on the wording of a provision regarding reservations. While the Soviet Union favoured an unrestricted permissibility[538], representatives of China, Egypt, Lebanon and the Philippines advocated a provision which would allow only such reservations compatible with the object and purpose of the Covenant.[539] There was also discussion as to the legal effects of reservations and the relevance of objections.[540] The proposal by the United Kingdom to allow only for reservations which were not objected to by two-thirds of the States parties was later withdrawn.[541] This was due to objections that under international law there was a right to formulate reservations unless they were incompatible with the object and purpose of the treaty.[542] An objection to a reservation would normally prevent the entry into force of the provision concerned between the reserving and the objecting State party.[543] An explicit provision on reservations was therefore deemed to be unnecessary.

The survey of the drafting history shows that the drafters anticipated some of the current problems regarding reservations, namely the potential for disintegration of a treaty because of a great number of reservations and the legal consequences of objections. They were aware of the problems resulting from the application of the law on reservations to human rights treaties. Though the particularities of human rights treaties, that is the difference to traditional reciprocal treaties, and the idea of unalienable rights

---

538 UN Doc. E/CN.4/L.349 (22.3.1954); UN Doc. E/CN.4/L.353 (24.3.1954), in: ESCOR (XVIII), Suppl.7, p. 29, para. 272.

539 UN Doc. E/CN.4/L.351 (24.3.1954), in: ESCOR (XVIII), Suppl.7, p. 29, para. 271.

540 UN Doc. E/2573 (E/CN.4/705) April 1954, in: ESCOR (XVIII), Suppl.7, p. 31f, paras. 290–293.

541 For the identical proposal for the ICESCR *see* UN Doc. A/6546 (13.12.1966), in: GAOR (XXI), Annexes, Vol.2, Agenda item 62, p. 43, paras. 139. For the withdrawal *see ibid.* p. 45, para. 146; p. 142, para. 564.

542 UN Doc. A/6546 (13.12.1966), in: GAOR (XXI), Annexes, Vol.2, Agenda item 62, p. 44, para. 143.

543 UN Doc. A/6546 (13.12.1966), in: GAOR (XXI), Annexes, Vol.2, Agenda item 62, S.44, para. 142.

were stressed[544] reservations were not entirely ruled out. The fact that in the end no reservation clause was included illustrates the intent of the drafters to make room for reservations albeit in limited terms. The object and purpose criteria as being part of customary international law were deemed to provide for the right balance between universality and integrity.

It is interesting to note that the decision to allow for reservations was informed by considerations similar to the ones underlying the 1951 ICJ *Advisory Opinion on Reservations to the Convention on the Prevention and Punishment of the Crime of Genocide.* The ICJ explained in its Advisory Opinion that the Genocide Convention was intended to be a universal instrument. Therefore '[t]he complete exclusion from the Convention of one or more States would not only restrict the scope of its application, but would detract from the authority of the moral and humanitarian principles'.[545] Minor reservations were deemed to be permissible. But the desire to secure universal ratification could not be pursued at all costs. The object and purpose of the Convention was considered to be a limit for the formulation of reservations.

Some of the statements regarding the permissibility and legal effect of reservations during the drafting of the ICCPR, namely the required compatibility with the object and purpose of the treaty, reflect the system which later found entry into the *Vienna Convention on the Law of Treaties*.[546] In sum, the drafting history of the ICCPR can be taken as an argument for the application of the Vienna regime on reservations while accommodating the particular exigencies of human rights treaties. Although the drafters succeeded in their objective to provide for broad ratification the practice of formulating numerous and general reservations under the ICCPR cannot be said to be in accordance with the understanding of the drafters.

3. RESERVATIONS SUBJECTING HUMAN RIGHTS TREATIES TO DOMESTIC LAW

Over the last 27 years since the entry into force of the *International Covenant on Civil and Political Rights* numerous reservations have been formulated. Of particular concern are reservations and declarations which make human rights treaties subject to domestic law. An example is the

---

544 UN Doc. (A/2929), 1.7.1955, in: GAOR (X), Annexes, Agenda item 28, part II, Ch. X, para. 27.

545 1951 ICJ Report, p. 24.

546 *See e.g.*, UN Doc. A/6546 (13.12.1966), in: GAOR (XXI), Annexes, Vol.2, Agenda item 62, S.44, para. 142.

interpretative declaration by Kuwait regarding Article 2, paragraphs 1 and 3 of the ICCPR which provides that 'the rights to which the articles refer must be exercised within the limits set by Kuwaiti law'.[547]

A number of reservations by Islamic States, especially those to the *Convention on the Elimination of All Forms of Discrimination against Women* (CEDAW), provide that the Convention is only binding as far as it is not in conflict with Sharia law.[548] For example, the Government of the People's Republic of Bangladesh declared that it did not consider as binding the provisions of Articles 2 (condemnation of discrimination and adoption of policies to eliminate discrimination) and 16(1)(c) CEDAW (same rights during marriage) 'as they conflict with *Sharia* law based on Holy Quran and Sunna'.[549] Similarly, Kuwait declared with regard to the provision on marriage and family (Article 23, ICCPR) that these matters were governed by personal-status law based on Islamic law and that it would apply domestic law in case of conflict.[550]

More subtle measures are reservations depriving human rights treaties of their autonomous meaning. Examples are the reservations, understandings and declarations of the United States to the ICCPR.[551] The reservation to the provision on torture, cruel, inhuman and degrading punishment (Article 7, ICCPR) provides '[t]hat the United States considers itself bound by Article 7 to the extent that "cruel, inhuman or degrading treatment or punishment" means the cruel and unusual treatment or punishment prohibited by the Fifth, Eighth, and/or Fourteenth Amendments to the Constitution of the United States'.[552] With regard to Article 10 (Human treatment of detainees) and

---

[547] United Nations Treaty Collection (as of 5 February 2002), Declarations and Reservations. <www.unhchr.ch/html/menu3/b/treaty9_asp.htm>, 15 October 2003.

[548] *See e.g.*, Reservations by Afghanistan and Brunei with regard to the *Convention on the Rights of the Child, ibid.*

[549] *Ibid. See also e.g.*, the reservations to CEDAW by Egypt, Libya and Morocco, *ibid.* For more on the practice of CEDAW Committee, *see* article by H. B. Schöpp-Schilling in this book above. – ed.

[550] *Ibid.*

[551] For a detailed analysis of the US reservations and their compatibility with the Covenant *see* A. Seibert-Fohr, 'Domestic Implementation of the International Covenant on Civil and Political Rights Pursuant to its article 2 para. 2', 5 *Max Planck Yearbook of United Nations Law* (2001), p. 399 (440 *et seq.*).

[552] Senate Comment on Foreign Relations, Report on the ICCPR, S. Exec. Rep. No. 23, 102d Cong., 2d Sess. 6-20 (1992), in: 31 *International Legal Materials* (ILM)

Article 14 (Right to fair trial) of the Covenant the United States declared '[t]hat the policy and practice of the United States are generally in compliance with and supportive of the Covenant's provisions regarding treatment of juveniles in the criminal justice system'.[553]

The US reservations have been subject to repeated criticism.[554] Argument was made that they violate the rule that a party may not invoke its domestic law to justify non-compliance with a treaty and that they pose serious questions of good faith.[555] The US reservations were even held to be contrary to the object and purpose of the Covenant.[556] Despite the criticism other States have followed this questionable practice. Botswana, for example, when ratifying the ICCPR, in its reservation to Article 7 declared in 2000 that it was bound 'to the extent that "torture, inhuman or degrading punishment or other treatment" means torture, inhuman or degrading punishment or other treatment prohibited by Section 7 of the Constitution of the Republic of Botswana'.

These are only some examples for a number of similar reservations which concern not only the ICCPR but also other universal human rights treaties. In the following such reservations will be analysed under the Vienna

(1992) pp. 651–657 at p. 645). For the same reservation under CAT, *see* article by B. Sørensen and P. Dalton in this book above. – ed.

[553] The proviso which was not included in the instrument of ratification even provides: 'Nothing in this Covenant requires or authorizes legislation, or other action, by the United States of America prohibited by the Constitution of the United States as interpreted by the United States.' In fact, the spokesman of the former Bush administration declared that implementing legislation was not necessary, because, as a result of the reservations such legislation was unnecessary. *See* Senate Comment on Foreign Relations, Report on the ICCPR, S. Exec. Rep. No. 23, 102d Cong., 2d Sess. 6-20 (1992), in: 31 *ILM* (1992), p. 645 (657).

[554] For objections against reservations designed to keep the *status quo* under U.S. law *see e.g.*, the objections of Finland, 1993, and of The Netherlands, 1993. Some States interpret these reservations as not affecting the obligations assumed by States parties on the basis of Article 2. *See* Objections of Italy, 1993, and of Germany 1993. For this issue *see* the Chapter on severability objections.

[555] O. Schachter, 'The Obligation to implement the Covenant in Domestic Law', in L. Henkin (ed.), *The International Bill of Rights* (Columbia Univ. Pr., New York, 1981), p. 311 (322); F. C. Newman and D. Weissbrodt, *International Human Rights* (Anderson, Cincinnati,1990), p. 590.

[556] L. Henkin, 'U.S. Ratification of Human Rights Conventions: The Ghost of Senator Bricker', 89 *American Journal of International Law* (AJIL) (1995), p. 341 (343).

regime in order to show that the VCTL provides for adequate answers to such reservations to human rights treaties.

4. THE POTENTIALS OF THE *VIENNA CONVENTION*

4.1. The Object and Purpose Criteria

As indicated earlier, the major key in the evaluation of reservations to human rights treaties is the determination of the object and purpose of the treaty. The drafting history of the ICCPR gives ample evidence for this understanding. That the object and purpose is an important element in determining the admissibility of reservations was later recognized under the *Vienna Convention on the Law of Treaties*.

The object and purpose criteria provides for the necessary flexibility to take the special nature of human rights treaties into due account.[557] This can be illustrated with the example of reservations subjecting human rights treaties to domestic law. International human rights treaties provide for minimum standards in the protection of human rights. The underlying idea is to set up standards which are universally accepted, independent of national law and require domestic implementation. If the application of the rights enshrined in the conventions is subjected to their conformity to domestic law, the whole system is set upside down. The idea of universal human rights is put into question if States simply declare that a right must be exercised within the limits of domestic law or if the obligation undertaken under a treaty is equated with domestic standards. The very idea of universality necessarily entails the notion of an autonomous meaning. The point of departure for evaluating a State's compliance with a human rights treaty are the obligations laid down in the treaty, not domestic law. If a reservation has the consequence that one has to go back to domestic law in order to determine the legal obligation undertaken, a human rights treaty is deprived of its essential function of providing for *international* standards.

That general reservations are not acceptable was pointed out by the Human Rights Committee in its *General Comment No. 24* on Reservations of 1994. It elaborated:

---

[557] *See also* Second Report on Reservations to Treaties by the ILC Special Rapporteur, UN Doc. A/CN.4/477/Add.1, para. 129 (1996), also printed in this book. –ed.

> 'Reservations must be specific and transparent, so that the Committee, those under the jurisdiction of the reserving State and other States parties may be clear as to what obligations of human rights compliance have or have not been undertaken. Reservations may thus not be general, but must refer to a particular provision of the Covenant and indicate in precise terms its scope in relation thereto . . . So that reservations do not lead to a perpetual non-attainment of international human rights standards, reservations should not systematically reduce the obligations undertaken only to those presently existing in less demanding standards of domestic law. Nor should interpretative declarations or reservations seek to remove an autonomous meaning to Covenant obligations, by pronouncing them to be identical, or to be accepted only in so far as they are identical, with existing provisions of domestic law.'[558]

The General Comment was criticized by the United States, France, Great Britain and Northern Ireland on various grounds.[559] But none of these States took issue with the statement on general reservations. Indeed, the United States in its *Observations on General Comment No. 24* explicitly acknowledged that

> 'There can be no serious question about the propriety of the Committee's concern about the possible effect of excessively broad reservations on the general protection and promotion of the rights reflected in the Covenant, nor any reasonable doubt regarding the general desirability of reservations that are specific, transparent and subject to review with an eye to withdrawal where appropriate.'

---

558 *General Comment No. 24/52 on Reservations (1994)*, para. 19, in: UN Doc. HRI/GEN/1/Rev.6.

559 Observations by the United States of America on General Comment No. 24/52 relating to Reservations, (1994–1995), HRC Report, in: GAOR, Suppl. No. 40, Doc. A/50/40, Vol. 1, 131, in 16 *HRLJ* (1995) p. 422 (423); Observations by France on General Comment No. 24/52 relating to Reservations, (1995–1996), HRC Report, in: GAOR, Suppl. No. 40, Doc. A/51/40; Observations by the United Kingdom of Great Britain and Northern Ireland on General Comment No. 24/52 relating to Reservations, (1994-1995), HRC Report, in: GAOR, Suppl. No. 40, Doc. A/50/40, Vol.1, 135, in 16 *HRLJ* (1995) p. 424 *et seq*.

According to the United States it is 'neither appropriate nor lawful' to generally subordinate the Covenant to the 'full unspecified range of national law'.[560] It goes without saying that the United States did not consider its reservations to be of this character. According to its observations it was not unlawful to declare a discrete reservation in which a State party declined to accept a particular provision of the Covenant in preference for existing domestic law.[561]

This view, however, cannot be shared. Reservations providing for the prevalence of domestic law even if they concern only one particular provision cannot be described as specific and transparent. This is not to deny States a right to formulate specific reservations in order to clear the way for domestic deviations. Reservations are regularly formulated with this motive.[562] But this can and must be done without subjecting a treaty obligation to domestic law. Reservations need to spell out in concrete terms which specific obligation is not accepted so that the scope of the reservation is comprehensible without reference to domestic law.[563] A reservation is not specific only because it concerns a particular provision. It must also be specific and transparent in its content.[564] This also applies to reservations and declarations which provide that a State is only bound by a provision to the

---

[560] Observations by the United States of America on General Comment No. 24/52 relating to Reservations, (1994-1995), HRC Report, in: GAOR, Suppl. No. 40, Doc. A/50/40, Vol. 1, 131, in 16 *HRLJ* (1995) p. 422 *et seq*.

[561] *Ibid.*

[562] *See also* Observations by the United States of America on General Comment No. 24/52 relating to Reservations, (1994–1995), HRC Report, in: GAOR, Suppl. No. 40, Doc. A/50/40, Vol. 1, 131, in: 16 *HRLJ* (1995) p. 422 *et seq*.

[563] This is what the Human Rights Committee envisages when it speaks of 'specific and transparent' reservations. *General Comment No. 24/52 on Reservations (1994)*, para. 19, in: UN Doc. HRI/GEN/1/Rev.6. For further reasons why general reservations are unlawful *see* A. Sassi, 'General Reservations to Multilateral Treaties', in *Six Studies on Reservations* (Università Degli Studi Di Milano), p. 91 (106), XXII *Comunicazioni e Studi* (Rome, 2002).

[564] But *see* the US observations on *General Comment No. 24*. Though the United States accepted the specific and transparent requirement they advocated a different meaning of specific and transparent. Observations by the United States of America on General Comment No. 24/52 relating to Reservations, (1994–1995), HRC Report, in: GAOR, Suppl. No. 40, Doc. A/50/40, Vol. 1, 131, in: 16 *HRLJ* (1995) p. 422 *et seq*.

extent that the meaning of a provision is identical to the terms of domestic law.

Apart from the fact that reservations subjecting the application of human rights provisions to domestic law are contrary to the object and purpose of a human rights treaty, they are also counterproductive. To formulate reservations in specific and transparent terms should be in a States party's own interest. It avoids objections and the risk that the reservation is misinterpreted. If States parties want to ensure that their reservations are respected, that is to be treated admissible and valid, they should avoid subjecting the application of human rights treaties to domestic law.

4.2. Objections to Reservations

In the preceding chapters the advantage of applying the object and purpose criteria to reservations was elaborated. But the potential of the Vienna regime with respect to human rights treaties does not only lie in these criteria. The fact that States parties may object to a reservation is also an important measure in preserving the integrity of a human rights treaty. This will be demonstrated below with objections raised by States to general reservations.

The usefulness of objections to reservations to human rights treaties has been repeatedly questioned. The reason given is that as a result of an objection the provision to which the reservation relates does not apply as between the reserving and objecting States to the extent of the reservation.[565] While this may provide for an incentive not to formulate a reservation or to withdraw from a reservation in case of traditional reciprocal treaties, it is not so with respect to human rights treaties where the beneficiaries are not the States parties but the individual. Objections, however, may serve the interest of preserving the integrity of human rights treaties in another way.[566] They show that a reservation is not acceptable for other States parties; they build up pressure to withdraw the reservation and may even play a role in the evaluation of the admissibility of a reservation.[567] An important aim of objecting States is also to avoid that reservations set bad precedents.[568]

---

[565] Article 21, para. 3 VCLT.

[566] To be clear, not an absolute integrity is envisaged, but one which preserves the underlying ideas of a human rights treaty.

[567] For this issue see below the chapter on objections to admissible reservations.

[568] An example is the objection by Belgium to Congo's reservation to Article 11 ICCPR (prohibition of detention for debt). Belgium feared that a reservation to Article 11 as a non-derogable right would set a bad precedent which might have

1) Objections to Inadmissible Reservations

Most of the current objections concern reservations which are held to be inadmissible. There are a number of objections to such general reservations as described above.[569] An example is the objection by Finland to Kuwait's above cited declarations and reservation to the ICCPR. Finland criticised that by means of the declarations and reservation the application of certain articles of the Covenant was subjected to Kuwait's national law. According to the Finish Government

> 'such general reservations raise doubts as to the commitment of Kuwait to the object and purpose of the Covenant and would recall that a reservation incompatible with the object and purpose of the Covenant shall not be permitted. . . .
>
> It is the common interest of States that treaties to which they have chosen to become parties are respected, as to their object and purpose, by all parties and that States are prepared to undertake any legislative changes necessary to comply with their obligations under the treaties.
>
> The Government of Finland is further of the view that general reservations of the kind made by the Government of Kuwait, which do not clearly specify the extent of the derogation from the provisions of the covenant, contribute to undermining the basis of international treaty law.
>
> The Government of Finland therefore objects to the aforesaid reservations made by the Government of Kuwait

---

considerable effects at the international level. Objections by Belgium of 6 November 1984, United Nations Treaty Collection (as of 5 February 2002), Declarations and Reservations.

[569] Some States have adopted a more cautious approach, calling on the reserving State to clarify or specify general reservations. See e.g., Objections by Austria of 18 June 1996 with regard to the reservations made by Malaysia upon accession to the Convention on the Rights of the Child, in United Nations Treaty Collection (as of 5 February 2002), Declarations and Reservations.

> to the [said Covenant] which are considered to be inadmissible.'[570]

Other objections concern reservations subjecting the application of a human rights treaty to Sharia law or to domestic Constitutional law.[571] The above cited reservations by the United States also met considerable objections.[572]

The totality of these objections underlines the above given analysis that reservations subjecting the application of human rights treaties to domestic law are contrary to the object and purpose of human rights treaties. This concerns also reservations to single provisions. As Sweden in its objections to the US reservations, declarations and understandings pointed out:

> 'A reservation by which a State . . . limits its responsibilities under that treaty by invoking general principles of national law, may cast doubts upon the commitment of the reserving State to the object and purpose of the Covenant. The reservations made by the United States of America include . . . general references to national legislation. Reservations of this nature contribute to undermining the basis of international treaty law. All States Parties share a common interest in the respect for the object and purpose of the treaty to which they have chosen to become parties.'[573]

Such objections apart from elaborating on the meaning of the object and purpose of a treaty demonstrate that States parties have an interest in preserving the integrity of human rights treaties even if they are not immediate beneficiaries.

A considerable number of objections refer to the non-derogability of certain human rights in order to determine the admissibility of reservations.[574] The underlying idea is that rights which may not be

[570] Objections by Finland to the declarations and reservation to the ICCPR by Kuwait of 25 July 1997, in United Nations Treaty Collection (as of 5 February 2002), Declarations and Reservations.

[571] *See* A. Sassi, 'General Reservations to Multilateral Treaties', in *Six Studies on Reservations* (Università Degli Studi Di Milano), p. 91 (97), XXII *Comunicazioni e Studi* (2002).

[572] *See* United Nations Treaty Collection (as of 5 February 2002), Declarations and Reservations.

[573] Objections by Sweden under the ICCPR of 18 June 1993, *ibid.*

[574] *See e.g.*, the objections by Belgium to the reservation by Congo to Article 11 of the ICCPR:

derogated from even in times of public emergency may neither be subjected to a reservation. This, apart from the above given explanation, was one of the reasons for numerous objections against the US reservation concerning capital punishment for crimes committed by persons below eighteen years of age (Article 6, ICCPR) and the reservation to the provision on cruel, inhuman and unusual punishment (Article 7, ICCPR). As the Government of Finland put it 'according to article 4(2), no restrictions of articles 6 and 7 of the Covenant are allowed for.[575] In the view of the Government of Finland, the right to life is of fundamental importance in the Covenant and the said reservation therefore is incompatible with the object and purpose of the Covenant'.[576] According to Denmark Article 6 and 7 were, as evidenced by the non-derogability pursuant to Article 4, paragraph 2, the 'most basic rights' of the Covenant[577] and the reservations thereto were 'incompatible with the object and purpose of the Covenant.[578] The Netherlands shared this view on incompatibility. In the opinion of the Dutch Government the US reservations to Article 7 had 'the same effect as a general derogation from

> 'By virtue of article 4, paragraph 2, of the aforementioned Covenant, article 11 is excluded from the sphere of application of the rule which states that in the event of an exceptional public emergency, the States Parties to the Covenant may, in certain conditions, take measures derogating from their obligations under the Covenant. Article 11 is one of the articles containing a provision from which no derogation is permitted in any circumstances. Any reservation concerning that article would destroy its effects and would therefore be in contradiction with the letter and the spirit of the Covenant.'

Objection by Belgium of 6 November 1984, United Nations Treaty Collection (as of 5 February 2002), Declarations and Reservations.

575 Objections by Finland to the US reservations concerning Articles 6 and 7 of the ICCPR, United Nations Treaty Collection (as of 5 February 2002), Declarations and Reservations.

576 *Ibid.*

577 *See also* objections by Germany to the US reservations concerning Article 6 and 7 ICCPR of 29 September 1993. United Nations Treaty Collection (as of 5 February 2002), Declarations and Reservations.

578 Objections by Denmark to the US reservations concerning Articles 6 and 7 of the ICCPR. See also objections by Italy. United Nations Treaty Collection (as of 5 February 2002), Declarations and Reservations.

this article, while according to article 4 of the Covenant, no derogations, not even in times of public emergency, are permitted'.[579]

These objections show that some human rights treaty provisions are deemed to be of such importance that reservations to these are held to be contrary to the object and purpose of the Covenant.[580] Examples for such essential rights are the minimum standards for the protection of the right to life[581], the prohibition of torture[582] and the prohibition of discrimination.[583] It is interesting to note that some of the above cited objections go even beyond *General Comment No. 24* by the Human Rights Committee. The Comment elaborates that there is no automatic correlation between the admissibility of reservations and the derogation clause, but that a State has a 'heavy onus to justify' reservations to non-derogable rights.[584] Taking these statements together they provide evidence for a growing consensus that reservations to the most fundamental rights are not compatible with the object and purpose of human rights treaties which may even culminate in a corresponding customary international law rule.

The observations outlined above are only illustrative. They are evidence of an increased trend to object to reservations since the 1990s. Unfortunately, the right to object is exercised predominantly by European States. The Netherlands, Germany, Sweden, Austria, Denmark, Finland, Norway, Ireland, Portugal and Italy are at the forefront of this development.[585] Since 1996 there have been efforts by the European Union

---

[579] *See also* Objections by Norway and Spain to the US reservations concerning Articles 6 and 7 of the ICCPR. United Nations Treaty Collection (as of 5 February 2002), Declarations and Reservations.

[580] Objections by Finland to the US understanding pertaining to Articles 2, 4 and 26 of the ICCPR, *ibid.*

[581] *See* Objections by Germany to the US reservations concerning Article 6 of the ICCPR of 29 September 1993; Objections by The Netherlands to the US reservations concerning Article 6 ICCPR of 28 September 1993; Objections by The Netherlands to Thailand's declaration with respect to Article 6, para. 5 of 26 December 1997. United Nations Treaty Collection (as of 5 February 2002), Declarations and Reservations.

[582] *See* the above cited objections against the US reservation to Article 7 ICCPR.

[583] Objections by Finland to the US understanding pertaining to Articles 2, 4 and 26 of the ICCPR. United Nations Treaty Collection (as of 5 February 2002), Declarations and Reservations.

[584] *General Comment No. 24/52 on Reservations (1994)*, para. 10, in: UN Doc. HRI/GEN/1/Rev.6.

[585] Further objections have been raised by Belgium, France and Spain. At times Canada, Mexico and Australia, New Zealand have submitted objections to

and the Council of Europe to collectively screen and evaluate reservations to international treaties.[586] The EU Working Party on Public International Law (COJUR) discusses the issue of reservations on a regular basis.[587] In this Group legal advisers to foreign ministries of EU Member States exchange their evaluation of reservations to multilateral treaties with the aim to harmonize their responses to reservations.[588] A similar purpose is pursued by the Council of Europe with the Ad Hoc Committee of Legal Advisers on Public International Law (CAHDI).[589] It functions as a European Observatory of reservations to international treaties. For this purpose its Group of Experts on Reservations to International Treaties systematically examines and prepares reports on the admissibility of reservations to and interpretations of multilateral treaties of significant importance to the international community. The Committee is further called upon to propose ways and guidelines to assist member States of the Council of Europe with regard to responses to reservations and to consider the establishment of a systematic screening procedure with respect to inadmissible reservations.[590] As a result of its work the Council of Europe's Committee of Ministers adopted a Recommendation on responses to inadmissible reservations to

---

reservations. Under CERD there are a number of objections from non-European States. *See* United Nations Treaty Collection (as of 5 February 2002), Declarations and Reservations.

[586] On the work of the Council of Europe in this respect, *see also* article by J. Polakiewicz earlier in this book. – ed.

[587] For a detailed account of this practice *see* F. Cede, 'European Responses to Questionable Reservations', in W. Benedek, H. Isak and R. Kicker (eds.) *Development and Developing International and European Law, Essays in Honour of Konrad Ginther on the Occasion of his 65th Birthday* (Lang, Frankfurt a.M., 1999), p. 21 (27 *et seq.*).

[588] In practice resort has been made to standardized models of objections. This explains the similarities between the objections of European States against a number of reservations by other States.

[589] *See* F. Cede, 'European Responses to Questionable Reservations', in W. Benedek, H. Isak and R. Kicker (eds.) *Development and Developing International and European Law, Essays in Honour of Konrad Ginther on the Occasion of his 65th Birthday* (Lang, Frankfurt a.M., 1999), p. 21 (30 *et seq.*); S. S. Akermark, 'Reservations: breaking new ground in the Council of Europe', 24 *European Law Review* (ELR) (1999) 499.

[590] CAHDI (97) 14. Also: *supra* note 586.

international treaties which includes model response clauses to reservations.[591]

2) Severability Objections

Some of the recent objections even pronounce on the legal effects of inadmissible reservations. For example, Italy in its objections against the US reservation to Article 6, paragraph 5, stated that this reservation was incompatible with the object and purpose and therefore null and void.[592] At the same time, Italy did not consider the objections an obstacle to the entry into force of the Covenant between Italy and the United States. With regard to a reservation made by the Democratic People's Republic of Korea upon accession to CEDAW[593] the Government of Sweden objected holding it to be incompatible with the object and purpose of the treaty. While Article 28, paragraph 2, of CEDAW provides that reservations incompatible with the object and purpose of the Convention shall not be permitted Sweden went a step further. It considered the reservation null and void and ascertained that the Convention entered into force 'in its entirety between the two States, without the Democratic People's Republic of Korea benefiting from its reservation'.[594] Similarly, the Finish Government objected to Kuwait's reservations to CEDAW and noted that the reservations were 'devoid of legal effect'.[595] The severability doctrine was also expressed by further European States with regard to other universal human rights treaties, such as for example Denmark,[596] Belgium[597] and Norway.[598]

---

[591] Recommendation No. R (99) 13, adopted by the Committee of Ministers on 18 May 1999.
[592] Objections by Italy of 5 October 1993. United Nations Treaty Collection (as of 5 February 2002), Declarations and Reservations.
[593] The reservation concerned Articles 2, lit. f and 9, para. 2, of the CEDAW.
[594] Objections by Sweden of 25 July 2001. *See also* Objections by Sweden with respect to the reservation and declarations by Kuwait to the ICCPR, 23 July 1997. This approach replaced an older approach by Sweden with regard to the reservations by Maldives, where the Swedish Government considered that the reservations constituted an obstacle to the entry into force of the Convention between the two States. Objection of 26 October 1994. United Nations Treaty Collection (as of 5 February 2002), Declarations and Reservations.
[595] *See also* the Finish Objections regarding the reservations by Kuwait of 25 July 1997. United Nations Treaty Collection (as of 5 February 2002), Declarations and Reservations.
[596] Objections by Denmark with regard to the reservations made by the Botswana upon ratification of the ICCPR, 4 October 2001, *ibid.*

The Special Rapporteur of the ILC, Alain Pellet, in his eighth report on reservations to treaties of 2003 has put into question whether such statements qualify as objections within the meaning of the Vienna Convention.[599] The fact that these statements challenge the legal effects of reservations was deemed by the Special Rapporteur as 'contrary to the very essence of an objection'.[600] According to his definition '[o]bjection means a unilateral statement . . . whereby the State . . . purports to prevent the application of the provisions of the treaty to which the reservation relates between the author of the reservation and the State . . . which formulated the objection, to the extent of the reservation, or to prevent the treaty from entering into force in the relations between the author of the reservation and the author of the objection'.[601] This very narrow reading is problematic, taking into account that the above cited statements are clearly intended as objections. It is beyond doubt that they are not the kind of objections envisaged by Articles 20 and 21, because they deal with the issue of admissibility under Article 19 of the VCTL.[602] But they are clearly objections which include a statement regarding the legal effect of an inadmissible reservation. A definition which is not based on the purported legal effects but on the natural meaning of the word 'objection' is therefore preferred in the context of this article. It is to be hoped that in the search for the applicable rules on reservations such statements will not be left unconsidered by excluding them from the definition of objections.

So far, the Special Rapporteur apart from questioning the legal nature of statements which refer to the concept of severability has indicated his disagreement with the content of such statements. He held that they are 'hardly compatible' with the Preliminary conclusions of the International

---

597 Objections by Belgium of 4 October 2001 with regard to the reservations made by the Botswana upon ratification of the ICCPR, *ibid.*

598 Objections by Norway of 11 October 2001 with regard to the reservation made by Botswana upon ratification of the ICCPR; *ibid. See also* the Objections by Sweden and Norway of 2002 against Qatar's reservation to the *Convention on the Rights of the Child*, *ibid.*

599 Eighth report on reservations to treaties, UN Doc. A/CN.4/535/Add.1, para. 97 (2003).

600 *Ibid.*

601 *Ibid.* at para. 98.

602 For the difference between inadmissible and merely objectionable reservations *see* the chapter below.

Law Commission (ILC) on reservations to normative multilateral treaties including human rights adopted in 1997 or with the principle *par in parem non habet juridictionem*.[603] The preliminary conclusions leave the responsibility for taking action in case of inadmissibility of a reservation to the reserving State.[604] The work of the ILC, however, is not yet finalized. The final decision on the validity of such statements is explicitly left to further study when the question of the effects of objections is taken up.[605] In this study current developments will certainly not go unnoticed. In this regard it will be of interest that there are obvious parallels between recent State practice pronouncing on the legal effects of inadmissible reservations and *General Comment No. 24* where the Human Rights Committee elaborated that the consequence of an unacceptable reservation is that 'the Covenant will be operative for the reserving party without benefit of the reservation'.[606] This statement was contested by the United States[607], France[608], the United Kingdom of Great Britain and Northern Ireland on grounds of traditional principles of international law.[609] But the above cited statements by other States, along with the jurisprudence of the European Court of Human Rights show that this issue is currently subject to evolution.[610] This may even lead to a customary international rule with respect to human rights treaties filling the often deplored lacuna of the

---

603 *Ibid.* at note 154. Reference is made to the Arbitral award in the *Mer d'Iroise Case* of 1977, XVIII RIAA p. 42, para. 60.

604 Preliminary Conclusions of the International Law Commission on Reservations to Normative Multilateral Treaties including Human Rights Treaties, para. 10. in ILC Report of 1997, Chapt. 5, para. 157.

605 *See* Eighth report on reservations to treaties by Allain Pellet, UN Doc. A/CN.4/535/Addd.1, para. 97 and note 154 (2003).

606 *General Comment No. 24/52 on Reservations (1994)*, para. 18, in: UN Doc. HRI/GEN/1/Rev.6.

607 Observations by the United States of America on General Comment No. 24/52 relating to Reservations, (1994-1995), HRC Report, in: GAOR, Suppl. No. 40, Doc. A/50/40, Vol. 1, 131, in: 16 HRLJ (1995) p. 422 *et seq.*

608 Observations by France on General Comment No. 24/52 relating to Reservations transmitted by letter dated 8 September 1995, at paras. 12–13. (1995-1996), HRC Report, in: GAOR, Suppl. No. 40, Doc. A/51/40.

609 Observations by the United Kingdom of Great Britain and Northern Ireland on General Comment No. 24/52 relating to Reservations, at para. 15 (1994-1995), HRC Report, in: GAOR, Suppl. No. 40, Doc. A/50/40, Vol.1, 135.

610 *Belilos* v. *Switzerland*, (1987) 132 Eur. Ct. H.R. (ser. A); *Chrysostomos Case*, 12 *HRLJ* (1991) p. 113; *Loizidou Case*, 16 *HRLJ* (1995) p. 15.

Vienna Convention on the Law of Treaties with respect to the legal consequences of inadmissible reservations.[611]

3) Objections to Admissible Reservations

Unfortunately, the potential of formulating objections to reservations has not been fully realized. As indicated above, objections are usually made because a reservation is deemed to be incompatible with the object and purpose of a treaty. What is overlooked is that the objections may also be formulated with respect to admissible reservations.[612] The *Vienna Convention on the Law of Treaties* distinguishes between inadmissible reservations (Article 19) and reservations which are admissible but may be subject to objections (Article

[611] For the shortcomings B. Simma, 'Reservations to Human Rights Treaties-Some Recent Developments', in G. Hafner *et al.* (eds.), *Liber Amicorum- Prof. Seidl-Hohenveldern in honour of his 80th birthday* (Kluwer, The Hague, 1998), p. 659 (662–663); F. Cede, 'European Responses to Questionable Reservations', in W. Benedek, H. Isak and R. Kicker (eds.) *Development and Developing International and European Law, Essays in Honour of Konrad Ginther on the Occasion of his 65th Birthday* (Lang, Frankfurt a.M., 1999), p. 21 (21–23). In order to fill this lacuna a severance presumption is for example advocated by R. Goodman, 'Human Rights Treaties, Invalid Reservations, And State Consent', 96 *AJIL* (2002) p. 531. For this issue *see also* R. W. Edwards Jr., 'Reservations to Treaties: The Belilos Case and the Work of the International Law Commission', 31 *The University of Toledo Law Review* (*UTLR*) (2000) p. 195; R. Baratta, 'should Invalid Reservations to Human Rights Treaties be Disregarded?' 11 *EJIL* (2000) p. 413.

[612] *But see* ICJ *Advisory Opinion on Reservations to the Convention on the Prevention and Punishment of the Crime of Genocide* of 28 May 1951, at p. 24. The Court held that the compatibility of a reservation with the object and purpose of the Convention must furnish the criterion for the appraisal by a State objecting to a reservation. It feared that otherwise States parties would have the power of excluding a reserving State due to minor reservations. The interest of the ICJ was to secure a broad participation of States. Under the regime of the VCTL, however, an objection to a reservation which is compatible with the object and purpose is not that the reserving State is excluded. The interest of securing a broad application of human rights treaties, therefore, is not put into question by an objection. Nonetheless objections should be based on valuable reasons (reasons which are in the interest of human rights protection) in order not to lead to a fragmentation of human rights treaty.

20 et seq.).[613] This becomes apparent in Article 21, paragraph 1, which spells out the legal effects of reservations and objections. It only applies to reservations 'in accordance with articles 19, 20 and 23'. Thus, if a reservation is inadmissible pursuant to Article 19 because of incompatibility with the object and purpose of the treaty the legal consequences of reservations and objections spelled out in Article 21 do not apply.[614] The inadmissibility of a reservation is to be determined on the basis of objective grounds, namely the object and purpose of a treaty.[615] It does not depend on objections by other States parties.[616] That there is a difference between inadmissible reservations and those which are merely opposable is the underlying concept of the above cited severability objections which in effect did not refer to the legal consequences set out in Article 21 for objections but held reservations which are incompatible with the object and purpose of a treaty to be null and void.[617]

---

613 D. Bowett, 'Reservations to Non-Restricted Multilateral Treaties', 48 *British Yearbook of International Law* (BYIL) (1976–1977) p. 67 (88); C. Redgwell, 'some Reflections on reservations to general multilateral treaties', 63 *BYIL* (1993) p. 245 (254 *et seq.*); Horn, *supra* note 1, p. 121; B. Simma, 'Reservations to Human Rights Treaties-Some Recent Developments', in G. Hafner *et al.* (eds.) *Liber Amicorum-Prof. Seidl-Hohenveldern in honour of his 80th birthday* (Kluwer, The Hague, 1998), p. 659 (663). The Special Rapporteur of the ILC, Alain Pellet, speaks of the schools of 'admissibility' and 'opposability'. He refused to take a position on this issue in his Second Report on Reservations to Treaties. UN Doc. A/CN.4/477, para. 44 (1996).

614 G. Dahm *et al.*, *Völkerrecht*, Band I/3, (2nd. ed., De Gruyter, Berlin, 2002), § 148.

615 According to the United Kingdom the 'test of incompatibility is and should be an objective one, in which the view of competent third parties would carry weight'. Observations by the United Kingdom of Great Britain and Northern Ireland on General Comment No. 24/52 relating to Reservations, (1994-1995), HRC Report, in: GAOR, Suppl. No. 40, Doc. A/50/40, Annex VI, para. 15.

616 This is also the interpretation given by the Human Rights Committee. General Comment No. 24/52 on Reservations (1994), para. 17, in: UN Doc. HRI/GEN/1/Rev.6.

617 It should be noted that even traditional objections cannot be interpreted as an argument against the admissibility doctrine. The statement that on objection does not constitute an obstacle to the entry into force of the treaty between the reserving and the objecting state does not mean that the legal consequences of an inadmissible reservation are merely to be determined on the basis of objections. *But see* F. Cede, *European Responses to Questionable Reservations*, in W. Benedek *et al.* (eds.) *Development and Developing International and European Law, Essays in Honour of*

The distinction between inadmissible and merely opposable reservations does not mean that objections are entirely irrelevant if it comes to the question whether a reservation is admissible.[618] Objections may inform the question whether a reservation can be considered to be inadmissible.[619] It is an important form of State practice which evidences *opinio juris* and informs the meaning of 'object and purpose'. Therefore, objections have the potential of further developing the applicable rules on reservation.[620]

Turning again to objections to admissible reservations the following examples show that objections are not limited to reservations incompatible with the object and purpose of a treaty. France and The Netherlands objected to the declaration of India to the *International Covenant on Economic, Social and Cultural Rights* (ICESCR) according to which the right of self-determination applied only to the peoples under foreign domination and not to sovereign independent States or to a section of a people or nation. The

---

Konrad Ginther on the Occasion of his 65th Birthday (Lang, Frankfurt a.M., 1999), p. 21 (23).

618 Any reservation may be subject to an objection. The difference between inadmissible and merely opposable reservations are the legal consequences of an objection. The fact that there has been no objection does not render a reservation valid whereas the consequences of an objection to an admissible reservation is to be evaluated on the basis of Article 21 VCT.

619 It has even been argued by scholars advocating the admissibility doctrine that in absence of an international mechanism for the determination of admissibility the decision is up to the States parties. C. Redgwell, 'some Reflections on Reservations to General Multilateral Treaties', 63 *BYIL* (1993) p. 245 (264); B. Simma, 'Reservations to Human Rights Treaties-Some Recent Developments', in G. Hafner *et al.* (eds.) *Liber Amicorum- Prof. Seidl-Hohenveldern in honour of his 80th birthday* (Kluwer, The Hague, 1998), p. 659 (663). According to the Human Rights Committee objections may provide guidance to the Committee in its interpretation as to its compatibility with the object and purpose of the Covenant. General Comment No. 24/52 on Reservations (1994), para. 17, in: UN Doc. HRI/GEN/1/Rev.6.

620 The fact that a considerable number of States parties do not make use of the possibility to object cannot be interpreted as evidence for a contrary *opinio juris* because inaction may have different reasons. Most States do not object because they are not aware of a reservation or due to political reasons. Thus, the fact that a State party does not object to a reservation entered by another State party does not mean that the reservation is deemed to be compatible with the object and purpose of a treaty.

French Government objected because the declaration attached conditions to the exercise of the right of self-determination which were not provided for by the UN Charter.[621] The Dutch Government gave the following explanation for its objection to the Indian declaration:

> '[T]he right of self determination as embodied in the Covenants is conferred upon all peoples. This follows not only from the very language of article 1 common to the two Covenants but as well from the most authoritative statement of the law concerned, i.e., the Declaration on Principles of International Law concerning Friendly Relations and Co-operation among States in accordance with the Charter of the United Nations. Any attempt to limit the scope of this right or to attach conditions not provided for in the relevant instruments would undermine the concept of self-determination itself and would thereby seriously weaken its universally acceptable character.'[622]

Sweden objected to a similar declaration made by Bangladesh, pointing out:

> 'The declaration concerning article 1 places on the exercise of the right of peoples to self-determination conditions not provided for in international law. To attach such conditions could undermine the concept of self-determination itself and would thereby seriously weaken its universally acceptable character.'

The reasons for these objections were not grounded in the object and purpose of the ICESCR, but on principles to be found in other sources of international law. The concept of self-determination was considered to be pre-existing and indivisible. The objecting States feared that the reservation would give rise to a narrow construction of this international principle. Though no mention was made of customary international law, the objections again show certain parallels to the Human Rights Committee's *General Comment No. 24*.[623]

---

[621] United Nations Treaty Collection (as of 5 February 2002), Declarations and Reservations.

[622] Objections by the Netherlands of 12 January 1981, *ibid.*

[623] General Comment No. 24/52 on Reservations (1994), paras. 8,9 in: UN Doc. HRI/GEN/1/Rev.6.

4.3. The Vienna Regime and Current Practice

Though it has been questioned whether the Vienna regime on reservations suits the special exigencies of international human rights treaties the following needs to be considered: To accommodate the special exigencies of human rights treaties is not contrary to the *Vienna Convention on the Law of Treaties* but rather encouraged. The text of the Convention clarifies in several provisions that the evaluation of reservations depends heavily on the nature of a treaty. According to Articles 19 –22, the permissibility of reservations, the consequences of acceptance and objections to reservations, the withdrawal of reservations depend on the specifics of a treaty. Especially in applying the object and purpose test there is room to take the nature of human rights treaties into due account.

When it comes to the applicable rules for reservations to human rights treaties regard should be made to current State practice, especially the objections made by other States parties. The increasing number of objections shows States' willingness to stand up for the integrity of human rights treaties with regard to their object and purpose. At the same time, they evidence a trend to further develop the regime on inadmissible reservations. Though the lacking coherence of the objection practice and the inadequacy of State reaction to inadmissible reservations has been criticized[624], there are efforts, especially by European States to comprehensively scrutinize reservations and to harmonize their practice. This is done in institutionalised procedures for the evaluation of reservations which shows a growing concern about troublesome reservations.[625] This does not only concern European instruments, but also universal human rights instruments. Globally, there is at least evidence for a consensus among States and monitoring bodies that general reservations to human rights treaties are not admissible.[626]

---

[624] B. Simma, 'Reservations to Human Rights Treaties-Some Recent Developments', in G. Hafner *et al.* (eds.) *Liber Amicorum- Prof. Seidl-Hohenveldern in honour of his 80th birthday* (Kluwer, The Hague, 1998), p. 659 (664).

[625] F. Cede, 'European Responses to Questionable Reservations', in W. Benedek *et al.* (eds.) *Development and Developing International and European Law, Essays in Honour of Konrad Ginther on the Occasion of his 65th Birthday* (Lang, Frankfurt a.M., 1999), p. 21 (34).

[626] There are, however, divergent views on what exactly qualifies as a general reservation.

To be clear, the absence of an objection does not mean that a reservation is compatible with the object and purpose of a treaty. This is a question which needs to be determined on objective grounds. But this does not render objections obsolete.[627] As the above analysis shows objections serve several purposes. An objection is a statement intended to secure a comprehensive application of the treaty in question and to preserve its overall integrity. At times, objections have even given rise to a withdrawal of the criticized reservations. For example, Azerbaijan reformulated and narrowed its reservation to the *Second Optional Protocol* to the ICCPR aiming at the abolition of the death penalty after Finland, Germany, Sweden and The Netherlands had objected. This is certainly an incentive to make more active use of objections in the future in order to help preserve the integrity of human rights treaties and to further their application.

Though mention has been made of the shortcomings of objections which are bilateral in nature and therefore lack an *erga omnes* effect[628] the following should not be overlooked: Objections to reservations give insight into States parties' understanding about incompatibility. They have the potential to further develop the applicable rules for evaluating reservations. Taken together they shape the meaning of the concept of incompatibility which is reflected in Article 19 of the VCTL. Instead of deploring the shortcomings of the Vienna regime with regard to inadmissible reservations and their legal effects, use should be made of the existing ways to further develop the meaning of the 'object and purpose' criteria and the consequences of inadmissible reservations. It is to be hoped that the ILC will take the practice of objecting States into due account in the formulation of the applicable rules for reservations to human rights treaties.

It is interesting to note that there are parallels between the often criticized *General Comment No. 24* by the Human Rights Committee and a number of recent objections to reservations formulated under universal human rights treaties. It is thus fair to say that despite the criticism by the United States, the United Kingdom and France, the General Comment reflects in several aspects an understanding which is now shared by a number of States parties to the ICCPR.

---

[627] Though objections do not determine the admissibility of the concerned reservation, they have their own value.

[628] Simma even speaks of 'old bilateralist mechanisms'. B. Simma, 'Reservations to Human Rights Treaties-Some Recent Developments', in G. Hafner *et al.* (eds.) *Liber Amicorum- Prof. Seidl-Hohenveldern in honour of his 80th birthday* (Kluwer, The Hague, 1998), p. 659 (669, 679).

5. CONCLUSION AND OUTLOOK

In determining which reservations are permissible under the ICCPR the intent of the drafters to achieve the most comprehensive application of the Covenant standards should be taken into due account. It was not only in the interest of the drafters to facilitate ratification but also to bind the ratifying States as far as possible. Broad ratification was not to be achieved at all costs. Though the drafters wanted to make allowance for domestic deviations from single standards in order to facilitate ratification, the current practice of perpetuating domestic legal standards by formulating reservations is not in line with the aim to seek the most comprehensive application of the Covenant. In this respect a proposal by the United Kingdom is noteworthy. It called on the States parties to change domestic legislation in order to withdraw from reservations as soon as possible.[629]

The Vienna regime on reservations despite obvious lacunae offers several potentials with respect to human rights treaties. By allowing the formulation of reservations compatible with the object and purpose the objective to provide for a broad application of universal human rights treaties while preserving their essential integrity is adequately taken care of if properly implemented. The example of reservations subjecting human rights treaties to domestic law shows that the object and purpose test of the Vienna regime provides a valuable tool in the evaluation of reservations to human rights treaties. This test provides for the necessary flexibility in order to accommodate the special exigencies of human rights treaties. This was affirmed by the ILC's Special Rapporteur on Reservations, Alain Pellet,[630] and the flexibility approach will certainly be reflected in his future work.

Since the *Vienna Convention on the Law of Treaties* is silent on the legal consequences of inadmissible reservations and the competent organ to determine whether a reservation is admissible, it is open for development. It is just the question if this opportunity is realized and taken advantage of. Objections by States may inform the interpretation of what is the object and purpose of a treaty. They may even give rise to a customary international law regime specifying the legal consequences of inadmissible reservations. In this respect objections to reservations with regard to non-derogable rights

[629] UN Doc. E/CN.4/L.345/Add.1 (24.3.1954), in: ESCOR (XVIII), Suppl.7, S.28f, para. 267.
[630] Second Report on Reservations to Treaties, UN Doc. A/CN.4/477/Add.1, para. 129 (1996).

should be taken note of. What is advocated here is a development of specific rules on the basis of the general rules spelled out by the *Vienna Convention*. Thus, instead of deploring that the cup is half-empty, it is preferable to picture it as half-full focusing on the potentials for future development.

The current trend pursued by European States is a first step into the direction of developing a systematic approach by States parties with regard to reservations. It is to be hoped that more States will follow this example in order to enhance the coherence of State practice. Institutionalized procedures for the evaluation of reservations similar to the ones used by the European Union and the Council of Europe may prove to be useful also in other regions of the world.

The encouragement of States parties to object to reservations should not be understood as putting the role of international human rights treaty bodies in evaluating reservations into question. But especially those States parties which refuse to accept the competence of the international treaty bodies with regard to reservations should be prepared to play a more active role in the evaluation of reservations.[631] Each State party is called upon to continuously re-evaluate its own reservations and reservations made by other States parties in order to protect the overall integrity of the human rights treaties to which they are a party and to pursue the drafter's aim of broad application of the treaties. After all, human rights do not only concern the relationship between States and individuals but also the relationship among the States parties. International human rights treaties entail obligations *erga omnes*.[632] All States parties have a common interest to preserve the integrity of the treaty system established. Objections to reservations which endanger this

[631] The United Kingdom in its Observations on the Human Rights Committee's General Comment on Reservations elaborated on the limited role of the Committee in the evaluation of reservations and the determination of legal consequences. It held that more weight should be given to the views of the States parties. Observations by the United Kingdom of Great Britain and Northern Ireland on General Comment No. 24/52 relating to Reservations, paras. 9–12, 15 (1994–1995), HRC Report, in: GAOR, Suppl. No. 40, Doc. A/50/40, Annex VI. It is, however, deplorable that the United Kingdom has not made more use of this role of States parties in objecting to reservations.

[632] As the Human Rights Committee recently put it, 'every State Party has a legal interest in the performance by every other State Party of its obligations'. According to the Committee the Covenant enjoins the States parties to view violations by any State party as deserving their attention. Draft General Comment on The Nature of the General Legal Obligation Imposed on States Parties to the Covenant of 5 May 2002, UN Doc.CCPR/C/74/CRP.4/Rev.3, para. 1.

integrity, therefore, should be viewed as a measure in furtherance of this aim. They are expression of a common responsibility of every State party to stand up for the inviolability of the treaty system. The question thus is not whether States parties can be adequate guardians of the common interest of human rights treaties but how States should exercise this role in cooperation with the international monitoring bodies. The above described trend to increasingly scrutinize and object to reservations deemed to be incompatible with the object and purpose of human rights treaties is just one example of the growing understanding of a new role and responsibility of States in preserving their common interest in the protection of human rights.

RESERVATIONS TO TREATIES AND NORMS OF JUS COGENS – A COMMENT ON HUMAN RIGHTS COMMITTEE GENERAL COMMENT NO. 24

Ulf Linderfalk[*]

TABLE OF CONTENTS

1. INTRODUCTION

On 2 November 1994, the Human Rights Committee adopted *General Comment No. 24 (52)*,[633] which was clearly provoked by the great number of reservations deposited by States to the *International Covenant on Civil and Political Rights* (ICCPR) and its two *Optional Protocols*.[634] In this decision, the Committee states its opinion on a variety of matters. All relate to the permissibility and effect of reservations. Among the issues addressed is the question of how to determine whether a reservation is compatible or not with the objects and purposes of the Covenant and the two Optional Protocols. The question is of great import; for – according to a recognised rule of international law laid down in Article 19 of the 1969 *Vienna Convention on*

---

[*] LLD (University of Lund); Assistant Professor, Faculty of Law, University of Lund.

[633] 'Issues relating to reservations made upon ratification or accession to the Covenant or the Optional Protocols thereto, or in relation to declarations under article 41 of the Covenant', *General Comment No. 24*, adopted on 4 November 1994, by the Human Rights Committee at its 52nd session.

[634] The Comment opens up with the following statement: 'As of 1 November 1994, 46 of the 127 States parties to the International Covenant on Civil and Political Rights had, between them, entered 150 reservations of varying significance to their acceptance of the obligations of the Covenant.' (Para. 1.)

the Law of Treaties (Vienna Convention, VCLT),[635] – when a State finds itself in the process of ratifying or acceding to the Covenant or to any of the two Protocols, it may only make such reservations as are compatible with that treaty's object and purpose.[636]

Approaching in an uncommonly straight-forward way the task it had apparently set out to achieve, the Committee establishes a series of propositions:

(1) 'Reservations that offend peremptory norms would not be compatible with the object and purpose of the Covenant.' (Paragraph 8.)
(2) '[P]rovisions in the Covenant that represent customary international law . . . may not be the subject of reservations'. (Paragraph 8.)
(3) '[T]here is no automatic correlation between reservations to non-derogable provisions, and reservations which offend against the object and purpose of the Covenant'. (Paragraph 10.)
(4) 'A State may not reserve the right not to present a report and have it considered by the Committee.' (Paragraph 11.)
(5) '[A] reservation that rejects the Committee's competence to interpret the requirements of any provisions of the Covenant would also be contrary to the object and purpose of that treaty.' (Paragraph 11.)
(6) '[B]ecause the object and purpose of the first Optional Protocol is to allow the rights obligatory for a State under the Covenant to be tested before the Committee, a reservation that seeks to preclude this would be contrary to the object and purpose of the first Optional Protocol.' (Paragraph 13.)
(7) '[R]eservations relating to the required procedures under the first Optional Protocol would not be compatible with its object and purpose'. (Paragraph 14.)

Simple as it might seem, this list of propositions makes an important contribution to legal discourse. Certainly, not all propositions are such that they may be whole-heartedly adopted and acknowledged, at least not at face

[635] *UNTS*, Vol. 1155, p. 331 *et seq.*
[636] Article 19 reads as follows: 'A state may, when signing, ratifying, accepting, approving or acceding to a treaty, formulate a reservation unless:
(a) The reservation is prohibited by the treaty;
(b) The treaty provides that only specified reservations, which do not include the reservation in question, may be made; or
(c) In cases not falling under subparagraphs (a) and (b), the reservation is incompatible with the object and purpose of the treaty.'

value. On the contrary; several of them are counter-intuitive and clearly in need of further justification. Not surprisingly, therefore, the statement represented by propositions (1) through (8) has, since it was made been the subject of recurring scholarly attacks,[637] and the discussion appears to continue.[638]

This article is a contribution to the overall assessment of *General Comment No. 24*. It will focus attention on one of the less debated aspects of the Comment, that represented by proposition (1). Consider again the way it was stated: 'Reservations that offend peremptory norms would not be compatible with the object and purpose of the Covenant'. Quite clearly,

---

[637] *See*, for instance, W. Schabas, 'Reservations to Human Rights Treaties: Time for Innovation and Reform', 32 *Canadian Yearbook of International Law* (1994), pp. 39–81; W. Schabas, 'Invalid Reservations to the International Covenant on Civil and Political Rights: Is the United States Still a Party?', 21 *Brooklyn Journal of International Law* (1995), pp. 277–325; M. Nowak, 'The Activities of the UN Human Rights Committee: Developments from 1 August 1992 through 31 July 1995', 16 *Human Rights Law Journal* (1995), pp. 380–382; G. Jonathan-Cohen, "Les réserves dans les traités institutionnels relatifs aux droits de l'homme: Nouveaux aspects européens et internationaux', *Revue générale de droit international public* (1996), pp. 915–949; C. Redgwell, 'Reservations to Treaties and Human Rights Committee General Comment No. 24 (52)', 46 *International and Comparative Law Quarterly* (1997), pp. 390–412; B. Simma, 'Reservations to Human Rights Treaties: Some Recent Developments', in G. Hafner *et al.* (eds.), *Liber Amicorum- Prof. Seidl-Hohenveldern in honour of his 80th birthday* (Kluwer, The Hague, 1998), pp. 659–682; E. Baylis, 'General Comment 24: Confronting the Problem of Reservations to Human Rights Treaties', 17 *Berkeley Journal of International Law* (1999), pp. 277–329; R. Baratta, 'should Invalid Reservations to Human Rights Treaties Be Disregarded?', 11 *European Journal of International Law* (2000), pp. 413–425; Y.K. Tyagi, 'The Conflict of Law and Policy on Reservations to Human Rights Treaties', 71 *British Yearbook of International Law* (2000), pp. 181–258; G. McGrory, 'Reservations of Virtue? Lessons from Trinidad and Tobago's Reservation to the First Optional Protocol', 23 *Human Rights Quarterly* (2001), pp. 769–826; K. Korkelia, 'New Challanges to the Regime of Reservations Under the International Covenant on Civil and Political Rights', 13 *European Journal of International Law* (2002), pp. 437–477; R. Goodman, 'Human Rights Treaties, Invalid Reservations, and State Consent', 96 *American Journal of International Law* (2002), pp. 531–560.

[638] Proof of this, if anything, is the work done by the International Law Commission on the law and practice relating to reservations to treaties, reports and summary records are available at the ILC homepage <www.un.org/law/ilc/convents.htm#current>.

when a State makes a reservation to a treaty, and the reservation is in conflict with a norm of *jus cogens* ('a peremptory norm of general international law'), it will not have effect. This was observed some years ago by the late judge Tanaka in his dissenting opinion to the judgment of the International Court of Justice in the *North Sea Continental Shelf Cases*:

> [I]f a reservation [to article 6] were concerned with the equidistance principle, it would not necessarily have a negative effect upon the formation customary international law, because in this case the reservation would in itself be null and void as contrary to an essential principle of the continental shelf institution which must be recognized as *jus cogens*.[639]

Of course, Judge Tanaka was speaking of the 1958 *Geneva Convention on the Continental Shelf*,[640] and not of the ICCPR and its two Optional Protocols. But the argument he expresses applies with equal force to all international treaties.[641]

Hence, when a reservation is made to the Covenant or to any of the two Optional Protocols, and that reservation is in conflict with a norm of *jus cogens*, the interesting question is not so much whether the reservation shall have effect or not. Clearly, it shall not have effect. The interesting question to be dwelled upon is for what reason this is the case. The question is interesting since evidently it can be answered in two different ways. According to the first alternative – what we will here term as *thesis A* – if a reservation is made to the Covenant or to any of its two Protocols, and the reservation is in conflict with a *jus cogens* norm, it is to be considered a nullity, this being prescribed in Article 19 of the 1969 Vienna Convention.[642]

---

[639] *North Sea Continental Shelf Cases* (Federal Republic of Germany/Denmark; Federal Republic of Germany/Netherlands, Judgment of 20 February 1969, Dissenting Opinion of Judge Tanaka, *ICJ Reports*, 1969, p. 182.

[640] UNTS, Vol. 499, p. 311 *et seq.*

[641] *See*, for instance, M. Shaw, *International Law*, 5th ed. (Cambridge, 2003), p. 118; A. Casseese, *International Law* (Oxford, 2001), p. 144; T. Mann, *Further Studies in International Law* (Oxford, 1990), pp. 88–89; L. Hannikainen, *Peremptory Norms in International Law* (Helsinki, 1988), p. 149.

[642] Today, it is generally recognised that Article 19 of the Vienna Convention not only confirms the obligations of the States parties to that treaty. It is also reproduces a rule of customary international law that entails obligations for all States, whether they are parties to the Vienna Convention or not. For reasons of simplicity, I will

According to a second alternative – *thesis B* – the reason lies elsewhere: if a reservation in conflict with a *jus cogens* norm is to be considered a nullity, this is not because of Article 19 of the Vienna Convention, but because of some other rule of international law.[643] The thesis adopted by the Human Rights Committee is clearly the first of the two. I, for my part, make a stand for the second – thesis B.

In this article I will attempt to show that out of theses A and B the latter is the more well-founded one; consequently, the position taken by the Human Rights Committee should be looked upon with suspicion. To achieve this purpose, I will begin by making an inventory of the different arguments that can be adduced in support of thesis A and B respectively. Certainly, at least as concerns thesis A, it can be defended in more than one way. On a careful analysis, the matter indeed reveals itself to be a very complex one. Proposition no. 1 (in the list provided by the Human Rights Committee) – seemingly pertaining to the relationship between a reservation in conflict with a *jus cogens* norm and the rule laid down in Article 19 of the Vienna Convention – brings to the fore a number of difficult questions, concerning not so much the rules on reservations as the concept of *jus cogens* as such:

– What is the source of *jus cogens*?
– What does it mean for a treaty or a unilateral act to be in conflict with a norm of *jus cogens*?
– What is the effect of a treaty or a unilateral act being in conflict with a norm of *jus cogens*?

Depending on the thesis defended (A or B), these questions will be answered differently – a fact that I think needs to be brought into the open. Whether we finally opt for thesis A or thesis B, we will be making assumptions as to the concept of *jus cogens*. It is important that these assumptions be conscious. Second – to achieve the purpose set forth – I will investigate further into the different arguments put on the inventory, making them subject to evaluation. I will briefly indicate what I consider to be the pros and cons of each respective argument. By so doing, I will provide the reasons for finally concluding that, all things considered, the position

continue to speak solely about the provisions of Article 19 of the Vienna Convention, and not about the identically similar rule of international custom.

[643] *See*, for instance, L. Lijnzaad, *Reservations to Human Rights Treaties: Ratify and Ruin?* (Martinus Nijhoff, Dordrecht, 1995), p. 82.

adopted by the Human Rights Committee in its *General Comment No. 24* should be conceived of as groundless. As such, it should be discarded.

2. OBJECT AND PURPOSE CRITERION AS A MEANS OF PRESERVING THE *TELOI* OF A TREATY

Since the adoption of the 1969 Vienna Convention, the following description has been commonly used as the general definition of a *jus cogens* norm:

> 'a peremptory norm of general international law is a norm accepted and recognized by the international community of States as a whole as a norm from which no derogation is permitted and which can be modified only by a subsequent norm of general international law having the same character'.[644]

Clearly, if we decide to stand by this practice, a *jus cogens* norm will in most instances be a norm belonging to the realm of customary international law. According to some international law scholars, there is however nothing compelling about this observation. A *jus cogens* norm – this is what they suggest – might also be a norm laid down in an international multilateral treaty.[645] Adopting this view, we will have at our disposal an argument clearly (if only partly) in support of thesis A.[646] It will run as follows:

[644] Vienna Convention, Article 53.

[645] *See*, for instance, M. Shaw, *International Law*, 5th ed. (Cambridge, 2003), p. 118; K. Bartsch och B. Elberling, '*Jus Cogens* vs. State Immunity, Round Two: The Decision of the European Court of Human Rights in the *Kalogeropoulou et al.* v. *Greece and Germany* Decision', 4 *German Law Journal* (2003), p. 485.

[646] Of course, this very blunt qualification – 'if only partly' – needs to be further explained. The explanation is given below.

Premise 1	Some of the norms laid down in the Covenant and its two Optional Protocols have the character of *jus cogens*.
Premise 2	If a reservation is made to the Covenant or to any of its two Protocols, in accordance with the rule laid down in Article 19 of the Vienna Convention, then the application of that treaty, in the relationship between the reserving State and (at least) the parties that have decided not to object, shall be modified along the lines of the reservation.
Premise 3	A norm of *jus cogens* contained in the Covenant or in any of its two Optional Protocols must not be excluded or modified, if all the *teloi* of that treaty are to be attained.
Premise 4	According to the rule laid down in Article 19 of the Vienna Convention, a reservation to a treaty is to be considered a nullity, when applied along the lines of the reservation it would run counter to one of that treaty's *teloi*.
Conclusion	According to the rule laid down in Article 19 of the Vienna Convention, when a reservation is made to the Covenant or to any of its two Protocols, it is to be considered a nullity, when applied along the lines of the reservation it would run counter to a norm contained in that very same treaty having the character of *jus cogens*.

The argument consists of four premises. Premise (4) restates the commonly accepted reading of Article 19(c) of the Vienna Convention. According to the wording of Article 19(c), reservations to a treaty must not be made, if it is not of such a character as to be compatible with that treaty's object and purpose.[647] Of course, the exact content of the object and purpose criterion is still left to be defined.[648] However, it is a view generally held in the

[647] According to the provisions of Article 19 of the Vienna Convention, a prohibited reservation is one to which any of the following descriptions applies: (1) The reservation is of a kind expressly prohibited by the treaty. (2) The reservation is not of such a kind that according to an express provision in the treaty shall be allowed. (3) The reservation, not fitting any one of the descriptions above, is incompatible with the object and purpose of the treaty.

[648] *See* U. Linderfalk, 'On the meaning of the 'object and purpose' criterion, in the context of the Vienna Convention on the Law of Treaties, article 19', 72 *Nordic Journal of International Law* (2003), pp. 429–448.

literature,[649] confirmed by the practice of international courts and tribunals,[650] that by the 'object and purpose' of a treaty we shall understand at least that treaty's *telos* or (in plural) *teloi* – the State or States of affairs that the parties (according to what is assumed) intend to attain by applying the treaty. As concerns premise (4), then, its correctness can hardly be doubted.

Premise (2) is the commonly accepted reading of Article 21 of the Vienna Convention. According to Article 21, paragraph 1,

> '[a] reservation established with regard to another party in accordance with articles 19, 20 and 23: (a) Modifies for the reserving State in its relations with that other party the provisions of the treaty to which the reservation relates to the extent of the reservation; and (b) Modifies for those provisions to the same extent for that other party in its relations with the reserving State'.

According to Article 21, paragraph 3, '[w]hen a State objecting to a reservation has not opposed the entry into force of the treaty in relations between itself and the reserving State, the provisions to which the reservation relates do not apply as between the two States to the extent of the reservation'. Of course, it can be asked whether these rules apply to all international treaties – as suggested by the wording of the Vienna Convention – or only to some.[651] Take for instance the reservation made by the United States relating to Article 6 in connection with its ratification of the *International Covenant on Civil and Political Rights*:

> [T]he United States reserves the right, subject to its Constitutional constraints, to impose capital punishment on any person (other than a pregnant woman) duly convicted under existing or future laws permitting the imposition of

---

[649] For references, *see* U. Linderfalk, *On the Interpretation of Treaties*, chapter 7 (forthcoming).

[650] *Ibid.*

[651] The issue has been excellently analysed by the late professor Horn. *See* F. Horn, *Reservations and Interpretative Declarations to Multilateral Treaties* (Kluwer, The Hague, 1988), pp. 145–169. *See also* Korkelia, *supra* note 5, pp. 439–440.

> capital punishment, including such punishment for crimes committed by persons below eighteen years of age.[652]

The duty incumbent upon the United States under Article 6 is one towards all other State parties to the Covenant – it is an obligation *erga omnes partes*.[653] Let us assume that an American court decides that a person convicted of murder be sentenced to death, although at the time of the crime he was still underage. We would then have to say that the United States – given the traditional reading of Article 21 of the Vienna Convention – by the one and very same sentence, is acting towards some parties in violation of its obligations under Article 6, whereas in relation to others it is acting in perfect compliance with those very same obligations. In the eyes of international law, the sentence imposed would have to be considered both lawful and non-lawful. The question is whether this is at all a logical possibility. To avoid the dilemma, caused by the existence of obligations *erga omnes partes*, premise (2) has been phrased to include the traditional reading of Article 21 of the Vienna Convention as well as the more careful interpretation of the article as excluding from its scope all such obligations. Thus, premise (2) – like premise (4) – seems to form a very strong proposition.

The weakness of the argument obviously lies in the remaining two premises (1) and (3). First, as concerns premise (1), the assumption that a *jus cogens* norm can be a norm laid down in a treaty meets with strong opposition in the literature. It is generally held that a *jus cogens* norm, by its very definition, cannot be anything but a norm belonging to the realm of customary international law.[654] Second, even if we were to accept the

---

[652] United Nations, Status of Multilateral Treaties Deposited with the Secretary General, as of 29 January 2004. Available at <http://untreaty.un.org/ENGLISH/bible/englishinternetbible/partI/chapterXXI/treaty4.asp>.

[653] We should be careful not to confuse the two concepts obligations *erga omnes* and obligations *erga omnes partes*. (*See* L.A. Sicilianos, 'The Classification of Obligations and the the Multilateral Dimension of the Relations of International Responsibility', 13 *European Journal of International Law* (2003), pp. 1134–1137.)

[654] *See*, for instance, I. Brownlie, *Principles of Public International Law*, 6th ed. (Oxford University Press, 2003), p. 488; *Oppenheim's Internationa Law*, 9th ed. (Harlow, Essex, 1992), p. 1293, M. Byers, 'Conceptualising the Relationship Between *Jus Cogens* and *Erga Omnes* Rules', 66 *Nordic Journal of International Law* (1997), pp. 220–229, Mann, *supra* note 9, p. 86; J. Paust, 'The reality of *Jus Cogens*', 7 *Connecticut Journal of International Law* (1991), p. 81. *See also* the following statement of the International Criminal Tribunal for the Former Yugoslavia: 'Because of the importance of the values it protects, [the prohibition

suggestion that it is indeed possible that a *jus cogens* norm take the form of a treaty provision, no one provision in the Covenant and its two Protocols seems to contain such a norm. The number of States presently party to the three treaties – 151, 104, and 51, respectively – is simply too low.[655] Indeed, some norms contained in the Covenant and its two Protocols may very well be thought to have a counterpart in customary international law;[656] and some of those customary norms may very well be part of *jus cogens*.[657] But this in itself would not confer upon the treaty norms existing in parallel that very same character. Granted that a norm contained in an international multilateral treaty may have a content identical to that of a norm in international custom, the two norms are still being products of two separate legal sources, leading two separate lives.

Third, as concerns premise (3), it is obviously taken for granted that if a norm of *jus cogens* is contained in a multilateral treaty, then by the very character possessed by that norm it is necessary for attaining that treaty's *telos* or *teloi*. This is an assumption that does not fully accord with the contents of Article 60 of the Vienna Convention. According to Article 60, when a *material breach* of a multilateral treaty is committed by one of its parties, the other parties are entitled to invoke the breach as a ground for terminating the treaty, or suspending its operation in whole or in part, *the violated provision included*.[658] A material breach consists, *inter alia*, in '[t]he violation of a provision essential to the accomplishment of the object and purpose of the treaty'.[659] Given the assumption underlying premise (3), it seems that a violation of a *jus cogens* norm contained in a multilateral treaty,

---

against torture] has evolved into a peremptory norm of jus cogens, that is, a norm that enjoys a higher rank in the international hierarchy than treaty law and even *'ordinary'* customary rules.' (*Prosecutor* v. *Anto Furundzija*, ICTY Trial Chamber, Judgment of 10 December 1998, para. 153. Italics are added.)

655 United Nations, Status of Multilateral Treaties Deposited with the Secretary General, as of 29 January 2004. Available at <http://untreaty.un.org/ENGLISH/bible/englishinternetbible/partI/chapterXXI/treaty4.asp>.

656 *See* the very long list provided by the Human Rights Committee, in its *General Comment No. 24*, para. 8.

657 Conspicious examples include the prohibition of torture and the prohibition of slavery. *See*, for instance, the Commentaries of the International Law Commission to the Draft Articles on Responsibility of States for Internationally Wrongful Acts, adopted by the Commission at its 53rd session (2001), *Report of the International Law Commission* (A/56/10), p. 208, para. 5.

658 *See* Article 60, para. 2(a).

659 Article 60, para. 3.

committed by one of its parties, would entitle the other parties to suspend the operation of that very same norm (if not unilaterally, then at least by agreement).[660] The proposition is clearly incompatible with the definition of *jus cogens* as consisting of norms, 'from which no derogation is permitted'.[661] If a *jus cogens* norm were to be contained in a treaty and the norm was breached by one of its parties, this violation could not be used as an excuse for suspending the provision.[662]

Apart from the obvious weak points inherent in the two premises (1) and (3), there is still one difficulty that cannot be ignored in assessing the argument at issue. Even if we were to accept the argument in full, it is still not sufficient justification for the position that thesis A represents. According to the claim implicit in this thesis, a reservation made to the Covenant or to any of its two Protocols is to be considered a nullity when in conflict with a *jus cogens* norm, *whatever the source of that norm.* In the argument, we are instructed how to deal with situations where a reservation is in conflict with a *jus cogens* norm contained in the Covenant or in any one of its two Optional Protocols. But we are *not* instructed how to deal with situations where the *jus cogens* norm is a norm belonging to the realm of customary international law. If we finally settle for thesis A as being a perfectly sound proposition, and we consider the above argument to be part of the justification, one part is still missing. If a reservation is to be considered a nullity, not only in those cases where it is in conflict with a *jus cogens* norm contained in the Covenant or in any of the two Protocols, but also where the *jus cogens* norm is one belonging to the realm of customary international law, the question 'why?' is still left unanswered. This immediately brings us to the second section of this article.

3. OBJECT AND PURPOSE CRITERION AS A MEANS OF PRESERVING INTERNATIONAL PUBLIC ORDER

Even if we choose to accept – with the great majority of international law scholars – that a norm of *jus cogens* is a norm belonging to the realm of customary international law, thesis B does not necessarily follow. There are indeed other ways to substantiate thesis A. The justifying argument would inevitably take a different form, however. It would run as follows:

---

660 *See* Article 60, para 2(a).

661 The Vienna Convention, Article 53. *See also* above, Section 2.

662 Nor could it be used as an excuse for terminating the provision. *See* Vienna Convention, Article 42, paragraph 2.

Premise 1	Every norm of *jus cogens* is a norm belonging to the realm of customary international law.
Premise 2	If a reservation is made to the Covenant or to any of its two Protocols, in accordance with the rule laid down in Article 19 of the Vienna Convention, then the application of that treaty, in the relationship between the reserving State and (at least) the parties that have decided not to object, shall be modified along the lines of the reservation.
Premise 3	According to the rule laid down in Article 19 of the Vienna Convention, a reservation to a treaty is to be considered a nullity, when applied along the lines of the reservation it would run counter to a norm of *jus cogens*.
Conclusion	According to a rule laid down in Article 19 of the Vienna Convention, when a reservation is made to the Covenant or to any of its two Protocols, it is to be considered a nullity, when applied along the lines of the reservation it would run counter to a *jus cogens* norm.

Assessing this argument, little needs to be said about the first two premises. Premise (1) restates the general opinion prevailing among international law scholars.[663] Premise (2) is the commonly accepted reading of Article 21 of the Vienna Convention, already commented upon in the above section 1. Quite clearly, both are premises carrying considerable weight. Premise (3) is not as easily assessed. The relevant task is to identify the assumption or assumptions underlying the premise. What reason can be adduced to support the proposition that – according to the rule laid down in Article 19 of the Vienna Convention – a reservation to a treaty is to be considered a nullity, when applied along the lines of the reservation it would run counter to a *jus cogens* norm?

One possible answer would present itself, if we were to regard the provisions of Article 19 of the Vienna Convention as a means of preserving the very values represented by the *jus cogens* concept as such – often referred to as *international public order.*[664] The assumption is this: If a

[663] *See* above, Section 2.

[664] *See*, for instance, J. A. Frowein, 'Reservations and the International Ordre Public', in J. Makarczyk (ed.) *Theory of International Law at the Threshold of the 21st Century*, (The Hague, London, Boston, 1996), p. 411; C.L. Rozakis, "The Law on Invalidity of Treaties', *Archiv des Vökerrechts*, Vol. 16 (1974/1975), pp.

reservation to a treaty runs counter to a *jus cogens* norm it is considered a nullity, this being necessary for preserving international public order. International public order cannot be fully upheld, if reservations to treaties are not set aside when in conflict with a norm of *jus cogens*. Thus understood, the provision contained in Article 19(c) of the Vienna Convention – according to which a reservation to a treaty is allowed only insofar as it is compatible with the treaty's object and purpose – would be a means of preserving values external to a treaty. The object and purpose of preserving international public order would have to be conferred on each and every treaty made between States, no matter the content and subject matter covered. This appears to give treaties a role far greater than the one usually expected.

Doubts aside, let us assume for a moment that it is indeed the intention of States when concluding a treaty – whatever the content of that treaty – to preserve international public order. Other problems persist. Even if we accept as a perfectly sound proposition the assumption, upon which premise (3) is said to be based, the argument can still be made that the premise is only partly valid. According to the assumption, international public order cannot be fully upheld, if reservations to treaties are not set aside when in conflict with a *jus cogens* norm. If we consider the issue from the perspective of the States parties to a treaty, this assumption is clearly erroneous. Suppose that there is in customary international law a rule that makes the practice of torture illegal, and that this rule is part of *jus cogens*.[665] Let us further assume that a State S, in ratifying the *International Covenant on Civil and Political Rights,* reserves the right of military agents to continue practicing torture in accordance with domestic law, to the extent that torture is performed on the order of a superior officer.[666] And, lastly, let us assume

---

165–177; Mann, *supra* note 9, pp. 84–85, *et passim*; E. Wyler, 'From 'state Crime' to 'serious Breaches of Obligations under Peremptory Norms of General International Law', 13 *European Journal of International Law* (2002), p. 1150 *et passim*; A.J. de Hoogh, 'The Relationship Between *Jus Cogens*, Obligations *Erga Omnes* and International Crimes: Peremptory Norms in Perspective', 42 *Austrian Journal of Pubic International Law* (1991), p. 186.

[665] *See*, once again, the above quoted statement by the International Criminal Tribunal for the Former Yugoslavia in the case of Furundzija, *supra* note 22.

[666] Compare the reservation made by Chile to Article 2, paragraph 3, of the 1984 *Convention Against Torture and Other Cruel, Inhuman or Degrading Treatment or Punishment* at the ratification of that treaty. United Nations, *Multilateral Treaties Deposited with the Secretary General, Status as of 31 December 1989*, p. 186. The reservation has later been redrawn.

that the reservation made by State S to Article 7 of the Covenant is compatible with that treaty's object and purpose. Inevitably situations will occur where the obligations of State S under customary international law will be in conflict with its obligations under Article 7 of the Covenant. Such conflicts are to be resolved to the benefit of *jus cogens*. It is a recognised rule of customary international law, that in cases where a conflict occurs in the application of two rules, of which the one is a rule contained in an international treaty and the other a rule of *jus cogens*, the latter is to prevail.[667] Thus, it seems that from the perspective of the States parties to a treaty – considering the obligations incumbent upon them under international law in general – international public order can indeed be upheld, notwithstanding the fact that reservations to the treaty, when in conflict with a *jus cogens* norm, are not considered as nullities.

A somewhat different picture emerges if we instead were to take the perspective of a treaty monitoring body such as the Human Rights Committee. Consider again the reservation made by State S to Article 7 of the Covenant. It might be that there is a conflict between the obligations of State S under Article 7 and its obligations under customary international law; and it might be that this conflict shall be resolved to the benefit of the latter since they derive from a *jus cogens* norm. But, from the perspective of the Human Rights Committee, this is entirely irrelevant. Under the Covenant, the Human Rights Committee is given the power to monitor compliance with the rights recognised therein. In considering reports submitted by State S under Article 40 of the Covenant – possibly also communications submitted under the First Optional Protocol – it may state its opinion as to whether State S is fulfilling its obligations under Article 7 of the Covenant. It may *not* state its opinion as to whether State S is fulfilling its obligations under customary international law. Thus, from the perspective of the Human Rights Committee – considering the powers given to it under the Covenant and its two Optional Protocols – it seems that international law cannot be fully upheld, if reservations to treaties are not set aside when in conflict with a *jus cogens* norm.

---

[667] *See*, for instance, the following statement recently made by the International Law Commission: 'Where there is an apparent conflict between primary obligations, one of which arises for a State directly under a peremptory norm of general international law, it is evident that such an obligation must prevail.' (Draft Articles on the Responsibility of States for Internationally Wrongful Acts, with Commentaries, adopted by the ILC at its 53rd session (2001), *Report of the International Law Commission* (A/56/10), p. 207, para. 3.)

In sum, then, the soundness of premise (3) obviously depends on whether thesis A is seen as a proposition confined to the application of the International Covenant and its two Protocols, or as a general proposition valid for all international treaties irrespective of their content. If we opt for the former alternative, we have to face up to the fact that from the perspective of general legal discourse thesis A will not be of very great interest. If, on the other hand, we opt for the latter alternative, then, of course, the reason that makes premise (3) into an acceptable proposition is still left to be identified. Surely, if the provisions of Article 19(c) of the Vienna Convention are to be regarded as a means of preserving international public order, then the latter alternative emerges as the more appealing. Hence, let us turn our attention to the next section of this article

4. OBJECT AND PURPOSE CRITERION AS A MEANS OF PRESERVING THE CONTINUED EXISTENCE OF A TREATY

We will not rashly do away with the argument, over which we have been carefully pondering in the above section 2. Accepting the conclusion that the provisions of Article 19(c) of the Vienna Convention are *not* to be regarded as a means for the preservation of international public order, there is still one possible way of rescuing premise (3). Let us return to the imaginary case of State S:

> State S is a party to the *International Covenant on Civil and Political Rights*. It has reserved the right of military agents to continue practicing torture in accordance with domestic law, to the extent that torture is performed on the order of a superior officer. The reservation made by State S to Article 7 of the Covenant – although in conflict with a *jus cogens* norm – is compatible with the object and purpose of the Covenant.

According to the provisions of Article 21 of the Vienna Convention, the reservation of State S would be modifying the content of Article 7 in the relationship between State S and (at least) the parties that have decided not to object. Thus, in the relationship between these very same States the Covenant would be in conflict with a norm of *jus cogens*. It is arguable that in a situation like this, the provisions of Article 53 of the Vienna Convention apply. Given that they do, the Covenant – as a consequence of State S' reservation – would be null and void, not only in the relationship between State S and the parties that have decided not to object, but as between all

States parties to the treaty.[668] Assumedly, this is something that the parties wish to avoid. Hence the assumption: if a reservation to a treaty is in conflict with a *jus cogens* norm, it is to be considered a nullity, this being necessary for preserving the treaty's very existence.

Thus understood, the provisions of Article 19(c) of the Vienna Convention would be turned into a means of preserving values that are no longer external to a treaty – as suggested in the above section 2 – but *internal*. As already noted, there are strong reasons to reject the assumption that it be the object and purpose of treaties in general to preserve international public order, no matter their content. However, I take it no one would argue against me if I suggested that, whatever the treaty, it is the object and purpose of that instrument to ensure that its entire existence does not turn on the making of single reservations. In that sense, the latter proposition is a far more promising alternative.

This is not to say that the proposition is free from all difficulties. First of all, the argument may be made that if it is the object and purpose of a treaty to ensure that its entire existence does not turn on the making of single reservations, then surely there are other means to fulfil that intention than the ones envisaged in Article 53 of the Vienna Convention. If it is clear to everyone that a reservation to a treaty is at variance with a *jus cogens* norm, and the parties wish to prevent the treaty from turning into a complete nullity, then they may easily do so by objecting to the reservation. The argument does not convince. According to the commonly accepted reading of Article 21 of the Vienna Convention, objections to a reservation will only preclude the effect of that act in the relationship between the reserving State and the objecting State or States.[669] Hence, to prevent the situation described in Article 53 from occurring, it is not enough that a great number of parties to a treaty object to a reservation. *All* parties need to object. This seems to

[668] The conclusion is based on the implicit assumption that the reservation of State S is made at the time of the Covenant's 'conclusion'. When the treaty is concluded, the rule of *jus cogens* already exists. But it is also possible that the rule of *jus cogens* is developed later, after the conclusion of the Covenant. In that case, the applicable rule would not be that of Article 53 but of Article 64 of the Vienna Convention. The Covenant would then necessarily not be null and void in its entirety. Granted that the conflict is due only to a particular clause of the Covenant, or to a few particular clauses, it is possible that the clause or clauses in question is severed from the Covenant and the remainder retained. (Compare the provisions of Vienna Convention, Article 44.) Article 19(c) would then have to be seen as a means of preserving the existence, not of the entire Covenant, but only of particular clauses.

[669] *See* the qualifications above, Section 2.

demand too much. We have to remember that for a State to be able to consistently object to reservations according to the standard of *jus cogens*, some very careful monitoring is required. The treaties to which the State is a party may be counted in the thousands – each and every reservation made to each and every one of those treaties has to be analysed and assessed. This is indeed a very time-consuming task requiring vast resources. It is a fact of life that such resources are not held by all States.

A more serious objection to the view of Article 19(c) of the Vienna Convention as a means of preserving the very existence of a treaty is the observation that it is based on a rather precarious interpretation of Article 53 of the Vienna Convention. Reading the text of Article 53 – 'A treaty is void if, at the time of its conclusion, it conflicts with a peremptory norm of general international law' – two questions arise. A first question concerns the meaning of 'treaty'. What is the situation envisaged in Article 53, when speaking of a conflict between a *jus cogens* norm and a *treaty*? Does it really include situations of the kind here confronted? The suggestion that the provisions of Article 19(c) of the Vienna Convention should be seen as a means of preserving a treaty's existence obviously presupposes a very specific idea of a treaty. A treaty is defined as consisting of a series of bilateral legal relationships. There is no one treaty apart from the number of bilateral relationships created by States when consenting to be bound. A treaty – this is the assumption – is in conflict with a *jus cogens* norm as soon as there is one single bilateral relationship that does not live up to the standards inherent in that concept. In the literature this is an assumption that meets with very strong opposition. It is simply not the way Article 53 generally is understood. Commenting upon the content of Articles 46–53 of the Vienna Convention – setting forth the various grounds of invalidity – writers tend to distinguish between Articles 46–51, on the one hand, and Articles 52–53, on the other hand, the former being designed to address defects in a party's consent, the latter dealing with defects in the treaty as such.[670] Clearly, reservations in conflict with a *jus cogens* norm belong in the former category and not in the latter.

A second question provoked by reading the text of Article 53 of the Vienna Convention concerns the meaning of a treaty's 'conclusion'. What, more specifically, is it that allows us to talk about a certain point in time, or a certain time period, as the 'conclusion' of a treaty? Considering the language of the Vienna Convention in general, the question may be

[670] *See* Rozakis, *supra* note 32, pp. 170–171.

answered in three different ways.[671] The 'conclusion' of a treaty might refer to the point in time when the treaty was established as definite; it might refer to the time period from when negotiations on the treaty started to when the treaty first entered into force; or it might refer to the time period from when negotiations on the treaty started to when the treaty entered into force for each respective party.[672] The suggestion that the provisions of Article 19(c) of the Vienna Convention should be seen as a means of preserving a treaty's very existence clearly presupposes the last of these three alternatives. This is however a reading that does not fit very well with the context of Article 53. Article 53 – let us repeat – reads as follows: 'A treaty is void if, at the time of its conclusion, it conflicts with a peremptory norm of general international law'. According to the ordinary meaning of this text, a treaty in conflict with a *jus cogens* norm will be considered a nullity already from the outset.[673] If the 'conclusion' of a treaty, in the sense of Article 53, is defined according to the alternative indicated above, there is the possibility of a treaty entering into force and remaining in force up to a certain time, when all of a sudden – as a consequence of a newly made reservation – it becomes void and terminates. Thus, the distinction between the two different types of situations described in Articles 53 and 64 respectively will be almost entirely blurred.

All things considered, I find it difficult indeed to accept that the provisions of Article 19(c) of the Vienna Convention should be looked upon as a means for the preservation of a treaty's existence. Given that the provisions are not to be regarded as a means for the preservation of a treaty's *teloi*, nor as a means for the preservation of international public order – both alternatives which, for reasons already explained, I have strongly suggested

[671] Throughout the text of the Vienna Convention, the conclusion of a treaty is frequently referred to. It is a matter of some concern that the term is not used with a consistent meaning. Compare for instance the provisions of Article 49 with those of Article 7, paragraph 2. In the former case, the 'conclusion' of a treaty is quite clearly the point in time when a treaty is established as definite; in the latter, it is the time period from when negotiations on a treaty started to when the treaty enters into force. On this problem in general, *see* the excellent article written by professor Vierdag. (B. Vierdag, 'The time of the 'Conclusion' of a Multilateral treaty': Article 30 of the Vienna Convention on the Law of Treaties and related provisions', 59 *British Yearbook of International Law*, (1988), pp. 75-111.) On the problems caused in the application specifically of Articles 31 and 32, *see* U. Linderfalk, *On the Interpretation of Treaties*, forthcoming, in particular chapters 5, 6 and 8.

[672] *Ibid.*

[673] *See*, for instance, T.O. Elias, *The Modern Law of Treaties* (Leiden, 1974), p. 182; B. Vierdag, *supra* note 39, p. 90.

against – a convincing argument in support of thesis A has still not been produced. Personally, I can see no such further arguments. It is my conclusion that thesis A is simply erroneous, and as such it should be discarded. The question remains whether a convincing argument can be produced in support of the opposing thesis – thesis B. My suggestion is that such an argument can indeed be produced. This is what I will attempt to show in the next section, section 5.

5. OBJECT AND PURPOSE CRITERION HAVING NOTHING TO DO WITH JUS COGENS

As an argument in support of thesis B, the following can be adduced:

Premise 1	Every *jus cogens* norm is a norm belonging to the realm of customary international law.
Premise 2	If a reservation is made to the Covenant or to any of its two Protocols, in accordance with the rule laid down in Article 19 of the Vienna Convention, then the application of that treaty, in the relationship between the reserving State and (at least) the parties that have decided not to object, shall be modified along the lines of the reservation.
Premise 3	According to a rule of customary international law, any legal act shall be void, if and to the extent that the purport of that act is in conflict with a norm of *jus cogens*.
Conclusion	If a reservation is made to the Covenant or to any of its two Protocols, according to a rule of customary international law, it is to be considered a nullity, when applied along the lines of the reservation it would run counter to a norm of *jus cogens*.

The argument consists of three premises. Premise (1) restates the general opinion prevailing among international law scholars.[674] Premise (2) is the commonly accepted reading of Article 21 of the Vienna Convention, already commented upon in the above section 2.[675] Quite clearly, both are premises of considerable weight.

The part of the argument, to which critics will most certainly direct their attacks, is the last of the three premises – premise (3). They will then have to deal with the following inferential evidence:

[674] *See* above, Section 2.
[675] *See* above, Section 2.

(1) By a claim of sovereignty a State may purport to procure for itself the title to a certain territory. The claim will not have purported effect if originating in a use of force violating a *jus cogens* norm.[676]
(2) By an act of recognition a State may purport to procure for another State the title to a certain territory occupied by that other State. The act will not have the purported effect, if the occupation is contrary to a *jus cogens* norm such as that relating to the use of force.[677]
(3) By unilateral consent a State may purport to create, on the part of itself, an undertaking to accept, on the part of some other State, an action that would otherwise be considered unlawful. The consent will not have the purported effect, if the action consented to, for that other State, would imply a violation of *jus cogens* norm.[678]
(4) By invoking *force majeure*, distress, or a State of necessity, a State may purport to justify, on the part of itself, an action that would otherwise be considered unlawful. No one of these circumstances will ever justify a breach of a *jus cogens* norm.[679]
(5) By persistently objecting to the binding nature of a rule of customary international law, a State may purport to evade obligations that would otherwise be the consequence of that rule. The objection will not have the purported effect, if the rule to which the objection relates is of a *jus cogens* character.[680]
(6) By adopting resolutions, the UN Security Council may purport to create on the part of Member States an obligation to adapt their behaviour in accordance with the decisions. No such resolution will

---

[676] *See*, for instance, Resolution 662 (concerning the purported Iraqi annexation of Kuwait), adopted by the UN Security Council on 9 August 1990, operative paragraph 1.
[677] *See*, for instance, Brownlie, *supra* note 22, p. 490; Mann, *supra* note 9, p. 100; Hannikainen, *supra* note 9, pp. 302–305.
[678] *See*, for instance, Article 20, compared to Article 26, of the Draft Articles on the Responsibility of States for Internationally Wrongful Acts, adopted by the International Law Commission in 2001, *supra* note 35.
[679] *See*, for instance, Articles 23–25, compared to Article 26, of the Draft Articles on the Responsibility of States for Internationally Wrongful Acts, adopted by the International Law Commission in 2001, *supra* note 35.
[680] *See*, for instance, Brownlie, *supra* note 22, p. 12, n. 56; Byers, *supra* note 22, pp. 217–218; H. Thirlway, *International Customary Law and Codification* (Leiden, 1972), p. 110.

> have the purported effect, if the behaviour required amounts to a violation of *jus cogens*.[681]
> (7) By concluding a treaty, two States may purport to create, each on the part of itself, an undertaking to accept, on the part of the other State, an action that would otherwise be considered unlawful. The treaty will not have the purported effect, if the action consented to amounts to a breach of *jus cogens*.[682]

The evidence is persuasive indeed. Only a short remark may be added concerning the last of the above seven paragraphs.

According to the content of premise (3) in the argument presented in this section, a legal act shall be void if the purport of that act is in conflict with a *jus cogens* norm; but the act is void *only to the extent of the conflict*. This proposition is fully in accordance with the content of Article 64 of the Vienna Convention compared to that of Article 44. If a new norm of a *jus cogens* character develops, any existing treaty in conflict with that norm becomes void and terminates. But granted that the conflict is due only to a particular clause of the treaty, in the normal course of events that clause will be severed from the treaty and the remainder of the treaty retained.[683] This is not a possibility where a treaty is in conflict with a *jus cogens* norm already at the time of its conclusion. In those cases, according to the wording of Article 53 compared to that of Article 44, the treaty will be void in its entirety.[684] However, it seems that this difference of treatment should be explained more for reasons of penalising bad faith rather than securing compliance with *jus cogens* norms. In the words of professor Rozakis,

> '[t]he drafters of the Convention felt that in cases falling under article 64, unlike those falling under article 53, the parties acted legitimately at the time of the conclusion of the treaty and therefore deserve a different treatment. Thus they

---

[681] *See*, for instance, Byers, *supra* note 22, pp. 216–217; Paust, *supra* note 22, pp. 139–140; D. Schweigman, *The Authority of the Security Council under Chapter VII of the UN Charter* (The Hague, 2001), p. 197. *See also* the statement made by Judge Lauterpacht in his separate opinion to the judgment of the International Court of Justice in the *Convention on the Prevention and Punishment of the Crime of Genocide Case* (*Bosnia and Herzegovina* v. *Yugoslavia*), Provisional Measures, *ICJ Reports* (1993), p. 440, para. 100.
[682] *See* Vienna Convention, Articles 53 and 64.
[683] Compare the provisions of Article 44, paragraph 3, of the Vienna Convention.
[684] *Contra*: Mann, *supra* note 9, p. 87, n. 14.

> were not punished by a total extinction of their instrument as are the parties to an originally illegal treaty.'[685]

So, whatever impressions are created by a mere reading of the Convention, the overall picture need not be disturbed. All things considered, I cannot come to any other conclusion than this: a convincing argument in support of thesis B has indeed been produced. If a reservation in conflict with a norm of *jus cogens* is to be considered a nullity, this is not because of Article 19 of the Vienna Convention, but because of some other rule of international law.

[685] Rozakis, *supra* note 32, p. 176.

ANNEX 1

EXCERPTS FROM THE SECOND REPORT ON RESERVATIONS TO TREATIES*

Report prepared by Alain Pellet, Special Rapporteur on the International Law Commission.

CONTENTS

* United Nations, General Assembly, Distr., General, A/CN.4/477/Add.1, 13 June 1996, English, Original: French, International Law Commission, Forty-eighth session, Geneva, 6 May-26 July 1996. Published with the permission of the Publication Board of the United Nations.

CHAPTER II UNITY OR DIVERSITY OF THE LEGAL REGIME FOR RESERVATIONS TO TREATIES (RESERVATIONS TO HUMAN RIGHTS TREATIES)

55. This chapter relates to item I of the general outline proposed on a provisional basis in chapter I above.[686] Its object is to determine if the rules applicable to reservations to treaties, whether codified in articles 19 to 23 of the 1969 and 1986 Conventions, or customary, are applicable to all treaties, whatever their object, and in particular to human rights treaties.

(a) Necessity and urgency of consideration of the question by the Commission

56. As recalled above, the question was raised with some insistence both in the Commission at its forty-seventh session and in the Sixth Committee of the General Assembly at its fiftieth session.[687] It is easy to understand these concerns.

57. Their origin doubtless lies in initiatives in respect of reservations taken recently by certain monitoring bodies established by human rights treaties, which in recent years have considered themselves entitled to assess the permissibility of reservations formulated by States to the instruments under which they are established, and, where appropriate, to draw far-reaching conclusions from such observations.

---

[686] See para. 37.
[687] See above, paras. 10 and 12, and footnotes 19 and 22.

58. The origins of this development may be found in the practice of the Commission and of the European Court of Human Rights, which, in several significant decisions, have noted that a reservation (or an 'interpretative declaration' which, on analysis, proves to be a reservation) was impermissible or did not have the scope attributed to it by the respondent State, and have drawn the conclusions both that the State concerned could not invoke the impermissible reservation before them and that the State was no less bound by its ratification of the Rome Convention.[688] The Inter-American Court of Human Rights has taken a similar position.[689]

59. The monitoring bodies established by human rights treaties concluded under United Nations auspices, traditionally cautious in this regard,[690] have thereby been encouraged to be somewhat bolder:

The persons chairing the human rights treaty bodies have twice expressed their concern at the situation arising from reservations to treaties under their scrutiny and recommended that those bodies should draw the attention of States to the incompatibility of some of those reservations with the applicable law;[691] The Committee on the Elimination of Discrimination against Women amended its guidelines on the preparation of initial and periodic reports by the inclusion of a section indicating the form in which States parties making reservations were to report them,[692] and 'Welcomed the request of the Sub-Commission on Prevention of Discrimination and Protection of Minorities of the Commission on Human Rights, in its resolution 1992/3 on contemporary forms of slavery, to the Secretary-General:

> 'To seek the views of the Committee on the Elimination of Discrimination against Women and the Commission on the Status

[688] See the cases of Temeltasch v. Switzerland (European Commission of Human Rights, 5 May 1982, Yearbook of the European Convention on Human Rights, vol. 31, p. 120); Belilos v. Switzerland (European Court of Human Rights, Series A, vol. 132, p. 1, 29 April 1988), Chrysostomos et al. v. Turkey (European Commission of Human Rights, 4 March 1991, Revue universelle des droits de l'homme, 1991, p. 193); F and ML v. Austria (European Commission of Human Rights, 6 September 1994); Gradinger v. Austria (European Commission of Human Rights, 19 May 1994; European Court of Human Rights, 23 October 1995); Loizidou v. Turkey (European Court of Human Rights, Series A, vol. 310, p.1, 23 March 1995); and Fischer v. Austria (European Court of Human Rights, 26 April 1995). These decisions are analysed in more detail in sect. 3 of this chapter.

[689] Inter-American Court of Human Rights, The effect of reservations on the entry into force of the American Convention (arts. 74 and 75), advisory opinion OC-2/82 of 24 September 1982, Series A, No. 2; and Restrictions to the death penalty (arts. 4(2) and 4(4)), advisory opinion OC-3/83 of 8 September 1983, Series A, No. 3.

[690] See below sect. 3, paragraph 1.

[691] See the reports of the fourth and fifth meetings of persons chairing the human rights treaty bodies, A/47/628, 10 November 1992, paras. 36 and 60-65, and A/49/537, 19 October 1994, para. 30.

[692] See fifteenth session, 15 January-2 February 1986, Guidelines regarding the form and content of initial reports of States parties, CEDAW/C/7/Rev.2.

> of Women on the desirability of obtaining an advisory opinion on the validity and legal effect of reservations to the Convention on the Elimination of All Forms of Discrimination against Women [...]' '[and] decided that it should support steps taken in common with other human rights treaty bodies to seek an advisory opinion from the International Court of Justice that would clarify the issue of reservations to the human rights treaties and thereby assist States parties in their ratification and implementation of those international instruments. Such an opinion would also help the Committee in its task of considering the progress made in the implementation of the Convention';[693]

Above all, perhaps, the Human Rights Committee, on 2 November 1994, adopted its 'General Comment No. 24 on issues relating to reservations made upon ratification or accession to the Covenant or the Optional Protocols thereto, or in relation to declarations under article 41 of the Covenant', in which it took a clear position in favour of a broad view of its own powers to examine the compatibility of such reservations and declarations with the purpose and object of the International Covenant on Civil and Political Rights.[694]

60. These positions have provoked some disquiet among States and drawn strong criticism from some of them,[695] probably linked to the review of the question of reservations to treaties being undertaken in various forums, in particular, the Council of Europe.[696]

61. It is thus certainly not redundant for the International Law Commission to take a position on these questions at an early date. The position of the Special Rapporteur, which induced him to amend somewhat the order in which he proposed

[693] Report of the Committee on the Elimination of Discrimination against Women, (twelfth session), A/48/38, 28 May 1993, paras. 3 and 5.

[694] See CCPR/C/21/Rev.1/Add.6, 11 November 1994.

[695] See, in particular, the extremely critical remarks on General Comment No. 24 by the United States of America, the United Kingdom (reproduced in the nineteenth Report of the Human Rights Committee to the General Assembly, A/50/40, pp. 131 and 135) and France (to appear in the 1996 Report, A/51/40).

[696] See in particular recommendation 1223 (1993) on reservations by member States to Council of Europe conventions, adopted by the Parliamentary Assembly on 1 October 1993, and the recommendation of the Committee of Ministers on the same question of 17 February 1994, and the work of the Committee of Legal Advisers on Public International Law (CAHDI) at its meeting of 21 and 22 March 1995 (cf. Meeting Report, CAHDI(95)5, paras. 23-34); at the conclusion of the meeting it was decided that '[t]he Secretariat will submit this document [i.e. a working paper submitted by the Austrian delegation, CAHDI(95)7], together with a copy of the meeting report to the Special Rapporteur of the ILC, indicating at the same time that the CAHDI takes a keen interest in this issue and was willing to contribute to the study. This item will be kept on the agenda for the Spring 1996 meeting of the CAHDI when first indications will have been received on how the ILC study was progressing'.

to take up the questions raised in connection with the matter entrusted to him, does not spring from any desire to follow a trend.

62. While it is obviously fundamental for human rights bodies to state their views on the question, the Commission must also make heard the voice of international law[697] in this important domain, and it would be unfortunate for it not to take part in a discussion which is of concern to the Commission above all: on the one hand, the questions raised by States and human rights bodies relate to the applicability of the rules on reservations codified by the 1969 Vienna Convention, in the drafting of which the Commission played such an influential role; on the other hand, under its statute, the Commission 'shall have for its object the promotion of the progressive development of international law and its codification',[698] meaning 'the more precise formulation and systematization of rules of international law in fields where there has already been extensive State practice, precedent and doctrine'.[699] These two aspects are at the centre of the debate, one of the prerequisites being to determine whether the problem arises in terms of codification or of progressive development.

63. Given the opposing views which have emerged, the Special Rapporteur considers that the Commission might usefully seek to clarify the terms of the problem as it arises with respect to general public international law and adopt a resolution on the question which could be brought to the attention of States and human rights bodies by the General Assembly. A draft resolution along these lines is included in the conclusion of this chapter.

(b) Object and plan of the chapter

64. However, since the function of the International Law Commission is to contribute to the codification and progressive development of international law as a whole, and as the question of 'reservations to treaties' covers treaties as a whole, it seems appropriate to resituate the specific problems raised by reservations to human rights treaties in a broader context and to consider the more general question of the unity or diversity of the legal regime or regimes applicable to reservations.

65. A first element of diversity could stem in this respect from the opposition between treaty norms laid down in articles 19 and 23 of the 1969 and 1986 Vienna

---

697 In its formulation of General Comment No. 24, the Human Rights Committee did not focus its attention on the general rules of international law on reservations but on the 1966 Covenant itself; cf. the comment by Mrs. Higgins who criticized the initial draft for making excessive reference to the Vienna Convention on the Law of Treaties in comparison with the Covenant, which should be the central concern of the Committee (CCPR/C/SR.1366, para. 58).

698 Article 1, para. 1.

699 Article 15.

Conventions[700] and customary rules in this area. There is, however, no reason to make such a distinction: while it can doubtless be maintained that at the time of their adoption the Vienna rules stemmed, at least in part, from the progressive development of international law rather than its codification in the strict sense, that is certainly no longer true today; relying on the provisions of the 1969 Convention, confirmed in 1986, practice has been consolidated in customary norms.[701] In any event, notwithstanding the nuances which may be ascribed to such an opinion,[702] the concern expressed by Commission members as well as within the Sixth Committee of the General Assembly to preserve what has been achieved under the existing Conventions[703] renders the question somewhat moot: it must be placed in the context of the norms set out in these conventions.

66. This artificial problem being set aside, the question of the unity or diversity of the legal regime governing reservations may be stated thus: do, or should, certain treaties escape application of the 'Vienna regime' by virtue of their object? Should the answer be yes, to what specific regime or regimes are, or should, these treaties be subject with respect to reservations?[704] If the treaties which are recognized by the 1969 and 1986 Conventions themselves as having a specific status are set apart, the problem has essentially been posed with respect to the 'normative' treaties, of which it has been affirmed that they would be antinomical with the very idea of reservations (sect. 1).

67. In this view (but with the specific problem of human rights treaties still in the background), it has been remarked that the general question leads to another, more specific: 'There are in effect two separate but related issues: should

[700] It would appear prudent to leave to one side, at this stage, the problems raised by article 20 of the 1978 Vienna Convention on Succession of States in respect of Treaties; besides the fact that a consensus seems to have emerged within the Commission that it is not a priority problem (see above footnote 20), it arises in quite specific terms. Suffice to say that the question of succession to reservations (and to acceptances and objections) appears prima facie only as ancillary to the more general question of succession to the treaty itself. This being so, the Commission, when it considers the problems of succession to reservations, will perhaps need to reflect, at least incidentally, on the question of determining whether the object of a treaty plays a role in the modalities for succession to treaties. It is possible that, in the meantime, the judgment soon to be delivered by the International Court of Justice on preliminary objections raised by the Federal Republic of Yugoslavia (Serbia and Montenegro) in the case of the Application of the Convention on the Prevention and Punishment of the Crime of Genocide will offer new elements in this regard.

[701] See preliminary report (footnote 2 above) paras. 153–157.

[702] See ibid., paras. 158–162.

[703] See above, paras. 2–4 and 18–20.

[704] The problem has been put in more or less exactly these terms with regard to reservations to human rights treaties: 'The basic question concerning treaties on human rights is whether or not they are to be considered as a category separate from other multilateral treaties and in particular, whether the rules on reservations [...] apply to them with equal force'. (Massimo Coccia, 'Reservations to Multilateral Treaties on human rights', California Western International Law Journal, 1985, p. 16).

reservations to normative treaties be permitted, and should the validity of such reservations be assessed by a system other than that pertaining to treaties in general?'[705] If the problem is put thus, 'the reality is that we are speaking of two sorts of rules - substantive and procedural'.[706]

68. These two categories of rules may be linked, and here again it may be imagined that the monitoring bodies established by certain multilateral treaties have specific powers with regard to reservations by virtue of the object of the treaty. But it may also be considered that the problem of the extent of these powers arises in many forms, independently of the object of the treaty, in all cases where a treaty instrument creates a body responsible for monitoring its implementation; in such a case, the specificity of the reservations regime would stem from the existence of the body and not from the specific characteristics of the treaty - unless it is considered that treaties establishing monitoring bodies constitute a separate category.

69. It thus appears methodologically sound to distinguish the problem of principle - substantive - of the unity or diversity of the rules applicable to reservations (sect. 2) from that - procedural - of the application of such rules, and, in particular, of the powers of monitoring bodies where they exist (sect. 3).

SECTION 1. DIVERSITY OF TREATIES AND THE LEGAL REGIME FOR RESERVATIONS

(a) Limitation of the study to normative treaties

70. Two conflicting considerations may lead to expansion or, conversely, to limitation of the scope of this chapter: on the one hand, the question of the unity or diversity of the legal regime of reservations arises with some acuteness and urgency only with regard to human rights treaties; but, on the other hand, it is the case that other categories of treaties present particular problems with regard to the nature of the applicable rules or the modalities of their application; this is very certainly true of:

- Limited treaties,
- Constituent instruments of international organizations, and
- Bilateral treaties.

71. It would seem wise, however, to exclude these various categories of treaties from consideration at this stage, for both theoretical and practical reasons. While the 'unity or diversity' problem is partially common to all treaties, it is also, as a logical necessity, specific to each category; after all, it is in the light of the particular features of each category that the question arises of whether common rules are

[705] Catherine Redgwell, 'Universality or integrity? Some reflections on reservations to general multilateral treaties', British Yearbook of International Law, 1993, p. 279.

[706] Rosalyn Higgins, 'Preface' to appear in 1996 in British Institute of International and Comparative Law, Reservations and Human Rights Treaties, p. 7 (manuscript version), underlining in the original.

applicable to all treaties or whether, on the contrary, they should be ruled out. Put differently, the problem of unity is one thing by definition, but, by the same token, the problem of diversity is many things.[707] In other words, it may be necessary to consider each individual category separately, and there is no disadvantage in giving such consideration to certain types of treaties and not to others for the time being, since they pose different problems, at least in part.

72. Moreover, in the 1969 and 1986 Vienna Conventions themselves, limited treaties and constituent instruments of international organizations are given separate treatment which is reflected in specific rules.[708] Reservations to bilateral treaties, meanwhile, pose very specific problems relating to the very definition of the concept of reservations,[709] and it would probably be advantageous to address them in the chapter devoted to that definition.[710]

73. Codification treaties raise more difficult questions. The belief has occasionally been expressed that reservations to such treaties pose specific problems.[711] However widespread,[712] this notion is not devoid of ambiguity; the boundary between the codification of international law on the one hand and its progressive development on the other is, to say the least, unclear (assuming that it exists);[713] many treaties contain 'codification clauses', in other words, provisions which reproduce customary norms, without constituting 'codification treaties' as such, since these provisions are set forth alongside others that are not of the same nature (this, incidentally, is the problem posed by numerous human rights treaties).[714] It is quite unlikely, then, that the category of codification treaties would, in and of itself, be 'operational' for the purposes of this chapter.[715]

---

[707] See the similar comments made by Mr. de Saram in the debate on the preliminary report, A/CN.4/SR.2404, pp. 6-7.

[708] Cf. article 20, paras. 2 and 3.

[709] Cf. the doubts expressed during the forty-seventh session of the Commission by Mr. Idris (A/CN.4/SR.2407, pp. 5-6), Mr. Kabatsi (ibid., p. 7) and Mr. Yamada (ibid., p. 11) concerning the appropriateness of the topic itself.

[710] See above, chap. I, para. 37, 'Provisional general outline of the study', II (e), and para. 40.

[711] See, for example, Gérard Teboul, 'Les réserves aux conventions de codification', Revue générale de droit international public, 1982, pp. 679-717, and the literature cited on p. 684, footnotes 9 and 10.

[712] See, for example, P.-H. Imbert, op. cit. (footnote 43 above), pp. 239-249, and G. Teboul, op. cit. (footnote 103 above).

[713] Cf. The Work of the International Law Commission, United Nations, New York, 1989, pp. 15-16.

[714] See below, paras. 85-86.

[715] It is chiefly for similar reasons, moreover, that the once important distinction between 'law-making treaties' and 'contractual treaties' has now fallen into disfavour: '... il est certain que la plupart des traités n'ont pas un contenu homogène. Ils constituent un moule dans lequel on peut couler des dispositions qui présentent des caractères très différents; [...] Si l'on devait donc appliquer des distinctions juridiques materielles aux dispositions des traités, il faudrait de toute façon examiner leurs dispositions séparément sans pouvoir se contenter d'une analyse globale rudimentaire' (It is undeniable that most treaties do not have a uniform

74. Unquestionably, however, there is a need to determine whether a reservation to a customary norm repeated in a treaty provision is permissible.[716] In keeping with the 'provisional general outline' contained in chapter I above,[717] the Special Rapporteur promises to deal more fully with this complex problem at a later stage in the study. This decision seems to him justified by the fact that what is at issue is not the subject but the dual nature (both contractual and customary) of the provision to which the reservation relates.

75. Nevertheless, the problem is clearly not wholly unrelated to the one with which this chapter deals. In the view of the Special Rapporteur, a practical approach is called for in this regard. Some of the questions being addressed at this stage are unavoidably of a 'vertical' nature and relate to the entire topic under consideration; they cannot be ignored altogether, as the Commission must feel completely free to make subsequent improvements in the provisional and partial conclusions reached at the current session.

76. Conversely, it is the conviction of the Special Rapporteur that consideration of the 'vertical' problem addressed in this chapter, which runs through the whole topic of reservations to treaties, can be very beneficial for the rest of the study, by providing it with useful reference points and analysing it from a particular angle.

(b) Normative treaties and provisions

77. 'Normative' treaties pose special problems. It is in discussing them that the academic writers have not only dwelt most heavily on the unsuitability of the general legal regime governing reservations, but have even gone so far as to assert that such instruments, by their nature, do not permit reservations. Before considering these questions, however (which are, to a large extent, separate),[718] it is necessary to inquire into the substance and the very existence of this category of treaties.

78. According to some writers, '[l]es conventions multilatérales sont devenues un des moyens les plus couramment employés pour établir des règles de conduite pour l'ensemble des Etats, non seulement dans leurs relations mais aussi au profit des individus. Par ces instruments, les Etats tendent ainsi à apporter leur contribution à la formation du droit international en se faisant les interprètes d'une exigence générale de la communauté internationale.' (Multilateral conventions have become one of the most common means of establishing rules of conduct for all States, not

---

content. They are a mould into which provisions having very different characters can be fitted. [...] If, therefore, one were to apply material legal distinctions to the provisions of treaties, it would still be necessary to consider their provisions separately, with no possibility of limiting oneself to a rudimentary overall analysis) (Paul Reuter, op. cit. (footnote 43 above), p. 24).

[716] See preliminary report (footnote 2), paras. 143-144, and the statement made by Mr. Lukashuk during the debate on the preliminary report, A/CN.4/SR.2402, p. 15.

[717] Para. 37, IV.A. (c).

[718] See paragraph 3 below.

only in their relations with other States, but also in their relations with individuals. States thus tend to make their contributions to the formation of international law through such instruments, by articulating a general requirement of the international community.)[719] 'It is this peculiarity of `normative' Conventions, namely, that they operate in, so to speak, the absolute, and not relatively to the other parties - i.e., they operate for each party per se, and not between the parties inter se - coupled with the further peculiarity that they involve mainly the assumption of duties and obligations, and do not confer direct rights or benefits on the parties qua States, that gives these Conventions their special character.'[720]

79. Treaties of this type are found in widely differing fields, such as the legal ('conventions on codification'[721] of public and private international law, including uniform law conventions), economic, technical, social, humanitarian, and other fields. General conventions on environmental protection usually have this character, and disarmament conventions frequently do so as well.

80. It is in the human rights field, however, that these peculiarities have most frequently come to light,[722] the term 'human rights' being understood here in the broad sense. For the purposes of this chapter, there are no grounds for distinguishing between humanitarian law on the one hand and human rights, strictly speaking, on the other; considerations which apply to one term apply just as well to the other.[723]

81. Nevertheless, even from a broad standpoint, the categorization of a treaty as a 'human rights' (or disarmament or environmental protection) treaty is not always problem-free;[724] a family law or civil status convention may contain some provisions which relate to human rights and others which do not. Moreover, assuming that this problem can be solved, two other difficulties arise.

82. First, the category of 'human rights treaties' is, by all indications, far from homogeneous. 'Il n'est pas possible de mettre sur le même plan [...] les Pactes des Nations Unies ou la Convention européenne, qui régissent presque tous les aspects de la vie en société et des conventions comme celles sur le génocide ou la discrimination raciale qui ne tendent à protéger qu'un seul droit'. (The United Nations Covenants or the European Convention [on Human Rights], which regulate nearly all areas of life, and conventions such as those on genocide or racial discrimination, which tend to protect only a single right, cannot be placed on an

---

[719] P.-H. Imbert, op. cit. (footnote 43 above), pp. 435-436; see also the extensive bibliography cited by this author, particularly footnotes 92 and 95.

[720] G. G. Fitzmaurice, 'Reservations to multilateral conventions', International and Comparative Law Quarterly 1953, p. 15 (italics in original).

[721] See above, para. 73.

[722] See below, paras. 84 and 148-152.

[723] For an outline and a justification of the distinction, see Karel Vasak, 'Le droit international des droits de l'homme', Collected Courses of The Hague Academy of International Law (Collected Courses), 1974-IV, vol. 140, pp. 350 ff.

[724] See, in this regard, C. Redgwell, op. cit. (footnote 97), p. 280.

equal footing.)[725] These two subcategories of 'human rights treaties' pose quite different problems as regards the definition of their object and purpose, which plays such a central role in evaluating the permissibility of reservations.[726]

83. Second, within a single treaty, clauses that vary greatly in their 'importance' (which, legally speaking, can be reflected in whether they are binding or non-binding and whether they may or may not be derogated from),[727] their nature (customary or non-customary)[728] or their substance ('normative' or contractual) can be set forth side by side. While all these factors have a bearing on the question under consideration,[729] it is clearly this last factor, the 'normative' character attributed to human rights treaties, which has the greatest impact.

84. According to a widely held view, the main peculiarity of such treaties is that their object is not to strike a balance between the rights and advantages which the States parties mutually grant to one other, but to establish common international rules, reflecting shared values, that all parties undertake to observe, each in its own sphere. As the International Court of Justice stated forcefully, with regard to the Convention on the Prevention and Punishment of the Crime of Genocide:

> 'In such a convention the contracting States do not have any interests of their own; they merely have, one and all, a common interest, namely, the accomplishment of those high purposes which are the raison d'être of the convention. Consequently, in a convention of this type one cannot speak of individual advantages or disadvantages to States, or of the maintenance of a perfect contractual balance between rights and duties.'[730]

85. It is, however, necessary to beware of taking an overly straightforward and simplistic view of things. While, as a rule, provisions that protect human rights have a marked 'normative' character, human rights treaties also include typically contractual clauses. Awkward as this may be, the 'Hague law' applicable to the

---

[725] P.-H. Imbert, 'La question des réserves et les conventions en matière de droits de l'homme'. Actes du Cinquième colloque sur la Convention européenne des droits de l'homme, (Paris, Prédone, 1982), p. 99; also published in English as 'Reservations and human rights conventions', The Human Rights Review (HRR), 1981, pp. 28-60 (p. 28).

[726] See, in this regard, Jeremy McBride, 'Reservations and the capacity to implement human rights treaties', forthcoming in op. cit. (footnote 98 above), p. 32 (manuscript version), and William A. Schabas, 'Reservations to human rights treaties: time for innovation and reform', Annuaire canadien de droit international, 1995, p. 48.

[727] See, on this point, the moderate position taken by the Human Rights Committee in its General Comment No. 24, cited above (footnote 86 above), para. 10, and the commentary by J. McBride, op. cit. (footnote 119 above), pp. 33-34; see also P.-H. Imbert, op. cit. (footnote 117 above), pp. 105-106 (HRR 1981, pp. 31-32).

[728] See above, paras. 73 and 74.

[729] See below, sect. 2, paragraph 1.

[730] Advisory opinion cited above (footnote 46 above), p. 23; see also below, paras. 148-152.

conduct of warring parties in armed conflicts remains fundamentally contractual, and the 1899 and 1907 Conventions are still applied on a reciprocal basis (despite the lapsing of the celebrated 'si omnes' clause);[731] similarly, the inter-State application machinery established by article 24 of the European Convention on Human Rights[732] and article 45 of the Inter-American Human Rights Convention is based on reciprocity, and it has even been possible, in speaking of the 1948 Convention on the Prevention and Punishment of the Crime of Genocide, to state that it

> 'contains stipulations of a normative character and stipulations of a contractual character. However, as is clear from its text and from the whole history of United Nations dealing with the problem of genocide, the intention of its framers was equally to codify, at least in part, substantive international law and to establish international obligations to facilitate international cooperation in the prevention and punishment of the crime. Consequently, the Convention cannot be regarded as a single indivisible whole, and its normative stipulations are divisible from its contractual stipulations.'[733]

86. Here again, the problem does not seem to have been posed in the proper terms. While this has been done with respect to 'human rights treaties', all that is involved is 'human rights clauses' of a normative character, or, more broadly, 'normative clauses', regardless of the subject of the treaty in which they are articulated.

87. Indeed, while it is clear that human rights treaties display these characteristics in a particularly striking way, it must also be recognized that they are not unique in doing so. The same is true of most environmental protection or disarmament treaties and, in a broader sense, all 'normative' treaties by which the parties enact uniform rules which they undertake to apply.

88. Naturally, this observation does not obviate the need to inquire whether there are subcategories within this category - if it does in fact have legal status - which pose specific problems with regard to reservations and, in particular, whether

---

731 See, on this point, P.-H. Imbert, op. cit. (footnote 43 above), pp. 256-257.

732 See P.-H. Imbert, op. cit. (footnote 109 above), p. 115 (HRR 1981, p. 36).

733 Statement made by Mr. Shabtai Rosenne on behalf of the Government of Israel during consideration of the request by the General Assembly for an advisory opinion concerning Reservations to the Convention on the Prevention and Punishment of the Crime of Genocide, International Court of Justice, Pleadings, Oral Arguments, Documents, 1951, p. 356; see also Tullio Scovazzi, Esercitazioni di diritto internazionale, (Milan, Giuffrè, 1994), pp. 69-71. Likewise, in a Memorandum concerning the 'Admissibility of reservations to general conventions' submitted to the Council of the League of Nations on 15 June 1927, the Director of the International Labour Office noted that international conventions 'appear to be legal instruments partaking of the nature both of a law and of a contract' (League of Nations, Official Journal, July 1927, p. 883).

human rights treaties pose such problems. Nevertheless, thinking must start from more general premises, unless conclusions are to be posited at the outset of the process. Hence, while human rights treaties will be emphasized for the reasons outlined above,[734] the body of law-making multilateral treaties will form the broader focus of this chapter.

SECTION 2. UNITY OF THE MAIN RULES APPLICABLE TO RESERVATIONS

89. The adaptation to normative multilateral treaties of the 'Vienna rules' relating to reservations cannot be evaluated in the abstract. It must be viewed in the light of the functions assigned to reservations regimes and the intentions of their authors.

Paragraph 1. Functions of the legal regime of reservations

90. 'Deux intérêts contradictoires sont en cause. Le premier intérêt est l'extension de la convention. On désire que cette convention fasse la loi pour le plus grand nombre d'Etats possible et, par conséquent, on accepte les aménagements qui permettront d'obtenir le consentement d'un Etat. L'autre préoccupation est celle de l'intégralité de la Convention: les mêmes règles doivent être valables pour toutes les parties; on n'a pas intérêt à avoir un régime conventionnel dans lequel il y aura des lacunes ou des exceptions, dans lequel les règles varieront suivant les Etats considérés.' (Two opposing interests are at stake. The first interest is the extension of the convention. It is desirable for this convention to be ratified by the largest possible number of States; consequently, adjustments which make it possible to obtain the consent of a State will be accepted. The other concern relates to the integrity of the Convention. The same rules must apply to all parties; there is no point in having a treaty regime that has loopholes or exceptions, in which the rules vary according to the States concerned.)[735] The function of the rules applicable to reservations is to strike a balance between these opposing requirements: on the one hand, the search for the broadest possible participation; on the other hand, the preservation of the ratio contrahendi (ground of covenant), which is the treaty's reason for being. It is this conflict between universality and integrity which gives rise to all reservations regimes,[736] be they general (applicable to all treaties which do not provide for a

[734] Under letter (a) above, paras. 56-63.

[735] Suzanne Bastid, Les traités dans la vie internationale - conclusions et effets (Paris, Economica, 1985), pp. 71-72.

[736] See, in this regard, B. T. Halajczuk, 'Les conventions multilatérales entre l'universalité et l'intégrité', Revue de droit international, de sciences diplomatiques et politiques, 1960, pp. 38-50 and 147-158; J. M. Ruda, op. cit. (footnote 43 above), p. 212; John King Gamble Jr., 'Reservations to multilateral treaties: a macroscopic view of State practice', American Journal of International Law (AJIL), 1980, pp. 372-373; Catherine Logan Piper, 'Reservations to multilateral treaties: the goal of universality', Iowa Law Review, 1985, pp. 295-322,

specific regime) or particular (established by express clauses incorporated into the treaty).

91. As far as human rights treaties are concerned, Judge Rosalyn Higgins has expressed the problem in the following terms: 'The matter is extremely complex. At the heart of it is the balance to be struck between the legitimate role of States to protect their sovereign interests and the legitimate role of the treaty bodies to promote the effective guarantee of human rights.'[737]

92. The first of these requirements, universality, militates in favour of widely expanding the right of States to formulate reservations, which clearly facilitates universal participation in 'normative' treaties. And the same applies with respect to human rights: '... the possibility of formulating reservations may well be seen as a strength rather than a weakness of the treaty approach, in so far as it allows a more universal participation in human rights treaties'.[738]

93. Nevertheless, such freedom on the part of States to formulate reservations cannot be unlimited. It clashes with another, equally pressing requirement - preserving the very essence of the treaty. For instance, it is absurd to believe that a State could become a party to the Genocide Convention while objecting to the application of articles I, II and III, i.e., the only substantial clauses of the Convention.

94. The problem can also be posed in terms of consent.[739]

95. By its very definition, the law of treaties is consensual. 'Le traité lie les Etats parce que ceux-ci ont voulu par lui être liés. Le traité est donc un acte juridique, mettant en oeuvre des volontés humaines.' (Treaties are binding on States because States have wished to be bound by them. A treaty is thus a legal instrument which implements human wishes.)[740] States are bound by treaties because they have undertaken - because they have consented - so to be bound. They are free to make this commitment or not, and they are bound only by obligations which they have

particularly pp. 297, 305 and 317; Rebecca J. Cook, 'Reservations to the Convention on the Elimination of All Forms of Discrimination Against Women', Virginia Journal of International Law, 1990, pp. 683-684 and 686; Samuel K. N. Blay and B. Martin Tsamenyi, 'Reservations and declarations under the 1951 Convention and the 1967 Protocol relating to the Status of Refugees', International Journal of Refugee Law, 1990, p. 557; Patrick Daillier and Alain Pellet, Droit international public (Nguyen Quoc Dinh) (Paris, Librairie générale de droit de jurisprudence, fifth edition, 1994), p. 178; etc.

[737] Op. cit. (footnote 98 above), p. 1 (manuscript version).

[738] M. Coccia, op. cit. (footnote 96 above), p. 3. The author refers to O. Schachter, M. Nawaz and J. Fried, Toward Wider Acceptance of United Nations Treaties, 148 (1971), and adds: 'This UNITAR study shows statistically that `the treaties ... which permit reservations, or do not prohibit reservations, have received proportionally larger acceptance than the treaties which either do not permit reservations to a part or whole of the treaty, or which contain only one substantial clause, making reservations unlikely'.'

[739] See the first report by Hersch Lauterpacht on the law of treaties, in which he explains that the problem of consent 'is a question closely, though indirectly, connected with that of the intrinsic justification of reservations....' (Yearbook ... 1953, A/CN.4/63, p. 125).

[740] Paul Reuter, op. cit. (footnote 43 above), pp. 20-21.

accepted freely, with full knowledge of the consequences.[741] 'No State can be bound by contractual obligations it does not consider suitable.'[742]

96. The same applies to reservations: 'The fundamental basis remains, that no State is bound in international law without its consent to the treaty. This is the starting-point for the law of treaties, and likewise for our international rules dealing with reservations.'[743] As the International Court of Justice has stated:

> 'It is well established that in its treaty relations a State cannot be bound without its consent, and that consequently no reservation can be effective against any State without its agreement thereto.'[744]

Likewise, in the arbitration of the dispute between France and the United Kingdom with regard to the Mer d'Iroise Continental Shelf, the Tribunal emphasized the need to respect the 'principle of mutuality of consent' in evaluating the effects of reservations.[745]

97. The rules applicable to reservations must therefore strike a dual balance between (a) the requirements of universality and integrity of the treaty and (b) the

---

[741] Unless they are otherwise bound, but this is a different problem. See also, in this regard, the statement made by the United States representative in the Sixth Committee during the fiftieth session of the General Assembly (A/C.6/50/SR.13, para. 53).

[742] Christian Tomuschat, 'Admissibility and legal effects of reservations to multilateral treaties - comments on articles 16 and 17 of the International Law Commission's 1966 Draft Articles on the Law of Treaties', Zeitschrift für ausländisches öffentliches Recht, 1967, p. 466. See, for example, in this regard, Permanent Court of International Justice, judgment of 17 August 1923, ss 'Wimbledon' case, Series A, No. 1, p. 25, and International Court of Justice, advisory opinion of 11 July 1950, International Status of South-West Africa, Reports, 1950, p. 139.

[743] William W. Bishop, Jr., 'Reservations to treaties', Collected Courses, 1961 II, vol. 103, p. 255.

[744] International Court of Justice, opinion cited above (footnote 46 above), Reports, 1951, p. 21. The authors of the dissenting opinion express this idea still more strongly: 'The consent of the parties is the basis of treaty obligations. The law governing reservations is only a particular application of this fundamental principle, whether the consent of the parties to a reservation is given in advance of the proposal of the reservations or at the same time or later' (ibid., p. 32). Moreover, it is clear that the majority and the dissenting Judges held very divergent views on the way in which consent to a reservation should be expressed, but this difference does not affect the 'principle of mutuality of consent' (see footnote 137 below), and it seems debatable to assert, as some eminent writers do, that in the opinion of the majority (which is the source of the Vienna regime), 'le principe même du consentement est ébranlé' (the very principle of consent has been shaken) (P.-H. Imbert, op. cit. (footnote 43 above), p. 69; see also pp. 81 and 141 ff.).

[745] Award of 30 June 1977, paras. 60 and 61, Reports of International Arbitral Awards, vol. XVIII, p. 42.

freedom of consent of the reserving State and that of the other States parties, it being understood that these two 'dialectical pairs' overlap to a large extent.

98. In the light of these requirements, it is necessary to inquire whether the legal regime for reservations envisaged by the 1969 and 1986 Vienna Conventions is generally applicable, and, in particular, whether it is suited to the particular natures of normative treaties (or, more specifically, of the 'normative clauses' articulated in general multilateral treaties).[746] As a first step, it can be determined that the authors of this regime showed themselves to be mindful of these requirements, and that they intended to adopt generally applicable rules to satisfy them.

Paragraph 2. A regime designed for general application

99. Since the very beginning of its work on reservations, the Commission has been aware of the need to strike the above-mentioned dual balance[747] between the requirements of universality and integrity on the one hand and, on the other, between respect for the wishes expressed by the reserving State and that of the other parties, although the Commission has taken a number of very different positions as to the best way of achieving such a balance.

100. In accordance with its position of principle in favour of the rule of unanimity, the first report by James L. Brierly merely stresses the need for consent to the reservation, while admitting - and this is in itself an element of flexibility - that such consent could be implicit.[748] However, beginning the following year, in response to the General Assembly's invitation to the Commission to study the question of reservations to multilateral conventions,[749] the Special Rapporteur fully discussed the question:

> 'In approaching this task it would appear that the Commission has o bear in mind two main principles. First there is the desirability of maintaining the integrity of international multilateral conventions. It is to be preferred that some degree of uniformity in the obligations of all parties to a multilateral instrument should be maintained. [...]
>
> Secondly, and on the other hand, there is the desirability of the widest possible application of multilateral conventions. [...] If they are to be effective multilateral conventions must be as widely in force or as generally accepted as possible.'[750]

---

[746] See below, paras. 73-74 and 85-86; in the rest of this report, the two terms are used interchangeably.

[747] See above, para. 97.

[748] Yearbook ... 1950, vol. II, p. 224.

[749] General Assembly resolution 478 (V) of 16 November 1950; see preliminary report (footnote 2 above), para. 14.

[750] A/CN.4/41, paras. 11-12. See also ibid., para. 16.

101. The Commission agreed with the Special Rapporteur on this question but at the same time was somewhat uneasy:

> 'When a multilateral convention is open for States generally to become parties, it is certainly desirable that it should have the widest possible acceptance. [...] On the other hand, it is also desirable to maintain uniformity in the obligations of all the parties to a multilateral convention, and it may often be more important to maintain the integrity of a convention than to aim, at any price, at the widest possible acceptance of it.'[751]

Faced with this dilemma,

> 'The Commission believes that multilateral conventions are so diversified in character and object that, when the negotiating States have omitted to deal in the text of a convention with the admissibility or effect of reservations, no single rule uniformly applied can be wholly satisfactory.'[752]

It concludes, none the less, 'that its problem is not to recommend a rule which will be perfectly satisfactory, but that which seems to it to be the least unsatisfactory and to be suitable for application in the majority of cases.'[753] it being understood that this rule can always be rejected, since States and international organizations are invited to 'consider the insertion [in multilateral conventions]' of provisions relating to reservations.[754]

102. It does not make much difference which system is decided on at this stage. It is significant that, the Commission, while perfectly aware of the diversity of situations, has shown a firm determination since the outset to separate out a single, unique system of ordinary law, one that does the least possible harm and can be applied in all cases where the treaty is silent.

103. The reports submitted by Hersch Lauterpacht in 1953 and 1954 are written along the same lines.[755] However, it is important to note that after a long section on the debates concerning reservations in the draft[756] Covenant on Human Rights,[757] the Special Rapporteur on the law of treaties concluded that it was incumbent on the General Assembly to choose a suitable system, and that the great variety of existing

[751] Yearbook ... 1951, A/1858, para. 26.
[752] Ibid., para. 28.
[753] Ibid.
[754] Ibid., para. 28.
[755] See preliminary report (footnote 2 above), paras. 23-29.
[756] The only one at the time.
[757] A/CN.4/87, commentary on draft article 9, pp. 28-34.

practice suggested 'that it is neither necessary nor desirable to aim at a uniform solution'; he nevertheless went on to say:

> 'What is both necessary and desirable is that the codification of the law of treaties shall contain a clear rule for the cases in which the parties have made no provision on the subject'.[758]

104. The only report in which Fitzmaurice dealt with the question of reservations is the first one, submitted in 1956.[759] It is of twofold interest with regard to the problem at issue here:

1. Endorsing the views of his predecessor, the Special Rapporteur felt that 'even as a matter of lex lata, the strict traditional rule about reservations could be regarded as mitigated in practice by the following considerations which, taken together, allow an appreciable amount of latitude to States in this matter, and should meet all reasonable needs',[760] thus reaffirming the idea that flexibility is a gauge of adaptability.

2. In addition, Fitzmaurice again pointed out the difference noted in an article published in 1953[761] between 'treaties with restricted participation' on the one hand and, on the other, 'multilateral treaties'.[762]

105. This distinction, mentioned again in 1962 by Sir Humphrey Waldock in his first report,[763] is the direct source of the current provisions of paragraphs 2 and 3 of the 1969 and 1986 conventions. This result was not without its problems, however. The lengthy discussions on the Special Rapporteur's suggestions[764] bear witness to profound differences on this point among the members of the Commission. The controversy was mainly about the validity of the exception to the general rule, as proposed by the Special Rapporteur and discussed in another form by the Drafting Committee, concerning 'multilateral treaties concluded by a restricted group of States'.[765] Summarizing the debate, the Special Rapporteur noted that two courses were open to the Commission:

> 'One was to draw a distinction between general multilateral treaties and other multilateral treaties; the other was to draw a distinction between treaties which dealt with matters of concern

758 Ibid., p. 34.
759 See preliminary report (footnote 2 above), paras. 30-33.
760 Yearbook ... 1956, vol. II, A/CN.4/101, para. 92, p. 126.
761 Op. cit. (footnote 112 above), p. 13.
762 Yearbook ...1956, vol. II, paras. 97-98, p. 127. Note, however, that while Fitzmaurice spoke expressly in the abovementioned article about 'conventions of the 'normative' types' (ibid.), he did not use that expression in his report.
763 Yearbook ... 1962, vol. II, A/CN.4/144, draft articles 17, para. 5, and 18, para. 3 (b).
764 For a brief discussion of these debates, see the preliminary report (footnote 2 above), paras. 43-45.
765 See especially Yearbook ... 1962, vol. I. pp. 229-237.

> only to a restricted group of States and treaties which dealt with matters of more general concern.'[766]

106. The first of these two courses was defended by some members,[767] while others, even more clearly, asked expressly that the criterion of the object of the treaty should be reintroduced.[768] These views, strongly opposed by other members,[769] none the less remained minority views and, after referral to the Drafting Committee, they were ultimately rejected. In its report, the Commission merely stated the following:

> '... the Commission also decided that there were insufficient reasons for making a distinction between multilateral treaties not of a general character between a considerable number of States and general multilateral treaties. The rules proposed by the Commission therefore cover all multilateral treaties, except those concluded between a small number of States, for which the unanimity rule is retained.'[770]

107. Neither the States in their commentaries on the draft articles nor the Commission itself ever returned to this point,[771] and in 1966, in its final report on the law of treaties, the Commission used the same formula – almost word-for-word - as in 1962:

> '... The Commission also decided that there were insufficient reasons for making a distinction between different kinds of multilateral treaties other than to exempt from the general rule those concluded between a small number of States for which the unanimity rule is retained.'[772]

108. The problem resurfaced briefly during the Vienna Conference after the United States of America proposed an amendment which sought to introduce the nature of the treaty as one of the criteria to be taken into consideration in determining whether

---

766 Ibid., p. 233.
767 See ibid., the positions of Verdross (642nd meeting, para. 56) or Waldock (p. 77).
768 See ibid., the positions of Jiménez de Aréchaga (p. 78), Yaseen (p. 83) or Bartoš (p. 82).
769 See especially the very firm position of Ago, ibid., pp. 79-80.
770 Yearbook ... 1962, vol. II, A/5209, p. 180. See also pp. 178 and 181.
771 Except in passing; see the statement by Briggs during the 1965 debates, Yearbook ... 1965, vol. I., p. 177.
772 Yearbook ... 1966, vol. II, A/6309/Rev.1, p. 223. At the forty-seventh session, Mr. de Saram drew attention to this sentence (A/CN.4/SR.2404, p. 6); see also the position of Mr. Rao (ibid., pp. 19-20) and that of the United States of America during the Sixth Committee debate (A/C.6/50/SR.13, p. 6, para. 50).

a reservation was permissible.[773] Supported by some States[774] and opposed by others,[775] the proposal was sent to the Drafting Committee,[776] which rejected it.[777] The Conference does not seem to have discussed the view expressed by the World Health Organization that draft article 19[778] should be 'interpreted as authorizing reciprocity only to the extent to which it is compatible with the nature of the treaty and of the reservation'.[779]

109. The travaux préparatoires for the Vienna Convention on the Law of Treaties between States and International Organizations or between International Organizations do not reflect the substantive debate on this question. At the most, one can observe that, after some discussion,[780] the International Law Commission disregarded the wishes of certain members to have a special regime for reservations by international organizations; in its 1982 report it stated:

> 'After a thorough review of the problem, a consensus was reached in the Commission, which, choosing a simpler solution than the one it had adopted in first reading, assimilated international organizations to States for the purposes of the formulation of reservations'.[781]

110. Bringing the regime of reservations to treaties to which international organizations are parties into line with the regime applicable to treaties involving only States was highlighted once again at the 1986 Vienna Conference.[782] Here the fundamental unity of the reservation regime laid out in the two Vienna Conventions was made complete and confirmed, the sole exceptions being certain treaties concluded between a limited number of States and constituent instruments of international organizations.[783]

---

[773] A/CONF.39/C.1/L.126 and Add.1.

[774] Cf. United Nations Conference on the Law of Treaties, first session, Vienna, 26 March - 24 May 1968, Official Records, summary records of plenary meetings and meetings of the Committee of the Whole: United States of America (pp. 118 and 141-142), Spain (p. 119) and China (p. 131), (all page numbers refer to the French text).

[775] Cf. ibid.: Ukrainian SSR (p. 125), Poland (p. 128), Ghana (p. 130), Italy (p. 131), Hungary (p. 132), Argentina (p. 140) or the USSR (p. 146) (all page numbers refer to the French text).

[776] See ibid., p. 147 of the French text.

[777] See the reaction of the United States of America in United Nations Conference on the Law of Treaties, second session, Vienna, 9 April-22 May 1969, Official Records, summary records of plenary meetings and meetings of the Committee of the Whole, p. 37 of the French text.

[778] Became article 21.

[779] Analytical compilation comments and observations made in 1966 and 1967 with respect to the final draft Articles on the Law of Treaties, A/CONF.39/5 (vol. I), p. 166.

[780] See preliminary report (footnote 2), paras. 72-85.

[781] Yearbook ... 1982, vol.II, p. 34.

[782] See preliminary report (footnote 2), paras. 87 and 88.

[783] See above, para. 72.

EXCERPTS FROM THE SECOND REPORT ON RESERVATIONS TO TREATIES

111. The documents tracing the drafting of the 1969 and 1986 Conventions leave no doubt whatsoever: the International Law Commission and, later, the codification Conferences deliberately, and after a thorough debate, sought to establish a single regime applicable to reservations to treaties regardless of their nature or their object. The Commission did not set out with any preconceived ideas to this end; as it clearly stated in 1962 and in 1966,[784] it had observed that there were no specific reasons for proceeding differently - and it is interesting to note, first, that the Commission adopted this reasoned position by looking specifically at the regime governing reservations to human rights treaties[785] and, second, that in the two cases in which it felt special rules were needed on certain points, it did not hesitate to derogate from the general regime.[786]

Paragraph 3. The legal regime of reservations is generally applicable

112. This argument is a familiar one. Whatever manifestation it takes, it holds that, given the importance of normative treaties for the international community as a whole, reservations to such instruments must be excluded, or at least discouraged, whereas the 'flexible system' of the 1969 and 1986 Conventions unduly facilitates their formulation and amplifies their effects.

113. However, it is doubtless a matter of good doctrine to draw a distinction between two separate problems even if they are related: the very general problem of whether or not reservations to such instruments are appropriate and the more technical question of determining whether the 'Vienna regime' addresses the various concerns expressed. But if the answer to the first question cannot be objective and depends far more on political - indeed, ideological - preferences than on legal technicalities, the latter considerations in turn make it possible to take a firm position with regard to the second question. And the two can in fact be considered separately.

A. A debate with no possible conclusion: the appropriateness of reservations to normative treaties

114. The terms of the debate are clearly evident in the opposition between the majority and the dissenting judges in the Reservations to the Convention on the Prevention and Punishment of the Crime of Genocide case. The former held that:

> 'The object and purpose of the Genocide Convention imply that it was the intention of the General Assembly and of the States which voted it that as many States as possible should participate. The

[784] See above, paras. 106 and 107.

[785] Particularly with regard to the International Covenants on Human Rights; see above, para. 103 and footnote 147.

[786] Cf. article 20, paragraphs 2 and 3, of the 1969 and 1986 Conventions.

> complete exclusion from the Convention of one or more States would not only restrict the scope of its application, but would detract from the authority of the moral and humanitarian principles which are its basis'.[787]

For the minority judges, on the other hand,

> 'It is [...] not universality at any price that forms the first consideration. It is rather the acceptance of common obligations - keeping step with like-minded States - in order to attain a high objective for all humanity, that is of paramount importance. [...] In the interests of the international community, it would be better to lose as a party to the Convention a State which insists in face of objections on a modification of the terms of the Convention, than to permit it to become a party against the wish of a State or States which have irrevocably and unconditionally accepted all the obligations of the Convention'.[788]

> 'These ['multilateral conventions of a special character'[789]], by reason of their nature and of the manner in which they have been formulated, constitute an indivisible whole. Therefore, they must not be made the subject of reservations, for that would be contrary to the purposes at which they are aimed, namely, the general interest and also the social interest.'[790]

115. This marked opposition of points of view elicits three observations:
- It arises at the outset of the controversy in connection with a human rights treaty par excellence, which as such falls in the sub-category of normative treaties, the category around which the debate has recently resurfaced;[791]
- The two 'camps' start from exactly the same premises (the aims of the Convention, which are pursued in the interest of all mankind) to reach radically opposing conclusions (reservations to the Convention must/must not be permitted);
- Everything was said in 1951; the ensuing dialogue of the deaf has gone on unabated for 45 years without either side displaying any fundamental change in its position.

116. As there is no possible way of ending the debate, let us content ourselves with setting out the undisputed facts.[792]

---

[787] Advisory opinion (footnote 46), Reports, 1951, p. 24.
[788] Joint dissenting opinion of Judges Guerrero, Sir Arnold McNair, Read and Hsu Mo. Ibid., p. 47.
[789] Dissenting opinion of Judge Alvarez, ibid., p. 51.
[790] Ibid., p. 53.
[791] See above, paras. 56-62.
[792] Subject to the more technical aspects of the debate, see sect. B below.

EXCERPTS FROM THE SECOND REPORT ON RESERVATIONS TO TREATIES

117. Reservations to 'normative' treaties are deleterious because:
- Permitting them is tantamount to encouraging partial acceptance of the treaty[793]
- And less careful drafting, since the parties can in fact modify their obligations later;[794]
- The accumulation of reservations ultimately voids these treaties of any substance where the reserving State is concerned[795]
- And, in any event, compromises their quasi-legislative functioning and the uniformity of their implementation.[796]

118. More specifically, as regards human rights treaties,
- There is 'une contradiction entre les deux expressions 'reserves' et 'droits de l'homme'. On conçoit mal qu'un Etat qui a accepté de se lier par un traité en cette matière n'ait pas tout fait pour être en mesure de remplir toutes ses obligations, [...] veuille encore se protéger par un 'domaine reservé''. (A contradiction exits between the terms 'reservations' and 'human rights'. It is hard to believe that a State that agreed to be bound by a treaty in this area would not do everything it could to fulfil its obligations, [...] yet seek to protect itself by means of a 'reserved domain';[797]
- It would be 'desirable in principle that States accept the full range of obligations, because the human rights norms are the legal expression of the essential rights that every person is entitled to as a human being';[798]
- Accompanying ratification with a series of reservations could give the reserving State an opportunity to enhance its international 'image' at little cost without having to really accept any restrictive commitments.[799]

119. Conversely, it is argued that:
- Reservations are a 'necessary evil'[800] resulting from the current state of international society; they 'cannot be qualified at the ethical level; they reflect a fact,

---

[793] G. G. Fitzmaurice, op. cit. (footnote 112 above), pp. 17 and 19-20.
[794] Ibid., p. 19.
[795] Cf. W. A. Schabas, op. cit. (footnote 118 above), p. 41.
[796] Cf., in the area of environmental protection, Gwyneth G. Stewart, 'Enforcement problems in the endangered species Convention: reservations regarding the reservation clause', Cornell International Law Journal, 1981, p. 438, and, albeit indirectly, in the field of disarmament, Pascal Boniface, Les sources du désarmement, (Paris, Economica, 1989), p. 68.
[797] P.-H. Imbert, op. cit. (footnote 117 above), p. 99 (HRR, 1981, p. 28); see also M. Coccia, op. cit. (footnote 96 above), p. 16; both authors endorse this opinion but do not claim it as their own. See also the position of Mr. Robinson during the debate on the preliminary report (A/CN.4/SR.2402, pp. 11 and 12).
[798] See the Human Rights Committee, General Comment No. 24 (footnote 86, above), para. 4.
[799] See R. P. Anand, 'Reservations to multilateral treaties', Indian Journal of International Law, 1960, p. 88; P.-H. Imbert, op. cit. (footnote 43 above), p. 249; and W. A. Schabas, op. cit. (footnote 118 above), p. 41.
[800] R. Ago, Yearbook ... 1965, vol. I, p. 151.

namely that there are minorities whose interests are as respectable as those of majorities';[801]

- More positively, they are an essential condition of life, of the dynamics of treaties[802] that promotes the development of international law in the process;[803]
- By facilitating the conclusion of multilateral conventions;[804] and
- By allowing a greater number of States to become parties;[805]
- Since, ultimately, partial participation is better than no participation at all.[806]

120. These considerations carry even more weight in the area of human rights:

- 'The possibility of entering reservations may encourage States which consider that they have difficulties in guaranteeing all the rights in [such treaties] none the less to accept the generality of obligations in that instrument';[807]
- 'Indeed, it could be argued that there is a particular need for a margin of flexibility in respect of human rights treaties which tend to touch on matters of particular sensitivity to States ...';[808]

---

[801] Paul Reuter, fourth report on the question of treaties concluded between States and international organizations or between two or more international organizations, A/CN.4.285, Yearbook ... 1975, vol. II, p. 36.

[802] P.-H. Imbert, op. cit. (footnote 43 above), p. 463.

[803] Ibid., p. 464.

[804] International Court of Justice, advisory opinion (footnote 46 above), Reports, 1951, p. 22. See also the position of Mr. Rao during the debate on the preliminary report (A/CN.4/SR.2404, pp. 18-19).

[805] Cf. for example Manfred Lachs, 'Le développement et fonctionnement des traités multilatéraux', Collected Courses, 1957 II, vol. 92, pp. 229-230. See also the views expressed during the debate on the preliminary report by Mr. Villagran Kramer (A/CN.4/SR.2403, p. 8) and Mr. Elaraby ('In a sense, reservations were the price paid for broader participation', A/CN.4/SR.2404, p. 16) and, in the area of the environment, G. G. Stewart, op. cit. (footnote 188 above), p. 436.

[806] This is what Fitzmaurice called, speaking in highly critical terms, 'the half-a-loaf doctrine' (op. cit. (footnote 112 above), p. 17): '...that in any case half a loaf is better than no bread - that it is better (especially as regards the lawmaking, social and humanitarian type of Convention) that States should become parties even if they cannot (or will not) carry out certain of the obligations involved, and that they should be bound by at least some of the obligations of the Convention, even if they disengage themselves from the rest', (ibid., p. 11). For examples in a similar vein, see Charles de Visscher, Théories et réalités en droit international public, Paris, Pédone 1970, pp. 292-293, or P.-H. Imbert, op. cit. (footnote 43 above), p. 372 or p. 438.

[807] Human Rights Committee, General Comment No. 24, (footnote 86 above), para. 4.

[808] C. Redgwell, op. cit. (footnote 97 above), p. 279; see also P.-H. Imbert, op. cit. (footnote 117 above), pp. 102-103 (HRR 1981, p. 30). Thomas Giegrich shows how 'kulturellen Relativismus' (cultural relativism) is often invoked in the area of human rights ('Vorbehalte zu Menschenrechtsabkommen: Zulässigkeit, Gültikeit und Prüfungskompetenzen von Vertragsgremien - Ein konstitutioneller Ansatz', pp. 713-715, English summary pp. 778-779). See also the position of Mr. Rao during the debate on the preliminary report (A/CN.4/SR.2404, pp. 18-19).

- Particularly when the terms of the convention are backed up by a monitoring mechanism which ensures a dynamic interpretation of the instrument;[809]
- The formulation of reservations would seem to constitute proof that States take their treaty obligations seriously; and
- Gives them an opportunity to harmonize their domestic law with the requirements of the convention while obligating them to abide by the most important provisions;
- Especially since the implementation of human rights treaties takes time;[810] and
- Takes more resources, particularly financial resources, than it would appear at first.[811]

121. Similarly, it is argued that the usefulness of reservations in the area of human rights is borne out concretely by the fact that very few conventions concluded in this area exclude reservations[812] and that this option is available even when a treaty is concluded among a small number of States.[813] It is also obvious that the periodic calls for withdrawal of reservations to human rights treaties elicit only a faint response,[814] which would seem to point up the usefulness of such reservations.

122. The same authors maintain that in reality, the scope of reservations to law-making treaties, including those in the field of human rights, is limited,[815] a view contested by the doctrine opposing the use of reservations.[816] Again, the question is one of appreciation, and this serves merely to confirm that there can be no objective answer to the question of whether the drawbacks of reservations to these instruments outweigh their advantages or vice versa.

---

[809] P.-H. Imbert, ibid.

[810] Cf. J. McBride, op. cit. (footnote 118 above), pp.2-4 (manuscript version). See also the position of Mr. Rao during the debate on the preliminary report (A/CN.4/SR.2404, pp. 18-19).

[811] See J. McBride, ibid., pp. 4-13.

[812] See para. 124 below.

[813] As in the case of the Council of Europe; cf. article 64 of the European Convention on Human Rights (see P.-H. Imbert, op. cit. (footnote 117 above), p. 119; HRR 1981, p. 38).

[814] Cf. the response dated 17 February 1994 from the Committee of Ministers of the Council of Europe concerning Parliamentary Assembly recommendation 1223 (1993); see also Belinda Clark, 'The Vienna Convention reservations regime and the Convention on Discrimination against Women', American Journal of International Law 1991, p. 288.

[815] Cf. M. Coccia, op. cit. (footnote 96 above), p. 34; J. K. Gamble, op. cit. (footnote 128 above), pp. 372-394, passim; P.-H. Imbert, op. cit. (footnote 43 above), pp. 347 ff., and op. cit. (footnote 117 above), p. 105 (HRR 1981, p. 31); Dinah Shelton, 'state practice on reservations to human rights treaties', Annuaire canadien des droits de la personne 1983, pp. 205-234, passim, note pp. 225-227; Markus G. Schmidt, 'Reservations to United Nations human rights treaties - the case of the two Covenants', to be included in op. cit. (footnote 98 above), pp. 18-20 (manuscript version), or Sir Ian Sinclair, The Vienna Convention on the Law of Treaties (Manchester University Press), 1984, p. 77.

[816] Cf. W. A. Schabas, op. cit. (footnote 118 above), pp. 42 and 64; see also the concerns expressed by the Human Rights Committee, the Committee on the Elimination of Discrimination against Women and the chairpersons of human rights treaty bodies (see above, para. 59).

123. The 'truth' probably lies somewhere in between; everything depends on the circumstances and the purpose of the provisions in question. However, leaving the question unanswered presents few drawbacks: it is true that the first subparagraph of article 19 of the Vienna Conventions on the law of treaties sets out the principle of the right to formulate reservations; however, like all rules governing reservations (and like the vast majority of other rules) set out in these Conventions, this is an optional residual rule which negotiators can reject if they find it useful to do so. If they feel that the treaty does not lend itself to the formulation of reservations, they need only insert a clause expressly excluding them, which is precisely the case contemplated in article 19, subparagraph (a).

124. It is remarkable, however, that such provisions should be so rare in normative human rights treaties;[817] they seem to be equally rare in disarmament treaties.[818]

125. This infrequency of clauses prohibiting reservations would seem to be explained by the ordinary-law regime laid down in the Vienna Conventions which is applied owing to the frequent silence[819] of these treaties on the matter of reservations. Another striking phenomenon seems prima facie to lead to this conclusion: this is the wide range of reservation clauses found in normative treaties. While these treaties might seem by their very nature to warrant a different reservation regime than that applicable to other types of treaties, one might also expect to see parties use this system, if not regularly, then at least frequently. This is not the case, however.

Where reservation clauses do exist in such treaties, including human rights treaties, they are notable for their great diversity.[820] These hints of the Vienna regime's 'acceptability' are confirmed when one looks at the special treatment given to this regime in human rights treaties.

---

[817] See, however, examples in the Supplementary Convention on the Abolition of Slavery, the Slave Trade, and Institutions and Practices Similar to Slavery of 7 September 1956 (article 9), the Convention against Discrimination in Education of 14 December 1960 (article 9), Protocol 6 to the European Convention on Human Rights, on abolition of the death penalty, of 28 April 1983 (article 4) or the European Convention against Torture of 26 November 1987 (article 21), all of which prohibit any reservations to their provisions.

[818] See, however, article 22 of the Paris Convention of 13 January 1993 on the prohibition of chemical weapons. The clauses prohibiting reservations seem to be more common in the field of environmental protection.; cf. the Madrid Protocol of 4 October 1991, on protection of the Antarctic environment (article 24), the New York Convention of 9 May 1992, on climate change (article 24), or the Rio Convention of 5 June 1992, on biological diversity (article 37), all of which exclude reservations.

[819] See para. 134 below.

[820] On this question see P.-H. Imbert, op. cit. (footnote 43 above), pp. 193-196, or W. A. Schabas, 'Invalid reservations to the International Covenant on Civil and Political Rights: is the United States still a party?', Brooklyn Journal of International Law, 1995, p. 286.

EXCERPTS FROM THE SECOND REPORT ON RESERVATIONS TO TREATIES

B. ADAPTING THE 'VIENNA REGIME' TO THE PARTICULAR CHARACTERISTICS OF MULTILATERAL NORMATIVE TREATIES

126. In the Special Rapporteur's view, the real legal question here is not whether or not it is appropriate to authorize reservations to multilateral normative treaties, but whether, when contracting parties remain silent on the legal regime of reservations, the rules set out in the 1969 and 1986 Conventions can be adapted to any type of treaty, including 'normative' treaties, including in the field of human rights.

127. In truth, it would seem had to argue that the answer to this question must be in the affirmative. Should one do so, however, it is not because reservations are a 'good' thing or a 'bad' thing in general or for normative treaties or for human rights, but because the rules which are applicable to them under the Vienna conventions strike a good balance between the concerns raised by the advocates of reservations and those raised by their opponents, and provide a reasonable answer to their respective arguments on which a position need no longer be taken.

128. The general and uniform applicability of the legal regime of reservations set out in the Vienna Conventions of 1969 and 1986 is related to the particular characteristics of this regime, which its architects sought to make flexible and adaptable precisely so that it could be applied in all situations. In fact, the system is adapted to the special features of general multilateral law-making treaties, including the requirements of human rights conventions.

(a) Flexibility and adaptability of the 'Vienna regime'

129. The unique nature of the regime of reservations to treaties is due to the regime's fundamental features, which enable it to meet the specific needs of all types of treaties and related instruments. Its flexibility guarantees its adaptability.

130. The system of unanimity which was the rule, at least at the universal level, until the advisory opinion of the International Court of Justice on Reservations to the Convention on the Prevention and Punishment of the Crime of Genocide,[821] was cumbersome and rigid. It was this rigidity that led to a preference for the Pan-American system, which became widespread after 1951. As the Court noted with regard to the 1948 Convention:

> 'Extensive participation in conventions of this type has already given rise to greater flexibility in the international practice concerning multilateral conventions. More general resort to reservations, very great allowance made for tacit assent to reservations, the existence of practices which go so far as to admit that the author of reservations which have been rejected by certain contracting parties is nevertheless to be regarded as a party to the convention in relation to those contracting parties that have

[821] See above, footnote 46.

accepted the reservations - all these factors are manifestations of a new need for flexibility in the operation of multilateral conventions.'[822]

131. 'Flexibility' - this is the key word of the new legal regime of reservations which is gradually replacing the old regime and becoming enshrined in the Vienna Conventions.

132. The first report of Sir Humphrey Waldock in 1962, which marks a departure by the International Court of Justice from the old reservation regime, contains a lengthy appeal, which is particularly eloquent and complete, in favour of a 'so-called flexible system' under which, 'as under the unanimity system, the essential interests of each individual State are to a very great extent safeguarded ...'.[823] The Special Rapporteur wishes to stress that the rules he is proposing - which have their origin largely in the rules set out in the Vienna Conventions - are most likely to promote the universality of treaties yet will have only a minimal effect on both the integrity of the text of the treaty and the principle of agreement.[824]

133. The principal elements that make this possible are the following:

(1) The permissibility of reservations must be considered in the light of the object and purpose of the treaty;[825] this fundamental rule in itself makes it pointless to modify a reservation regime in terms of the object of the treaty, for the object is taken into account in the very wording of the basic rule;

(2) The freedom of the other contracting parties to agree is entirely preserved, since they can change the scope of the reservations as they choose practically without restriction, through the mechanism of acceptances and objections;[826]

(3) 'The right to 'formulate' reservations instituted by the Vienna Conventions is in no way residual in nature: every treaty can limit this freedom and, in particular, prohibit any or certain reservations';[827] it can also institute its own regime for admissibility and monitoring reservations. Accordingly, the Vienna rules are simply a safety net which negotiators are free to reject or modify, particularly if they find it useful to do so because of the nature or the object of the treaty.

134. Moreover, it is not immaterial that, notwithstanding this possibility, many treaties do not contain reservation clauses, but simply refer implicitly to the regime set out in the 1969 and 1986 Conventions. '[C]e silence n'a pas du tout la même signification qu'autrefois: il n'est pas uniquement une conséquence du besoin de ne pas remettre en cause un compromis ou de l'impossibilité pour les Etats de

---

[822] Ibid., Reports 1951, pp. 21-22; underlining added.

[823] Op. cit. (footnote 155 above), pp. 64-65. See the preliminary report (footnote 2 above), para. 36.

[824] Ibid., pp. 64-65.

[825] Cf. article 19, subparagraph (c), of the Vienna Conventions.

[826] Cf. article 20, paras. 3, 4 and 5, and articles. 21 and 22. See the preliminary report (footnote 2 above), para. 61.

[827] Paul Reuter, op. cit. (footnote 43 above); see also para. 26 above and the other references cited in footnote 43.

s'entendre sur un texte commun; il correspond essentiellement au désir de la majorité d'entre eux de soumettre les réserves au 'système souple' élaboré dans le cadre des Nations Unies. Le silence du traité devient ainsi le résultat d'un choix positif.' (This silence no longer means what it once did: it is not solely a consequence of the need to avoid questioning an agreement of the inability for States to agree on a joint text; it corresponds largely to the desire of most States to submit reservations to the 'flexible' system developed by the United Nations. The treaty's silence then becomes the result of a positive choice),[828] and the residual rules thus become the ordinary law deliberately chosen by the parties.[829]

135. It is likewise not immaterial that this solution of implicit - and, occasionally, explicit[830] - reference was used in a number of general multilateral normative treaties, in fields including human rights. This would seem to establish that the Vienna regime is suited to the particular characteristics generally attributed to treaties of this type.

(b) The 'Vienna regime' is suited to the particular characteristics of normative treaties

136. The objections made to the 'flexible' regime of Pan-American origin[831] used in the Vienna Conventions on the Law of Treaties were synthesized forcefully and with skill by Fitzmaurice in an important article published in 1953. In it he stressed in particular the drawbacks the regime would present in the case of reservations to 'normative' treaties.[832] These arguments have been repeated numerous times since and revolve principally around three ideas: the Pan-American or 'Vienna' regime[833] is ostensibly unsuitable to this type of treaty and especially to human rights treaties because:

- It would undermine the integrity of the rules set out therein, and uniform implementation of these rules is essential for the community of contracting States;
- It would be incompatible with the absence of reciprocity in commitments undertaken by the parties under such instruments; and
- It would fail to preserve equality between the parties.

[828] P.-H. Imbert, op. cit. (footnote 43), pp. 226-227.
[829] Cf. ibid., p. 226.
[830] See footnotes 18 and 19 above.
[831] This origin was rightly emphasized by Mr. Barboza during the debate on the preliminary report (A/CN.4/SR.2404, p. 12).
[832] Op. cit. (footnote 112 above), pp. 15-22 in particular.
[833] In reality, the two regimes differ somewhat in the way they are implemented, but they are identical in spirit, and have thus received similar criticism.

(i) Problems related to the 'integrity' of normative treaties

137. It is undeniable that the 'Vienna regime' does not guarantee the absolute integrity of treaties. Furthermore, the very concept of reservations is incompatible with this notion of integrity;[834] by definition, a reservation 'purports to exclude or to modify the legal effect of certain provisions of the treaty'.[835] Thus far the only way to preserve this integrity completely has been to prohibit any reservations whatsoever; this, it cannot be repeated too often, is perfectly consistent with the 1969 and 1986 Conventions.[836]

138. The fact remains that, where a treaty is silent, the rules set out in the Vienna Conventions, by not fully addressing the concerns of those who would defend the absolute integrity of normative treaties, guarantee, to all intents and purposes, that the essence of the treaty is preserved.

139. Article 19, subparagraph (c), in fact prohibits the formulation of reservations that are incompatible 'with the object and purpose of the treaty', which means that in no case can the treaty be weakened by a reservation, contrary to the fears occasionally expressed by the proponents of the restrictive school.[837] And this can lead to the prohibition of any reservations, because it is perfectly conceivable that a treaty on a very specific topic may have a small number of provisions that form an indissoluble whole. This situation, however, is probably the exception, if only because 'purely normative' treaties are themselves rare.[838]

140. This, however, is the rationale given by the representative of the International Labour Office in his statement on 1 April 1968 to the Vienna Conference in support of the traditional prohibition of any reservation to international labour conventions.[839] According to Mr. C. Wilfred Jenks, 'ILO practice concerning reservations is based on the principle recognized in Article 16[840] that reservations incompatible with the object and purpose of the treaty are inadmissible. Reservations to international labour Conventions are incompatible with the object and purpose of these Conventions.'[841] Actually, this explanation seems somewhat artificial, and it is probably better to assume that in this specific case the prohibition of reservations is based on a practice which, most likely,

[834] As the International Court of Justice noted, '[i]t does not appear, moreover, that the conception of the absolute integrity of a convention has been transformed into a rule of international law'. (See advisory opinion (footnote 46 above), Reports 1951, p. 24.)
[835] Art. 2, para. 1 (d), of the 1969 and 1986 Conventions.
[836] See above, para. 133.
[837] See above, para. 117.
[838] See above, para. 85.
[839] To which Mr. Razafindralambo drew attention during the debate on the preliminary report (cf. A/CN.4.SR.2042, pp. 5-6).
[840] Became art. 19 of the Convention.
[841] The text of this statement was transmitted to the Special Rapporteur by the ILO Legal Counsel.

assumed a customary value owing more to do with the tripartite structure of ILO than with the object and purpose of the treaty.[842]

141. The reserving State's obligation to respect them is not the only legal guarantee against the weakening of a treaty, normative or not, by means of reservations. Indeed, there can be no doubt that the provisions concerning peremptory norms of general international law (jus cogens) cannot be the subject of reservations. *General Comment No. 24* of the Human Rights Committee links this prohibition with the prohibition against any action contrary to the object and purpose of the treaty:

> 'Reservations that offend peremptory norms would not be compatible with the object and purpose of the Covenant'.[843]

This wording is open to discussion[844] and cannot, in any event, be generalized: one can well imagine a treaty referring, very indirectly, to a norm of jus cogens without that norm having anything to do with the object and purpose of the treaty. A reservation to such a provision would still be impermissible, for one cannot imagine a State using a reservation to a treaty provision, to avoid having to respect a rule which it was in any case obliged to respect as 'a norm from which no derogation is permitted'.[845]

142. Whatever its basis, the rule is no less definite and can have concrete effects in the area of human rights. There is no question that certain rules which seek to protect human rights are of a peremptory character; the International Court of Justice in fact provided two such examples in the commentary to draft article 50 (which became article 53 of the 1969 Convention) in its 1966 report: the prohibition of genocide and of slavery.[846] However, this is not the case with all rules that seek to protect rights,[847] and the identification of these norms is not easy; this is in fact the main flaw in the notion of jus cogens. Yet the principle is not really debatable:

---

842 Jenks, in the same statement, added that '[t]he procedural arrangements concerning reservations embodied in the Draft Articles are entirely inapplicable to the ILO by reason of its tripartite character as an organization in which, in the language of our Constitution, "representatives of employers and workers" enjoy "equal status with those of governments"'. See also the Report of the Director-General of the International Labour Office submitted to the International Labour Conference in 1921, International Labour Conference - Third session, vol. III, annex XVII, p. 1046, and the Memorandum by the Director-General of ILO dated 15 June 1927 (footnote 125 above), p. 882.

843 See above, footnote 86, para. 8.

844 Cf. the doubts expressed in this connection by the United States of America in its commentary (footnote 87) to General Comment No. 24 (52).

845 Cf. art. 53 of the 1969 and 1986 Vienna Conventions.

846 Yearbook ... 1966, vol. II, p. 248.

847 See, for example, M. Coccia, op. cit. (footnote 96 above), p. 17; J. McBride, op. cit. (note 118 above), pp. 1 and 32 ff; W. A. Schabas, op. cit. (footnote 118 above), pp. 49-50; however, see also the doubts raised by Éric Suy, 'Droits des traités et droits de l'homme' in Völkerrecht

peremptory provisions in treaties cannot be the subject of reservations, and this, taken together with respect for the object and purpose of the treaty, provides a further guarantee for the integrity of normative conventions, particulary in the field of human rights.

143. Should one go further and consider that reservations to treaties which reflect the rules of customary international law are always impermissible? The Human Rights Committee affirmed this, basing itself on the special characteristics of human rights treaties:

> 'Although treaties that are mere exchanges of obligations between States allow them to reserve inter se application of rules of general international law, it is otherwise in human rights treaties, which are for the benefit of persons within their jurisdiction'.[848]

144. This would seem to be debatable prima facie.

145. One might, after further study,[849] agree with the Human Rights Committee that reservations to customary norms are not excluded a priori - such norms are binding on States independently of whether they have expressed their acceptance of the treaty norm; however, unlike the case of peremptory norms, States can derogate from customary norms by agreement inter se. And one should not overlook the phenomenon of the 'persistent objector', the party who can indeed refuse to apply a rule which it cannot oppose under general international law. As the United Kingdom pointed out in its observations on *General Comment No. 24*, 'there is a clear distinction between choosing not to enter into treaty obligations and trying to opt out of customary international law'.[850] But if this reasoning is correct, it is hard to see why it would not apply also to reservations to human rights treaties.

146. By way of justification, the Human Rights Committee limits itself to noting that these instruments are designed to protect the rights of individuals. What is involved is a simple matter of principle: implicitly, the Committee starts from the assumption that human rights treaties are legislative, not only in the material sense - which, with some reservations, is acceptable[851] - but also in the formal sense, which is not acceptable and is the product of a highly questionable amalgam.

---

als Rechtsordnung Internationale Gerichtsbarkeit, Menschenrechte - Festschrift für Hermann Mosler (Berlin, Springer-Verlag, 1983), pp. 935-939.

[848] General Comment No. 24 (footnote 86 above), para. 8. (France, in its remarks (see footnote 87 above), rightly pointed out that 'paragraph 8 is worded in such a way that the document seems to associate, to the point of confusing them, two separate legal notions - that of "peremptory norms' and that of 'rules of international customary law"'.

[849] See above, para. 74.

[850] Commentary (footnote 87 above), para. 7, p. 154. (However, one may well question what real motives a State might have for doing so.)

[851] See above, para. 85.

147. In making this assumption, the Committee is forgetting that these instruments, even though they are designed to protect individuals, are still treaties: it is true that they benefit individuals directly, but only because - and after - States have expressed their willingness to be bound by them. The rights of the individual derive from the State's consent to be bound by such instruments. Reservations are inseparable from such consent, and the Special Rapporteur believes that the order of factors cannot be reversed by stating - as the Committee does - that the rule exists as a matter of principle and is binding on the State, at least by virtue of the treaty, if the State has not consented to it. If, as the Committee maintains, States can 'reserve inter se application of rules of general international law', there is no legal reason why the same should not be true of human rights treaties; in any event, the Committee does not give any such reason.

(ii) Problems with regard to the 'non-reciprocity' of undertakings

148. In fact, this somewhat marginal issue of whether reservations can be made to treaty provisions reproducing rules of customary law ties in with another, broader issue, that of whether the 'Vienna regime' is not incompatible with the non-reciprocity that is one of the essential characteristics of human rights treaties and, more generally, normative treaties.

149. According to a recent article, '[i]n contrast to most multilateral treaties, human rights agreements do not establish a network of bilateral legal relationships among the states parties, but rather an objective regime for the protection of values accepted by all of them. A reservation entered by one state therefore cannot have the reciprocal effect of releasing one or all the other states parties from its or their treaty obligations'.[852]

150. These arguments are largely correct, but while they may perhaps lead one to think that reservations to human rights treaties should be prohibited or permitted restrictively[853] - a decision that is solely up to the contracting parties - they do not in any way allow one to conclude that the common regime of reservations is inapplicable to such instruments.

151. These statements should first of all be qualified:

1. If they are valid, they are not valid only for human rights, and while a rigorous quantitative analysis is not possible here, one might ask whether normative treaties are not the largest category of multilateral treaties so far concluded;

[852] T. Giegerich, op. cit. (footnote 200 above), English summary, p. 780; see also, inter alia: Antonio Cassese, 'A new reservations clause (art. 20 of the United Nations Convention on the Elimination of All Forms of Racial Discrimination', in Recueil d'études de droit international en hommage à Paul Guggenheim, (Geneva, Institut Universitaire des Hautes Etudes Internationales 1968), p. 268; B. Clark, op. cit. (footnote 205 above); R.J. Cook, op. cit. (footnote 128 above), p. 646.

[853] See above, sect. 1, para. 3, paras. 97-105.

2. While it is true that human rights treaties assume that the parties accept certain common values, it is still an open question whether they must necessarily accept all the values conveyed by a complex human rights treaty;
3. It must also be admitted that the concept of reciprocity is not totally absent from normative treaties, including those in the area of human rights.[854]

152. It is nevertheless true that reciprocity is certainly less omnipresent in human rights treaties than in other treaties and that, as the European Commission of Human Rights has noted, the obligations resulting from such treaties 'are essentially of an objective character, being designed rather to protect the fundamental rights of individual human beings from infringement by any of the High Contracting Parties than to create subjective and reciprocal rights for the High Contracting Parties'.[855] Or, in the words of the Inter-American Court of Human Rights:

> 'In concluding these human rights treaties, the States can be deemed to submit themselves to a legal order within which they, for the common good, assume various obligations not in relation to other States, but towards all individuals within their jurisdiction.'[856]

153. Secondly, however, it is highly doubtful that this specific feature of human rights treaties would make the reservations regime inapplicable as a matter of principle.

154. Of course, force of circumstance and the actual nature of the 'non-reciprocal' clauses to which the reservations apply result in a situation where 'the reciprocal function of the reservation mechanism is almost meaningless'.[857] 'It would be simply absurd to conclude that the objections by the various European states to the United States reservations on the death penalty discharge them from their obligations under Articles 6 and 7 [of the 1966 Covenant on Civil and Political Rights] as concerns the United States, and this is surely not their intention in making the objection'.[858]

155. But all that we can deduce from this is that when a State enters a reservation to a treaty provision that must apply without reciprocity, the provisions of article 21, paragraph 3, of the Vienna Conventions of 1969 and 1986 do not apply; that is all. Moreover, the same is true when it is not the provision to which the

---

[854] See above, para. 85.
[855] Austria v. Italy case, decision on admissibility, 11 January 1961, Yearbook of the European Convention on Human Rights, 1961, p. 140; see also the advisory opinion (footnote 81 above), para. 30.
[856] Advisory opinion 2/82 (footnote 81 above).
[857] Rosalyn Higgins, 'Human rights: Some questions of integrity', M.L.R., 1989, p. 9; see also op. cit. (footnote 99 above), pp. 13 and 14 (manuscript version).
[858] W. A. Schabas, op. cit. (footnote 118 above), p. 65. In the same vein, see G. G. Fitzmaurice, op. cit. (footnote 112 above), pp. 15 and 16, of R. Higgins, op. cit. (footnote 98 above), p. 13.

reservation applies but the reservation itself that, by its nature, does not lend itself to reciprocity.[859] This is the case with reservations that are territorial in scope: it is hardly conceivable, for instance, that France might respond to a reservation by which Denmark reserved the right not to apply a treaty to Greenland by deciding not to apply that treaty to its own overseas departments. Besides, very generally speaking, the principle of reciprocity assumes a certain equality in the positions of the parties in order for a State to be able to 'respond' to a reservation.[860]

156. But, unless it is by 'doctrinal decree', reciprocity is not a function inherent in a reservations regime and is not in any way the object of such a regime.[861] Integrity and universality are reconciled in a treaty by preserving its object and its purpose, independently of any consideration having to do with the reciprocity of the parties' undertakings, and it is hard to see why a reciprocity that the convention rules out would be reintroduced by means of reservations.

157. In fact, we have two choices:

- Either the provision to which the reservation applies imposes reciprocal obligations, in which case the exact balance of rights and obligations of each party is guaranteed by means of reservations, acceptances and objections, and article 21, paragraph 3, can and must be applied in full;
- Or the provision is 'normative' or 'objective', and States do not expect reciprocity for the undertakings they have given; there is no point then in speculating about possible violations of a 'reciprocity' which is not a precondition for the parties' undertakings, and the provisions of article 20, paragraph 3, are not relevant. One simply cannot say here that the reservation is 'established with regard to another party'.

158. This does not mean that the reservations regime instituted by the Vienna Conventions does not apply in this second case:

- The limitations imposed by article 19 on the freedom to formulate reservations remain entirely valid;
- Under article 20, paragraph 4 (b), an objecting State is always free to refuse to allow the treaty to enter into force as between itself and the reserving State;
- Even if this is not the case, objections are not without effect. In particular, they can play a major role in the interpretation of a treaty either by any bodies which the treaty may set up[862] or by external mechanisms for the settlement of disputes,[863] or even by national jurisdictions.

---

[859] See to this effect P.-H. Imbert, op. cit. (footnote 43 above), p. 258 and the somewhat diverse examples given by this author, pp. 258-260.

[860] Ibid.

[861] See above, para. 1.

[862] See P.-H. Imbert, op. cit. (footnote 117 above) and the examples cited on pp. 116 and 117 (HRR 1984, pp. 37 and 38); see also B. Clark, op. cit. (footnote 205 above), p. 318, or W. A. Schabas, op. cit. (footnote 212 above), pp. 313 and 314.

[863] In the Loizidou case (footnote 80 above), the European Court of Human Rights based itself on 'the subsequent reaction of various Contracting Parties to the Turkish declarations', in

(iii) Problems of equality between the parties

159. Many authors link so-called problems of reciprocity to the fact that the reservations regime instituted by the Vienna Conventions allegedly violates the principle of equality between the parties to normative treaties. Professor Pierre-Henri Imbert sums up this argument[864] as follows: the absence of reciprocity means that reservations may violate another fundamental principle, that of equality between the contracting parties. States which have not entered reservations are required to comply with the entire treaty, including the provisions whose application has been evaded by the reserving State. The latter State will thus be at an advantage. This inequality cannot be counterbalanced by objections to the reservations, since the objecting State will still be required to fulfil all its obligations, even if it refuses to be bound with regard to the reserving State.[865]

160. In his first report, Sir Humphrey Waldock countered this argument, noting that:

> 'Too much weight ought not, however, to be given to this point. For normally the State wishing to make a reservation would equally have the assurance that the non-reserving State would be obliged to comply with the provisions of the treaty by reason of its obligations to other States,[866] even if the reserving State remained completely outside the treaty. By entering into the treaty subject to its reservation, the reserving State at least submits itself in some measure to the regime of the treaty. The position of the non-reserving State is not made in any respect any more onerous if the reserving State becomes a party to the treaty on a limited basis by reason of its reservation'.[867]

view of Turkey's 'awareness of the legal position' created by declarations which the Court deemed invalid (para. 95).

864 Of which Sir Gerald Fitzmaurice was an ardent proponent (cf. op. cit. (footnote 112 above), p. 16, or 'The law and procedure of the International Court of Justice, 1951-1954: treaty interpretation and other treaty points', B.Y.B.I.L., 1957, pp. 278, 282 and 287).

865 Op. cit. (footnote 127), p. 110. The Commission showed itself sympathetic to this argument in its Report for 1951 (footnote 47 above), in which it noted that, in treaties of a law-making type: 'each State accepts limitations on its own freedom of action on the understanding that the other participating States will accept the same limitations on a basis of equality' (para. 22).

866 And, one might add, by reason of the very nature of the treaty.

867 Yearbook ... 1962, vol. II, p. 64. The Commission endorsed this reasoning (cf. its reports to the General Assembly in 1962, ibid., p. 198, and 1966, Yearbook ... 1966, vol. II, p. 224).

The reservation does not create inequality, but attenuates it by enabling the author of the reservation, who without it would have remained outside the circle of contracting parties, to be partially bound by the treaty.[868]

161. Once the reservation[869] has been made, article 19 and subsequent articles of the Vienna Conventions guarantee the equality of the contracting parties in that:

- 'The reservation does not modify the provisions of the treaty for the other parties to the treaty inter se' (article 21, paragraph 2); and
- These other parties may formulate an objection and draw whatever inferences they see fit.

However, by virtue of article 20, paragraph 4, the objecting State may restore the equality which it considers threatened by the reservation by preventing the entry into force of the treaty as between itself and the reserving State. This puts the two States in the same position as if the reserving State had not expressed its consent to be bound by the treaty.

162. Furthermore, both the argument based on the loss of equality between the parties and that based on non-reciprocity are difficult to comprehend in that it is hard to see why and how they could apply in the case of treaties which are specifically not based on reciprocity of obligations between the parties but rather constitute clusters of unilateral undertakings pursuing the same ends. It is illogical to suggest that each contracting party should consent to be bound only because the others will do likewise, since its obligations are not the counterpart of those assumed by the others.[870] And it is not a little ironic that it is precisely the authors who insist most on the non-reciprocal nature of normative treaties, beginning with human rights instruments, who also invoke the adverse effects which the formulation of reservations has on reciprocity and equality: how could reservations affect the reciprocity ... of non-reciprocal undertakings?

CONCLUSION OF SECTION 2: THE 'VIENNA REGIME' IS GENERALLY APPLICABLE

163. In concluding this analysis, it appears that:

1. The reservations regime embodied in the 1969 and 1986 Conventions was conceived by its authors as being able to be, and being required to be, applied to all

---

[868] Mr. Cassese rightly emphasizes that equality could be adversely affected by the implementation of certain 'collegiate' mechanisms for monitoring the permissibility of reservations (op. cit. (footnote 244 above), pp. 301 and 302). However, this is a very different problem, involving the possible breakdown of equality between reserving States, and is in any case caused not by the 'Vienna regime' (which is not collegiate) but by the waiving of that regime.

[869] Which, it will be recalled, is a unilateral statement (art. 2, para. 1 (d), of the 1969 Convention).

[870] P.-H. Imbert, op. cit. (footnote 43 above), p. 372.

multilateral treaties, whatever their object,[871] with the exception of certain treaties concluded among a limited number of parties and constituent instruments of an international organization, for which some limited exceptions were made;
2. Because of its flexibility, this regime is suited to the particular characteristics of normative treaties, including human rights instruments;[872]
3. While not ensuring their absolute integrity, which would scarcely be compatible with the actual definition of reservations, it preserves their essential content and guarantees that this is not distorted;
4. This conclusion is not contradicted by the arguments alleging violation of the principles of reciprocity and equality among the parties; if such a violation occurred, it would be caused by the reservations themselves and not by the rules applicable to them; moreover, these objections are hardly compatible with the actual nature of normative treaties, which are not based on reciprocity of the undertakings given by the parties;
5. There is no need to take a position on the advisability of authorizing reservations to normative provisions, including those relating to human rights: if it is felt that they must be prohibited, the parties are entirely free to exclude them or to limit them as necessary by including an express clause to this effect in the treaty, a procedure which is perfectly compatible with the purely residual rules embodied in the Vienna Conventions.

SECTION 3. IMPLEMENTATION OF THE GENERAL RESERVATIONS REGIME (APPLICATION OF THE 'VIENNA REGIME' TO HUMAN RIGHTS TREATIES)

164. The current controversy regarding the reservations regime applicable to human rights treaties[873] is probably based, in part at least, on a misunderstanding. Despite what may have been understood from certain ambiguous or clumsy formulas, the monitoring bodies established by the human rights instruments do not challenge the principle of the applicability to these treaties of the rules relating to reservations contained in the Vienna Conventions and, in particular, they do not deny that the

---

[871] To use the formula adopted by Mr. Rao in discussing the preliminary report, it achieves 'a certain diversity in unity' (A/CN.4/SR.2404, p. 19).

[872] This was, moreover, the position taken by most States whose representatives spoke on this point in the Sixth Committee at the fiftieth session of the General Assembly; see, inter alia, the statements on behalf of Algeria (A/C.6/50/SR.23, para. 65), India (A/C.6/50/SR.24, para. 43) or Sri Lanka (ibid., para. 82) emphasizing the desirable unity of the reservations regime, or the United States of America (A/C.6/50/SR.13, paras. 50-53), Pakistan (A/C.6/50/SR.18, para. 62), Spain (A/C.6/50/SR.22, para. 44), France (ibid., para. 54), Israel (A/C.6/50/SR.23, para. 15), the Czech Republic (ibid., para. 46) or Lebanon (A/C.6/50/SR.25, para. 20) rejecting the idea of a special regime for human rights treaties; see also the more tentative statements by the representatives of Australia (A/C.6/50/SR.24, para. 10) and Jamaica (ibid., paras. 19 and 21).

[873] See paras. 56-60 above.

permissibility of reservations must be determined, where the treaty is silent on the matter, on the basis of the fundamental criterion of the object and purpose of the treaty. The real problems lie elsewhere and relate to the existence and extent of the determining powers of these bodies in this matter.

Paragraph 1. The fundamental criterion of the object and purpose of the treaty

165. An examination of the practice of States and international organizations and of the bodies established to monitor the implementation of treaties, including human rights treaties, confirms that the regime for reservations established by the Vienna Conventions is not only generally applicable, but is also very widely applied. This examination shows in particular that the criterion of the object and purpose of the treaty, referred to in article 19 (c), is used principally in the case where the treaty is silent, although it is also used in those cases where there are reservation clauses.

166. Although it marked the starting point of the worldwide radical transformation of the reservation regime,[874] the 1951 advisory opinion of the International Court of Justice was given on *Reservations to the Convention on the Prevention and Punishment of the Crime of Genocide* of 1948. It was, moreover, the special nature of this treaty which led the Court to distance itself from what was undeniably the dominant system at the time,[875] namely unanimous acceptance of reservations, and to favour the more flexible system of the Pan-American Union:

- the Court confined its answers strictly to the questions put to it, which related exclusively to the 1948 Convention:

> 'The questions [asked by the General Assembly] [...] having a clearly defined object, the replies which the Court is called upon to give to them are necessarily and strictly limited to that Convention',[876]

- it referred expressly to the special character of this Convention:

> 'The character of a multilateral convention, its purpose, provisions, mode of preparation and adoption, are factors which must be considered in determining, in the absence of any express

[874] See Karl ZEMANEK 'some Unresolved Questions in the Vienna Convention on the Law of Treaties', in Jerzy MAKARCZYK, ed. Etudes de droit international en l'honneur du Juge Manfred LACHS, Nijhoff. The Hague, 1984, p. 327.

[875] As is convincingly shown by the joint dissenting opinion quoted above (footnote 130), ICJ Reports 1951, pp. 32-42.

[876] Ibid. p. 20; see also the operative part, pp. 29-30. Several statements made to the Court emphasized this point; one of these was the written statement of the United States (ICJ Pleadings, pp. 33 and 42-47); this is particularly noteworthy as that country then applied the rule of unanimous consent in the exercise of its functions as depositary State (see P.-H. IMBERT, op. cit. (footnote 43), p. 61, footnote 98).

> provision on the subject, the possibility of making reservations, as well as their validity and effect',[877] and

- it stressed the 'purely humanitarian and civilizing purpose' of the contracting States and the fact that they did 'not have any interests of their own',[878]
- the Court concluded by stating:

> 'The complete exclusion from the convention of one or more States would not only restrict the scope of its application, but would detract from the authority of the moral and humanitarian principles which are its basis'.[879]

167. It was therefore difficulties connected with reservations to a highly 'normative' human rights treaty that gave rise to the definition of the present regime. As the United Kingdom pointed out in its observations on *General Comment No. 24* of the Human Rights Committee, 'It was in the light precisely of those characteristics of the Genocide Convention, and in the light of the desirability of widespread adherence to it, that the Court set out its approach towards reservations'.[880]

168. In this regard, Jude Rosalyn HIGGINS observed that:
'Although the Genocide Convention was indeed a 'human rights treaty', the Court was in 1951 concerned with the broad distinction between 'contract treaties' and 'normative treaties'. And the issue it was addressing was whether the old unanimity rule on reservations would prevail, and whether the contract/normative distinction was relevant to this answer. The only questions put to the Court related to the legal consequences, between ratifying States, of reservations made that had been objected to (and sometimes objected to by some States but not by others). 'The Court favoured a 'flexible' answer, rather than the unanimity rule, in respect of the precise questions asked to it; and it found no difference in that regard between contract and normative treaties'. She added, however: 'that cannot be said to determine the very different question: in a human rights treaty, in respect of which a monitoring body has been given certain functions, is it implicit in its functions and in the operation of the principles of Article 19 (3) of the Vienna Convention, that the treaty body rather than contracting States should decide whether a reservation is or is not compatible with the objects and purpose of the treaty?'[881]

169. This is, indeed, a different question, which will be examined in detail further on.[882] With regard to the question considered here, however, it will be noted that Mrs. HIGGINS recognizes that one can infer from the 1951 opinion that the Court rejected the distinction between 'contract treaties' and 'normative treaties' as

---

[877] Ibid. p. 22; see also p. 23.
[878] Ibid. p. 23; see para. 114 above.
[879] Ibid. p. 24.
[880] Observations (footnote 87 above), para. 4, p. 152.
[881] Op. cit. (footnote 98), p. 6 (typewritten version), underlining in the text.
[882] See para. 2 above and, in particular, para. 178.

regards the implementation of the reservations regime and that, in its view, *General Comment No. 24*, in the preparation of which she played a determining role,[883] does not reject this conclusion.

170. Quite surprisingly, moreover, the Human Rights Committee itself, in this General Comment, considers that, in the absence of any express provision on the subject in the Covenant on Civil and Political Rights, 'the matter of reservations [...] is governed by international law'[884] and goes on to make express reference to article 19, paragraph 3, of the 1969 Convention. Admittedly, it considers this as providing only 'relevant guidance',[885] but the Committee immediately adds, in a footnote:

> 'Although the Vienna Convention on the Law of Treaties was concluded in 1969 and entered into force in 1980 - i.e. after the entry into force of the Covenant - its terms reflect the general international law on this matter as had already been affirmed by the International Court of Justice in The Reservations to the Genocide Convention Case of 1951',[886]

and makes use of this provision to give its view on the admissibility of reservations to the Covenant[887] by adding:

> 'Even though, unlike some other human rights treaties, the Covenant does not incorporate a specific reference to the object and purpose test, that test governs the matter of interpretation and acceptability of reservations'.[888]

The Committee again applied this criterion in 1995, during the consideration of the first report of the United States of America. Applying the principles enunciated in *General Comment No. 24*, it noted that it believed certain reservations to the Covenant by the United States[889] 'to be incompatible with the object and purpose of the Covenant'.[890]

171. This position seems to apply to all cases, including those where there are no reservation clauses. Thus, although the practice of the ILO, which results in a

---

[883] See CCPR/C/SR.1366, para. 53, CCPR/C/SR.1380, para. 1 or CCPR/C/SR.1382, para. 1.
[884] General Comment above (footnote 36), para. 6.
[885] Ibid.
[886] Ibid. footnote 3.
[887] The question of the validity of this position cannot be dealt with in the present report.
[888] Above-mentioned General Comment (footnote 86), para. 6.
[889] In particular the reservations to article 6, para. 5, and article 7.
[890] Consideration of reports submitted by States parties under article 40 of the Covenant. Comments of the Human Rights Committee, 'United States of America', CCPR/C/79/Add.50, 7 April 1995, para. 14; see also the above-mentioned Report of the Committee (footnote 87), para. 279; see also the observations made by the Chairman of the Committee, Mr. Aguilar, during the consideration of the report, CCPR/C/SR.1406, paras. 2-5.

prohibition of reservations to the international labour conventions, is due, in fact, to other factors, that organization nevertheless justifies it on grounds based on respect for the object and purpose of those instruments.[891] Similarly, in 1992 the persons chairing the human rights treaty bodies noted that some of the reservations lodged 'would appear to give rise to serious questions as to their compatibility with the object and purpose of the treaties in question'[892] and, even more characteristically, they recommended in 1984 that treaty bodies: 'state clearly that certain reservations to international human rights instruments are contrary to the object and purpose of those instruments and consequently incompatible with treaty law';[893] it should be noted that, in doing so, they addressed bodies charged with monitoring treaties that contained or did not contain reservation clauses, thus showing their belief that this criterion constitutes a principle applying generally.

172. This same position is shown by the actual wording of the reservation clauses contained in international instruments, the variety of which has already been pointed out.[894] However, despite this diversity, the constant desire of the drafters of the treaties to promote a reservations regime based on that of article 19 of the Vienna Conventions[895] is very striking:

- as far as the Special Rapporteur is aware, it is in the area of human rights that the only treaty clause is to be found that expressly refers to the provisions of the Convention of 23 May 1969 relating to reservations;[896]
- many human rights treaties make express reference to the object and purpose as a criterion for determining the permissibility of reservations,[897] and
- it is clear from the travaux préparatoires of treaties which do not contain reservations clauses that this silence must be interpreted as an implicit but deliberate reference to the ordinary law regime established by the Convention of 23 May 1969.

173. Here too, the example of the 1996 Covenant on Civil and Political Rights is significant. After much tergiversation,[898] it was decided not to include any reservations clause in this treaty, but the treaty silence on this matter must be interpreted, not as a rejection of reservations, but as reflecting the intention of the negotiators to rely on the 'accepted principle of international law' that any State had

---

[891] See para. 140 above.

[892] See the previous Report A/47/628 (footnote 83), para. 60; see also para. 36.

[893] See the previous Report A/49/537 (footnote 83) para. 30.

[894] See para. 125 above.

[895] or, in the case of earlier treaties, on the Pan-American 'flexible regime' adopted in the ICJ's opinion of 1951.

[896] Article 75 of the American Convention on Human Rights, footnote 48 above. In its 1983 advisory opinion on restrictions to the death penalty (footnote 81 above), the Inter-American Court of Human Rights considered that the reservations of Guatemala to paragraphs 2 and 4 of article 4 of the Pact of San José were permissible in view of their compatibility with the object and purpose of the Pact.

[897] See the examples given above (footnote 49).

[898] See P.-H. IMBERT, op. cit. (footnote 43), pp. 223-224 and Rosalyn HIGGINS, 'Derogations under Human Rights Treaties', B.Y.B.I.L. 1976-1977, pp. 317-318.

the right 'to make reservations to a multi-lateral treaty [...] subject to the proviso that such reservations were not incompatible with the object and purposes of the treaty'.[899]

174. The Rome Convention of 1950, for its part, includes a reservations clause, but the clause make no reference to this criterion.[900] The view that reservations to this instrument must not only fulfil the requirements of article 64, but must also be consistent with the purpose and object of the treaty seems difficult to support, according to some commentators.[901] Nevertheless, the Commission - quite clearly - and the European Court of Human Rights - less clearly - consider reservations whose permissibility is challenged before them in the light of the fundamental criterion of the object and purpose of the treaty.[902] This approach, which seems quite a logical one - provided it is recognized that a reservation may distort the meaning of a treaty - confirms the universality of the object and purpose criterion and would seem to imply that every treaty includes an implicit clause limiting in this way the possibility of making reservations.

175. The objections of States to reservations to human rights treaties are frequently also expressly motivated by the incompatibility of the reservations with the object and purpose of these instruments. This is all the more true as States generally seem disinclined to express objections[903] and, when they do so, they rarely

---

[899] General Assembly, twenty-first session, Report of the Third Committee, A/6546; see also the statements by the representatives of several States quoted by P.-H. IMBERT, ibid., pp. 224 and 411-412.

[900] Article 64: '1. Any State may, when signing this Convention or when depositing its instrument of ratification, make a reservation in respect of any particular provision of the Convention to the extent that any law then in force in its territory is not in conformity with the provision. Reservations of a general character shall not be permitted under this Article; 2. Any reservation made under this Article shall contain a brief statement of the law concerned'.

[901] William A. SCHABAS, commentary on article 64, in Louis-Edmond PETTITI, Emannuel DECAUX and Pierre-Henri IMBERT dirs. La Convention européene des droits de l'homme - commentaire article par article. Économica, Paris, 1994, p. 938; *contra*: J. VELU et R. ERGEG, La Convention européene des droits de l'homme, Bruylant, Brussels, 1990, pp. 159-160.

[902] See the Commission's decision in the *Chrysostomos and others v. Turkey* case above (footnote 80), para. 19, and the Court's judgement in the *Loizidou* case, above (ibid.), in which the Court bases its decision on the object and purpose of articles 25 and 46 of the Convention but appears to refer more to the rules concerning the interpretation of treaties than to those concerning reservations (cf. paras. 73 and 75). In the *Temeltasch v. Switzerland* case above (*ibid.*), the Commission considered that the provisions of the Convention on the law of treaties of 23 May 1969 enunciated essentially customary rules relating to reservations (para. 68) and based itself on the definition in article 2, 1, (d), of the Convention in determining the true nature of an interpretative declaration by the defending State (paras. 69 et seq.); see, on this point, M. COCCIA, *op. cit.* (footnote 96), pp. 14-15.

[903] Cf. M. COCCIA, ibid., pp. 34-35 and appendix pp. 50-51; P.-H. IMBERT, op. cit. (footnote 43), pp. 419-434 and D. SHELTON, op. cit. (footnote 207), pp. 227-228.

give the reasons for their actions.[904] It is therefore highly symptomatic that, for example, nine States parties to the Convention on the Elimination of All Forms of Discrimination against Women[905] gave this as the reason for their objections to certain reservations,[906] one of them[907] referring expressly to article 19 (c) of the Vienna Convention on the law of treaties.[908] Similarly, several objections to reservations to the Covenant on Civil and Political Rights advanced as their justification, the incompatibility of the reservations with the object and purpose of the treaty. Thus the 11 European States which filed objections to the reservations of the United States[909] gave as justification for their position the incompatibility of some of these reservations with the object and purpose, either of the Covenant as a whole, or of some of its provisions.[910]

176. It is therefore undeniable that 'there is a general agreement that the Vienna principle of 'object and purpose' is the test'.[911] With regard to this fundamental point, the central element of the 'flexible system' adopted by the ICJ in 1951 and enshrined in the Vienna Conventions of 1969 and 1986, namely the special nature of human rights treaties or, more generally, of normative treaties, therefore does not affect the reservations regime.

Paragraph 2. The machinery for monitoring implementation of the reservations regime

177. One of the main 'mysteries' of the reservations regime established by the Vienna Conventions on the Law of Treaties is clearly that of the relations which exist, might exist, or should exist, between article 19, on the one hand, and the following articles, on the other. There can be no question of attempting, within the framework of the present report, to dispel this mystery, as this would be tantamount

---

904 Cf. D. BOWETT, 'Reservations to non-restricted multilateral treaties', B.Y.B.I.L. 1976-77, p. 75; C. REDGEWELL op. cit. (footnote 97), p. 276 and K. ZEMANEC, op. cit. (footnote 266), p. 334; See also the views expressed by the Human Rights Committee in General Comment No. ..., above, (footnote 86), para. 17.

905 Austria, Canada, Finland, Germany, Mexico, Netherlands, Norway, Portugal and Sweden.

906 Including those of Bangladesh, Brazil, Egypt, India, Iraq, Jamaica, Jordan, Libyan Arab Jamahiriya, Malawi, Maldives, Mauritius, Morocco, New Zealand, Republic of Korea, Thailand and Tunisia.

907 Portugal.

908 Concerning these objections (and, more generally, concerning the reservations to the Convention of 18 December 1979), see B. CLARK, op. cit. (footnote 205), pp. 299-302 and R. COOK, op. cit. (footnote 128), pp. 687-707; see also: Anna JENEFSKY, 'Permissibility of Egypt's Reservations to the Convention on the Elimination of All Forms of Discrimination Against Women', Maryland Journal of International Law and Trade, pp. 199-233.

909 See para. 170 above. These States are Belgium, Denmark, Finland, France, Germany, Italy, Netherlands, Norway, Portugal, Spain and Sweden.

910 See W.A. SCHABAS, op. cit. (footnote 212), pp. 310-314; for other examples, see ibid., p. 289.

911 R. HIGGINS, op. cit. (footnote 98), p. 9 (typewritten version).

to taking sides, prematurely, in the quarrel concerning 'opposability' and 'admissibility'.[912]

178. It is perhaps sufficient to note that '[d]e façon générale, la plupart des problèmes posés par l'alinéa c) de l'article 19 disparaissent dans la pratique ...',[913] and that the modalities and effects of monitoring the permissibility of reservations are problems that are, primarily, of a practical nature. It would not be correct, however, to say that these problems 'disappear' when a treaty establishes machinery for monitoring its implementation. In addition to the uncertainties inherent in the 'Vienna regime', there are other ones which the drafters of the 1969 and 1986 Conventions do not seem to have thought of[914] and which are due to the concurrence of systems for verifying the permissibility of reservations that may be envisaged: in accordance with the - more 'imprecise' than 'flexible' - rules on this point, deriving from these conventions, on the one hand, or by the monitoring mechanisms themselves, on the other? And if the answer to this question leads to these mechanisms being taken into account, a second question has immediately to be answered: what is or what should be the effect of the verification they perform?

A. DETERMINATION BY THE MONITORING BODIES OF THE PERMISSIBILITY OF RESERVATIONS

179. As was seen earlier,[915] the 'Vienna regime', intended to be of general application, is substantively adapted to the particular requirements of the human rights treaties and the general mechanisms for determining the permissibility of reservations can also apply to reservations made in this area. However, the last 15 years have seen the development of additional forms of control carried out directly by the human rights treaty monitoring bodies, the existence, if not the permissibility,

---

912 See above paras. 42-45 and Preliminary Report, above, (footnote 2), paras. 97-108 and 115-123.

913 P.-H. IMBERT, op. cit. (footnote 43), p. 138.

914 As Rosalyn HIGGINS wrote: 'This question was simply never before the International Court in the *Reservations* case - nor at issue in the preparation of the Vienna Convention. Indeed, it could not have been. Neither in 1951 nor in 1969 did there exist a web of multilateral human rights treaties with their own treaty bodies. That phenomenon was to come later' (op. cit. footnote 98; see also *supra*, para. 168) and, similarly: D. SHELTON, op. cit. (footnote 207), p. 229. Some commentators soon revealed their perplexity on this point. See, for example, A. MARESCA: 'Perplessita possono sorgere, ed interrogativi possono porsi, in particulare su *tre punti della codificata normativa*: (a) a quale soggetto, a quale organo, a quale ente competente, il potere di valutare se la formulata riserva sia *compatibile*, oppure no. con l'oggetto e con il fine del trattato? ...' (There may be some perplexity and questions may need to be answered, particularly regarding Three Aspects of the Codified Norm: (a) what subject, what body and what entities have the power of determining whether the reservation made is compatible or not with the object and purpose of the treaty? ...) (op. cit., note 43, p. 304, italics in the text).

915 Section 1 above.

of which can scarcely be questioned. This raises the problem of the coexistence and combination of these two types of control.

(a) Role of the traditional mechanisms

180. Apart from any uncertainties which may exist regarding the link between articles 19 and 20 of the Vienna Conventions, there is general agreement that the reservations regime which they establish 'is based on the consensual character of treaties'.[916] This view constitutes the fundamental '*creed*' of the 'opposability' school, which is based on the idea that 'the validity of a reservation depends solely on the acceptance of the reservation by another contracting State'.[917] It is not rejected, however, by the supporters of 'admissibility'. Thus, for example, Professor BOWETT points out that where a treaty contains no provisions concerning the settlement of disputes, 'there is at present no alternative to the system in which each party decides for itself whether another party's reservations are permissible'.[918]

181. This conventional - and imperfect - mechanism for verifying the permissibility of reservations is employed in the case of the human rights treaties:
- certain reservations clauses included in these treaties 'expressly make these clauses subject to the acceptance-objection process ...',[919]
- States do not hesitate to object to reservations to such treaties made by other parties, even in the absence of any express provision in the treaties,[920] and
- the other parties may induce the State making the reservation to withdraw the latter,[921]
- while the treaty monitoring bodies may take account of this in interpreting the treaty or determining the fate of the reservation,[922] and
- the persons chairing the human rights treaty bodies believe:

> 'it is essential, if the present system relating to reservations is to function adequately, that States that are already parties to a

[916] Taslim O. ELIAS. The Modern Law of Treaties, Oceana, Dobbs Ferry, 1974, p. 34. See also W.W. BISHOP, op. cit. (footnote 135), C. REDGWELL, op. cit. (footnote 97), p. 268 and Ch. TOMUSCHAT, op. cit. (footnote 134), p. 466.
[917] J.M. RUDA, op. cit. (footnote 128), p. 190. See also the Preliminary report above (footnote 2), para. 102.
[918] Op. cit. (footnote 296), p. 81.
[919] P.-H. IMBERT, op. cit. (footnote 117), p. 122 (H.R.R. 1951, p. 40); see for example article 8 of the Convention on the Nationality of Married Women of 29 January 1957 and article 75 of the American Convention on Human Rights, above (footnote 48), which makes reference to the 1969 Convention.
[920] See para. 175, above.
[921] Australia and the Republic of Korea withdrew some of their reservations to the 1966 Covenant on Civil and Political Rights following objections lodged by other States parties (cf. Multilateral Treaties Deposited with the Secretary- General: status as at 31 December 1994, ST/LEG/SER.E/13, p. 123 and 127-130).
[922] See para. 158 above.

> particular treaty should give full consideration to lodging an objection on each occasion when that may be appropriate'.[923]

182. There is nothing, of course, to prevent the parties from adopting a different system - either collegial or jurisdictional - for determining the validity of reservations. Both of these possibilities were envisaged on various occasions during the travaux préparatoires for the 1969 Convention, but were eventually rejected. Thus, the first two of the four 'alternative drafts' proposed *de lege ferenda* by LAUTERPACHT in his first Report on the law of treaties in 1953 was based on a collegial control of the validity of reservations by two thirds of the States concerned,[924] while under the two other drafts this control was entrusted to a committee appointed by the parties,[925] or to a chamber of summary procedure of the International Court of Justice.[926][927]

183. Although these proposals were not incorporated in the Vienna Conventions, they were included in some of the reservations clauses inserted in multilateral treaties. Thus, in the area of human rights, article 20, paragraph 2, of the International Convention on the Elimination of All Forms of Racial Discrimination of 21 December 1965 provides as follows:

> 'A reservation incompatible with the object and purpose of this Convention shall not be permitted, nor shall a reservation the effect of which would inhibit the operation of any of the bodies established by this Convention be allowed. A reservation shall be considered incompatible or inhibitive if at least two thirds of the States parties to this Convention object to it.'[928]

923 Report above (footnote 83) of 10 November 1992, para. 64: see also para. 36 and the Report of the Committee on the Elimination of Discrimination against Women, A/48/38, mimeographed version, p. 7.

924 Yearbook ... 1953, pp. 124-133.

925 Ibid., pp. 133-134.

926 Ibid., pp. 134-135.

927 See also the position taken by Hersch LAUTERPACHT *in* 'some Possible Solutions of the Problem of Reservations to Treaties', Transactions of the Grotius Society, vol. 39, 1964, pp. 108 et seq. Surprisingly, Sir Gerald FITZMAURICE, who considered a collegial system to be 'an ideal system' (op. cit. (footnote 112) pp. 23-26), did not take up this idea in his first Report (see Yearbook ... 1956, pp. 129-130). During the deliberations in 1962 several members of the Commission supported the adoption of such a system, while others successfully opposed the idea (see A. CASSESE, op. cit. (footnote 244) p. 272); some States also submitted amendments to this effect at the Vienna Conference: see, for example, the proposals of Japan (A/CONF.39/C.1/L.133 and Summary Records above (footnote 166) pp. 199-120 and of the United Kingdom (ibid., pp. 123-124).

928 For a detailed commentary on this provision, see A. CASSESE, ibid., pp. 266-304. Comparable clauses exist in other areas; see, for example, article 39 of the Customs

184. In cases such as these, determination of the admissibility of a reservation is entrusted, not to each State acting for itself, but to the totality of the parties as a collective body. This does not, however, modify the essence of the system: the consent of the parties is expressed (i) by adoption of the reservations clause itself (ii) collectively by the traditional system of acceptance (which may be tacit) or objection.

185. This second element of the consensual principle disappears if control of the admissibility of the reservation is entrusted to a jurisdictional or quasi-jurisdictional type of body.

186. As far as the Special Rapporteur is aware, there is no express reservations clause providing for this last arrangement. We may however consider that the mere fact that a treaty provides for the settlement of disputes connected with its implementation through a jurisdictional or arbitral body, automatically empowers the latter to determine the admissibility of reservations or the validity of objections. 'The question of permissibility, since it is governed by the treaty itself, is eminently a legal question and entirely suitable for judicial determination and, so far as the treaty itself or some other general treaty requiring legal settlement of disputes requires the parties to submit this type of legal question to adjudication, this would be the appropriate means of resolving the question.'[929] Here too, we remain in the context of mechanisms that are well established in general international law.

187. There does exist, moreover, an arbitral and judicial practice of this nature, although it is admittedly limited.

188. In the *Mer d'Iroise* case, for example, the United Kingdom maintained before the arbitral tribunal to which the dispute was submitted, that the three French reservations to article 6 of the Continental Shelf Convention 'should be left out of consideration altogether as being either inadmissible or not true reservations'[930] In its decision of 30 June 1977, the tribunal implicitly recognized itself competent to rule on these matters and considered 'that the three reservations to article 6 are true reservations and admissible'.[931]

189. Similarly, in the case concerning *Right of Passage over Indian Territory*, the International Court of Justice examined, and rejected, India's first preliminary objection that 'the Portuguese Declaration of acceptance of the jurisdiction of the court of 19 December 1995, is invalid for the reason that the Third Condition of the

---

Convention on the Temporary Importation of Private Road Vehicles of 4 June 1954, article 20 of the Convention of the same date concerning customs facilities for touring (and article 14 of the Additional Protocol thereto) and article 50 of the Single Convention on Narcotic Drugs of 30 March 1961. Other treaties, including treaties concluded under the auspices of FAO, incorporate the principle of the unanimous consent of the parties (see P.-H. IMBERT, op. cit. (footnote 43) pp. 174-175).

[929] D.W. BOWETT, op. cit. (footnote 296), p. 81. Likewise: M. COCCIA op. cit. (footnote 96), p. 26. The latter considers, however, that a State which accepts a reservation is no longer entitled to take advantage of its inadmissibility.

[930] Decision of 30 June 1977 (footnote 137 above), para. 49.

[931] Ibid., para. 56; see paras. 50-55.

Declaration is incompatible with the object and purpose of the optional clause'.[932] Although the Court itself never declared impermissible a reservation to an optional declaration of acceptance of its compulsory jurisdiction, Sir Hersch LAUTERPACHT twice held in well-supported opinions, that the Court should have done so.[933][934]

190. What the Court can do in litigious cases, it can obviously also do in consultative matters. As the Court observed, the questions submitted to it in 1951 were:

> 'purely abstract in character. They refer neither to the reservations, which have, in fact, been made to the Convention by certain States, nor to the objections which have been made to such reservations by other States. They do not even refer to the reservations which may in future be made in respect of any particular article; nor do they refer to the objections to which these reservations might give rise'.[935]

However, there is nothing to prevent this being the case and the human rights treaty monitoring bodies would be perfectly entitled to seek an advisory opinion regarding the permissibility of reservations to these instruments, as some have, moreover, contemplated doing,[936] and, juridically, there is nothing to prevent such a body requesting the Economic and Social Council or the General Assembly, as appropriate, 'to request an advisory opinion on the issue from the International Court of Justice' in relation to reservations with the object and purpose of the treaty, nor, from a legal standpoint, is there anything to prevent the inclusion in a future human rights treaty of 'a provision permitting the relevant treaty body to request an advisory opinion from the International Court of Justice in relation to any reservation that it considers might be incompatible with the object and purpose of

[932] Judgement of 26 November 1957, Reports of ICJ 1957, p. 141; see the Court's response, pp. 141-144.

[933] Case of *Certain Norwegian loans*, separate opinion, ICJ Reports, 1975, pp. 43-55 and *Interhandel* case, dissenting opinion, ICJ Reports, 1959, pp. 103-106; see also the dissenting opinions of President Klaestad and of Judge ARMANDHUGON, ibid., pp. 76 and 93.

[934] In its judgement in the *Loizidou* case, the European Court of Human Rights considered that reservations concerning its competence could not be judged according to the same criteria as those applicable to determination of the permissibility of reservations to declarations made under article 36, paragraph 2, of the Statute of the International Court of Justice (footnote 80 above, paras. 83-85). While there may be doubts regarding this distinction, it relates to the substance of the applicable law and not to the modalities of control.

[935] Advisory opinion (footnote 46 above), ICJ Reports, 1951, p. 21.

[936] See above Report of the Committee on the Elimination of Discrimination against Women (footnote 85).

the treaty', as was suggested by the chairpersons of the human rights treaty bodies in 1992.[937]

191. The Inter-American Court of Human Rights could also exercise its consultative competence in this area, including the matter of problems that might arise in the interpretation or implementation of treaties other than the Pact of San José,[938] and the same applies to the Strasbourg Court,[939] to which it was proposed to submit, preventively, the question of the conformity of future reservations with article 64 of the Rome Convention.[940]

192. From all these standpoints, the mechanisms for verifying the permissibility of reservations to human rights treaties are entirely conventional:

(1) The ordinary law mechanism is the ordinary law inter-State system, as reflected in article 20 of the Vienna Conventions of 1969 and 1986;

(2) It is sometimes modified or corrected by specific reservation clauses calling for majority or unanimous determination of permissibility;

(3) The jurisdictional or arbitral organs having competence to settle disputes connected with the implementation of treaties have never hesitated to give their opinion, where necessary, regarding the permissibility of reservations made by the parties;

(4) a fortiori, these organs have the competence to give advisory opinions on this matter.

(b) Role of the human rights treaty monitoring bodies

193. To these traditional mechanisms for determining the permissibility of reservations have been added, since the early 1980s, other such mechanisms in the area of human rights, because the bodies for monitoring the implementation of treaties concluded in this area have deemed themselves to have in this regard a right and a duty of control which do not, in principle, seem likely to be challenged.

(i) Development of the practice of the monitoring bodies

194. Initially, it is true these bodies showed themselves to be very hesitant and reserved on this point:

---

[937] Report above (footnote 83), paras. 61 and 65.

[938] See article 64, paragraph 1, of the Convention and the advisory opinion OC-1/82 of 24 September 1982, series A; see also R.J. COOK, op. cit. (footnote 128), p. 711.

[939] See the Second Protocol to the European Convention for the Protection of Human Rights, dated 6 May 1963.

[940] See the partly dissenting opinion of Judge VALTICOS attached to the judgement of the European Court of Human Rights of 25 August 1993, Chorherr v. Austria, p. 16 of the judgement.

- In 1978, in accordance with a very firm legal opinion given to the Director of the Human Rights Division by the Office of Legal Affairs,[941] the Committee on the Elimination of Racial Discrimination decided:

> 'The Committee must take the reservations made by States parties at the time of ratification or accession into account: it has no authority to do otherwise. A decision - even a unanimous decision - by the Committee that a reservation is unacceptable could not have any legal effect.'[942]

- The Legal Counsel of the United Nations took the same position regarding the powers of the Committee for the Elimination of Discrimination against Women,[943] and, although some members of the Committee questioned the government representatives, during the consideration of the country reports, regarding the scope of the reservations made,[944] the Committee itself always refrained from taking a position on the matter until 1987.[945]
- The Human Rights Committee, for its part, has long maintained a prudent waiting policy in this regard. During the examination of country reports some of its members expressed themselves in favour of consideration of the validity of reservations to the Covenant, while others opposed the idea,[946] however, it is felt that the Committee, although prepared to 'reclassify' an interpretative declaration as a reservation, if necessary, seemed not inclined to determine the permissibility of reservations.[947]

195. At the regional level, the bodies established under the European Convention for the Protection of Human Rights also adopted, for a long time, a

---

[941] Memorandum of 5 April 1976 (see in particular para. 8, whose wording was almost fully repeated by the Committee) reproduced *in* United Nations, Juridical Yearbook, 1976, pp. 220-221. See also Note by the Secretary-General, CERD/C/R.93.

[942] Report of the Committee to the General Assembly, A/33/18, para. 374. See in this connection the observations of P.-H. IMBERT, op. cit. (footnote 117), pp. 125-126 (H.R.R. 1981, pp. 41-42) and D. SHELTON, op. cit. (footnote 207), pp. 229-230.

[943] See the Report of the Committee on its third session, A/39/45, vol. II, annex III.

[944] See the examples given in this connection by R.J. COOK, op. cit. (footnote 128, p. 708, to footnote 303).

[945] See B. CLARK, op. cit. (footnote 205), pp. 283-289.

[946] See the examples of this given by P.-H. IMBERT, op. cit. (footnote 117), pp. 127-128 and D. SHELTON, op. cit. (footnote 207), pp. 230-231.

[947] 339/ See the decisions of 8 November 1989 in M.K. v. France and T.K. v. France (CCPR/C/37/D/220 and 222/1987) in which the Committee declares the complaints inadmissible on the ground that the French 'declaration' relating to article 27 of the Covenant constitutes a genuine reservation; *contra*: the opinion of R. HIGGINS, appended to the decisions, who considers that the declaration is one that is not binding on the Committee, which, *a contrario*, seemed to indicate, in both cases, that the Committee lacked the competence to determine the permissibility of reservations formulated by the States parties. See, on this point: M. SCHMIDT, op. cit. (footnote 207), pp. 6-7 (typewritten version).

waiting attitude and avoided taking sides in the debate between the experts on the question whether those bodies were entitled to give an opinion on the question of the permissibility of reservations to the Convention.[948] From the outset, the Commission and the Court considered that they should interpret these reservations and give them practical meaning,[949] but the bodies themselves refrained from going any further or even implying that they might undertake a verification of permissibility.

196. The report adopted by the Commission on 5 May 1982 in the *Temeltasch* case,[950] constitutes a turning point in this regard. The Commission points out:

> 'that, even if an acceptance or an objection formulated with respect to a reservation to the Convention can be seen as having any value, that does not mean that the Commission does not have competence to express an opinion regarding the conformity with the Convention of any given reservation or interpretative declaration',[951] [provisional translation]

and, basing itself on the 'special nature' of the Convention, it 'believes that the very system of the Convention confers upon it competence to consider whether in a specific case, a reservation or interpretative declaration has or has not been made in conformity with the Convention',[952] [provisional translation] consequently, the Commission finds that the Swiss interpretative declaration concerning article 6, paragraph 3 (e), of the Convention constitutes a reservation[953] and it finds, also, that the declaration is not in conformity with the provisions of article 64 of the Convention.[954]

---

[948] See in particular the controversy between Professor Héribert GOLSONG (statement at the Colloque de Rome, 5-8 November 1975, Actes du quatrième colloque international sur la Convention européenne des droits de l'homme, Council of Europe, Strasbourg, 1976, pp. 269-270 and 'Les réserves aux instruments internationaux pour la protection des droits de l'homme', *in* Université catholique de Louvain, Quatrième colloque du Département des Droits de l'homme, 7 December 1978, Les clauses échappatoires en matière d'instruments internationaux relatifs aux droits de l'homme, Bruylant, Brussels, 1982) and Professor Pierre-Henri IMBERT (op. cit., footnote 117, pp. 11-114).

[949] See, for example, the reports of the Committee on Applications, No. 473/59 (Annuaire C.E.D.H., vol. 2, p. 405) and 1008/61 (ibid., vol. 5, p. 87) and, in particular, the extracts referred to by P.-H. IMBERT, op. cit. (footnote 43), pp. 176-277.

[950] Application No. 9116/30, (footnote 30 above); see Gérard COHEN-JONATHAN, La Convention européenne des Droits de l'homme, Economica, Paris, 1989, pp. 36-93; Pierre-Henri IMBERT, 'Les réserves à la Convention européenne des Droits de l'homme devant la Commission de Strasbourg (Affaire Temeltasch)', R.G.D.I.P., 1983, pp. 580-625 (also published in English: 'Reservations to the European Convention on Human Rights Before the Strasbourg Commission: The *Temeltasch* Case', I.C.L.Q., 1984, pp. 558-595.

[951] Para. 61.

[952] Para. 65.

[953] Paras. 68 to 82.

[954] Paras. 83 to 92.

197. As the Commission, surprisingly, did not refer this matter to the Court, it was the Committee of Ministers that, pursuant to article 32 of the Convention, approved the Commission's report on this case[955] and it was only six years later, by its judgement in the *Belilos* case of 29 April 1988, that the Strasbourg court adopted the Commission's position of principle.[956] In its turn, it proceeded to 'reclassify' as a reservation an 'interpretative declaration' of Switzerland (concerning art. 6, para. 1, of the Convention)[957] and held that 'the declaration in litigation does not meet the two requirements of article 64 of the Convention and must therefore be treated as invalid',[958] [Provisional translation] after having noted that

> 'the competence of the court to determine, in the light of article 64, the validity of a reservation or of an interpretative declaration, as the case may be, was not in fact challenged. It derives both from articles 45 and 49 of the Convention [...] and from article 19 and the jurisprudence of the Court (see, finally, the judgement in the Ettl and other cases of 23 April 1987, series A No. 117, p. 19, section 42)'[959] [Provisional translation]

198. Since that time, the Commission and the European Court of Human Rights have made use of this jurisprudence on a virtually routine basis[960] and have extended it to reservations formulated by States in respect of their own competence. Thus, in its decision of 4 March 1991 concerning the admissibility of three applications made against Turkey,[961] the Commission considered that certain restrictions of its competence formulated by the respondant State in its declaration of acceptance of individual applications under article 25 were 'not authorized by that article'.[962]

---

[955] Resolution DH (83) 6 of 24 March 1983 (Annuaire C.E.D.H., 1980, p. 5.

[956] Judgement (footnote 80 above); see Henri J. BOURGUIGNON, 'The Belilos Case: New Light on Reservations to Multilateral Treaties', Virginia Journal of International Law, 1989, pp. 347-386; Iain CAMERON and Frank Horn, 'Reservations to the European Convention on Human Rights: The Belilos Case', G.Y.B.I.L. 1990, pp. 69-129; Gérard COHEN-JONATHAN, 'Les réserves à la Convention européenne des Droits de l'homme (à propos de l'arrêt Belilos du 29 avril 1988)', R.G.D.I.P. 1989, pp. 273-314; R.J. Stuart MACDONALD, 'Reservations Under the European Convention on Human Rights', Revue belge de droit international, 1988, pp. 429-450 and Susan MARKS, 'Reservations Unhinged: The Belilos Case Before the European Court of Human Rights', I.C.L.Q., 1990, pp. 300-.

[957] Paras. 40 to 49.

[958] Para. 60; see paras. 51 to 59.

[959] Para. 50; in para. 42 of the *Ettl* judgement, the Court made use of the reservation of Austria to article 6, paragraph 1, of the Convention and referred to its judgement in *Ringeisen* (series A No. 13, pp. 40-41, para. 98), which merely draws the consequences of this reservation, which is interpreted in a very liberal manner (in favour of the State).

[960] See the examples quoted above, footnote 80.

[961] *Chrysostomos and others*, see above (footnote 80).

[962] Para. 42.

[provisional translation]. More categorically, in its judgement in the *Loizidou* case of 23 March 1995,[963] the Strasbourg Court held that 'the object and the purpose of the Convention's system'[964] precludes States from limiting the scope of their declarations under articles 25 and 46 of the Convention by means of declarations or reservations, which confirms the practice followed by the States parties:

> 'Given the nature of the Convention and the ordinary meaning of articles 25 and 46 in their context and in the light of their object and their purpose, and having regard to the practice of the Contracting Parties, the Court concludes that the restrictions *ratione loci* attached to the declarations of Turkey relating to articles 25 and 46 are invalid'.[965] [Provisional translation]

199. As far as the Special Rapporteur is aware, the Inter-American Court of Human Rights has not as yet had to determine, in contentious proceedings, the permissibility of reservations formulated by States parties under article 75 of the Convention of 22 November 1969. It can, however, be deduced from some of its advisory opinions that, in appropriate cases, it would adopt a position similar to that of the Strasbourg Court. Thus, in its second advisory opinion concerning the *Effects of reservations on the entry into force of the Convention*,[966] [provisional translation] it considered that the parties have a legitimate interest in opposing reservations incompatible with the purpose and object of the Convention and 'are free to assert that interest through the adjudicatory and advisory machinery established by the Convention'.[967] In particular, in its third advisory opinion, given on 8 September 1983 in the *Restrictions on the death penalty* case,[968] the San José Court held that certain reservations by Guatemala were inadmissible.[969]

200. It is in this context that the monitoring bodies established under the universal human rights instruments adopted a much more critical attitude regarding the validity of reservations, compared with the very prudent attitude they had traditionally maintained.[970] This is particularly noteworthy in the case of the Committee on the Elimination of Discrimination against Women[971] and, especially, the Human Rights Committee.

201. In General Comment No. 24,[972] the Committee states:

---

[963] Footnote 80 above.
[964] Para. 75.
[965] Para. 89; see paras. 65 to 89.
[966] See note 81 above.
[967] Para. 38.
[968] See note 81 above.
[969] See note 288 above.
[970] See para. 194 above.
[971] See para. 59 above.
[972] Footnote 86 above.

> 'It necessarily falls to the Committee to determine whether a specific reservation is compatible with the object and purpose of the Covenant. This is in part because [...] it is an inappropriate task for States parties in relation to human rights treaties, and in part because it is a task that the Committee cannot avoid in the performance of its functions. In order to know the scope of its duty to examine a State's compliance under article 40 or a communication under the first Optional Protocol, the Committee has necessarily to take a view on the compatibility of a reservation with the object and purpose of the Covenant and with general international law. Because of the special character of a human rights treaty, the compatibility of a reservation with the object and purpose of the Covenant must be established objectively, by reference to legal principles,'.[973]

(ii) Basis of the control exercised by the monitoring bodies

202. This ground, which is similar to that invoked by the European and inter-American regional organs,[974] is also the one invoked by some of those writers who believe the human rights treaty monitoring bodies have competence to verify the permissibility of reservations. For example, it has been asserted that:

- the special character of these treaties excludes 'the possibilities of objection or acceptance by the other contracting States which customary international law has developed since the advisory opinion of the International Court of Justice in the case of the Convention on the Prevention and Punishment of the Crime of Genocide, traces of which are to be found in articles 19 to 23 of the Vienna Convention on the Law of Treaties,'[975] [provisional translation]
- their objective character would seem to call for an objective control,[976]
- it would be impossible for the bodies they establish to perform their general monitoring functions 'without establishing which obligations bind the party concerned';[977]
- in practice, the objections system would not really function.[978]

---

[973] Para. 18.

[974] See paras. 196 to 199 above.

[975] H. GOLSONG, statement at the Colloque de Rome (footnote 240 above), p. 269; see also (footnote 332 above) the opinion of Judge VALTICOS attached to the judgement of the European Court of Human Rights in the *Chorherr* case, p. 15.

[976] See Th. GIEGERICH, op. cit. (footnote 200), pp. 780-781 and R. HIGGINS, op. cit. (footnote 98), p. 10 (typewritten version).

[977] W.A. SCHABAS, op. cit. (footnote 118), p. 68.

[978] See J. MCBRIDE, op. cit. (footnote 118), p. 48 (typewritten version) and R. HIGGINS, op. cit. (footnote 98), p. 13 (typewritten version).

203. These arguments have been challenged and are certainly not all of equal validity.

204. In the first place, as is made clear in the preceding section of the present report,[979] neither the allegedly 'objective' character of human rights treaties, nor the absence of reciprocity characterizing most of their substantive provisions, constitute convincing reasons for a regime departing from the ordinary law. This might at most be a ground for saying that it might be desirable for the permissibility of reservations to those instruments to be determined by an independent and technically qualified body, but that would not result in the existing machinery being vested with such competence if it was not provided for in the treaties by which the bodies were established.[980]

205. As for the claim that the acceptance and objection mechanism does not function satisfactorily, that is a matter of judgement, which, in any event, does not constitute an argument either; the fact that the existing mechanism may be questionable does not mean that the alternative system would be legally acceptable. In particular, the criticisms of the effectiveness of the 'Vienna regime' are, in fact, tantamount to a challenging of the very bases of contemporary international law. As was noted by Sir Humphrey WALDOCK, speaking as expert-consultant of the Vienna Conference on the Law of Treaties:

> 'It was true that, although the International Law Commission had intended to state an objective criterion, the method of application proposed in the draft articles was subjective, in that it depended on the judgement of States. *But that situation was characteristic of many spheres of international law in the absence of a judicial decision, which in any case would bind only the State concerned and that only with respect to the case decided.*[981]

This may be seen as an unfortunate situation, but it is a fundamental characteristic of international law as a whole and, as such, affects the implementation of any treaty, irrespective of its object.

206. In fact, from the standpoint of the reservations regime, the truly special nature of the 1966 Covenant on Civil and Political Rights and the European and Inter-American Conventions on human rights, as well as many instruments of more limited scope, is not that they are human rights treaties, but that they establish bodies for monitoring their implementation. Once such bodies are established, they have, in accordance with a general legal principle that is well established and recognized in general international law, the competence that is vested in them by their own powers. This is the only genuinely convincing argument in favour of determination of the permissibility of reservations: these bodies could not perform the functions

[979] See, in particular, paras. 136 to 162.
[980] See the statement by the representative of Jamaica in the Sixth Committee at the fiftieth session of the General Assembly (A/C.6/50/SR.24, para. 20).
[981] United Nations Conference on the Law of Treaties, op. cit. (footnote 166), p. 137.

vested in them if they could not determine the exact extent of their competence vis-à-vis the States concerned, whether in examining applications by States or by individuals or periodic reports or in exercising a consultative competence.

207. The point has been made, in this connection, that these bodies function in a context that is 'quite different' from that of the International Court of Justice, which 'is required, in particular, to hear, in the light of the principles of international law, any legal dispute among States arising in any part of the world' and 'any question of international law', whereas the monitoring bodies exercise only verification functions in connection with a normative treaty', and that, consequently, there can be no possible analogy between the competencies of these bodies and those of the Court.[982] This is a very debatable and even harmful argument.

208. The first ground justifying the exercise by human rights treaty monitoring bodies of the power to determine the permissibility of reservations lies in the need for these bodies to check their own competence, and therefore to determine the exact extent of the commitments entered into by the State involved; and this is possible only on the basis of any reservations which that State has attached to its undertaking. As the possibility of formulating reservations is not unlimited, this necessarily implies that the reservations must be permissible. This reasoning applies to these bodies as it does to the International Court of Justice'[983] or any other jurisdictional or quasi-jurisdictional organ which has to apply any treaty, and is based on the principle of 'mutual consent'[984] which must be respected, in particular, in the case of a dispute between States. It is pointed out in this connection that the functions of human rights treaty monitoring bodies are never limited exclusively to the consideration of applications from individuals; these bodies are all also vested with certain powers to hear complaints from other States parties[985] and, in the circumstances, they have, undeniably, to determine the extent of their competence.

209. It is therefore not because of their undeniably special nature that human rights treaties require determination of the permissibility of reservations formulated in respect of them, by monitoring bodies, but rather because of the 'ordinariness' of these bodies. Being established by treaties, they derive their competence from those instruments and must verify the extent of that competence on the basis of the consent of the States parties and of the general rules of the law of treaties.

210. To this it may be added that, even if the validity of this conclusion were to be challenged, the now many concurring positions taken by the human rights treaty monitoring bodies have probably created a situation which it would probably be

---

982 European Court of Human Rights, judgement of 23 March 1995, *Loizidou*, (footnote 80 above), paras. 84-85.

983 See para. 189 above.

984 See para. 96 above.

985 See article 41 of the 1966 Covenant on Civil and Political Rights, article 24 of the European Convention and article 45 of the American Convention on Human Rights; see the observations of the United Kingdom concerning General Comment No. 24, (footnote 87 above), para. 5.

difficult to alter. Particularly since, regarding the very principle of control, the attitude of the States concerned is not such as would establish the existence of a contrary *opinio juris*:
- Switzerland, although it contemplated doing so,[986] did not denounce the European Convention for the Protection of Human Rights following the judgements of the European Court of Human Rights in the *Belilos* and *Weber* cases,
- nor did Turkey do so following the *Loizidou* judgement;
- the Committee of Ministers of the Council of Europe approved the solution adopted by the European Commission in the *Temeltasch* case,[987]
- the Parliamentary Assembly of the Council of Europe wishes to develop the jurisprudence of the organs of the Convention in this area,[988]
- Guatemala appears to have taken the desired action following the advisory opinion given by the Inter-American Court of Human Rights in the matter of *Restrictions on the death penalty*[989]
- and, although some States reacted negatively to the Human Rights Committee's General Comment No. 24,[990] their criticisms related more to the Committee's consequential action following its verification of the permissibility of reservations than to the actual principle of such verification.[991]

(c) Combination of different methods of determining the permissibility of reservations

211. The present situation regarding verification of the permissibility of reservations to human rights treaties is therefore one in which there is concurrence, or at least coexistence, of several mechanisms for determining the permissibility of these reservations:
- one of these - which constitutes the ordinary law, is the purely inter-State one provided for in the Vienna Conventions on the Law of Treaties of 1969 and 1986. This can be adapted by special reservation clauses contained in the treaties concerned;
- where the treaty establishes a body to monitor its implementation, it is now accepted - for reasons which are not all improper – that that body can also give its view on the permissibility of reservations;

[986] See I. CAMERON and F. HORN, op. cit. (footnote 343), p. 117.
[987] See para. 197 above.
[988] See recommendation 1223 (1993) (footnote 88), para. 7.A.ii.
[989] See Christina M. CERNA, 'La Cour interamericaine des Droits de l'homme - ses premières affaires', A.F.D.I. 1983, p. 312.
[990] See para. 60 above.
[991] Thus: 'The United Kingdom endorses the view that the Committee must necessarily be in a position to determine the status and effects of a reservation when obliged to do so in order to be able to perform its basic functions under the Covenant' (Observations, note 87 above, para. 11). [Provisional translation]

- but this still leaves the possibility for the States parties to have recourse, where appropriate, to the customary methods of peaceful settlements of disputes, including jurisdictional or arbitral methods, in the event of a dispute arising among them concerning the permissibility of a reservation;[992]
- it may well be, moreover, that national courts, like those in Switzerland,[993] also consider themselves entitled to determine the validity of a reservation in the light of international law.

212. The number of these various possibilities of verifying permissibility presents certain disadvantages, not least of which is the risk of conflict between the positions different parties might take on the same reservation (or on two identical reservations of different States.[994] However, this risk is in fact inherent in any verification system - over time, any given body may take conflicting decisions - and it is perhaps better to have too much verification than no verification at all.

213. A more serious danger is that constituted by the succession of verifications over time, in the absence of any limitation of the duration of the period during which the verifications may be carried out. The problem does not arise in the case of the 'Vienna regime' because article 20, paragraph 5, of the 1969 and 1986 Conventions sets a time-limit of 12 months following the date of receipt of notification of the reservation (or expression by the objecting State of its consent to be bound by the Treaty[995]) on the period during which a State may formulate an objection. A real problem arises, however, in all cases of jurisdictional or quasi-jurisdictional control, which must be assumed to be aleatory and to depend on reference of the question to the monitoring or settlement body. In order to overcome this problem, it has been proposed that the right of the monitoring bodies to give their opinion should also be limited to a twelve-month period.[996] Apart from the fact that none of the relevant

[992] Subject, however, to the existence of 'self-contained regimes'. These certainly include those established by the European and Inter-American Conventions on Human Rights (see Bruno SIMMA, 'self-Contained Regimes'. Netherlands Yearbook of International Law, 1985, pp. 130 et seq. and Theodor MERON, Human Rights and Humanitarian Norms as Customary Law, Clarendon Press, Oxford, 1989, pp. 230 et seq.).

[993] See the decision of the Federal Tribunal of 17 December 1992, *Elisabeth B. c. Conseil d'Etat du canton de Thurgovie* EuGRZ 1993, p. 17; see, more generally, the very well-informed article by Jean-François FLAUSS, 'Le contentieux de la validité des réserves à la CEDH devant le Tribunal federal suisse: Requiem pour la déclaration interprétative relative à l'article 6 § 1', R.U.D.H. 1993, pp. 297-303.

[994] See, in particular, P.-H. IMBERT, op. cit. (footnote 342), pp. 617-619 (I.C.L.Q. 1984, pp. 590-591); the writer draws attention to the risks of incompatibility within the European Convention system, in particular between the position of the Court and the position of the Committee of Ministers.

[995] It should be noted, however, that a problem nevertheless arises owing to the spreading over time of ratifications and accessions.

[996] See P.-H. IMBERT, op. cit. (footnote 43), p. 146, footnote 25, (footnote 117), pp. 113-114 and 130-131 (H.R.R. 1981, pp. 36 and 44); *contra*: H. GOLSONG, Report above, (footnote

texts currently in force provides for such a limitation, the limitation seems scarcely compatible with the very basis for action by monitoring bodies, which is designed to ensure respect for the general principles of international law (preservation of the purpose and object of the treaty). Furthermore, as has been pointed out, one of the reasons why States lodge few objections is precisely that the twelve-months rule often allows them insufficient time;[997] the same problem is liable to arise a fortiori in the case of the monitoring bodies, as a result of which the latter may find themselves paralysed.

214. It seems, moreover, that the possibilities of cross-verifications in fact strengthen the opportunity for the reservations regime to play its real role. The problem is not one of setting one up against the other or, in the case of a single system, of seeking to affirm its monopoly over the others,[998] but of combining them so as to strengthen their overall effectiveness, for while their modalities differ, their end purpose is the same: the aim is always to reconcile the two conflicting but fundamental requirements of integrity of the Treaty and universality of participation.[999] It is only natural that the States, which wished to conclude the Treaty, should be able to express their point of view; it is also natural that the monitoring bodies should play fully the role of guardians of the Treaty entrusted to them by the parties.

215. This does not exclude - in fact it implies - a degree of complementarity among the different control methods, as well as cooperation among the bodies responsible for control. In particular, it is essential that, in determining the permissibility of a reservation, the monitoring bodies (as well as the organs for the settlement of disputes) should take fully into account the positions taken by contracting parties through acceptances and objections. Conversely, the States, which are required to abide by the decisions taken by the monitoring bodies, when they have given those bodies a power of decision, should pay serious attention to the well-thought-out and reasoned positions of those bodies, even though they may not be able to take legally binding decisions.[1000]

---

240), para. 7 and Richard W. EDWARDS Jr., 'Reservations to Treaties', Michigan Journal of International Law 1989, pp. 387-388.

[997] See B. CLARK, op. cit. (footnote 206), pp. 312-314.

[998] This is in fact their natural tendency; see the conflict between the points of view of the Human Rights Committee 'it is an inappropriate task for States parties in relation to human rights treaties' General Comment No. 24, (para. 18) (see above, para. 201) and France ('it is the responsibility [of the States parties] and of them alone, unless the treaty provides otherwise, to decide in the case of incompatibility between a reservation and the object and purpose of the treaty' [provisional translation] - see observations (footnote 87 above), para. 7).

[999] See above, paras. 90-98.

[1000] See, however, the extremely strong reaction to General Comment No. 24 reflected by the Bill submitted in the United States Senate by Senator Helms on 9 June 1995, which provided that 'No funds authorized to be appropriated by this Act nor any other Act, or otherwise made available may be obligated or expended for the conduct of any activity which has the purpose of effect of:

EXCERPTS FROM THE SECOND REPORT ON RESERVATIONS TO TREATIES

B. CONSEQUENCES OF THE FINDINGS OF MONITORING BODIES

216. This raises, very directly, the question of the consequences of a finding of impermissibility of a reservation by a human rights treaty monitoring body.

217. Once it is recognized that such a body can determine whether a reservation meets the permissibility requirements of ordinary law (compatibility with the object and purpose of the treaty) or of a special reservations clause, 'it remains to be determined what [the body] is empowered to do should it consider that a particular reservation does not meet this requirement', a 'particularly important and delicate' question, [provisional translations] as Mrs. HIGGINS pointed out during the preparation of General Comment No. 24,[1001] and one which in fact gave rise to a very lively debate. To this question must be added another, which is closely linked to it, but which it seems preferable to deal with separately for reasons of clarity. This is the question of the obligations (and the rights) of the State whose reservation has been considered inadmissible.

(a) Rights and duties of the monitoring body

218. The problem of the action to be taken by the monitoring body if it finds that a reservation is impermissible is generally stated in terms of 'divisibility',[1002] in the sense that commentators and the monitoring bodies themselves wonder whether the reservation can be separated from the consent to be bound and whether the State making the reservation can and should be regarded as being bound by the treaty as a whole despite the impermissibility of the reservation it has formulated.

219. All the monitoring bodies which have asked themselves this question have so far answered in the affirmative:

'(A) reporting to the Human Rights Committee in accordance with Article 40 of the International Covenant on Civil and Political Rights, or '(B) responding to any effort by the Human Rights Committee to use the procedures of Articles 41 and 42 of the International Covenant on Civil and Political Rights to resolve claims by other parties to the Covenant that the United States is not fulfilling its obligations under the Covenant, until the President has submitted to the Congress the certification described in paragraph (2).
'(2) CERTIFICATION. The certification referred to in paragraph (1) is a certification by the President to the Congress that the Human Rights Committee established under the International Covenant on Civil and Political Rights has:
'(A) revoked its General Comment No. 24 adopted on 2 November 1994; and '(B) expressly recognized the validity as a matter of international law of the reservations, understandings, and declarations contained in the United States instrument of ratification of the International Covenant on Civil and Political Rights'. (A Bill to authorize appropriations for the Department of State for fiscal years 1996 through 1999 ..., 104th Congress, 1st session, S. 908-Report No. 104-95, pp. 87-88).

[1001] CCPR/C/SR.1366, para. 54.

[1002] Cf. R.W. EDWARDS Jr., op. cit. (footnote 388), p. 376.

- In the *Belilos* case, the European Court of Human Rights, indicating the grounds for its judgement, stated, laconically:

> 'There is no doubt that Switzerland considers itself bound by the Convention, independently of the validity of the Declaration'.[1003] [provisional translation]

- The court was more explicit in the *Loizidou* case, in which, after recalling its judgement of 1988,[1004] it dismisses the 'statements made by Turkey during the course of the proceedings' but 'notes that the respondent Government cannot fail to have been conscious, having regard to the uniform practice of the contracting parties in relation to articles 25 and 46, consisting in accepting unconditionally the competence of the Commission and of the Court, of the fact that the denounced restrictive clauses had an undeniable validity under the system of the Convention and that the Convention bodies might hold them to be inadmissible.
[...]

> 'The subsequent reaction of several contracting Parties to the Turkish statements [...] gives full support to the previous comment to the effect that Turkey was not unaware of the legal situation. [...], that being the case, the responding Government cannot invoke the ex post facto statements of the Turkish representatives in order to retreat from the basic intention - despite some compromises - to accept the competence of the Commission and of the Court.
>
> 'The Court therefore has, in the exercise of the responsibilities entrusted to it by article 19, to deal with this question by reference to the text of the respective declarations, in the light of the special character of the Convention regime. The latter, however, militates in favour of separation of the clauses attacked, because this is the means of guaranteeing the rights and freedoms enunciated by the Convention in all areas under Turkey's 'jurisdiction' within the meaning of article 1 of the Convention.
>
> 'The Court examined the text of the declarations and the wording of the restrictions in order to determine whether the restrictions that have been challenged could be dissociated from the instruments of acceptance, or whether they formed an integral and indivisible part of them. Even taking the texts of the declarations relating to articles 25 and 46 as a whole, it considers that the restrictions that have been challenged cannot be dissociated from

---

[1003] Judgement (note 80 above), para. 60.
[1004] Judgement (footnote 80 above), para. 94.

> the remainder of the text, leaving intact the acceptance of the optional clauses.'[1005] [provisional translation]

- And the Human Rights Committee stated that:

> 'The normal consequence of an unacceptable reservation is not that the Covenant will not be in effect at all for a reserving party. Rather, such a reservation will generally be severable, in the sense that the Covenant will be operative for the reserving party without benefit of the reservation.'[1006]

220. Although the European Court of Human Rights emphasizes the differences between the context in which it operates and that in which the International Court of Justice functions,[1007] the similarities between this reasoning and that of Sir Hersch LAUTERPACHT in his separate opinion attached to the judgement of the International Court of Justice in the *Norwegian loans* case[1008] are very striking, although the Strasbourg Court is more circumspect than the judge of the Hague Court in making use of it and, above all, the Court totally ignores the starting-point of all his reasoning, which was based on a clear alternative:

> 'If the clause of the Acceptance reserving to the declaring Government the right of unilateral determination is invalid, then there are only two alternatives open to the Court: it may either treat as invalid that particular part of the reservation or it may consider the entire Acceptance to be tainted with invalidity. (There is a third possibility - *which has only to be mentioned in order to be dismissed* - namely, that the clause in question invalidates not the Acceptance as a whole but the particular reservation. This would mean that the entire reservation of matters of national jurisdiction would be treated as invalid while the Declaration of Acceptance as such would be treated as fully in force).'[1009]

221. It is precisely this 'third possibility' (which LAUTERPACHT mentions only immediately to reject it) that the Strasbourg Court utilizes in the judgements cited above and that the Human Rights Committee contemplates in General Comment No. 24.

222. These positions are perhaps due to the confusion of two very different concepts:

[1005] Ibid., paras. 95-97.
[1006] General Comment No. 24 (footnote 86 above), para. 18.
[1007] See above footnote 326.
[1008] See footnote 325 above, ICJ Reports 1957, pp. 56-59.
[1009] Ibid., pp. 55-56; italics added.

- First of all there is the concept of 'severability' of the provisions of the treaty itself,[1010] which, in relation to reservations, raises the question whether the provision in respect of which the reservation is made can be separated from the treaty without compromising the latter's object and purpose. This may probably be deemed a prerequisite for permissibility of the reservation, since otherwise the provisions of article 20, paragraph 4, and of article 21, paragraph 1, of the Vienna Conventions would be meaningless;[1011]
- then there is the concept of the 'severability' of the reservation from the consent of the State making the reservation to be generally bound by the treaty, which is something quite different[1012] and raises the question whether the reservation was or was not a prerequisite for the State's commitment.

223. It is by no means impossible to foresee what might be the consequences of the 'severability' of the provision in respect of which the reservation was made that is held to be unlawful. In its observations on General Comment No. 24 of the Human Rights Committee, the United Kingdom, supporting LAUTERPACHAT's argument,[1013] 'agrees that severability[1014] of a kind may well offer a solution in appropriate cases, although its contours are only beginning to be explored in State practice. However, the United Kingdom is absolutely clear that severability would entail excising both the reservation and the parts of the treaty to which it applies. Any other solution they would find deeply contrary to principle, notably the fundamental rule reflected in Article 38 (1) of the Statute of the International Court of Justice, that international conventions establish rules 'expressly recognized by' the Contracting States'.[1015]

224. The 'severability' practised by the European Court of Human Rights and contemplated by the Human Rights Committee leads precisely to this other solution.[1016]

225. During the discussion of General Comment No. 24 in the Human Rights Committee, Mrs. HIGGINS explained that 'in the case of the human rights treaties, it is undesirable to exclude States parties; it is preferable, on the contrary, to keep them; hence the formulation employed in the penultimate sentence of paragraph 20'.[1017][1018] [provisional translation] As far as the Special Rapporteur is aware, this is

---

[1010] See P. REUTER, op. cit. (footnote 43), p. 33.

[1011] It is in accordance with this first meaning that the most authoritative commentators on the question of reservations refer to 'divisibility' (see, for example P. REUTER, ibid., pp. 76-77; D.W. BOWETT, op. cit. (footnote 296), p. 89 and Sir Ian SINCLAIR, op. cit. (footnote 207), p. 68).

[1012] This appears to have been confused with the preceding concept by the European Court of Human Rights in the *Loizidou* case (see para. 219 above).

[1013] See para. 220 above.

[1014]

[1015] Observations (footnote 87 above), para. 14, underlining in the text; this possibility is likely to occur only rarely in practice.

[1016] See para. 219 above.

[1017] Later para. 18.

the only explanation of 'severability' to be found in the travaux préparatoires for General Comment No. 24, and it is also the principal justification given by the commentators who expressed support for it.[1019]

226. This explanation presents very serious legal difficulties. In law, it is not a question of determining whether or not reserving States parties should be 'kept', but whether or not they have consented to be bound and, to paraphrase the Committee, it is the States themselves - and not external bodies, however well-intentioned and technically above criticism they may be - who are 'particularly well placed to perform this task';[1020] moreover it is difficult to see how such external bodies could replace the States in carrying out the determination. The opposite solution could give rise to serious political and constitutional difficulties for the reserving State, particularly where the Parliament has attached conditions to the authorization to ratify or accede.[1021]

227. It would seem odd, moreover, for the monitoring bodies to be able to go further than the States themselves can do in their relations *inter se*. Under the Vienna Conventions and in accordance with practice, only two possibilities are open to them: exclusion of application of the provision that is the subject of the reservation (art. 21, para. 1 (a)) or of the treaty as a whole (art. 20, para. 4 (b)); but the Conventions do not even contemplate 'the possibility that the full treaty might come into force for the reserving State'.[1022]

228. However, the most serious criticism one might level at 'severability' is that it takes no account whatsoever of the consensuality that is the very essence of any treaty commitment. The three States which have so far reacted to General Comment No. 24 are in agreement on this point. Their view was expressed particularly clearly by France, which stated that 'agreements, whatever their nature, are governed by the law of treaties; they are based on the consent of States and the reservations are the conditions which the States attached to their consent. Necessarily, therefore, if the reservations are deemed incompatible with the purpose and object of the treaty, the only consequence that may be drawn from this is to state that the consent is not valid and to decide that the States are considered not to be parties to the instrument concerned'.[1023] [provisional translation]

1018 CCPR/C/SR.1382, para. 11.

1019 See Th. GIEGERICH, op. cit. (footnote 200), p. 782 (surprisingly, however, this commentator adds that this solution 'also prevents legal uncertainty as to the status of the reserving State as a contracting party').

1020 See General Comment No. 24 (footnote 86 above), para. 18.

1021 See, in this connection, the statement by the United States representative in the Sixth Committee at the fiftieth session of the General Assembly, A/C.6/50/SR.13, para. 53.

1022 Observations of the United States (footnote 89 above), sect. 5, p. 134.

1023 Comments (footnote 87 above), sect. 7. See also above (ibid.) observations of the United States, sect. 5, and of the United Kingdom, para. 14.

229. Subject to the possible consequences of the 'severability' of the provision that is the subject of the reservation,[1024] this conclusion seems to be the correct one. Irrespective of its object, a treaty remains a juridical act based on the will of States, whose meaning cannot be presumed or invented. Human rights treaties do not escape the general law: their object and purpose do not effect any 'transubstantiation' and do not transform them into international 'legislation' which would bind States against their will.

230. This is the risk monitoring bodies take if they venture to determine what was the intention of a State when it bound itself by a treaty, while it was, at the same time, formulating a reservation. Not only may the determination of this intention prove extremely delicate,[1025] and not only are the precedents constituted by the *Belilos* and *Loizidou* cases very unconvincing in this regard,[1026] but the very principle of such determination gives rise to serious objections.

(b) Rights and duties of the reserving State

231. If the points made above are considered accepted,
1. The human rights treaty-monitoring bodies may determine the permissibility of reservations formulated by States in the light of the applicable reservations regime;
2. If they consider the reservation to be impermissible, they can only conclude that the reserving State is not currently bound;[1027]
3. But they cannot take the place of the reserving State in order to determine whether the latter wishes or does not wish to be bound by the treaty despite the impermissibility of the reservation accompanying the expression of its consent to be bound by the treaty.

232. The attitude of the reserving State is therefore crucial and the question is whether that State is bound by legal rules or enjoys a purely discretionary competence.

233. Here again, it is convenient to divide the problem into two questions that are separate even though linked:
- Are the findings of the monitoring body binding on the reserving State?

[1024] See above, para. 223.
[1025] See the opinion (footnote 325 above) of Sir Hersch LAUTERPACHT in the *Interhandel* case, Reports 1959, pp. 112-116; see also R.W. EDWARDS Jr., op. cit. (footnote 388), p. 375.
[1026] In the *Belilos* case, the European Court of Human Rights very clearly underestimated the importance of the reservation in the eyes of the Swiss authorities, as is shown by Switzerland's reluctance to remain a party to the Convention following the handing down of the judgement (see footnote 378 above). Furthermore, the entirely contrary grounds given by the Strasbourg Court in support of its decision in the *Loizidou* case reflect an offhand attitude, to say the least, on the part of the Court, towards a sovereign State, in simply casting doubt on formal statements made before it in the written proceedings (see para. 219).
[1027] Except in the case of 'severability', which is difficult to conceive in practice (see paras. 220 to 223 above).

- Irrespective of the answer to the preceding question, has the State a choice between several types of reaction?

(i) Binding force of the findings of the monitoring body

234. Although it seems controversial,[1028] the answer to this first question does not present any problem. Indeed, it seems almost obvious that the authority of the findings made by the monitoring body on the question of reservations will depend on the powers with which the body is invested: they will have the force of *res judicata* where the body is jurisdictional in character, or is arbitral and adjudicates and will have the status of advisory opinions or recommendations in other cases.

235. Admittedly, things are somewhat more complex in practice. On the one hand, it is not always easy to determine the exact nature of the body required to make a determination, especially as one and the same body may successively exercise different competences. Furthermore, the latter do not necessarily fall into well-defined categories that are clearly identified in law. Finally, the exact scope of certain instruments is the subject of doctrinal controversy and, even where this is not the case, practical problems may also arise.[1029] Real as they are, these problems are not specific to the area of reservations. It is therefore sufficient to rely on the very general directive set out above.[1030]

236. It should be noted, however, that, even on this point, the Human Rights Committee's General Comment No. 24 has not escaped criticism. In particular, the United Kingdom criticized it for having used 'the verb 'determine' in connection with the Committee's functions towards the status of reservations' and of having done so, moreover, 'in the context of its dictum that the task in question is inappropriate for the States parties'.[1031]

237. Although the Committee meant by this that it had to take decisions that were binding on the States parties, this objection is very probably well-founded: the 'comments', 'reports' and 'finding' adopted by the Committee under articles 40 and 41 of the Covenant or article 5 of the first Protocol are certainly not legally binding.[1032] 'Findings' would have been more accurate, but it is certainly true that 'too much is not to be read into the verb 'determine'':[1033] the Committee can take a position regarding the permissibility or impermissibility of reservations formulated by the States parties to the Covenant in the exercise of its general functions of monitoring the implementation of that instrument, but 'a competence to do

[1028] See paras. 236 et seq.
[1029] See, for example, para. 241 above.
[1030] Para. 234.
[1031] Observations (footnote 87 above), para. 11.
[1032] 'The legally binding nature of any 'determination' of the Committee, whether on the issue or otherwise, is problematic' (R. HIGGINS, op. cit. (footnote 98), p. 5, footnote 7 (typewritten version).
[1033] Ibid.

something' should not be confused with 'the binding effect of that which is done'.[1034]

238. Furthermore, when it considered the first report of the United States of America, following the adoption of General Comment No. 24, the Committee confined itself to 'regretting' the extent of the State party's reservations, declarations and understandings to the Covenant, stating that it was 'also particularly concerned at reservations to article 6, paragraph 5, and article 7 of the Covenant, which it believes to be incompatible with the object and purpose of the Covenant'.[1035] Furthermore, at the last meeting devoted to consideration of this report, the Chairman of the Committee, responding to the concerns expressed by the United States of America, pointed out that:

> 'The Committee's interpretations as set out in its general comments were not strictly binding, although it hoped that the comments carried a certain weight and authority.'[1036]

239. The formulas used by the chairpersons of the bodies set up under international human rights instruments in their 1992 and 1994 reports[1037] call for similar comments. They are of different types and in any event cannot imply that the bodies concerned have greater powers in this area than those conferred on them by their statutes.

240. These powers also vary greatly, depending on circumstances and from body to body. It is nevertheless clear that by ratifying the treaties which establish these bodies, the States parties undertake to execute them in good faith, which implies at least that they will examine in good faith the comments and recommendations made to them by bodies concerned.[1038]

(ii) The reactions expected from the reserving State

241. The juridical value of the findings of the monitoring bodies naturally has some bearing on the nature and scope of the consequential obligations for a reserving

---

[1034] Ibid., p. 10 (typewritten version).

[1035] Comments (footnote 282 above), para. 14.

[1036] CCPR/C/SR.1406, para. 3.

[1037] 'The treaty bodies should systematically review reservations made when considering a report and include in the list of questions to be addressed to reporting Governments a question as to whether a given reservation was still necessary and whether a State party would consider withdrawing a reservation that might be considered by the treaty body concerned as being incompatible with the object and purpose of the treaty. (Report above, A/47/628, footnote 83, para. 36); 'They recommend that treaty bodies state clearly that certain reservations to international human rights instruments are contrary to the object and purpose of those instruments and consequently incompatible with treaty law.' (Report above, A/49/537, footnote 83, para. 30).

[1038] See R. HIGGINS, op. cit. (footnote 98), p. 5, footnote 11 (typewritten version); and, more generally, P. DAILLIER and A. PELLET, op. cit. (footnote 128), p. 372.

State whose reservation is declared inadmissible. Where the body concerned is vested with decision-making powers, the State must conform to the body's decisions. However, this rule is tempered by two factors:

- in the first place, it is not entirely obvious, from the strictly legal standpoint, that a State would be legally bound to withdraw a reservation declared impermissible if this question does not constitute the actual subject of the decision; in the case of the human rights treaty-monitoring bodies this is likely to occur only rarely,[1039]
- secondly, and again from a strictly legal standpoint, assuming that such a decision were handed down, it would have the relative authority of *res judicata* and would therefore impose an obligation on the defending State only in relation to the applicant or applicants.[1040]

242. Too much importance should not, however, be attached to these strictly technical considerations: it is scarcely conceivable that a State anxious to observe the law - and to preserve its international image - would adopt such a restrictive position. This applies at least to any findings that might be made in such circumstances and to the recommendations made or advisory opinions given. While such instruments have no binding force, they do grant permission[1041] and States parties cannot, without breaching the principle of good faith, remain indifferent to findings regarding the scope of their commitments, made, in the exercise of its functions (contentious, consultative or other), by an organ established under a treaty by which they have wished to be bound.

243. In all cases where such a body has found a reservation to be impermissible, the State therefore finds itself confronted with a choice. Except in special cases, it alone must determine whether the impermissible reservation that it attached to the expression of its consent to be bound constituted an essential element of that consent.[1042]

244. The State has two options:

- simply to withdraw the reservation, or

[1039] This might, however, be the case if a State (the reserving State or the objecting State) were to submit to the European Court of Human Rights a dispute relating to reservations under article 46 of the European Convention on Human Rights or article 62 of the American Convention. On the other hand, it is generally considered that the principle of *res judicata* extends only to the substantive provisions of jurisdictional or arbitral decisions and to the grounds on which they are necessarily based, but not to those decisions as a whole. While a jurisdictional organ may give its views on the permissibility of a reservation when an individual or inter-State application is made to it in relation to the implementation of the Convention, it is doubtful that observations made in connection with the matter can be considered *res judicata*.

[1040] See para. 205 above, the position of Sir Humphrey WALDOCK.

[1041] See, for example: Jean-Paul Jacqué. Eléments pour une théorie de l'acte juridique en droit international public, L.G.D.J., Paris, 1975, p. 238 and P. DAILLIER and A. PELLET. op. cit. (footnote 128), pp. 373-374.

[1042] See above, paras. 228 to 231.

- to terminate its participation in the treaty.

245. In both these cases, it must be borne in mind that the State's decision produces its effects, or in any event certain effects, *ab initio*. By definition, if the reservation is incompatible with the object and purpose of the treaty,[1043] it alters the latter's nature, emptying it of its substance, so that it is difficult to consider that the reserving State was really a party to the treaty.[1044] Consequently, we cannot regard as too absolute the nullity which would result from incompatibility of the reservation with the object and purpose of the Treaty; the finding of impermissibility of the reservation may be made a long time after expression by the State of its consent to be bound[1045] and may, in the meantime, have produced affects in law which it may be difficult or impossible to alter.

246. Certainly, the decision of the reserving State to end its relationships under the Treaty following a finding that its reservation is impermissible presents real drawbacks. In particular, as was noted by Judge MACDONALD, 'to exclude the application of an obligation by reason of an invalid reservation is in effect to give full force and effect to the reservation'.[1046] [provisional translation] This statement calls for two comments, however:

1. the Judge assumes here the case of 'severability';[1047] but what is envisaged here is different: in this case the State renounces the benefits of the Treaty as a whole (or withdraws the challenged reservation);
2. consequently, a decision of the reserving State to terminate its relationships under the Treaty simply has the effect of restoring the *statu quo ante*.

247. Yet if we relate this 'all or nothing' situation to the functions of the reservations regime,[1048] it is unsatisfactory and is liable to compromise the objective of universality by encouraging the reserving State to leave the Treaty circle. The question therefore is whether this State cannot move towards an intermediate solution that will preserve the integrity of the Treaty and yet allow the State to continue its participation without this causing it insuperable difficulties. In other words, is it conceivable, from a legal standpoint, for the State concerned to modify its reservation in order to make it compatible with the object and purpose of the Treaty?[1049]

1043 D.W. BOWETT makes a distinction between a reservation that is 'fundamentally inconsistent with the object and purpose of the treaty' and a reservation that is simply 'inadmissible' (op. cit., footnote 296, p. 77) and draws the conclusion that only the former is 'a nullity and if severable can be struck out' (ibid., p. 84). *Contra:* C. REDGWELL, op. cit. (footnote 97), pp. 267-268.

1044 Notwithstanding the point made in the preceding note, the situation may be different if a reservation is prohibited by the treaty - because of a reservations clause - but yet cannot be regarded as contrary to the object and purpose of the Treaty.

1045

1046 Op. cit. (footnote 348), p. 449.

1047 See para. 222 above.

1048 See paras. 90-98 above.

1049 Or could it rectify whatever was the cause of the impermissibility of its reservation?

248. Prima facie, such an intermediate solution seems scarcely compatible with the 'Vienna regime', since, under the provisions of article 19 of the 1969 and 1986 Conventions, the formulation of a reservation can take place only 'when signing, ratifying, accepting, approving or acceding to a treaty'. Furthermore, the possibility of raising an objection to a reservation is restricted by the time-limit set in article 20, paragraph 5.

249. However, the objection does not appear to be diriment. In the first place, if we consider that the State has never in fact expressed a valid consent to be bound by the Treaty,[1050] the 'regularization' of its reservation would seem, in fact, to be concomitant with the expression of its consent to be bound. Secondly, and above all, if, as seems inevitable without serious prejudice to the fundamental principle of consent which underlies every treaty commitment,[1051] the reserving State can give up its participation in the Treaty, it is difficult to see why it could not equally well modify the sense of its reservation, so as to make it compatible with the object and purpose of the Treaty, and thus permissible. This solution, which is not incompatible with the Vienna rules, has the advantage of reconciling the requirements of integrity and universality that are inherent in any reservations regime.

250. As Judge VALTICOS wrote in the partly dissenting opinion which he appended to the *Chorherr* judgement of the European Court of Human Rights, rejection of this possibility 'would be unreasonable, the Government concerned having been informed of the non-validity of its reservation only several years after the ratification. The Government concerned should therefore have the possibility of rectifying the situation and formulating a valid reservation within a reasonable period on the basis of its earlier reservation.'[1052] [provisional translation]

251. There is, moreover, at least one precedent for such action. Although, by the *Belilos* judgement, the European Court of Human Rights considered that Switzerland was bound 'irrespective of the validity of the declaration', which it had found not in conformity with article 64 of the Convention,[1053] that country, in accordance, moreover, with a suggestion it had made to the Court and which the latter had not adopted,[1054] formulated a new declaration,[1055] without, seemingly,

---

[1050] See para. 245 above.

[1051] See para. 228 above.

[1052] Opinion (footnote 332 above) pp. 16-17. Judge VALTICOS further suggests that any new declaration or reservation should be submitted to the European Court of Human Rights for the latter to determine its validity. There is nothing to prevent this *de lege ferenda*, but a text should expressly provide for this, or, alternatively, it would simply be possible to follow the advisory opinion procedure of the Second Protocol.

[1053] See para. 219 above.

[1054] See W.A. SCHABAS, op. cit. (footnote 118), pp. 76-77.

[1055] E.C.H.R. Yearbook, 1988, vol. 31, p. 5. Switzerland even modified its declaration again the following year and Liechtenstein - whose own, identical declaration had nevertheless not

giving rise to any objection or protest. More generally, moreover, it probably must be recognized that States, which can at any time withdraw their reservations, may also 'tone them down'; here again, the recent practice of the Secretary-General as depositary reflects the same approach.[1056]

CONCLUSION OF SECTION 3: COEXISTENCE OF MONITORING MECHANISMS

252. In conclusion, it would seem that:

1. While, as far as their content is concerned, the human rights treaties are not of such a special nature as to justify applying to them a different reservations regime, the establishment, by most of these treaties, of monitoring bodies influences the modalities of determination of the permissibility of reservations;
2. Although no provision is made for this in their statutes, these bodies have undertaken to determine the permissibility of reservations to their constituent instruments. Their competence to do so must be recognized: it is a prerequisite for the exercise of the general monitoring functions with which they are invested;
3. Like the contracting parties themselves in their relations inter se or any other bodies which may have competence to settle disputes, the monitoring bodies determine the permissibility of reservations to human rights treaties on the basis of the criterion of the Treaty's object and purpose, thus confirming the adaptation to these instruments of the flexible reservations regime provided for in the 1969 and 1986 Conventions;
4. The legal force of the findings made by these bodies in the exercise of this determination power cannot exceed that resulting from the powers given them for the performance of their general monitoring role; in all cases, however, the States must examine these findings in good faith and, where necessary, rectify the factors found to exist which render the reservation impermissible;
5. No organ for determining the permissibility of reservations can take the place of the reserving State in determining the latter's intentions regarding the scope of the treaty obligations it is prepared to assume. The State alone, therefore, is responsible for deciding how to put an end to the defect in the expression of its consent arising from the impermissibility of the reservation;

---

been declared invalid by the court – did likewise in 1992 (see W.A. SCHABAS, op. cit. (footnote 118), p. 77).

[1056] Following several objections, the Government of the Libyan Arab Jamahiriya informed the Secretary-General on 5 July 1995 of its intention to 'modify by making more specific' the general reservation it had formulated on its accession to the Convention on the Elimination of All Forms of Discrimination against Women. The Secretary-General communicated this modification (see ST/LEG/SR.E/24, pp. 172 and ...-182, footnote 21), without this giving rise to any objection or criticism. (See also the Finnish Government's notification to the Secretary-General dated 10 February 1994 to amend, by reducing its scope, a reservation to the International Convention for the Protection of Performers, Producers of Phonograms and Broadcasting Organizations of 26 October 1961 ibid, p. 670).

6. This 'action to ensure conformity' may consist simply in withdrawal of the inadmissible reservation or in its modification.

CONCLUSIONS OF CHAPTER II

253. In view of the importance of the problems raised by the recent practice of the human rights treaty monitoring bodies with regard to reservations and the extent of the controversy this practice has generated, the Special Rapporteur has thought it necessary to depart somewhat from his announced intentions at the time of submission of his preliminary report, regarding the order of dealing with the various issues raised by the question of 'reservations to treaties'. He believes it necessary for the International Law Commission to present in this debate the viewpoint of general international law, of which it is one of the organs, a debate that is sometimes obscured, and in any event distorted, by certain approaches, that are sometimes adopted with the best of intentions, but which, being too sectorial, tend to exaggerate the special aspects of particular areas, particular branches of law and particular treaties, to the detriment of the unity of the rules of international law.

254. Unity is not, of course, an end in itself and it is quite conceivable to envisage applying diverse rules to different situations when the situations so justify. Reservations to treaties do not, however, seem to require such a normative diversification: the existing regime is characterized by its flexibility and its adaptability and it achieves satisfactorily the necessary balance between the conflicting requirement of the integrity and the universality of the Treaty.

255. Whatever may have been said or written on the subject, this objective of equilibrium is universal. Whatever its object, a treaty remains a treaty and expresses the will of the States (or international organizations) that are parties to it. The purpose of the reservations regime is to enable these wishes of States to be expressed in a balanced fashion and it succeeds in doing so in a generally satisfactory manner. It would be unfortunate to bring the regime into question by attaching undue importance to sectorial considerations that can perfectly well be accommodated within the existing regime.

256. This general conclusion must nevertheless be tempered by two considerations:

- First, it is undeniable that the law was not frozen in 1951 or in 1969;[1057] issues which did not arise (or scarcely arose) at that time have since emerged and call for answers. The Special Rapporteur believes that the answers must be found in the spirit of the 'Vienna Rules', although these will have to be adapted and extended, as appropriate, whenever this is found to be necessary;
- Secondly, it should be borne in mind that the normal way of adapting the general rules of international law to particular needs and circumstances is to adopt appropriate rules by the conclusion of treaties. In the area of reservations, this can

[1057] See Preliminary Report (footnote 2 above), paras. 161 and 162.

easily be done through the adoption of derogating reservations clauses, if the parties see a need for this.

257. More specifically, no determining factor seems to require the adoption of a special reservations regime for normative treaties, or even for human rights treaties. The special nature of the latter was fully taken into account by the Judges in 1951 and the 'codifiers' of later years and it did not seem to them to justify an overall derogating regime. This view is shared by the Special Rapporteur.

258. There is reason to believe, however, that the drafters of the Vienna Conventions never envisaged the role which the bodies for monitoring the implementation of certain treaties would later have to play, especially in the area of protection of human rights, in applying the reservations regime which they established. This role can in fact be quite easily circumscribed by the application of general principles of international law and by taking account of both the functions of a reservations regime and the responsibilities vested in those bodies.

259. There are thus, however, two circumstances - the second one in particular - that may justify the adoption of special reservation clauses, a measure that will in any case help to avoid sterile controversy.

260. In the light of the forgoing, it seems to the Special Rapporteur that the Commission would be fully performing its role of promoting the progressive development of international law and its codification,[1058] by adopting a resolution addressed to the General Assembly, which the latter might wish to bring to the attention of States and the various parties concerned, in the hope of clarifying the legal aspects of the matter. It is in this spirit that he has prepared the draft resolution reproduced below.

DRAFT RESOLUTION OF THE INTERNATIONAL LAW COMMISSION ON RESERVATIONS TO NORMATIVE MULTILATERAL TREATIES INCLUDING HUMAN RIGHTS TREATIES

The International Law Commission,

Having considered, at its forty-eighth session, the question of the unity or diversity of the juridical regime for reservations,

Aware of the discussion currently taking place in other forums on the subject of reservations to normative multilateral treaties, and particularly treaties concerning human rights,

Desiring that the voice of international law be heard in this discussion,

1. Reaffirms its attachment to the effective application of the reservations regime established by articles 19 to 23 of the Vienna Conventions on the Law of Treaties of 1969 and 1986, and particularly to the fundamental criterion of the object and purpose of the treaty as the fundamental criterion for determining the permissibility of reservations;

[1058] See article 1 of the Statute.

EXCERPTS FROM THE SECOND REPORT ON RESERVATIONS TO TREATIES

2. Considers that, because of its flexibility, this regime is suited to the requirements of all treaties, of whatever object or nature, and achieves a satisfactory balance between the objectives of preservation of the integrity of the text of the treaty and universality of participation in the treaty;

3. Considers that these objectives apply equally in the case of reservations to normative multilateral treaties, including treaties in the area of human rights and that, consequently, the general rules enunciated in the above-mentioned Vienna Conventions are fully applicable to reservations to such instruments;

4. Nevertheless considers that the establishment of monitoring machinery by many human rights treaties creates special problems that were not envisaged at the time of the drafting of those conventions, connected with determination of the permissibility of reservations formulated by States;

5. Also considers that, although these treaties are silent on the subject, the bodies which they establish necessarily have competence to carry out this determination function, which is essential for the performance of the functions vested in them, but that the control they can exercise over the permissibility of reservations does not exclude the traditional modalities of control by the contracting parties, on the one hand, in accordance with the above-mentioned provisions of the Vienna Conventions of 1969 and 1986 and, where appropriate, by the organs for settling any dispute that may arise concerning the implementation of the treaty;

6. Is also firmly of the view that it is only the reserving State that has the responsibility of taking appropriate action in the event of incompatibility of the reservation which it formulated with the object and purpose of the treaty. This action may consist in the State either forgoing becoming a party or withdrawing its reservation, or modifying the latter so as to rectify the impermissibility that has been observed;

7. Calls on States to cooperate fully and in good faith with the bodies responsible for determining the permissibility of reservations, where such bodies exist;

8. Suggests that it would be desirable if, in future, specific clauses were inserted in multilateral normative treaties, including human rights treaties, in order to eliminate any uncertainty regarding the applicable reservations regime, the power to determine the permissibility of reservations enjoyed by the monitoring bodies established by the treaties and the legal effects of such determination;

9. Expresses the hope that the principles enunciated above will help to clarify the reservations regime applicable to normative multilateral treaties, particularly in the area of human rights; and

10. Suggests to the General Assembly that it bring the present resolution to the attention of States and bodies which might have to determine the permissibility of such reservations.

ANNEX 2

LIST OF PARTICIPANTS OF THE CONFERENCE

Mr. Gudmundur Alfredsson, Sweden
Ms. Jane Connors, UNHCHR, Switzerland
Mr. Cees Flinterman, The Netherlands
Ms. Mia Hallén, Sweden
Mr. Rainer Hofmann, Germany
Mr. Morten Kjærum, Denmark
Mr. Eckart Klein, Germany
Ms. Sigita Lidaka, Latvia
Mr. Ulf Linderfalk, Sweden
Mr. Percy MacLean, Germany
Mr. Miguel Alfonso Martínez, Cuba
Mr. Göran Melander, Sweden
Ms. Hanna Beate Schöpp-Schilling, Germany
Ms. Anja Seibert-Fohr, Germany
Mr. Martin Scheinin, Finland
Mr. Jerzy Sztucki, Sweden
Mr. Bent Sørensen, Denmark
Mr. Arist von Hehn, Germany
Ms. Brita Wagener, Germany
Mr. Roman Wieruszewski, Poland
Ms. Ineta Ziemele, Sweden

LIST OF CONTRIBUTORS

PAUL **DALTON**	BA, LLB. Assistant to Bent Sørensen
RAINER **HOFMANN**	Professor Dr.; Director, Walther-Schücking-Institute for International Law, University of Kiel, Germany; President of the Advisory Committee under the Council of Europe Framework Convention for the Protection of National Minorities
MORTEN **KJÆRUM**	Director, Danish Institute for Human Rights and member of CERD
JAN **KLABBERS**	Professor of International Law, University of Helsinki
ECKART **KLEIN**	Dr. iur., Professor for Constitutional Law, Public International Law and European Law, Director of the Human Rights Centre, University of Potsdam, Member of the UN Human Rights Committee 1995–2002
ULF **LINDERFALK**	JD, Assistant Professor of International Law at the Faculty of Law, Lund University
PERCY **MACLEAN**	Presiding judge at the Berlin administrative court, first Director of the German Institute for Human Rights (2002/2003)
GÖRAN **MELANDER**	Professor Emeritus, Faculty of Law, Lund University; Chairman of the Board of the Raoul Wallenberg Institute and the Member of the CEDAW Committee
JÖRG **POLAKIEWICZ**	Deputy Head of the Council of Europe's Legal Advice Department and lecturer at the Europainstitut of the University of Saarbrücken
MARTIN **SCHEININ**	Professor of Constitutional and International Law, Åbo Akademi

	University, Member, Human Rights Committee (1997–2004)
HANNA BEATE **SCHÖPP-SCHILLING**	Dr. Phil.; Consultant; Member of the UN Committee on the Elimination of All Forms of Discrimination of Women (CEDAW) since 1989
ANJA **SEIBERT-FOHR**	LL.M., S.J.D. cand., Senior Research Fellow at the Max Planck Institute for Comparative Public Law and International Law, Lecturer at Mannheim University Law School
BENT **SØRENSEN**	Professor of Law, MD, DMSc. Former member of both the UN Committee against Torture (CAT) (1988–1999) and the Council of Europe Committee for the Prevention of Torture (CPT) (1989–1997)
LUZIUS **WILDHABER**	President of the European Court of Human Rights, Dr.iur., LL.M., J.S.D. (Yale), Dres.h.c., LL.D.h.c., Professor at the University of Basel
INETA **ZIEMELE**	Söderberg Professor of International Law and Human Rights at the Riga Graduate School of Law, Visiting Professor at the Raoul Wallenberg Institute of Human Rights and Humanitarian Law, Lund University, Sweden

INDEX

MIX
Papier aus verantwortungsvollen Quellen
Paper from responsible sources
FSC® C105338

If you have any concerns about our products,
you can contact us on
ProductSafety@springernature.com

In case Publisher is established outside the EU,
the EU authorized representative is:
Springer Nature Customer Service Center GmbH
Europaplatz 3, 69115 Heidelberg, Germany

Printed by Libri Plureos GmbH
in Hamburg, Germany